Zondervan Illustrated Bible Backgrounds Commentary

Acts

Clinton E. Arnold

Clinton E. Arnold   *general editor*

ZONDERVAN®

ZONDERVAN.com/
AUTHORTRACKER
follow your favorite authors

About the Author

Clinton E. Arnold (PhD, University of Aberdeen), professor and chairman, department of New Testament, Talbot School of Theology, Biola University, Los Angeles, California

We want to hear from you. Please send your comments about this book to us in care of zreview@zondervan.com. Thank you.

Zondervan Illustrated Bible Backgrounds Commentary: Acts
Copyright © 2002 by Clinton E. Arnold

Requests for information should be addressed to:

Zondervan, *Grand Rapids, Michigan* 49530

Library of Congress Cataloging-in-Publication Data
Zondervan illustrated Bible backgrounds commentary / Clinton E. Arnold, general editor.
p.cm.
Includes bibliographical references.
ISBN-10: 0-310-27825-2
ISBN-13: 978-0-310-27825-2
1. Bible. N.T.—Commentaries.   I. Arnold, Clinton E.
BS2341.52.Z66 2001
225.7—dc21   2001046801
                                         CIP

Printed in China

Interior design by Sherri L. Hoffman

10 11 12 13/TPC/12 11 10 9 8 7 6 5 4 3

CONTENTS

INTRODUCTION

All readers of the Bible have a tendency to view what it says it through their own culture and life circumstances. This can happen almost subconsiously as we read the pages of the text.

When most people in the church read about the thief on the cross, for instance, they immediately think of a burglar that held up a store or broke into a home. They may be rather shocked to find out that the guy was actually a Jewish revolutionary figure who was part of a growing movement in Palestine eager to throw off Roman rule.

It also comes as something of a surprise to contemporary Christians that "cursing" in the New Testament era had little or nothing to do with cussing somebody out. It had far more to do with the invocation of spirits to cause someone harm.

No doubt there is a need in the church for learning more about the world of the New Testament to avoid erroneous interpretations of the text of Scripture. But relevant historical and cultural insights also provide an added dimension of perspective to the words of the Bible. This kind of information often functions in the same way as watching a movie in color rather than in black and white. Finding out, for instance, how Paul compared Christ's victory on the cross to a joyous celebration parade in honor of a Roman general after winning an extraordinary battle brings does indeed magnify the profundity and implications of Jesus' work on the cross. Discovering that the factions at Corinth ("I follow Paul . . .

I follow Apollos . . .") had plenty of precedent in the local cults ("I follow Aphrodite; I follow Apollo . . .") helps us understand the "why" of a particular problem. Learning about the water supply from the springs of Hierapolis that flowed into Laodicea as "lukewarm" water enables us to appreciate the relevance of the metaphor Jesus used when he addressed the spiritual laxity of this church.

My sense is that most Christians are eager to learn more about the real life setting of the New Testament. In the preaching and teaching of the Bible in the church, congregants are always grateful when they learn something of the background and historical context of the text. It not only helps them understand the text more accurately, but often enables them to identify with the people and circumstances of the Bible. I have been asked on countless occasions by Christians, "Where can I get access to good historical background information about this passage?" Earnest Christians are hungry for information that makes their Bibles come alive.

The stimulus for this commentary came from the church and the aim is to serve the church. The contributors to this series have sought to provide illuminating and interesting historical/cultural background information. The intent was to draw upon relevant papyri, inscriptions, archaeological discoveries, and the numerous studies of Judaism, Roman culture, Hellenism, and other features of the world of the New Testament and to make the results accessible to people in the church. We recognize that some readers of the commentary will want to go further, and so the sources of the information have been carefully documented in endnotes.

The written information has been supplemented with hundreds of photographs, maps, charts, artwork, and other graphics that help the reader better understand the world of the New Testament. Each of the writers was given an opportunity to dream up a "wish list" of illustrations that he thought would help to illustrate the passages in the New Testament book for which he was writing commentary. Although we were not able to obtain everything they were looking for, we came close.

The team of commentators are writing for the benefit of the broad array of Christians who simply want to better understand their Bibles from the vantage point of the historical context. This is an installment in a new genre of "Bible background" commentaries that was kicked off by Craig Keener's fine volume. Consequently, this is not an "exegetical" commentary that provides linguistic insight and background into Greek constructions and verb tenses. Neither is this work an "expository" commentary that provides a verse-by-verse exposition of the text; for in-depth philo-

logical or theological insight, readers will need to have other more specialized or comprehensive commentaries available. Nor is this an "historical-critical" commentary, although the contributors are all scholars and have already made substantial academic contributions on the New Testament books they are writing on for this set. The team intentionally does not engage all of the issues that are discussed in the scholarly guild.

Rather, our goal is to offer a reading and interpretation of the text informed by what we regard as the most relevant historical information. For many in the church, this commentary will serve as an important entry point into the interpretation and appreciation of the text. For other more serious students of the Word, these volumes will provide an important supplement to many of the fine exegetical, expository, and critical available.

The contributors represent a group of scholars who embrace the Bible as the Word of God and believe that the message of its pages has life-changing relevance for faith and practice today. Accordingly, we offer "Reflections" on the relevance of the Scripture to life for every chapter of the New Testament.

I pray that this commentary brings you both delight and insight in digging deeper into the Word of God.

Clinton E. Arnold
General Editor

LIST OF SIDEBARS

Acts

LIST OF CHARTS

INDEX OF PHOTOS AND MAPS

ABBREVIATIONS

1. Books of the Bible and Apocrypha

1 Chron.	1 Chronicles
2 Chron.	2 Chronicles
1 Cor.	1 Corinthians
2 Cor.	2 Corinthians
1 Esd.	1 Esdras
2 Esd.	2 Esdras
1 John	1 John
2 John	2 John
3 John	3 John
1 Kings	1 Kings
2 Kings	2 Kings
1 Macc.	1 Maccabees
2 Macc.	2 Maccabees
1 Peter	1 Peter
2 Peter	2 Peter
1 Sam.	1 Samuel
2 Sam.	2 Samuel
1 Thess.	1 Thessalonians
2 Thess.	2 Thessalonians
1 Tim.	1 Timothy
2 Tim.	2 Timothy
Acts	Acts
Amos	Amos
Bar.	Baruch
Bel	Bel and the Dragon
Col.	Colossians
Dan.	Daniel
Deut.	Deuteronomy
Eccl.	Ecclesiastes
Ep. Jer.	Epistle of Jeremiah
Eph.	Ephesians
Est.	Esther
Ezek.	Ezekiel
Ex.	Exodus
Ezra	Ezra
Gal.	Galatians
Gen.	Genesis
Hab.	Habakkuk
Hag.	Haggai
Heb.	Hebrews
Hos.	Hosea
Isa.	Isaiah
James	James
Jer.	Jeremiah
Job	Job
Joel	Joel
John	John
Jonah	Jonah
Josh.	Joshua
Jude	Jude
Judg.	Judges
Judith	Judith
Lam.	Lamentations
Lev.	Leviticus
Luke	Luke
Mal.	Malachi
Mark	Mark
Matt.	Matthew
Mic.	Micah
Nah.	Nahum
Neh.	Nehemiah
Num.	Numbers
Obad.	Obadiah
Phil.	Philippians
Philem.	Philemon
Pr. Man.	Prayer of Manassah
Prov.	Proverbs
Ps.	Psalm
Rest. of Est.	The Rest of Esther
Rev.	Revelation
Rom.	Romans
Ruth	Ruth
S. of III Ch.	The Song of the Three Holy Children
Sir.	Sirach/Ecclesiasticus
Song	Song of Songs
Sus.	Susanna
Titus	Titus
Tobit	Tobit
Wisd. Sol.	The Wisdom of Solomon
Zech.	Zechariah
Zeph.	Zephaniah

2. Old and New Testament Pseudepigrapha and Rabbinic Literature

Individual tractates of rabbinic literature follow the abbreviations of the *SBL Handbook of Style*, pp. 79–80. Qumran documents follow standard Dead Sea Scroll conventions.

2 Bar.	*2 Baruch*
3 Bar.	*3 Baruch*
4 Bar.	*4 Baruch*
1 En.	*1 Enoch*
2 En.	*2 Enoch*
3 En.	*3 Enoch*
4 Ezra	*4 Ezra*

3 Macc.	3 Maccabees
4 Macc.	4 Maccabees
5 Macc.	5 Maccabees
Acts Phil.	Acts of Philip
Acts Pet.	Acts of Peter and the 12 Apostles
Apoc. Elijah	Apocalypse of Elijah
As. Mos.	Assumption of Moses
b.	Babylonian Talmud (+ tractate)
Gos. Thom.	Gospel of Thomas
Jos. Asen.	Joseph and Aseneth
Jub.	Jubilees
Let. Aris.	Letter of Aristeas
m.	Mishnah (+ tractate)
Mek.	Mekilta
Midr.	Midrash I (+ biblical book)
Odes Sol.	Odes of Solomon
Pesiq. Rab.	Pesiqta Rabbati
Pirqe. R. El.	Pirqe Rabbi Eliezer
Pss. Sol.	Psalms of Solomon
Rab.	Rabbah (+biblical book); (e.g., Gen. Rab.=Genesis Rabbah)
S. ʿOlam Rab.	Seder ʿOlam Rabbah
Sem.	Semahot
Sib. Or.	Sibylline Oracles
T. Ab.	Testament of Abraham
T. Adam	Testament of Adam
T. Ash.	Testament of Asher
T. Benj.	Testament of Benjamin
T. Dan	Testament of Dan
T. Gad	Testament of Gad
T. Hez.	Testament of Hezekiah
T. Isaac	Testament of Isaac
T. Iss.	Testament of Issachar
T. Jac.	Testament of Jacob
T. Job	Testament of Job
T. Jos.	Testament of Joseph
T. Jud.	Testament of Judah
T. Levi	Testament of Levi
T. Mos.	Testament of Moses
T. Naph.	Testament of Naphtali
T. Reu.	Testament of Reuben
T. Sim.	Testament of Simeon
T. Sol.	Testament of Solomon
T. Zeb.	Testament of Zebulum
Tanh.	Tanhuma
Tg. Isa.	Targum of Isaiah
Tg. Lam.	Targum of Lamentations
Tg. Neof.	Targum Neofiti
Tg. Onq.	Targum Onqelos
Tg. Ps.-J	Targum Pseudo-Jonathan
y.	Jerusalem Talmud (+ tractate)

3. Classical Historians

For an extended list of classical historians and church fathers, see *SBL Handbook of Style*, pp. 84–87. For many works of classical antiquity, the abbreviations have been subjected to the author's discretion; the names of these works should be obvious upon consulting entries of the classical writers in classical dictionaries or encyclopedias.

Eusebius

Eccl. Hist.	Ecclesiastical History

Josephus

Ag. Ap.	Against Apion
Ant.	Jewish Antiquities
J.W.	Jewish War
Life	The Life

Philo

Abraham	On the Life of Abraham
Agriculture	On Agriculture
Alleg. Interp	Allegorical Interpretation
Animals	Whether Animals Have Reason
Cherubim	On the Cherubim
Confusion	On the Confusion of Thomas
Contempl. Life	On the Contemplative Life
Creation	On the Creation of the World
Curses	On Curses
Decalogue	On the Decalogue
Dreams	On Dreams
Drunkenness	On Drunkenness
Embassy	On the Embassy to Gaius
Eternity	On the Eternity of the World
Flaccus	Against Flaccus
Flight	On Flight and Finding
Giants	On Giants
God	On God
Heir	Who Is the Heir?
Hypothetica	Hypothetica
Joseph	On the Life of Joseph
Migration	On the Migration of Abraham
Moses	On the Life of Moses
Names	On the Change of Names
Person	That Every Good Person Is Free
Planting	On Planting
Posterity	On the Posterity of Cain
Prelim. Studies	On the Preliminary Studies
Providence	On Providence
QE	Questions and Answers on Exodus
QG	Questions and Answers on Genesis

Rewards	On Rewards and Punishments
Sacrifices	On the Sacrifices of Cain and Abel
Sobriety	On Sobriety
Spec. Laws	On the Special Laws
Unchangeable	That God Is Unchangeable
Virtues	On the Virtues
Worse	That the Worse Attacks the Better

Apostolic Fathers

1 Clem.	First Letter of Clement
Barn.	Epistle of Barnabas
Clem. Hom.	Ancient Homily of Clement (also called 2 Clement)
Did.	Didache
Herm. Vis.; Sim.	Shepherd of Hermas, Visions; Similitudes
Ignatius	Epistles of Ignatius (followed by the letter's name)
Mart. Pol.	Martyrdom of Polycarp

4. Modern Abbreviations

AASOR	Annual of the American Schools of Oriental Research
AB	Anchor Bible
ABD	Anchor Bible Dictionary
ABRL	Anchor Bible Reference Library
AGJU	Arbeiten zur Geschichte des antiken Judentums und des Urchristentums
AH	Agricultural History
ALGHJ	Arbeiten zur Literatur und Geschichte des Hellenistischen Judentums
AnBib	Analecta biblica
ANRW	Aufstieg und Niedergang der römischen Welt
ANTC	Abingdon New Testament Commentaries
BAGD	Bauer, W., W. F. Arndt, F. W. Gingrich, and F. W. Danker. Greek-English Lexicon of the New Testament and Other Early Christina Literature (2d. ed.)
BA	Biblical Archaeologist
BAFCS	Book of Acts in Its First Century Setting
BAR	Biblical Archaeology Review
BASOR	Bulletin of the American Schools of Oriental Research
BBC	Bible Background Commentary
BBR	Bulletin for Biblical Research
BDB	Brown, F., S. R. Driver, and C. A. Briggs. A Hebrew and English Lexicon of the Old Testament
BDF	Blass, F., A. Debrunner, and R. W. Funk. A Greek Grammar of the New Testament and Other Early Christian Literature
BECNT	Baker Exegetical Commentary on the New Testament
BI	Biblical Illustrator
Bib	Biblica
BibSac	Bibliotheca Sacra
BLT	Brethren Life and Thought
BNTC	Black's New Testament Commentary
BRev	Bible Review
BSHJ	Baltimore Studies in the History of Judaism
BST	The Bible Speaks Today
BSV	Biblical Social Values
BT	The Bible Translator
BTB	Biblical Theology Bulletin
BZ	Biblische Zeitschrift
CBQ	Catholic Biblical Quarterly
CBTJ	Calvary Baptist Theological Journal
CGTC	Cambridge Greek Testament Commentary
CH	Church History
CIL	Corpus inscriptionum latinarum
CPJ	Corpus papyrorum judaicorum
CRINT	Compendia rerum iudaicarum ad Novum Testamentum
CTJ	Calvin Theological Journal
CTM	Concordia Theological Monthly
CTT	Contours of Christian Theology
DBI	Dictionary of Biblical Imagery
DCM	Dictionary of Classical Mythology.
DDD	Dictionary of Deities and Demons in the Bible
DJBP	Dictionary of Judaism in the Biblical Period
DJG	Dictionary of Jesus and the Gospels
DLNT	Dictionary of the Later New Testament and Its Developments
DNTB	Dictionary of New Testament Background
DPL	Dictionary of Paul and His Letters
EBC	Expositor's Bible Commentary
EDBT	Evangelical Dictionary of Biblical Theology
EDNT	Exegetical Dictionary of the New Testament
EJR	Encyclopedia of the Jewish Religion
EPRO	Études préliminaires aux religions orientales dans l'empire romain
EvQ	Evangelical Quarterly
ExpTim	Expository Times

FRLANT	Forsuchungen zur Religion und Literatur des Alten und Neuen Testament
GNC	Good News Commentary
GNS	Good News Studies
HCNT	Hellenistic Commentary to the New Testament
HDB	Hastings Dictionary of the Bible
HJP	History of the Jewish People in the Age of Jesus Christ, by E. Schürer
HTR	Harvard Theological Review
HTS	Harvard Theological Studies
HUCA	Hebrew Union College Annual
IBD	Illustrated Bible Dictionary
IBS	Irish Biblical Studies
ICC	International Critical Commentary
IDB	The Interpreter's Dictionary of the Bible
IEJ	Israel Exploration Journal
IG	Inscriptiones graecae
IGRR	Inscriptiones graecae ad res romanas pertinentes
ILS	Inscriptiones Latinae Selectae
Imm	Immanuel
ISBE	International Standard Bible Encyclopedia
Int	Interpretation
IvE	Inschriften von Ephesos
IVPNTC	InterVarsity Press New Testament Commentary
JAC	Jahrbuch fur Antike und Christentum
JBL	Journal of Biblical Literature
JETS	Journal of the Evangelical Theological Society
JHS	Journal of Hellenic Studies
JJS	Journal of Jewish Studies
JOAIW	Jahreshefte des Osterreeichischen Archaologischen Instites in Wien
JSJ	Journal for the Study of Judaism in the Persian, Hellenistic, and Roman Periods
JRS	Journal of Roman Studies
JSNT	Journal for the Study of the New Testament
JSNTSup	Journal for the Study of the New Testament: Supplement Series
JSOT	Journal for the Study of the Old Testament
JSOTSup	Journal for the Study of the Old Testament: Supplement Series
JTS	Journal of Theological Studies
KTR	Kings Theological Review
LCL	Loeb Classical Library
LEC	Library of Early Christianity
LSJ	Liddell, H. G., R. Scott, H. S. Jones. A Greek-English Lexicon
MM	Moulton, J. H., and G. Milligan. The Vocabulary of the Greek Testament
MNTC	Moffatt New Testament Commentary
NBD	New Bible Dictionary
NC	Narrative Commentaries
NCBC	New Century Bible Commentary Eerdmans
NEAE	New Encyclopedia of Archaeological Excavations in the Holy Land
NEASB	Near East Archaeological Society Bulletin
New Docs	New Documents Illustrating Early Christianity
NIBC	New International Biblical Commentary
NICNT	New International Commentary on the New Testament
NIDNTT	New International Dictionary of New Testament Theology
NIGTC	New International Greek Testament Commentary
NIVAC	NIV Application Commentary
NorTT	Norsk Teologisk Tidsskrift
NoT	Notes on Translation
NovT	Novum Testamentum
NovTSup	Novum Testamentum Supplements
NTAbh	Neutestamentliche Abhandlungen
NTS	New Testament Studies
NTT	New Testament Theology
NTTS	New Testament Tools and Studies
OAG	Oxford Archaeological Guides
OCCC	Oxford Companion to Classical Civilization
OCD	Oxford Classical Dictionary
ODCC	The Oxford Dictionary of the Christian Church
OGIS	Orientis graeci inscriptiones selectae
OHCW	The Oxford History of the Classical World
OHRW	Oxford History of the Roman World
OTP	Old Testament Pseudepigrapha, ed. by J. H. Charlesworth
PEQ	Palestine Exploration Quarterly
PG	Patrologia graeca
PGM	Papyri graecae magicae: Die griechischen Zauberpapyri
PL	Patrologia latina
PNTC	Pelican New Testament Commentaries
Rb	Revista biblica
RB	Revue biblique

RivB	*Rivista biblica italiana*
RTR	*Reformed Theological Review*
SB	Sources bibliques
SBL	Society of Biblical Literature
SBLDS	Society of Biblical Literature Dissertation Series
SBLMS	Society of Biblical Literature Monograph Series
SBLSP	*Society of Biblical Literature Seminar Papers*
SBS	Stuttgarter Bibelstudien
SBT	Studies in Biblical Theology
SCJ	*Stone-Campbell Journal*
Scr	*Scripture*
SE	*Studia Evangelica*
SEG	*Supplementum epigraphicum graecum*
SJLA	Studies in Judaism in Late Antiquity
SJT	*Scottish Journal of Theology*
SNTSMS	Society for New Testament Studies Monograph Series
SSC	Social Science Commentary
SSCSSG	Social-Science Commentary on the Synoptic Gospels
Str-B	Strack, H. L., and P. Billerbeck. *Kommentar zum Neuen Testament aus Talmud und Midrasch*
TC	Thornapple Commentaries
TDNT	*Theological Dictionary of the New Testament*
TDOT	*Theological Dictionary of the Old Testament*
TLNT	*Theological Lexicon of the New Testament*
TLZ	*Theologische Literaturzeitung*
TNTC	Tyndale New Testament Commentary
TrinJ	*Trinity Journal*
TS	*Theological Studies*
TSAJ	Texte und Studien zum antiken Judentum
TWNT	*Theologische Wörterbuch zum Neuen Testament*

TynBul	*Tyndale Bulletin*
WBC	Word Biblical Commentary Waco: Word, 1982
WMANT	Wissenschaftliche Monographien zum Alten und Neuen Testament
WUNT	Wissenschaftliche Untersuchungen zum Neuen Testament
YJS	Yale Judaica Series
ZNW	*Zeitschrift fur die neutestamentliche Wissenschaft und die Junde der alteren Kirche*
ZPE	*Zeischrift der Papyrolgie und Epigraphkik*
ZPEB	*Zondervan Pictorial Encyclopedia of the Bible*

5. General Abbreviations

ad. loc.	in the place cited
b.	born
c., ca.	circa
cf.	compare
d.	died
ed(s).	editors(s), edited by
e.g.	for example
ET	English translation
frg.	fragment
i.e.	that is
ibid.	in the same place
idem	the same (author)
lit.	literally
l(1)	line(s)
MSS	manuscripts
n.d.	no date
NS	New Series
par.	parallel
passim	here and there
repr.	reprint
ser.	series
s.v.	*sub verbo*, under the word
trans.	translator, translated by; transitive

Zondervan Illustrated Bible Backgrounds Commentary

ACTS

by Clinton E. Arnold

Acts as a Second Volume

"Acts" is the second installment of Luke's two-volume account of the ministry, death, and resurrection of Jesus (volume 1) and the story of the beginning of the early church (volume 2). It is an account of God's plan of salvation consummated in Jesus Christ and going out to all peoples—both geographically (from Jerusalem to Samaria, Syria, Asia Minor, Greece, and Italy) and ethnically (not only to Jews, but now embracing Gentiles of every nationality). The book of Acts reflects the continuation of Jesus' ministry after his death and exaltation (Acts 1:1).

COASTLINE OF MYRA IN LYCIA (ASIA MINOR)

> ## Acts
> ## IMPORTANT FACTS:

- **AUTHOR:** Luke. He was a coworker of the apostle Paul, who ministered with him in Troas and Philippi, accompanied him with the collection to Jerusalem, and was with him during his Caesarean and Roman imprisonments. He was a physician who may have come from Syria.

- **PART TWO OF A TWO-VOLUME WORK:** Luke's Gospel is the first half of a single two-volume work ("Luke-Acts"), sharing purpose, themes, and theology with the book of Acts.

- **CENTRAL THEME OF LUKE-ACTS:** Luke seeks to show that *God's great plan of salvation has come to fulfillment in the life, death, resurrection, and ascension of Jesus the Messiah, and continues to unfold as the Spirit-filled church takes the message of salvation from Jerusalem to the ends of the earth.*

- **OTHER KEY THEMES:**
  1. Promise-Fulfillment: The age of salvation has arrived in Jesus the Messiah.
  2. The Age of the Spirit: The sign of the new age is the coming of the Spirit in the ministry of Jesus and the early church.
  3. The gospel is "good news" for all people, regardless of race, gender, or social status.

- **PURPOSE IN WRITING:** To defend and legitimize the claims of the church as the authentic people of God in the present age. To help believers grow in their faith and to inspire their evangelistic zeal.

- **RECIPIENT:** Theophilus, but intended for a larger Christian audience.

Acts is not a comprehensive history of the church, but rather a focused history centering on the beginnings and early development of the church in Jerusalem, the ministry of the apostle Peter (and to some degree, John), and a rather extensive account of the way God used the apostle Paul to take the gospel to Asia Minor, Greece, and Rome. A complete history of the church would have told us about the ministries of the other apostles, the development of the church in Galilee, the story of the spread of Christianity to Egypt, the origins of the church in Rome, and a variety of other topics.

Luke's primary burden is to give testimony to the fact that God's salvation has arrived in and through the Lord Jesus Christ. This salvation is the fulfillment of Israel's hope and is now being sent to Gentiles and to people throughout the entire world.

Luke

Although Luke never names himself as the author of Acts, ancient historians are unanimous in their assertion that Luke was the author of Acts and the third

Gospel. The earliest evidence comes from a late second-century papyrus (P[75]) that has the phrase "the gospel according to Luke" at the end of the scroll. The church father Irenaeus gives fairly extensive testimony about Luke:

> Luke also, the companion of Paul, recorded in a book the Gospel preached by him . . . . But that this Luke was inseparable from Paul, and his fellow-labourer in the Gospel, he himself clearly evinces, not as a matter of boasting, but as bound to do so by the truth itself.[1]

After summarizing the passages in Acts where Luke includes himself in the story (the so-called "we" sections), Irenaeus adds these remarks: "As Luke was present at all these occurrences, he carefully noted them down in writing, so that he cannot be convicted of falsehood or boastfulness."[2]

Another important ancient source, a second-century prologue to the Gospel of Luke, gives additional historical information: "Luke was a Syrian of Antioch, by profession a physician, the disciple of the apostles, and later a follower of Paul until his martyrdom. He served the Lord without distraction, without a wife, and without children. He died at the age of eighty-four in Boeotia [a region in central Greece], full of the Holy Spirit."[3] Eusebius and Jerome contain similar historical traditions about Luke.[4]

Paul refers to Luke three times in his letters.[5] The references in Philemon and Colossians place Luke with Paul in Rome during his imprisonment, which represents historical data that line up with the text of Acts. It was probably during this time that Luke engaged in writing his two-volume work while he served with the apostle Paul as his "fellow worker." In the Colossians passage, Paul speaks of Luke as the "doctor," but we know nothing else about Luke's background, training, or practice as a physician. The apostle extols Luke's faithfulness in 2 Timothy 4:11 when he says, "Only Luke is with me." Paul wrote this comment during his second imprisonment in Rome when he faced his impending martyrdom for the cause of Christ.

In summary, Luke was probably a Gentile Christian, possibly of Syrian (and thus Semitic) origin. He may have been a Jewish sympathizer ("God-fearer") prior to his conversion as his familiarity with Judaism and the Greek Old Testament might suggest. The story of when and how he was converted is unknown.

Theophilus—Luke's Literary Patron

In his introductions both to the Gospel and to the book of Acts, Luke addresses himself to a man named Theophilus. This individual is already a follower of Christ and Luke writes to him so that he may "know the certainty" of the things he has been taught (Luke 1:4). Acts is thus not an evangelistic tract, a defense brief for Paul's trial, or a piece of literature for its own sake. Acts is written by a believer to help another believer and probably a great many more.

In describing Theophilus as "most excellent," Luke uses the term *kratistos*, an expression typically used as a title of respect for a person of high social status and wealth, often a person of equestrian rank in Roman society. Paul uses this title, for instance, to respectfully address the Roman procurators of Judea (Acts 24:3; 26:25). The equestrian order ranked only below the senatorial order in status and had a minimum wealth qualification of

four hundred thousand sesterces.[6] It may well be that as a zealous new believer with a significant amount of wealth, Theophilus desires to use his resources for the sake of the cause of Christ. He finds opportunity for doing so by functioning as a literary patron for Luke.[7]

A possible reconstruction might look something like this: Theophilus is a new believer from the equestrian order in Rome—excited about his new faith, anxious to spread the word, and eager to learn more and grow. He meets Luke shortly after his arrival in Rome with Paul. Luke has already planned to write both the Gospel and Acts, but is unable both to support himself and devote his time to the arduous and time-consuming task of writing. As Theophilus gets to know Luke and hears of his plans, he becomes convinced (not least by the leading of the Holy Spirit) that he should use his resources to subsidize Luke for the period it would take to write the two volumes and then to support the publication of the work. Theophilus personally wants to benefit from Luke's account as a means of facilitating his own knowledge and growth as a Christian, but he also realizes that there are numerous others who could benefit similarly from such a production. Theophilus thus gives generously to support Luke in this endeavor and then funds scribes to make copies of the manuscript for distribution to churches.

Luke's Opportunity For Writing

Luke was uniquely positioned to write this two-volume work. He was a Gentile who had excellent training in Greek, knew the art of rhetoric, had superb research and compositional skills, and was familiar with the conventions of historical writing in the Hellenistic tradition (along the lines of Polybius and Thucydides). Yet Luke also had a strong familiarity with Judaism and the Greek Old Testament, which may have come as a result of involvement in a synagogue prior to becoming a Christian.

Since Luke was not one of the Twelve, he was not an eyewitness to the life and ministry of Jesus or the earliest days of the church. But Luke was a gifted researcher and had the time and opportunity to gather written sources and interview eyewitnesses. When Luke accompanied Paul to Jerusalem in A.D. 57 with the Gentile-Christian delegation, he probably had no idea that he would be spending the next two years in Palestine while Paul was in custody in Caesarea. Yet this time provided him with ample opportunity to collect the information he needed to write his planned account.[8] From Caesarea, Luke probably made repeated visits to Jerusalem to interview the leaders of the church (including a number of the apostles) and likely also had the opportunity to speak with believers who came to Caesarea to visit Paul in his chains.

The time in Caesarea would also have afforded him with many occasions to dialogue with the apostle Paul, who was in a light form of custody and was permitted visitors. After Paul's release, Luke accompanied him on the voyage to Rome, which Luke writes about in great detail as a participant in the events.

Why Did Luke Write Acts?

Luke's intention in writing Acts may best be summed up as "an account of Christian beginnings in order to strengthen faith and give assurance that its foundation is firm."[9] He does this on two levels: (1) by helping his readers understand the story of God's work in and through Jesus of Nazareth and the beginnings of the early church as a means of informing and establishing their beliefs, and (2) by providing them with instruction and inspiration—through moving examples—that will inform their lifestyles, affections, and priorities in life. More specifically, here are a few of the principal ways that Luke hopes to encourage and build up believers:

- He wants to give his readers further confidence in the truthfulness and reliability of their faith (Luke 1:4).
- He wants his readers to recognize that the advent of Christianity is according to God's plan. God himself providentially guided all of the events surrounding the development and growth of the church.[10]
- He wants to assure his readers that God's salvation has come both to Jews and to Gentiles of every social class and background. It represents the fulfillment of divine promises recorded throughout the Hebrew Scriptures. A new era of human history has begun.[11]
- He wants to inspire ongoing evangelistic outreach, prepare his readers with a better understanding of the heart of the gospel (the *kerygma*), and provide them with instructive models on how to proclaim it in a variety of circumstances—whether in a synagogue or in a room full of Greek philosophers.[12]
- He wants to encourage a greater dependence on the Spirit.
- He wants his readers to know that in spite of intense opposition and suffering, their faith is secure and the word of God will prevail.[13]

FIRST-CENTURY JERUSALEM

A reconstruction drawing of Jerusalem in A.D. 30.

When Did Luke Write This Book?

Luke probably wrote the Gospel and Acts during the two-year period of Paul's imprisonment in Rome: A.D. 60–62 (shortly after the last recorded events in Acts).[14]

Introduction (1:1–5)

Luke begins the second volume of his account of the person of Jesus Christ by recalling a series of incredible events immediately following the resurrection. Jesus appeared to his followers over a period of forty days. These appearances served to guarantee the reality of his coming to life again after his painful and torturous death. The Lord also used this time to instruct his disciples about the plan of God and their crucial role in it. He instructs them to wait for a short period of time until they would receive the abiding manifestation of God's empowering presence—the Holy Spirit.

My former book (1:1). The book of Acts complements the Gospel of Luke as the second part of his two-volume work. It was common in Greek, Latin, and even Jewish literature for an author to divide his work into volumes and begin the first with a preface for the whole. The succeeding volumes would each begin with a shorter preface summarizing with a few words the contents of the previous volume.[15] The Jewish historian Josephus, for instance, begins the second volume of his polemic against Apion with a comment similar to Luke's: "In the former book, most honored Epaphroditus, I have demonstrated."[16]

Theophilus (1:1). Luke wrote for the benefit of a person named Theophilus (see "Introduction" and comments on Luke 1:1).

All that Jesus began to do and to teach (1:1). The word "began" conspicuously implies that what Jesus did in his public ministry on earth until the time he was crucified was only a start. Jesus would now continue his proclamation of the kingdom of God and his redemptive ministry by working through his people. This continuation of Jesus' work is the story of Acts.

Gave many convincing proofs that he was alive (1:3). In the final chapter of his Gospel (Luke 24), Luke records some of these appearances (see comments on Luke 24:1–53). The apostle Paul records that Jesus appeared not only to the twelve apostles and to James, but even to five hundred brothers at the same time (1 Cor. 15:5–7). Paul adds that among these five hundred, many were still alive, meaning that anyone who needed eyewitness verification of this incredible claim of bodily resurrection from the dead could easily obtain it.

Spoke about the kingdom of God (1:3). The kingdom of God was the central message of Jesus' teaching during his three-year ministry. It continues to be the central theme of his teaching after his resurrection. The kingdom, however, took a substantially different form than what his Jewish followers were expecting.

The gift my Father promised, which you have heard me speak about (1:4). The Old Testament prophets announced the pouring out of the Holy Spirit in connection with the new covenant. Isaiah 32:15 looks forward to a time when "the Spirit is poured upon us from on high." God says through Ezekiel that, "I will put my Spirit in you" (Ezek. 37:14; cf. 36:27). On the day of Pentecost, Peter specifically connected the outpouring of the Spirit with the prophecy of Joel 2:28–32. Jesus gave his most extensive teaching about the coming Holy Spirit to his disciples in the night before he was crucified (John 14–16).

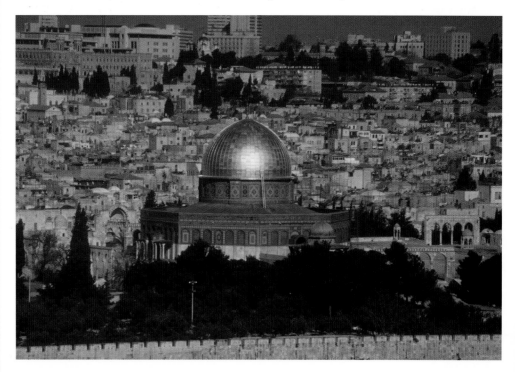

▶

MODERN JERUSALEM

The Muslim Dome of the Rock is prominent on the temple mount.

The Ascension (1:6–11)

Responding to a question that reveals the disciples' ongoing confusion about the nature of the kingdom of God, Jesus declares what is truly central to God's plan for the immediate future. First, this is not the time that God is coming in judgment on the nations and establishing a political earthly reign. Jesus warns his followers even to avoid speculating about the timing of this event; only the Father knows when this will happen. Second, they will soon receive the fulfillment of the new covenant promise of the Holy Spirit. Third, the Spirit will empower them to serve as witnesses of Christ throughout the world. As witnesses, they will testify to Jesus as the Messiah and to his sacrificial death on the cross, his resurrection, and his offer of salvation to all who believe. This task will not be limited to the borders of Israel. Rather, Christ calls them to take their testimony to the entire world.

Forty days after his resurrection, Jesus ascends to the Father. Two angels appear and assure the disciples that Jesus will return.

Are you at this time going to restore the kingdom to Israel? (1:6). Israel at this time was under the political domination of Rome. Most Jews were unhappy with this situation and longed for the time that God would sovereignly intervene in fulfillment of the prophetic texts and remove these impure and arrogant Gentiles from power. The nation took matters into their own hands in A.D. 66 and inaugurated a war with the Roman forces that eventually led to the destruction of Jerusalem and the temple. It appears that the disciples still did not completely understand the nature of this phase of the kingdom plan that Jesus was inaugurating. In fairness to them, however, we need to realize that they had not yet received the indwelling presence of the Holy Spirit. After Pentecost, there was no more misunderstanding about this issue.

In Jerusalem, and in all Judea and Samaria, and to the ends of the earth (1:8). The itinerary Jesus establishes becomes the outline for the book of Acts: "in Jerusalem" (Acts 1–7), "in all Judea and Samaria" (8:1–11:18), and the rest of the book tracks the spread of the gospel through Asia Minor, Greece, and on to Rome.

The ends of the earth (1:8). In a first-century Jewish manner of speaking, this could be a reference to Rome.[17] It is significant in this regard that Luke draws the book of Acts to a conclusion with Paul reaching Rome. Yet it is likely that Luke intends for his readers to see this commission from the Lord as extending far beyond the city of Rome or even the boundaries of the Roman empire. From the perspective of a Roman, the capital city was not on the extremities of the earth, but was rather the center. The empire itself extended far to the north

REFLECTIONS

THE TASK OF TAKING THE GOSPEL to the ends of the earth remains unfinished. As many as 12,000 distinct cultural groups around the world remain unreached, having no church in their language and culture. What is your church doing to support this ongoing mission given to us by the risen Lord? What role will you play?

glory of God (the *shekinah*). It was like the cloud that covered the tent of meeting when the glory of the Lord filled the tabernacle (Ex. 40:34) and the cloud that enveloped Jesus and the other two figures with him when he was transfigured in the presence of three of his disciples (Luke 9:34–36).

Two men dressed in white (1:10). These two men are actually angels. These messengers could manifest their appearance in dazzling white as the two did at the tomb: "Suddenly two men in clothes that gleamed like lightning stood beside them" (Luke 24:4). The fact that there are two is significant for establishing their credibility as witnesses in a Jewish context. The Jewish law stipulates that "a matter must be established by the testimony of two or three witnesses" (Deut. 19:15).

Will come back in the same way (1:11). The angels assure the amazed disciples not only that Jesus will return, but that it will be in a similar fashion. This accords with what Jesus himself taught: "At that time men will see the Son of Man coming in clouds with great power and glory" (Mark 13:26).

(as far as the province of Britannia, modern Great Britain) and a great distance to the west (Spain and Gaul). We know that the apostle Paul planned to preach the gospel as far as Spain (see Rom. 15:24). Jesus here echoes the language of Isaiah 49:6, which anticipates the light of the gospel extending throughout the inhabited earth: "I will also make you a light for the Gentiles, that you may bring my salvation to the ends of the earth."

A cloud hid him from their sight (1:9). This is not a normal cloud. Rather, it is a special cloud that shrouds the divine

The Disciples Wait and Pray (1:12–14)

In roughly the ten days between Jesus' ascension and the coming of the Spirit, the disciples devote themselves to prayer. They meet together in a private room where they spend long hours together calling on the Lord. Their sense of anticipation must have been high in light of Jesus' promise of an outpouring of the Spirit.

The Mount of Olives (1:12). Luke indicates that Jesus ascended not from within the city walls of Jerusalem, but from the Mount of Olives (see "Mount of Olives" at Luke 19:29). Following Jesus' ascension, the disciples return to the city.

A Sabbath day's walk (1:12). This Jewish expression referred to a distance between a half and three-quarters of a mile. The Rabbinic sources stipulate that a Sabbath day's journey was not to exceed two thousand cubits. Given that a cubit was about twenty-two inches, this would be a limit of 3,666 feet (a mile is 5,280 feet). The distance between the temple and the Mount of Olives was within this range.

They went upstairs to the room (1:13). The group met together in an upstairs room of a private home in Jerusalem. Most likely this was a home owned by someone sympathetic with the movement. To accommodate a crowd of this size (later 120 people meet in the room), the home was probably owned by a fairly wealthy person. Archaeologists have recovered the remains of a few homes in the Herodian quarter from this period owned by wealthy citizens.[18] One of these homes, the so-called "Palatial Mansion," had a room that measured thirty-six by twenty-one feet (nearly seven hundred square feet). Early Christian tradition, however, identifies this home with the "Cenacle" (see "The 'Cenacle' ").

The women (1:14). This refers to the same women who visited the tomb of

CENACLE

An historical tradition locates the "upper room" in the Cenacle on Mount Zion.

▶ The "Cenacle"

Christian tradition identifies a place called the "Cenacle" as the "upper room" where the 120 disciples met. The site of the *cenaculum,* a Latin expression meaning "dining room," is today located within the church of the Dormition (built in 1900) on Mount Zion in the southwest corner of the city near the Zion Gate. Although there is nothing visible on this site today that constitutes the upper room at the time of the apostles, there is historical evidence that demonstrates Christian veneration of this site as the location of the home with the upper room since the first century.[A-1] The church father Epiphanius notes that there was "a little church of God" on this site since the time of the emperor Hadrian.[A-2]

Beginning in 1971, excavations were undertaken in this area under the direction of M. Broshi.[A-3] The team found remains of a number of Herodian-era homes that would have been two- and three-story structures. The excavators also discovered a variety of water installations (rock-hewn and barrel-vaulted cisterns, pools, and baths), pottery, a sword, and a few fresco fragments. The finds are consistent with the historical evidence that this was a densely populated portion of the city with wealthy inhabitants living in splendid private homes.

One of these homes—and possibly the site identified as the "Cenacle"—may well have been the location of the upper room. It suggests that a wealthy follower of Jesus opened up his home as a meeting place for this group. Who owned this home is uncertain, but someone such as Mary, the mother of John Mark, is a distinct possibility.[A-4]

Jesus and discovered it was empty: Mary Magdalene, Joanna, and Mary (the mother of James) (see Luke 24:10).

Mary the mother of Jesus (1:14). This is the final time that Mary is mentioned in the New Testament. It is meaningful that the last image we have of her is in prayer.

His brothers (1:14). These brothers are named in only one place in the New Testament (Mark 6:4). They were James, Joseph (or Joses), Judas, and Simon. Before the cross, they were skeptical of his claims (see John 7:5), but now they are devoted to him. James will become the leader of the Jerusalem church and Judas (or Jude) will become the author of a New Testament letter.

Peter Addresses a Group of 120 (1:15–26)

In the ten days between Jesus' ascension and the coming of the Spirit, many of Jesus' followers meet in the upper room of a Jerusalem home and wait on God in prayer. During this time, Peter addresses the group regarding Judas Iscariot and announces the necessity of choosing a man to replace Judas in the special min-

istry that the Lord had entrusted to the Twelve. After calling on the Lord in prayer, the group is sovereignly guided to select a man named Matthias to serve as one of the twelve apostles. These twelve men would serve an important role as witnesses of the resurrection of Jesus, vindicating his claim of being the Messiah of Israel, who died on the cross for the sins of the world.

A hundred and twenty (1:15). It may be significant that according to Jewish tradition, it was necessary to have a hundred and twenty men in a city to have a legitimate Jewish community. The Mishnah says, "And how many should there be in a city that it may be fit to have a Sanhedrin? A hundred and twenty men."[19]

Judas (1:18). On the surface it appears that Luke's account of Judas's death differs from Matthew's in a few places. Matthew says that Judas is remorseful after his betrayal of Jesus, returns the thirty silver coins to the chief priests, and then hangs himself. The chief priests then use the money to buy a potter's field for the burial of foreigners (Matt. 27:1–10). Luke simply states that Judas buys a field with the money and there suffers a terrible fall. Rather than seeing two contradictory stories here, it is better to consider how the various elements combine to give us a more complete picture of what actually happened, especially regarding who buys the field (the priests or Judas?) and how Judas dies (by hanging himself or by taking a nasty fall?). Many interpreters throughout church history as early as Augustine have suggested that the Jewish leaders themselves buy the field in Judas's name (thus explaining Luke's, "Judas bought a field"). It is possible that the leaders pur-

chase the land before Judas's death, since no clear relative time coordinates are given for the purchase of the property and Judas's death. At some point after the priests take possession of the property, Judas decides to commit suicide on this piece of land. It is not surprising that he chooses to take his life there, given his frustration with the priests, initially expressed by his throwing the money into the temple (Matt. 27:5). He manages to devise a way to hang himself, but the rope (or tree branch) breaks under his weight, which results in his body tumbling to the ground (presumably on a rocky surface) and suffering fatal trauma.[20]

They called that field in their language Akeldama, that is, Field of Blood (1:19). *Akeldama* is a compound Aramaic expression. Over the centuries, many have identified Akeldama with a Jewish cemetery located about a half mile south of the Old City of Jerusalem, where the Hinnom Valley joins the Kidron Valley.

In this area, archaeologists have uncovered roughly eighty burial caves, most of which date to the Herodian period (37 B.C.–A.D. 70). Most archaeologists today would discount the identification of this area with the potter's field. The principal reason is that this was not a likely site for a potter's field or as a cemetery for strangers; rather, this was a burial place for the wealthy and priestly families of Jerusalem. One of the tombs probably belonged to the high priest Annas, who held office from A.D. 6–15.[21]

It is written in the book of Psalms (1:20). Peter quotes from two Psalms that he regards as predicting Judas's demise (Ps. 69:25) and the need to find someone to replace him (Ps. 109:8). Because these Psalms were authored by David, Peter understands them messianically and sees in them information that speaks directly to their situation.

It is necessary to choose this apostolic ministry (1:21, 25). Because Jesus had

AKELDAMA, THE FIELD OF BLOOD

The traditional site of Akeldama, the "field of blood," in the Hinnom Valley near the monastery of St. Onuphrius.

chosen *twelve* men to function as his witnesses, Peter and the others consider it essential that an additional witness be chosen by Jesus himself. The term "apostle" comes directly from the Greek word *apostolos* ("one who is sent; a messenger") and is used throughout the New Testament to designate someone sent by Christ to convey a message. The replacement for Judas needs to be one who had a close association with Jesus and the eleven from the beginning of Jesus' public ministry. Above all, this person would function as a witness to the fact of the bodily resurrection of Jesus and the saving significance of this event. These Twelve would pass on as well as safeguard the true tradition about Jesus. This "apostolic ministry" would be significant in laying the foundations for the church.

Joseph called Barsabbas (also known as Justus) (1:23). The name "Bar-Sabbas" is Aramaic for "Son of the Sabbath." We do not know if this was a nickname expressing his former zeal for Sabbath observance or a given name. His proper name was Joseph, but he also took a Roman (Latin) name, Justus.

Matthias (1:23). The lot fell to a man named Matthias. His name is an abbreviated form of "Mattathias," meaning, "the gift of God." The church historian Eusebius reports a tradition that Matthias had been one of the Seventy sent out by the Lord.[22] We know nothing else about either of these men.

They cast lots (1:26). By the casting of lots, Jesus himself would supernaturally make the choice, just as he had chosen the Twelve in his earthly ministry. When they prayed, they specifically asked the Lord Jesus to choose: "Show us which of these two you have chosen" (1:24). The typical method for casting lots involved writing the two names on stones, placing them into a jar, and shaking it until one fell out.[23] This decision-making procedure was not unusual in a Jewish context. The book of Proverbs says, "The lot is cast into the lap, but its every decision is from the LORD" (Prov. 16:33). Examples of this practice can be found in the Old Testament, for instance, in the distribution of responsibilities for working in the temple of the Lord (1 Chron. 26:14–16). After the coming of the Spirit on the day of Pentecost, we do not find this method used again elsewhere in the New Testament.

The Day of Pentecost (2:1–13)

The time finally came when the Lord poured out his Spirit on all the believers. It happened during the Feast of Weeks (which the Greeks called "Pentecost")— a time when many were once again gathered in Jerusalem. The Spirit did not come in a quiet and imperceptible way, but manifested his presence like a surging wind and like tongues of fire. The recipients of the Spirit were then empowered for witness and began immediately by magnifying the greatness of God. Leaving the upper room and moving into the streets, the disciples continued to speak and attracted a large crowd. The Jews who listened could not believe what they heard—Galileans speaking in languages and dialects they could not possibly have known.

▶

LOTS

Dice made of bone found in Jerusalem and dating to the early Roman period.

The coming of the Spirit marked the beginning of the church. The presence of the Spirit is what makes a person a Christian. The event fulfilled prophecies that spoke of the last days and that the Spirit would be imparted (see Isa. 32:15 and Joel 2:28–32). The last days had now arrived.

The day of Pentecost (2:1). The term "Pentecost" is a transliteration of the Greek word *pentēkostē*, which means "fiftieth." It referred to the fiftieth day after the Passover festival when the Jews celebrated the Feast of Weeks—the annual harvest festival (see Lev. 23:15–21 and Deut. 16:9–12). This was the second of three festivals (the others being Passover and Tabernacles) that all Jewish males were required to attend in Jerusalem (Deut. 16:16). It occurred in early summer after the conclusion of the grain harvest. This was a joyous occasion when the Israelites expressed their thanks to God for his provisions through the year and renewed their commitment to him. Later Jewish tradition associated this festival with the giving of the law at Sinai. If this tradition dated as early as the first century, the coming of the Spirit at Pentecost would underscore the Spirit's role in fulfilling and superseding the Mosaic law. This was also an opportune time since Pentecost was the next occasion after Passover that a large crowd would be assembled in Jerusalem.

The blowing of a violent wind ... tongues of fire (2:2–3). The Spirit is associated here with two symbols that often symbolized the manifestation of the presence of God. In Ezekiel's vision of the valley filled with dry bones, the life-giving breath of God comes as a wind and makes these dead bodies live again (Ezek. 37:1–14). This prophecy is linked to the new covenant promise of the indwelling Spirit (Ezek. 37:14). Alluding to Ezekiel's vision, Jesus himself described the coming Holy Spirit as a wind (John 3:8).

During the period of the Exodus, God appeared to Moses as fire. When the Lord revealed himself to Moses the first time, it was in a burning bush (Ex. 3:2–5). God called Moses to be his agent for rescuing the people of Israel from their bondage in Egypt and assured Moses of his enabling presence. After the Exodus, God appeared to Moses again on Mount Sinai. The Lord "descended on it in fire" and gave the law to Moses (Ex. 19:18).

With both the wind and the fire, Luke is careful to point out that the coming of the Spirit was *like* these two common natural phenomena. There was no actual wind or fire. Violent wind and fire represent powerful forces; a divine wind bringing life and fire from above suggests the empowering presence of God.

The image of tongues is probably meant to convey both the miraculous speaking in other languages that the disciples were about to accomplish as well as the ability the Spirit would provide to proclaim the gospel with power.

Staying in Jerusalem (2:5). Numerous Jews from all over the Mediterranean world came to this important festival. The population of Jerusalem swelled from about one hundred thousand inhabitants to around a million during each of the three festivals.[24] Many would stay in private homes and inns, but the majority would have camped in tents both within the city walls and in the vicinity of the city.[25]

In his own language (2:6). Since the time of Alexander the Great, who spread Greek culture all the way to Mesopotamia and beyond, Greek was the official language.

Official documents and letters were written in Greek from countries as far apart as Persia to Spain and North Africa to Gaul. Nevertheless, most people were multilingual and could also speak a local language. It was these local languages and dialects that the Holy Spirit enabled these believers to speak fluently, uttering praises to God.

Galileans (2:7). The majority of Jesus' followers at this point were from Galilee, where he had spent most of his time in his public ministry. The Galileans often bore the brunt of disparaging comments and stereotyping. Most Jewish Galileans were bilingual, speaking both Aramaic and Greek (with some also speaking Hebrew). They would not be capable of speaking the languages and dialects of the various countries represented in Jerusalem on this day.

Parthians . . . Arabs (2:9–11). Luke only gives us a representative list of the countries from which many Jewish pilgrims came. He does not mention many other countries from which a contingent of Jews would have arrived, such as Syria, many of the other Asia Minor territories (Galatia, Caria, Lydia, Cilicia), any territories in Greece (Macedonia, Achaia), other parts of North Africa, or the island of Cyprus.

Converts to Judaism (2:11). This is a translation of the Greek word *prosēlytoi*, from which we get "proselyte." For a male Gentile to become a proselyte, he was required to (1) be circumcised, (2) perform a baptismal rite of purification, and (3) offer a sacrifice at the Jerusalem temple. Only the latter two requirements were mandated for women. Most Gentiles attracted to the one true God preferred the looser requirements in obtaining the status of "God-fearer," especially the men, who could then avoid the rite of circumcision.

Our own tongues (2:11). Each person heard God exalted in his or her own native language or dialect.

THE ROMAN WORLD

The map shows the fifteen locations mentioned in Acts 2:9–11.

▼

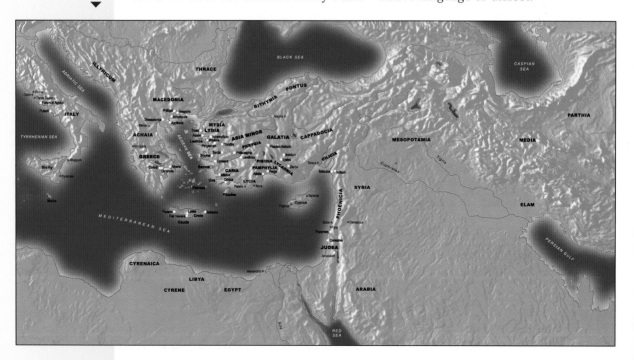

The Countries and Languages Refleccted in Acts 2:9–11		
Country	**Local Dialects**[A-5]	**What Is Known About Judaism There**[A-6]
1. Parthia 2. Media 3. Elam 4. Mesopotamia	Aramaic, *Parthian, Iranian*	It was to these countries in the East—in the area of modern-day Iran and Iraq—that the tribes of Israel were exiled over seven hundred years earlier under the Assyrians (722 B.C.) and later under the Babylonians (586 B.C.). Although they were given permission to return to Israel during the Persian empire (5th cent. B.C.), many chose to stay. By the time of the first century, the number of Jews in this region may have numbered in the hundreds of thousands.
5. Judea	Aramaic, Hebrew	This was the Roman province to which Jerusalem belonged. Jews from all of the surrounding villages streamed to Jerusalem for the festivals.
6. Cappadocia 7. Pontus 8. Asia 9. Phrygia 10. Pamphylia	*numerous local dialects include Phrygian, Pisidian, Lydian, Carian, Lycian, Celtic, Lycaonian, and others.*[A-7]	These five countries were all ethnic territories within the Roman province of Asia Minor (modern-day Turkey). There are numerous literary texts and archaeological evidences illustrating the extensive Jewish presence in Asia Minor from the second century B.C. The earliest Jewish presence can be traced to the late sixth or fifth century B.C.
11. Egypt	Coptic	This was the largest Jewish community in the world at that time. The largest community was in the city of Alexandria, where there may have been as many as a hundred thousand Jews.
12. Libya (Cyrene)	Latin, *Numidian*	There is considerable evidence for Jewish presence in North Africa, especially in the city of Cyrene.
13. Rome	Latin	Jews established a colony in Rome during the second century B.C. The Roman general Pompey brought a great number of Jews to the city from Palestine in 62 B.C. The Jewish population in Rome swelled to as high as twenty thousand by the first century A.D. Those who became Christians at Pentecost returned to Rome and planted the church there—the same church that Paul wrote to in his letter to the Romans.
14. Crete	Greek	This large Greek island had a sizeable Jewish population dwelling primarily in the area of Gorytna. In the second century B.C., they faced persecution from the Cretans, but later secured Roman support. The first-century Jewish writer Philo said that the islands of Euboea, Cyprus, and Crete were "full of Jewish colonies."[A-8]
15. Arabia	Nabatean (a branch of Aramaic), Aramaic, Arabic[A-9]	This would refer to the Nabatean Arabs who lived to the east of the Jordan River and to the south of Palestine. Their capital was Petra, about fifty miles south of the Dead Sea. There is ample evidence of Jewish presence in the key cities (Petra, Hegra) and in the territory.[A-10]

They have had too much wine (2:13). The literal translation of this phrase from the Greek is, "they are filled with sweet wine."

Peter Stands Up and Preaches the Gospel (2:14–36)

Reversing his previous public denial of Jesus, Peter now stands up in front of this large crowd and boldly declares that Jesus is in fact the awaited Messiah of Israel and the sovereign Lord. He cites three passages from the Old Testament demonstrating that the Messiah would be a descendent of David, that he would rise from the dead, and that he would be exalted to the right hand of God. He proclaims that these have all been fulfilled in Jesus of Nazareth.

The actual message Peter gave was probably much longer than what was recorded here. Luke provides us with an accurate abbreviation of this important address.

Peter . . . addressed the crowd (2:14). Peter takes the opportunity to address the gathered crowd by responding to their accusation that the followers of Jesus are drunk. Flanked by the eleven other apostles and inspired by the Holy Spirit, Peter embarks on a long address that elicits an incredible response with many people putting their faith in Jesus. Peter begins by pointing out the absurdity of thinking that over a hundred people would be drunk at nine o'clock in the morning.

In the last days, God says, I will pour out my Spirit (2:17). He immediately explains that what they are witnessing is nothing less than the outpouring of the Spirit predicted in Joel 2:28–32. This coming of the Spirit marks the beginning of the last days. The "age to come" has

arrived and the new covenant blessing of the Holy Spirit is now visibly manifest among those who have put their faith in Jesus.

Your sons and daughters will prophesy (2:17). According to the prophecy, one of the key features of the Spirit's coming would be men and women prophesying. What the crowd was hearing on the day of Pentecost was one form of prophetic utterance.

I will show wonders in the heaven above (2:19). The text of Joel also predicts the occurrence of miraculous signs in space involving the sun and the moon. These astral phenomena, however, will occur in connection with the coming future Day of the Lord. While the coming of the Spirit marks the beginning of the age to come and the commencement of the last days, the signs in heaven will point to the conclusion of the present evil age and the return of the Lord in judgment.

Everyone who calls on the name of the Lord will be saved (2:21). Joel's prophecy is not one of utter gloom and despair. It holds out the bright hope that anyone who calls on the name of the Lord will be saved.

Jesus of Nazareth (2:22). Peter now moves from his explanation about the outpouring of the Spirit to a proclamation of the person of Jesus Christ. He speaks specifically about Jesus' miraculous deeds (which point to the fact that God was active in him) and his violent death. Peter assumes that the crowd was familiar with Jesus' works of power— whether they would publicly admit it or not. He explains, however, that the death of Jesus was not something unexpected. It was an integral part of the plan of God.

God raised him from the dead (2:24). Peter then affirms the reality of Jesus' resurrection from the dead. He does not present an apologetic for an empty tomb at this point, but rather focuses on the Jewish issue of the resurrection as fulfillment of prophecy. To accomplish this, he cites Psalm 16:8–11, a psalm ascribed to David.

You will not abandon me to the grave, nor will you let your Holy One see decay (2:27). Peter's argument hinges on Psalm 16:10, where David declares that he would not be left in the grave nor would his body experience decay. Under the inspiration of the Spirit, Peter argues that this could not refer to David himself because he did in fact die and his tomb is present in Jerusalem for all to see. Rather, this psalm is a prophecy about the greater descendent of David who would sit on David's throne—Jesus the Messiah—whose body did not remain in a tomb nor did it experience decomposition because God raised him from the grave. Peter declares that he and all those with him are eyewitnesses to the fact that Jesus was resurrected.

His tomb is here to this day (2:29). The Jewish historian Josephus confirms that David's tomb was still present in Jerusalem in the first century. He tells the story about a Jewish priest named John Hyrcanus entering the tomb and taking out three thousand talents of silver to give to the invading Syrian king in 134 B.C. with the hope that the invasion could be forestalled.[26] Hearing of this, Herod the Great made a secretive entry into the tomb at night to retrieve more of this treasure. He did not find any money, but he found many gold furnishings. When he tried to penetrate further into the tomb, two of his guards were killed by what he considered to be an act of divine judgment. He fled the tomb and built a white marble monument hoping that this would help to make amends for his indiscretion.[27]

In 1913, the French archaeologist, Raymond Weill, discovered nine burial tombs in the southern portion of the City of David. He identified the largest and most magnificent of these as the tomb of David. This tomb was hewn out of rock and measured over fifty-two feet long, eight feet wide, thirteen feet high at the front and lowering to six feet at the deepest portion. Many archaeologists today dismiss Weill's identification because no corroborating evidence dating the tomb to the time of David has been discovered.[28] Nevertheless, other scholars believe that a reasonable case can be made that this is, in fact, David's tomb.[29]

The Lord said to my Lord: "Sit at my right hand" (2:34). Peter goes on to further establish that Jesus had ascended to heaven and once again argues that this was in fulfillment of prophecy, citing Psalm 110:1, the most frequently cited Old Testament passage in the entire New Testament. The Psalm speaks of the exaltation of Jesus to the right hand of God where he wields kingly authority over his enemies. Peter implicitly understands the address of the Psalm, the Lord said to my Lord, as God speaking to David's Lord, that is, to Jesus.

Both Lord and Christ (2:36). For Peter, the bottom line of his entire message is that Jesus is both Messiah (Christ) and Lord. As Messiah, he is the fulfillment of Israel's expectations for a descendent of David to come and sit on the throne. As Lord, Jesus is at the right hand of God and is *the* sovereign.

A Great Response to the Message (2:37–41)

The crowd had listened intently to everything Peter declared. Rather than rejecting what Peter said about who Jesus was and what he had accomplished on the cross, they became profoundly aware of their own sinfulness. Many in this crowd, no doubt, were among those in the Passover mob who yelled "Crucify! Crucify!" when Pilate mockingly presented Jesus to them as their king (John 19:14–15). They now plead with Peter and the other apostles to tell them how they should respond to his words.

Peter directly tells them to repent and to express their commitment to Christ through baptism. He assures them that Christ would forgive their sins and endow them with the promised Holy Spirit.

The response to this Spirit-inspired message is astonishing. Three thousand Jews from all over the Mediterranean world receive Christ. They are immediately baptized and become the first converts in the beginnings of a movement that would spread rapidly throughout the extent of the Roman empire and ultimately all over the world.

They were cut to the heart (2:37). Luke uses a term that literally means, "to be stabbed (with a knife)." It came to be used to express deep anxiety or profound regret. This is the only time the word is used in the New Testament.

Repent (2:38). This became the central call of early Christian preaching. Repentance (*metanoia*) involves primarily a radical change in a person's central affections, convictions, and life direction. It signifies a recognition that one's life has been oriented around self and sinful pursuits and an embracing of God's will and priorities.

The call to repent is a continuation of Jesus' own ministry introduced by John the Baptist with his call to repentance (Luke 3:3) and repreatedly urged by Jesus himself in his earthly ministry (Luke 13:3, 5; 24:47).

Be baptized. . . . Those who accepted his message were baptized (2:38, 41). From the beginning, baptism has been the central rite performed for incorporating new believers into the church. The word itself is a Greek term, a transliteration of *baptizō*, meaning "to dip (in water)," "immerse," "sink," or "drench."[30]

What Peter calls for here in conjunction with their repentance is an entirely new rite for the people of God. This is appropriate since baptism is associated with the new covenant and the gift of the Holy Spirit. There was some similarity in form, however, to contemporary practices in Judaism. Gentile converts to Judaism were required to be purified in a ritual bath. There is also evidence that many Jews throughout the land performed daily washings in special pools as a way of maintaining ritual purity. This was particularly true at Qumran, where numerous ritual baths (*miqva'ot*) have been discovered.

There were many places in Jerusalem where these new believers could have been baptized. A number of ritual baths were located within the walls of the temple as well as a number of installations west of the temple mount. There were also six large pools in Jerusalem (mentioned by Josephus): the pool of the Towers, the Strouthion Pool, the Sheep's Pool (Bethesda), the Serpents' Pool, Solomon's Pool (the Pool of Siloam), and the Pool of Israel.[31]

In the name of Jesus Christ for the forgiveness of your sins (2:38). This baptism is a one-time rite. It is also specifically a baptism in the name of Jesus Christ. The apostle Paul later characterizes it as vividly symbolizing a participation in Christ's burial and resurrection (Rom. 6:3–4). Identification with Christ—and not the water itself—is the basis for the forgiveness of sins (Acts 2:38).

For all who are far off (2:39). This phrase is an allusion to Isaiah 57:19 where the Prophet points to a day when it will be said, "Peace, peace, to those far and near." Peter applies this promise to all of the Jews who have come from faraway lands and are now recipients of the Spirit of peace. At this point he may not realize it, but the intent of the application of this promise is for Gentiles as well. God will show him this by a vision and by involving him in the conversion of the Gentile household of Cornelius (Acts 10). Paul will apply this prophecy to the inclusion of Gentiles into the one body of Christ (Eph. 2:13).

The Early Christian Experience and Practice (2:42–47)

Luke gives us the first of a series of summary statements about the life and Spirit-directed vitality of these early Christians (see also in 4:32–35; 5:12–16; 9:31; 12:24). So much was happening so fast, but these new believers were commiting themselves to learning more about Jesus, praying, worshiping, and

---

▶ Foundational Elements of Early Christian Life

In a summary statement, Luke lists four key features that characterize the lives of the first Christians. These believers made as a matter of the highest priority "devoting themselves" to these practices:

1. Instruction: The Apostles' Teaching: The twelve apostles had a significant role in the beginnings of the church. They passed on to these new Jewish believers a full account of Jesus' life and teaching. This would have included much of what came to be recorded in the four Gospels. In addition to this, they would have helped provide a new perspective on the Old Testament, explaining how Jesus was the fulfillment of many prophecies. Throughout the early history of the church, grounding new believers in the apostles' teaching was a major priority.

2. Fellowship: It was important to these early believers to spend much time together. These hours would have been passed in discussing the apostles' teaching, encouraging and challenging each other, and enjoying one another in the family bond that the Spirit created. This "fellowship" also extended to a tangible manifestation of love for one another that found expression in sharing with the poorer members of this new community.

3. Worship: The Breaking of Bread: This expression refers both to sharing ordinary meals together (furthering their fellowship) and to remembering the significance of the death of the Messiah by celebrating what came to be known as "the Lord's Supper." At this stage, the Lord's Supper was held in conjunction with a common meal in homes throughout the city. This remembrance would have been a time of quiet reflection, as well as an occasion for expressing thanks to the risen Jesus and praising him for what he had accomplished.

4. Prayer: The first Christians spent much time before the Lord in prayer. They prayed privately, but they often prayed together as a group. It appears that many maintained the Jewish pattern of setting aside three times a day for focusing on prayer. Some continued to go to the temple and pray at the customary Jewish hours of prayer. Their prayers probably centered on blessing and praising God as well as asking him for guidance and for boldness in proclaiming the Gospel.

enjoying a vibrant community life. They were also committed to proclaiming Jesus as the Messiah to others and God was powerfully at work through their testimony. Every day more people were confessing Jesus and joining their community.

Wonders and miraculous signs (2:43). The Spirit of God works through the twelve apostles to perform many healings and to cast demons out of people. These miracles contribute to the development of a climate of receptivity to the gospel message.

All the believers were together (2:44). They did not all move into a communal living arrangement together, but rather they develop a strong sense of community. They confess a common Lord, spend much time together, share with one another, and participate in a common vision and purpose.

REFLECTIONS

"FELLOWSHIP" AND SPENDING time together regularly to deepen relationships and serve one another is a significant challenge facing the church—especially in the larger churches of heavily populated areas. Work schedules, the pull of entertainment, and the proliferation of various activities undermine community. The result is that believers sometimes feel disconnected, uncared for, and unloved. Many Christians even see church as something that you do only once a week. What steps can be taken to develop more true fellowship among believers?

Had everything in common (2:44). Sometimes a false impression is gained that these early Christians sold everything they owned when they joined the church. This was, in fact, the practice of the Qumran community on the Dead Sea. When someone joined that group, his property and earnings were all handed over to a trustee in the community and it became part of a common fund.[32] This is not the case, however, for these first believers. Their commitment to Jesus and the work of the Spirit in their lives produce in them a completely new attitude to their property. No longer are they motivated to amass wealth for themselves, but they now view what they have as resources for the cause of Christ and for the care of his people. The verb tense for "selling" (the imperfect) implies that there was not one big sale of goods upon a person's conversion, but that individuals sold portions of their personal and real property as needs in the community surfaced. This was entirely voluntary and not mandated by the apostles.

The temple courts (2:46). The Greek text reads simply, "in the temple." Luke does not specify here exactly which part of the temple precincts these three to four thousand believers met each day, but later he tells us that they met "in Solomon's Colonnade" (see comments on 5:12).

In their homes (2:46). Some of the wealthier members of the church owned private residences in the city of Jerusalem. Rather than sell their homes, they opened them up for the Christians to meet. Private homes were the principal meeting places of early Christians for the first three centuries of the church's existence.

A WEALTHY HOME

A model of a typical affluent family house in Herodian upper Jerusalem.

Recent excavations in Jerusalem on the Western Hill (part of the Upper City) have resulted in the discovery of a residential district in the ancient city. There were many houses in this area that would have belonged to the wealthier inhabitants of the city.[33] It is not known whether any of these homes were the places where one or more of the groups of early Christians gathered, but they do help us to see the kind of setting for some of the home groups (see "The 'Cenacle'").

ENTRANCE TO A MIQVEH

The entrance to a ritual bath in the remains of a Herodian-era home on the western hill in upper Jerusalem.

Peter and John Heal a Lame Beggar (3:1–10)

Some time after the day of Pentecost—perhaps as much as a couple of years later (Luke does not tell us)—an amazing incident happens near a gate in the temple courts. Two of the apostles, Peter and John, are confronted by a lame beggar who asks them for money. They, in turn, manifest the healing power of Jesus to restore the paralyzed limbs of this destitute man. Cured of his paralysis, the man promptly makes a spectacle in the temple courts by demonstratively praising God for his healing. Such an incident of healing is not out of ordinary in these early days and months of the church. Luke has previously said that they are commonplace in the ministry of the apostles (see 2:43). Luke chooses to tell us about this episode because it attracts a large crowd and gives Peter

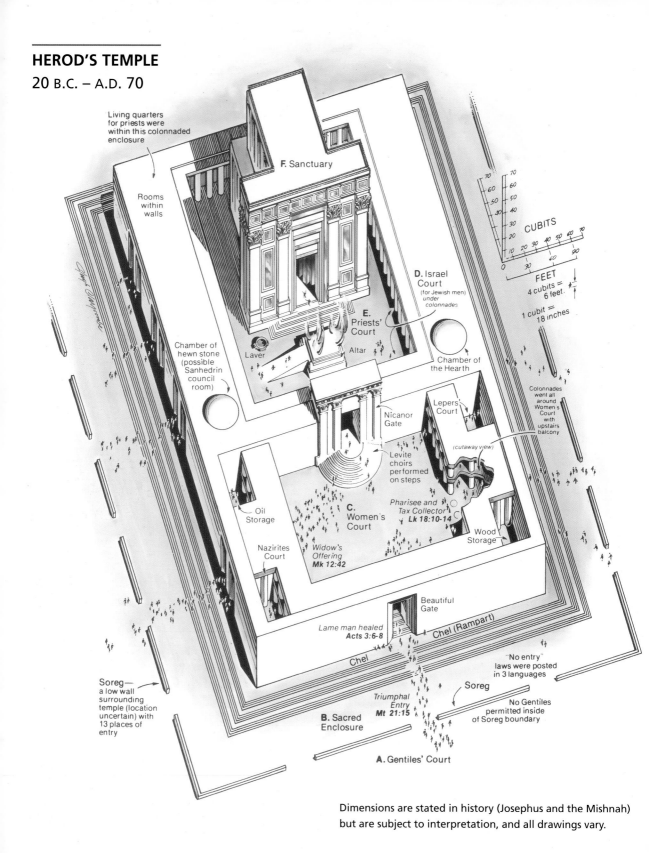

HEROD'S TEMPLE
20 B.C. – A.D. 70

Living quarters for priests were within this colonnaded enclosure

Rooms within walls

F. Sanctuary

D. Israel Court
(for Jewish men) under colonnades

E. Priests' Court

Chamber of hewn stone (possible Sanhedrin council room)

Laver

Altar

Chamber of the Hearth

CUBITS

FEET
4 cubits = 6 feet.

1 cubit = 18 inches

Nicanor Gate

Lepers' Court

Colonnades went all around Women's Court with upstairs balcony

Levite choirs performed on steps

(cutaway view)

Oil Storage

C. Women's Court

Pharisee and Tax Collector
Lk 18:10-14

Wood Storage

Nazirites Court

Widow's Offering
Mk 12:42

Beautiful Gate

Lame man healed
Acts 3:6-8

Chel (Rampart)

Chel

"No entry" laws were posted in 3 languages

Soreg

Soreg—
a low wall surrounding temple (location uncertain) with 13 places of entry

Triumphal Entry
Mt 21:15

No Gentiles permitted inside of Soreg boundary

B. Sacred Enclosure

A. Gentiles' Court

Dimensions are stated in history (Josephus and the Mishnah) but are subject to interpretation, and all drawings vary.

another unique opportunity to proclaim the gospel.

The time of prayer—at three in the afternoon (3:1). According to Josephus, the priests at the temple "twice each day, in the morning and about the ninth hour [= 3 P.M.]" offer the daily animal sacrifice prescribed by the law of Moses (see Num. 28:1–8) and referred to in Judaism as the *tamid*.[34] Following an offering of incense, a sacrificial lamb is slaughtered on the altar. This is accompanied by the priest presenting a cereal offering (an unleavened loaf of wheat flour and oil) and a drink offering (a libation of wine). The priests then lead those in attendance in a time of singing and prayer. The Mishnah describes this time of prayer following the sacrifice:

> When he stooped to pour out the drink offering the Prefect waved the towel and Ben Arza [a priest] clashed the cymbal and the levites broke forth into singing. When they reached a break in the singing they blew upon the trumpets and the people prostrated themselves [in prayer]; at every break there was a blowing of the trumpet and at every blowing of the trumpet a prostration [in prayer]. This was the rite of the daily whole-offering in the service of the House of our God.[35]

In these early stages of the church, the apostles and the other believers (who were all Jewish) continue to observe the set times of worship in the Jerusalem temple.

A man crippled from birth (3:2). It was not at all surprising to find poor and handicapped people begging for a handout in Jerusalem and particularly near the temple. Charitable giving was viewed as particularly meritorious when it was done here.[36]

The temple gate called Beautiful (3:2). This is most likely one of the gates in the Court of Women, either on the west side leading to the Court of the Israelites (also called the Corinthian gate or the gate of the Sanctuary) or on the east side leading to the Court of the Gentiles. Both of these gates were exceptionally grand and ornate in appearance, appropriately fitting the description "beautiful." Josephus describes their size and splendor well:

> Of the gates nine were completely covered with gold and silver, as were the posts and lintels, but the one outside the Sanctuary was of Corinthian bronze, and far more valuable than those overlaid with silver or even with gold. Every gateway had double doors, each half being 45 feet high and 22-1/2 wide. On the inner side

THE GOLDEN GATE (THE BEAUTIFUL GATE)

According to Jewish tradition, this gate (from the Early Islamic period) was built upon the foundations of the original Eastern Gate of the Temple Mount.

▼

however the gateways widened out, and on either hand there was a gate-room 45 feet square, shaped like a tower and over 60 feet high. Each room was supported by two pillars 18 feet round. The other gates were all of the same size, but the one beyond the Corinthian gate, opening out from the court of the Women on the east and facing the gate of the Sanctuary, was much bigger; for its height was 75 feet, that of the doors 50, and the decoration was more magnificent, the gold and silver plates being extremely thick.[37]

In the name of Jesus Christ of Nazareth, walk (3:6). Hoping to get a charitable handout from Peter and John as they pass through the gate, the lame man receives far beyond what he could have imagined. Staring at him, Peter says, "In the name of Jesus Christ of Nazareth, walk." By this statement, Peter acts not on his own authority, but he is appealing to the risen Jesus to manifest his healing power. Jesus himself, by contrast, heals on the basis of his own authority during his earthly ministry. Other itinerant healers of the time call on various kinds of deities (such as

Asclepius) or helper spirits to attempt their healings. Peter calls on the power of the exalted Lord. This healing marks yet another instance of the ongoing work of Christ through the church as Luke has announced at the beginning of his work when he says that his Gospel is an account of "all that Jesus *began* to do and to teach" (1:1).

The man's feet and ankles are miraculously strengthened—in fact so much so that he is able to run and jump. Staying close to the apostles' side, the man accompanies them into the temple courts unable to contain his exuberance over what God has done for him. Because all of the onlookers know well the pitiable state of the man before, they are astonished and wonder what has happened.

Peter Speaks at the Temple (3:11–25)

Taking advantage of this singular opportunity, Peter addresses the crowd. They give their full attention to Peter because there is incontrovertible evidence standing right before them that Peter and John could exercise some kind of supernatural power. What is this power that healed the crippled man so dramatically? Is this a sign to them from God?

In his message, Peter strongly emphasizes that the healing is performed in the power of the risen Jesus. He testifies to the crowd that Jesus is indeed the anticipated Messiah and offers his point on the basis of many Old Testament prophetic texts that find their precise fulfillment in the ministry of Jesus. This is not strictly an informational speech. Peter stresses to the crowd their guilt before God in rejecting the Messiah and, in fact, joining the rest of the mob in demanding his death. Peter then tells them that it is not too late for them to be reconciled to God if they repent of their sin and turn to God by embracing the risen Jesus as the Messiah who will forgive their sin and come again to fulfill God's kingdom program on earth.

Solomon's Colonnade (3:11). The entire temple platform was surrounded by beautiful colonnades on the perimeter of the outer court. The colonnade on the east side is referred to as "Solomon's Colonnade" (or "portico," "stoa," or "porch"). On the other side of the eastern temple wall would have been a steep hillside descending to the Kidron Valley. Josephus provides us with a detailed description of the colonnade:

> The colonnades were all double, the supporting pillars were 37 -1/2 feet high, cut from single blocks of the whitest marble, and the ceiling was panelled with cedar. The natural magnificence of it all, the perfect pol-

ish and the accurate jointing afforded a remarkable spectacle, without any superficial ornament either painted or carved. The colonnades were 45 feet wide and the complete circuit of them measures three quarters of a mile, Antonia being enclosed within them.[38]

This eastern colonnade would then have extended for over three hundred yards. One part of this large area apparently became a popular meeting spot for the first Christians in Jerusalem (see also Acts 5:12). The entire colonnade was destroyed during the Jewish war (A.D. 66–70); only the temple platform remains.

The God of Abraham, Isaac and Jacob (3:13). Peter seizes this unique opportunity to address the crowd and begins by immediately clarifying that the man is not healed by any inherent powers that he or John possesses. He points them to

SOLOMON'S COLONNADE

A model of the Royal Stoa as it would have appeared from the northeast.
▼

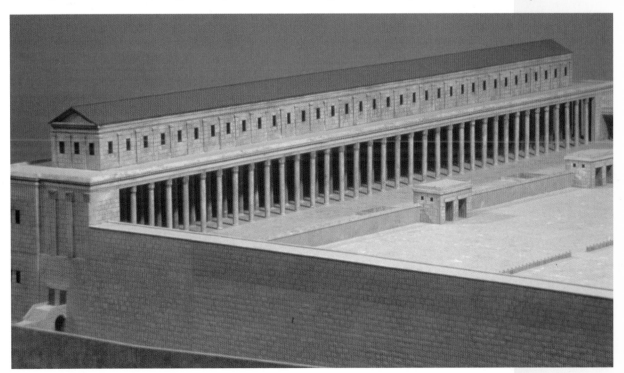

the one God that they all worship—the God who reveals himself to Moses at the burning bush as "I Am" (Yahweh), the God of Abraham, Isaac, and Jacob" (see Ex. 3:4–6).

Servant Jesus (3:13). Yet Peter attributes the healing to God's glorified servant, Jesus. For the Jew, "Servant" is a significant expression. It is an allusion to the Servant Songs of the prophet Isaiah. Isaiah 52:13 says that the servant "will be raised and lifted up and highly exalted." Yet this will only follow a period of suffering.

The author of life (3:15). Peter immediately moves on to speak of the suffering the Servant of God experienced. Peter directly accuses the assembled crowd of handing Jesus over to be killed. Presumably many of those present in this crowd are among those who join with the throng in demanding before the Roman proconsul that Jesus be crucified. Their assent makes them guilty of the most heinous crime imaginable. Peter accuses them of the amazing paradox of killing the author of life. This title points to Christ as the source of life, a function normally ascribed to the Father in the Old Testament. Using the same words, the writer of Hebrews later refers to Jesus as "the author of salvation" (Heb. 2:10). Jesus does not remain in the grave, however, for God raises him. Peter and John are now eyewitnesses of this important fact.

Peter once again makes it clear that it is the power of the risen Christ, represented by his name, that has healed the man. Belief in the person and the power of Jesus, not any kind of magic or personal power, has made the man well.

Foretold through all the prophets (3:18). Peter tells them that they acted in ignorance, although this is no excuse before God. It was in the predetermined plan of God that Jesus would die. For most Jews this would have been difficult to see. Where does it explicitly state in the Old Testament that the Messiah would suffer? Part of the difficulty for many Jews is that they do not understand some of the prophecies in the Old Testament as pointing to the Messiah and therefore do not expect a *suffering* Messiah. For instance, most Jews interpret the Suffering Servant in Isaiah 52–53 as referring to themselves (in a corporate sense): They are the ones who have suffered and there is atoning significance to their suffering. Jesus, however, has used the language and imagery of the Suffering Servant to characterize his own mission (see, for example, Mark 10:45). He would be the representative of the people who would die an atoning death. This prophecy of Isaiah then becomes a central part of early Christian preaching to demonstrate that the Messiah would suffer and die. Yet there are other Old Testament texts that speak in a typological or prophetic way of the suffering of the Messiah.[39] The whole sacrificial system, in fact, points to a final and effective sacrifice.

REFLECTIONS

"I KNOW DEEP DOWN THAT I WILL still pay for some of the terrible things I have done." This is the sentiment that some Christians cling to in their hearts (often secretly) because of sinful choices and behaviors prior to coming to know Christ or even after becoming a Christian. Yet this notion is patently false. God wipes away the *entire* record of our sinful misdeeds.

So that your sins may be wiped out (3:19). As in his preaching at Pentecost, Peter now calls on the people to repent and turn to God so that their sins could be wiped out. This is a rare and colorful word that only appears in the Gospels and here in Acts. The term (*exaleiphō*) is used in the contemporary literature for the erasure or blotting out of a written record. The point is that there would no longer be any record of their complicity in the death of Jesus or any of their transgressions before God. Paul uses the same word in Colossians 2:14 to describe the forgiveness of sins.

Times of refreshing (3:19). By repenting and turning to God's plan in Jesus as the Messiah, Peter announces that there will be a future blessing. They will be able to participate fully in the future times of refreshing when Jesus returns and the kingdom of God is fully realized. This will be the time when God restores everything, establishing his order on earth.

He must remain in heaven until the time comes (3:21). Peter's comment indicates that a certain amount of time must elapse until the Messiah returns. As Jesus said, "No one knows about that day or hour, not even the angels in heaven, nor the Son, but only the Father" (Matt. 24:36).

All the prophets . . . have foretold these days (3:24). In this latter part of Peter's message, he appeals to further prophetic texts that point to the Messiah. He begins with a prophecy of Moses who pointed to a coming "prophet like me" that would arise and lead God's people (see Deut. 18:15–19). He also points to the covenant promise that God made with Abraham indicating that God would bless the nations through Abraham's offspring (Gen. 12:3; 22:18; 26:4). For Peter, Jesus the Messiah is the means by which this promise will be realized. At this point, it is doubtful that Peter appreciates the full scope of this promise and that he will soon be proclaiming the gospel to Gentiles (see Acts 10). The first opportunity for responding to these blessings will be extended to Abraham's physical descendants, the Jews.

Peter and John Are Arrested (4:1–22)

The apostles' continued proclamation of Jesus in the temple courts and the incredible number of his followers cause great concern among the Jewish leaders. The crucifixion of the leader of the movement has by no means put a stop to it. After arresting Peter and John, the high court of Israel interrogates the two witnesses. The rulers are overwhelmed by their boldness and persuasive appeal and so order them never to speak about Jesus again.

The captain of the temple guard (4:1). The wording of the NIV text can give the impression that there is an armed temple security force distinct from the priesthood. There is, however, no professional police force; security is handled by the priests. This official (*stratēgos*) is a priest who is second in authority to the chief priest. He stands at the high priest's right hand during the Day of Atonement ritual and whenever the high priest offers the daily sacrifice.[40] He supervises the day-to-day activities of the temple and is in charge of keeping order. He possesses the legal right to make an arrest. The potential military skill of this official is well illustrated by the example of Eleazar (captain of the temple guard in A.D. 66), who was made a general in the Jewish war of independence.[41]

The Sadducees (4:1). Well known through their repeated appearances in the Gospels (see "Sadducees" at Luke 5:24), the Sadducees were a wealthy group of politically influential Jews, many of whom were priests. They held a more moderate attitude toward the Torah than the Pharisees or the Essenes and tended to be more open to Greek cultural influences (Hellenism). The name of this group most likely derives from Zadok, the high priest under David (the first Old Testament reference is 2 Samuel 8:17, where he was co-priest with Abiathar; his descendants held the priestly office in Jerusalem since Solomon's time).

Later in Acts 23:8, Luke tells us that the Sadducees refuse to accept the belief in a future resurrection of the dead, a view espoused by the Pharisees. This is confirmed by Josephus.[42] The Sadducees may have considered the idea of a resurrection as a liberal innovation since it is not perfectly clear in the Torah. Josephus says that "according to their teaching, souls perish together with bodies."[43]

The number of men grew to about five thousand (4:4). A short time earlier following Peter's sermon on the day of Pentecost, the community of believers in Jerusalem has increased by three thousand (2:41). To this number are added two thousand more. The fact that Luke uses the term *anēr* for men (versus the more generic *anthrōpos*), indicates that he has not included all of the women and young people in his figure.

The rulers, elders and teachers of the law (4:5). These three groups composed the Jewish ruling council, the Sanhedrin (see "The Sanhedrin" at 4:15). "Rulers"

(*archontes*) refers specifically to the high priest and the chief priests, the most prominent of whom are specifically named in verse 6. "Elders" (*presbyteroi*) is a special term used to designate the lay members of the council. These were probably representatives of the aristocratic families in Jerusalem and tended to ally themselves with the Sadducees.[44]

The final expression (*grammateus*) is translated by most other versions as "scribes." They were a professional class of scholars invested with the responsibility of interpreting, teaching, and preserving the Jewish law. They were esteemed as the spiritual leaders of the people and, for the most part, were allied with the Pharisees (although there were undoubtedly some scribes associated with the Sadducees).

Annas the high priest (4:6). Annas retired from his high priesthood some twenty years earlier. He bore the title "high priest" only in an emeritus sense. Nevertheless, his age, experience, and family associations gave him significant personal authority. Annas became high priest in A.D. 6 and served in that capacity for nine years (until A.D. 15). He played a significant part in the trial of Jesus (see John 18:13–14).

Caiaphas (4:6). Joseph Caiaphas became high priest in A.D. 18 and was able to retain his position for nineteen years (until A.D. 37). He was the son-in-law of Annas (John 18:13). As high priest, he not only officiated at the temple, but served as president of the Sanhedrin and as the political head of the Jewish nation.

John, Alexander and the other men of the high priest's family (4:6). All of these men were "rulers" in Jerusalem as members of the Sanhedrin. It is likely that

John (or Jonathan) was one of the five sons of Annas who later succeeded his brother-in-law as high priest in A.D. 37.[45] A recently discovered ossuary inscription found in the vicinity of Jerusalem mentions John. It reads: "Yehohanah, daughter of Yehohanah [John], son of Theophilus the high priest."[46] The Theophilus of this inscription, who began his service as high priest in A.D. 37, is the father of John.

By what power or what name did you do this? (4:7). These leaders of the Sanhedrin do not question the reality of the healing; the evidence is apparently beyond dispute. They assume, however, that the miracle is not done on the basis of power from the one true God. It was common in the Greco-Roman world to call on various deities, helper spirits, and magical names and symbols to effect healing. In response, Peter makes it clear that the healing has nothing to do with magic, but only with the Lord Jesus Christ.

He is "the stone you builders rejected, which has become the capstone" (4:11). Peter not only responds to their question, but offers an incisive rebuke. He claims that their rejection of Jesus and Jesus' current place of honor in God's plan fulfills Psalm 118:22, which he cites. By appealing to this passage, Peter follows the lead of Jesus himself (see Matt. 21:42). The force of this quotation and rebuke may be underlined by the fact that the scribes are described as "builders" in rabbinic literature.[47]

"Capstone" is an interpretation of the expression "head of the corner." As one author describes, "It expresses rather the

◄

CORNERSTONE

Herodian-era masonry in Jerusalem.

▶ The Appointments of Annas and Caiaphas (According to Josephus)

The Jewish historian Josephus gives a succinct account of the deposition of Annas from the high priesthood and the appointment of Caiaphas in the context of the Roman governorship of Judea:

Tiberius Nero, [Caesar Augustus's] wife Julia's son, succeeded. He was now the third emperor; and he sent Valerius Gratus to be procurator of Judea, and to succeed Annius Rufus. (34) This man deprived Ananus of the high priesthood, and appointed Ismael, the son of Phabi, to be high priest. He also deprived him in a little time, and

ordained Eleazar, the son of Ananus, who had been high priest before, to be high priest: which office, when he had held for a year, Gratus deprived him of it, and gave the high priesthood to Simon, the son of Camithus; (35) and when he had possessed that dignity no longer than a year, Joseph Caiaphas was made his successor. When Gratus had done those things, he went back to Rome, after he had tarried in Judea eleven years, when Pontius Pilate came as his successor.[A-11]

function of a main, often oversized, stone used at an important spot in the joining of two walls of a building, to bear their weight and stress."[48] This usage is well-illustrated by the *Testament of Solomon:* "So Jerusalem was being built and the temple was moving toward completion. Now there was a gigantic cornerstone which I [Solomon] wished to place at *the head of the corner* to complete the Temple of God."[49]

Unschooled, ordinary men (4:13). The point of their criticism is that Peter and John both lack formal scribal training in the law. This is seen clearly in the Greek where the contrast is between *grammateis* and *agrammatoi,* that is, between scribes and those without scribal training.

Judge for yourselves whether it is right in God's sight to obey you rather than God (4:19). Peter and John let it be known that they will defy the injunctions of the Sanhedrin if the council rules to prohibit them from proclaiming the gospel of Jesus Christ. They portray their decision as choosing to obey God rather than men thereby implying that the Sanhedrin's ruling on this matter is not from God. This is an extraordinarily bold and audacious statement. All Jews were accustomed to viewing the Sanhedrin as the final and binding interpreter of the Hebrew Scriptures. These two men, without any scribal training, now challenge the validity of the Sanhedrin's ruling and undermine the integrity of the supreme ruling body of all Israel.

A similar statement was uttered by Socrates when he stood trial in Athens and was ordered to stop teaching his philosophy or "if you are caught doing so again you shall die." Socrates declared, "Men of Athens, I respect and love you, but I shall obey the god rather than you, and while I live and am able to continue, I shall never give up philosophy or stop exhorting you and pointing out the truth to any one of you whom I may meet."[50]

▶ **The Sanhedrin**

The Sanhedrin was the ruling body of the Jewish people. It was composed of seventy people plus the high priest, who presided over the council. Although Palestine was ultimately under the control of the Romans through the appointed procurator, the emperor had granted the Jews a great deal of self-governing powers. The Sanhedrin was essentially a senate that directly governed the eleven districts (*toparchies*) of Judea. The group made judicial rulings and conducted the administrative affairs of Judea. But the decisions of the Sanhedrin carried substantial weight for Jews scattered throughout the Mediterranean world. It was the final board for deciding on matters connected with the Jewish law.

In the New Testament era, the Sanhedrin was controlled by the chief priests (most of whom were Sadducees) and the wealthy nobility of Jerusalem. The Pharisees had increasing representation on the council through some of their scribes who retained seats. The Pharisaic popularity with the masses, however, gave their voice significant power on the council.

The Sanhedrin met in a building to the west of the southern end of the temple precincts near the so-called Xystus/*Lishkath ha-Gazith* (an open square close to the palace).[A-12] The Talmud describes the council chamber as "like a great basilica."[A-13] A bridge led directly from the Sanhedrin's council building across the Tyropoeon valley directly to the temple mount. This bridge has been identified by archaeologists as "Wilson's Arch."[A-14] The council building and the bridge were completely destroyed by the Romans in A.D. 70.

It is not certain whether Peter would have been familiar with this statement (although Luke would probably have known it). The principle of obedience to God's commands as a matter of paramount importance, however, is deeply rooted in the Old Testament. After Saul's failure to obey God by completely routing the Amalekites, for instance, the prophet Samuel told Saul, "Does the LORD delight in burnt offerings and sacrifices as much as in obeying the voice of the LORD? To obey is better than sacrifice . . . . For rebellion is like the sin of divination, and arrogance like the evil of idolatry" (1 Sam. 15:22–23). The repeated mistake of many of the leaders of Israel in generations past was in following "the stubborn inclinations of their evil hearts" rather than obeying God (Jer. 7:23–26). This is how Peter and John interpret the stubbornness and intransigence of Israel's present leadership in not only refusing to recognize Jesus as Messiah, but also by ardently opposing the proclamation of this good news.

The Believers Gather and Pray for Confidence to Proclaim the Gospel (4:23–31)

Peter and John immediately return to their fellow believers and report all that has transpired in the hearing before the Sanhedrin. Undoubtedly feeling dismayed at the intransigence of the Jewish leaders and rather intimidated by the threats, they lift their voices as a group before God in prayer. Surprisingly, they don't ask for protection, but for boldness to continue sharing Christ. They also ask God to continue to manifest his healing power, as he has just done with the crippled man, to demonstrate the authenticity and source of the message they are proclaiming.

Sovereign Lord (4:24). The group addresses God as *despota*, from which is derived the English word "despot." But there are no overtones of tyranny in the Greek expression, only the idea of one who wields absolute and sovereign power. This same way of addressing God is found elsewhere in the New Testament (e.g. Luke 2:29; Rev. 6:10) and in the Greek Old Testament (Gen. 15:2, 8; Josh. 5:14). When Jeremiah was called by God as a prophet, he addressed God: "'Ah, Sovereign LORD (*despota*),' I said, 'I do not know how to speak; I am only a child.' But the LORD said to me, 'Do not say, "I am only a child." You must go to everyone I send you to and say whatever I command you. Do not be afraid of them, for I am with you and will rescue you,' declares the LORD" (Jer. 1:6–8).

Why do the nations rage? (4:25). These believers remind God of what he said through David in Psalm 2, a psalm that early Christians applied to Christ because of its reference to the "anointed one" and the similarities to their own situation. The raging of the "nations" (lit., the "Gentiles") is seen to correspond to the Romans who sentenced Jesus to death by crucifixion. The "peoples" of Israel conspired with the Romans to execute this sentence. The actions of the "kings" and "rulers" find their fulfillment in Herod and Pontius Pilate. This Herod is not Herod the Great, but his son, Herod Antipas.

Against his Anointed One (4:26). Their rage is directed at God's *christos*, his Messiah. In its original context, Psalm 2 refers to David as God's "anointed" king. Here it is interpreted as fulfilled in the descendent of David "whom you [God himself] anointed" (4:27). This becomes an explicit identification of Jesus of Nazareth as the Messiah and, of course, is what the Sanhedrin adamantly rejects.

They did what your power and will had decided beforehand should happen . . . . Stretch out your hand (4:28, 30). "Your power" is the NIV interpretation of "your hand." The hand of God is a common image in the Old Testament to represent the power and strength of God. It is by God's "mighty hand" that Pharaoh was forced to free the Israelite captives (see Ex. 3:19–29; 6:1; 7:4–5). When Moses stretched out his hand over Egypt, God performed many miraculous signs and wonders through him (see Ex. 8:5; 9:22; 10:12). The psalmist writes reassuringly, "Though I walk in the midst of trouble, you preserve my life; you stretch out your hand against the anger of my foes, with your right hand you save me" (Ps. 138:7).

The place where they were meeting was shaken (4:31). After these believers pray, God gives them this unmistakable sign that he has heard them and that he is present with them. The psalmist observes, "Nations are in an uproar, kingdoms fall; he lifts his voice, the earth melts [lit., *is shaken*]. The LORD Almighty is with us" (Ps. 46:6–7). The earth shakes when the Lord is present: "Tremble [lit., *shake*], O earth, at the presence of the Lord, at the presence of the God of Jacob" (Ps. 114:7).

The Community Experience of the Early Believers (4:32–37)

The Holy Spirit is powerfully at work in transforming the lives of these new believers and shaping this new community. Unity, generosity, and powerful witness are some of the key characteristics of this group.

They shared everything they had (4:32). See comments on 2:44.

There were no needy persons among them (4:34). At this early stage in the life of the church, the basic needs for day-to-day life of each person are met by the generosity of members of the community. About fifteen years later (A.D. 47–49) during the reign of Claudius, however, the Jerusalem church as well as the entire city and the whole surrounding area of Judea faced a terrible famine. This same principle of generosity was then exhibited by other churches. The believers at Antioch put together a relief fund for the sake of the churches in Judea (see 11:28–30; 12:25). Similarly, at the beginning of his second missionary journey, Paul began raising funds for the impoverished Christians in Judea to which the churches of the provinces of Galatia, Asia, Macedonia, and Greece gladly contributed. Detailed reference to this collection can be seen 1 Corinthians (16:1–4), 2 Corinthians (8–9), and Romans (15:25–27).

Put it at the apostles' feet (4:35). By placing the money at the feet of the apostles, these believers are recognizing and

submitting to their authority. In the Old Testament and Judaism, feet are sometimes referred to in contexts where someone's authority is stressed.[51] This image is also used to stress the authority of Christ over all things.[52] Falling at someone's feet is a sign of respect and compliance (Est. 8:3; 1 Sam. 25:24). By laying their money at the feet of the apostles, these believers are recognizing the authority of the apostles to administer the funds however they see fit.

REFLECTIONS

EXTRAORDINARY GENEROSITY AND a caring sensitivity to the poor characterized the life of the early church. These virtues are quite contrary to our natural tendency to focus on ourselves. It is the presence of the Holy Spirit that prompts a desire to give. Are you allowing the Spirit to warm the coldness of your heart? Do you periodically contribute to your church's common fund for the poor? Are you responsive when you hear of someone in need?

Joseph, a Levite from Cyprus, whom the apostles called Barnabas (which means Son of Encouragement) (4:36). Luke gives both a positive and negative example of contributions to the community life—Joseph and Ananias. Joseph is a Levite originally from the island of Cyprus (see comments on 13:4) but now apparently resides in Jerusalem. Clement of Alexandria reports that Barnabas was one of the seventy disciples sent out by Jesus (Luke 10:1).[53] The nickname "Barnabas" is most likely derived from the Aramaic expression *bar* (son of) *nabi* (prophet).[54] As such, "Son of Exhorta-

tion" is a better translation of the following expression than the NIV, "Son of Encouragement." The nickname thus expresses the apostles' recognition of Joseph's giftedness and ability as a preacher or missionary. This is precisely the role that Joseph/Barnabas assumes later in Acts when he becomes a prophet/teacher in the church at Antioch (Acts 13:1) and a missionary to his homeland (Cyprus) and to the province of Galatia with the apostle Paul (Acts 13–14).

Ananias and Sapphira (5:1–11)

The earliest church in Jerusalem gets off to a grand and exciting start. Incredible opposition comes from outside the church, but God works miracles, the proclamation of the gospel prevails, and the church continues to grow. Now there is a sudden change. There is a significant disruption from within when two members of the community sin and face sudden and direct divine retribution. But the opposition is not strictly from within. Satan is back on the scene attempting to derail what God is doing by exerting his powerful evil influence on these followers of Jesus.

Ananias (5:1). With a twist of irony, the name Ananias is derived from a Hebrew name meaning, "God is merciful." Apart from his appearance here, we know nothing else about Ananias or his wife.

Sapphira (5:1). Her name is a common Hebrew name meaning "beautiful." Her name is attested on a number of first-century Jewish ossuaries (containers for the bones of the dead).

CYPRUS

He kept back part of the money for himself (5:2). Ananias and his wife own a valuable piece of property, sell it, and give a portion of the money to the apostles while retaining some of the money for themselves. So far, there is nothing at all wrong with their actions. In fact, they are another exemplary illustration of the wealthier members of the community contributing to the well being of the whole. The relatively uncommon word that Luke uses for "kept back" (*nosphizō*) highlights a similarity between this episode and the sin of Achan in Joshua 7. Joshua gave the people of Israel firm instructions not to take as personal plunder any of the articles of the city of Jericho that had been dedicated to the Lord (Josh. 6:18–19). Achan sinned by taking some of the devoted materials and hid them in his tent. He lied and deceived the community, suffering his own death as a consequence. In a similar way, Ananias keeps back what he represents to the apostles as devoted to the Lord and lies to the leaders of the community.

Satan has so filled your heart (5:3). Although Ananias devises the plan and suffers the consequence for acting it out, Satan plays a role in this drama as well. This is his first recorded appearance after the death and resurrection of Christ when he suffered a massive defeat. He is portrayed here as actively opposed to God by attempting to destroy the well-being of this new community. He does so by his classic activity of enticing an individual to sin and defy God. He tried to derail Jesus at the outset of his ministry by tempting him in the desert (Luke 4:1–13), by influencing Judas to betray Jesus (Luke 22:3), and by enticing Peter to deny Jesus (Luke 22:31–32). He will continue his efforts unabated against the church and its mission. For Luke, the contrast here is in being filled with the Holy Spirit (see 4:31 as well as 2:4; 4:8; 13:52).

You have lied to the Holy Spirit (5:3). The sin of Ananias does not have to do with what percentage of the sale price of his property he gives to the apostles. His transgression is in lying to Peter and the apostles by misrepresenting the gift as the entire sale price. His lie is interpreted as a lie to the Holy Spirit because of the Spirit's dynamic presence in the body of believers and its leaders.

After it was sold, wasn't the money at your disposal? (5:4). This statement makes it clear that Ananias is under no obligation to give all or part of the money to the apostles. The practice of selling property to meet the needs of the community is strictly a Spirit-led voluntary expression of love for one another. It is not an experiment in communism or socialism. Neither is it an attempt to model the Christian community after the pattern of the Dead Sea community of Essenes as represented in the Dead Sea Scrolls.

When Ananias heard this, he fell down and died (5:5). The language of this passage points to divine judgment (not simply a sudden heart attack caused by the stress of the situation[55]). The same unique verb used here for dying is also used to refer to the death of Herod Agrippa I (in 12:23) when the Lord strikes him down through an infestation of worms.

The young men came forward, wrapped up his body, and carried him out and buried him (5:6). These young men

REFLECTIONS

IT IS EASY TO TREAT SINFUL BEHAVIOR lightly. Christians sometimes find ways to ignore it, overlook it, justify it, reexplain it, and not deal with it appropriately. Let us not forget that we are accountable to a perfectly holy God who took sin so seriously that he allowed his only Son to die an excruciating death for us.

(*neōteroi*) do not hold any kind of special office. They are merely young believers who are willing to help serve the church in any way they can. It is customary for the deceased to be buried on the same day as the day of death. It is unusual for Ananias' wife to know nothing of it. This can be explained, in part, by the supposition that Ananias is given a rapid and unceremonious burial without the traditional mourning as a result of the community's recognition that he has been struck down by the hand of God (see Lev. 10:1–5), as happened also in Israel's history with Achan (Josh. 7:25).[56]

How could you agree to test the Spirit of the Lord? (5:9) This deception goes beyond lying. They are "testing" (*peirazō*) the Spirit of God. The people of Israel have done the same through their rebellion in the desert after God redeems them from their bondage in Egypt (Ex. 17:2; Deut. 33:8).

The whole church (5:11). This is the first time that the word "church" (*ekklēsia*) is used to designate the Christian community in Luke's writings. As tempting as it might be to base the meaning on the etymology of the word and arrive at "called out ones" (from *ek*, "out of," and *kaleō*,

"call"), this is clearly not the background of the word. The word has a long history of usage in the Greek language for simply designating an "assembly" of people (as it is used in Acts 7:38) or, specifically, the assembly of citizens of a Greek city-state (and thus parallel in meaning to the Greek *dēmos*, from which is derived the English term "democracy").[57] This Greek term was used by the Greek translators of the Hebrew Scriptures to render the Hebrew term *qāhāl*, referring to the "assembly" of Israel, the people of God. This can be illustrated by a passage such as Deuteronomy 31:30: "And Moses recited the words of this song from beginning to end in the hearing of the whole assembly (*ekklēsia*) of Israel."[58] Luke reflects the early Christian application of this term to the Christian community.

Signs, Wonders, and the Growth of the Church (5:12–16)

God works powerfully through the apostles to bring healing and deliverance to many unbelieving Jews. This makes the crowds more receptive to the message they are proclaiming and many turn their hearts to Christ. Nevertheless, great awe

TOMBS IN JERUSALEM

These burial places are located in the Hinnom Valley where it joins to the Kidron.

fills the hearts of the local Jews and causes them to be apprehensive about joining the Christian meetings in the temple courts.

Solomon's Colonnade (5:12). See comments on 3:11.

No one else dared join them (5:13). Because people in Jerusalem hear about the Ananias and Sapphira episode, they have great respect for the Christians (especially the apostles), but they are also somewhat fearful. Whenever the believers meet in the colonnaded area of the temple courts to worship and hear the teaching of the apostles, unbelieving Jews are afraid to join their meetings. They are probably concerned that a half-hearted allegiance may cause them to experience the same kind of demise as the couple who are struck dead.[59] Nevertheless, many people continue to hear the gospel through the outreach and preaching of the apostles and the believing community and respond in faith to Christ.

So that at least Peter's shadow might fall on some of them as he passed by (5:15). In Jewish and Hellenistic folk belief, a shadow was believed to carry spiritual power. This could be harmful as well as beneficial depending on who or what cast the shadow. Cicero relates a belief that by touching the shadow of a criminal, harm would come to a person.[60] Another ancient writer wrote that a person or an animal could be injured if something violent was done to their shadow.[61] The Mishnah warns Jews of the danger of passing under the shadow of an Asherah[62] or the shadow of a corpse[63]; to do so rendered one unclean. In the present case, some of the people believe that Peter's shadow will convey a miraculous and beneficial power of healing. This does not mean that Peter believes this or condones it. The apostles, as well as Luke, tend to oppose a magical way of viewing spiritual power. Nevertheless, God in his mercy allows these people to be healed—a sign that ultimately attracts them to the message of the gospel.

Those tormented by evil spirits (5:16). The word translated "tormented" (*ochleō*) was used in Judaism to refer to any kind of trouble or affliction an evil spirit might cause. The book of Tobit says: "If a demon or evil spirit gives trouble to any one, you make a smoke from these [a fish liver and heart] before the man or woman, and that person will never be troubled again."[64] The crucial difference here is that the apostles never burned fish entrails or used any other magical means of deliverance. They relied strictly on the power and authority of the resurrected Christ.

"Evil spirits" is literally "unclean spirits." Jews commonly made a distinction between "clean" (*katharos*) and "unclean" (*koinon* or *akathartos*). Numerous laws determined what made a person ritually or morally impure. These included such things as the consumption of certain

---

SOLOMON'S COLONNADE

A portion of the Royal Stoa as it is reconstructed in the Jerusalem Temple model.

▼

kinds of foods, contact with a corpse, idolatry, and sexual promiscuity. Jews also regarded evil spirits as unclean, presumably because they promoted idolatry and enticed the people of God to defile themselves through a variety of impure actions. One Jewish document notes, "If you continue to do good, even the unclean spirits will flee from you."[65] Zechariah looked forward to the day when God would remove the "unclean spirit" from the land (Zech. 13:7). Jesus commonly referred to demons with this phrase.[66]

The Apostles Are Arrested and Then Set Free By an Angel (5:17–26)

Continuing to disobey the orders of the Jewish leaders to quit talking about Jesus, Peter and John are arrested again, but this time with the rest of the apostles. God dramatically intervenes by sending an angel to free them from their custody.

The party of the Sadducees (5:17). See comments on 4:1.

Filled with jealousy (5:17). The Jewish leaders are certainly jealous, but the word *zēlos* implies more than this. Behind it stands an Old Testament and Jewish tradition of zeal for the law, the temple, and the honor of God. Phineas the priest, grandson of Aaron, became legendary in Israel because of the way he burned with zeal for the law. When the men of Israel were indulging in sexual immorality with Moabite women and began worshiping their idols, Phineas drove a spear through an Israelite man and his Moabite companion. God commended Phineas because "he was zealous for the honor of his God" (Num. 25:13). Phineas was extolled to the people of

Israel during the time of the Maccabean revolt (1 Macc. 2:54). Here the high priest and the Sadducees are ready to resort to violence to squash this new movement that they perceive to be a threat to the honor of God.

They arrested the apostles (5:18). This time the Jewish officials arrest not only Peter and John, but all the apostles.

The public jail (5:18). In addition to Herod's prison on the west side of the city and a prison in the fortress of Antonia, the Sanhedrin had a place of incarceration either in the temple or below the building where it met (i.e., the Xystus or "the Gazith").[67]

An angel of the Lord (5:19). The entire group of apostles is able to escape from confinement in the prison through the direct intervention of an angel sent by God. In the Old Testament, "the angel of the Lord" appears at key times in Israel's history to guide, guard, and to reveal. For example, the angel of the Lord appeared to Moses in the burning bush (Ex. 3:1–6). The angel of the Lord also stopped Abraham from slaughtering Isaac, encouraged and strengthened Gideon and Elijah, and fought the Assyrian forces of Sennacherib.[68] Many have thought that some of the angel of the Lord passages in the Old Testament refer to the work of the preincarnate Jesus as the Logos.[69] Here it is clearly not a reference to the risen Christ, who mediates his presence directly or through the Holy Spirit, but to a special unnamed angel dispatched directly from the Father.

Stand in the temple courts (5:20). The angel tells the apostles to proclaim the gospel not throughout the cities and villages of Judea, but specifically "in the temple." The temple had been the center of spiritual life for the Jewish people, but that has now come to an end for God's people. No longer is it necessary for the daily animal sacrifices to be performed: One final sacrifice has been offered. No longer will the people of God need to stream to Jerusalem annually for the Passover celebration: Jesus has offered himself as the ultimate Passover sacrifice. No longer will there be a need for the Day of Atonement ritual: Jesus has provided atonement through his blood shed on the cross. All that had been represented by the temple has now reached its final purpose and fulfillment in Christ.

The full message of this new life (5:20). The temple was sometimes described by Jews as "the house of our life."[70] God has now intervened to bring *new* life to his people but apart from the temple.

The officers (5:22). These are the "attendants" or "servants" of the *stratēgos*, the captain of the temple guard (see comments on 4:1). They were not a specially trained Roman police force, but a group of Jewish Levites and priests responsible for security in the temple precincts.

The Apostles Appear Before the Sanhedrin (5:27–42)

Confronted with yet another miraculous event, it seems that the leaders finally recognize the hand of God on this movement, yet they remain staunchly opposed. Some members of the council want the apostles put to death not only because of their opposition to the Messianic sect, but also due to their own vindictiveness at the apostles' accusation of their complicity in the death of Jesus. One moderating voice among the Jewish rulers, however, advises proceeding with caution and discernment. Gamaliel's counsel prevails and the Apostles are flogged and released.

Determined to make us guilty of this man's blood (5:28). This is indeed the same council who a short time earlier sentenced Jesus of Nazareth to death. The chief priest and members of the Sanhedrin regarded Jesus' death as just punishment due to him for blaspheming God (Mark 14:63–64). They vehemently object to the apostles' accusation that there were other motives for inflicting the death penalty on Jesus.

The God of our fathers (5:30). This way of addressing God demonstrates that Peter does not now dissociate himself from his Judaism, but still embraces it as his heritage. "The Christian faith is the fulfilment, not the contradiction, of Judaism, if Judaism is rightly understood."[71] This was a common way of referring to God in the Old Testament and Judaism.[72] The title distinguished the one true God from the gods of the nations and highlighted the personal nature of God, who directly revealed himself to the patriarchs.

By hanging him on a tree (5:30). The "tree" does not indicate a live tree, but the wood used to construct a stake or a pole. Peter's remarks echo Deuteronomy 21:22–23: "If a man guilty of a capital offense is put to death and his body is hung on a tree, you must not leave his body on the tree overnight. Be sure to bury him that same day, because anyone who is hung on a tree is under God's curse." Of course, Jesus was accursed, but thereby freed us from the curse that the law brought on us (see Gal. 3:13–14).

Prince (5:31). As used here, this title is similar to "Lord" (*kyrios*). In the Greek Old Testament, "prince" (*archēgos*) was also used to refer to the head of a tribe (Num. 10:4), a commander in an army (1 Chron. 26:26), or a leader among the people (Isa. 3:6–7) (see comments on 3:15).

Savior (5:31). The prophet Isaiah declares, "The LORD has made proclamation to the ends of the earth, 'Say to the Daughter of Zion, See, your Savior comes'" (Isa. 62:11). Peter now announces to the chief priest and all the members of the Sanhedrin that the Savior has arrived. The Old Testament often speaks of God as Savior for his mighty deliverance of the people of Israel from their slavery in Egypt (see Ps. 95:1). Now the title is applied to Jesus, the Son of God, who has delivered people from a different type of bondage.

A Pharisee (5:34). One of the three major sects of Judaism, the Pharisees constituted the single most important party and come closest to representing "normative Judaism." In essence, Pharisaism was not a political party or a party of the "clergy." It was a lay society that emphasized a rigorous commitment to obeying the Torah. Not only was every word of the written Torah binding, but also the interpretation and explanation of Torah provided by the Scribes. Josephus notes, "the Pharisees have imposed on the people many laws from the tradition of the fathers not written in the Law of Moses."[73] A strong rivalry existed between

TORAH SCROLL
▼

▶ Rabban Gamaliel, the Elder

Gamaliel was famous in Judaism, recognized as the greatest teacher of his day (roughly A.D. 25–50). He was the grandson of Hillel, for whom an entire school of thought was named within Pharisaism. Among Christians, he is best known for his role as the spiritual father and teacher to the young Saul of Tarsus (Acts 22:3).

Although some scholars have erroneously regarded him as the president of the Sanhedrin at this time (an office that properly belonged to the high priest), he was nevertheless the most respected man of the Sanhedrin and the leader of the Pharisaic party.[A-15] It is said in the Mishnah that, "when Rabban Gamaliel the Elder died, the glory of the Law ceased and purity and abstinence died."[A-16]

The Mishnah refers to him repeatedly appealing to his authority for many of the laws regulating the Sabbath, certificates of divorce, the recitation of blessing at a meal, harvesting, tithing, dough offerings, among many others.

Gamaliel also left a significant legacy through his descendants. His son Yeshua served as high priest in A.D. 63–65. Another son, Simeon, became a famous rabbi who is cited repeatedly throughout the Mishnah. His grandson, Gamaliel II, also became a famous rabbi allegedly training over a thousand disciples.

the Pharisees and the Sadducees because the latter saw only the Torah as binding, not the many oral traditions of the Pharisees. Although the Sadducees had significant influence because of their wealth and control of the priesthood, the great majority of the people sided with the Pharisees, seeing them as the upholders of the law (see "Pharisees" at Luke 5:24).

Theudas (5:36). There is no information about this Theudas outside of the New Testament. There were many insurgents after the death of Herod the Great (4 B.C.) and, presumably, he was one of them. This Theudas has sometimes been confused with another revolutionary leader of the same name who led an uprising during the procuratorship of Cuspius Fadus (A.D. 44–46), but this does not take place for another ten years (if Josephus' dating of this Theudas can be trusted[74]). Nevertheless, the story of this later Theudas is instructive as an example of the insurgent activity.

Judas the Galilean (5:37). Gamaliel refers to the seditious activities of a man who came on the scene shortly after Herod the Great's son Archelaus was deposed from his rulership of Judea and a Roman procuratorship was established (A.D. 6). Josephus explains what happened: "The territory of Archelaus was brought under direct Roman rule, and a man of equestrian rank at Rome, Coponius, was sent as procurator with authority from Caesar to inflict the death penalty. In his time a Galilean named Judas tried to stir the natives to revolt, saying that they would be cowards if they submitted to paying taxes to the Romans, and after serving God alone accepted human masters. This man was a rabbi with a sect of his own, and was unlike the others."[75] Josephus credits Judas the Galilean and his companion, Sadduk the Pharisee, with the rise of the entire Zealot movement—the fourth Jewish "philosophy" that ultimately led to the revolt against Rome.

In the days of the census (5:37). Josephus informs us that this census took place under the direction of P. Sulpicius Quirinius, the governor of the Roman province of Syria. This is the same Quirinius who earlier directed a census on behalf of Caesar Augustus at the time of Jesus' birth (see comments on Luke 2:1). Quirinius came into Judea, now part of the Roman province of Syria, to take account of its wealth and to assess it for the purposes of taxation. The Jewish people were upset with this action, but the high priest Joazar intervened and

▶ A Later Theudas (according to Josephus)

Now it came to pass, while Fadus was procurator of Judea, that a certain magician, whose name was Theudas, persuaded a great part of the people to take their effects with them, and follow him to the river Jordan; for he told them he was a prophet, and that he would, by his own command, divide the river, and afford them an easy passage over it; and many were deluded by his words. However, Fadus did not permit them to make any advantage of his wild attempt, but sent a troop of horsemen out against them; who, falling upon them unexpectedly, slew many of them and took many of them alive. They also took Theudas alive, and cut off his head, and carried it to Jerusalem. This was what befell the Jews in the time of Cuspius Fadus's government.[A-17]

▶ Instructions on Flogging

An entire tractate of the Mishnah—*Makkoth* (stripes)—is devoted to delineating the infractions that warrant flogging as well as the methods and procedures for carrying it out. The following excerpt explains how it is to be done:

> How do they scourge him? They bind his two hands to a pillar on either side, and the minister of the synagogue lays hold on his garments . . . so that he bares his chest. A stone is set down behind him on which the minister of the synagogue stands with a strap of calf-hide in his hand, doubled and re-doubled, and two other straps that rise and fall are fastened thereto. . . . He must give him one-third of the stripes in front and two-thirds behind; and he may not strike him when he is standing or when he is sitting, but only when he is bending low, for it is written, "the judge shall cause him to lie down" [Deut. 25:2]. And he that smites, smites with his one hand with all his might. . . . If he dies under his hand, the scourger is not culpable.[A-18]

As the accused suffers his beating, another person stands by and reads from Deuteronomy 28:58–63 ("If you do not carefully follow all the words of this law. . .") repeatedly throughout the beating.

---

quelled their fears somewhat with a stirring appeal. It was this census that prompted Judas to revolt and excited the Jews about fighting for liberty from foreign rule and oppression. He admonished the people to take action by insisting that "taxation was no better than an introduction to slavery."[76]

But if it is from God, you will not be able to stop these men (5:39). Gamaliel gives sound and temporizing advice to the council—something that did not happen when Jesus stood before the same group. His comments echo the instructions given in the Torah about discerning a prophet that was sent from God: "You may say to yourselves, 'How can we know when a message has not been spoken by the LORD?' If what a prophet proclaims in the name of the LORD does not take place or come true, that is a message the LORD has not spoken. That prophet has spoken presumptuously. Do not be afraid of him" (Deut. 18:21–22). A later rabbi reflects a similar principle: "R. Johanan the Sandal-maker said: Any assembling together that is for the sake of Heaven shall in the end be established, but any that is not for the sake of Heaven shall not in the end be established."[77]

Had them flogged (5:40). Rather than let the apostles go again with a stern warning, the council orders a severe beating. The word used here, *derō*, literally means to "flay, skin," but it has come to be used in a figurative sense for a flogging. The law governing flogging is given in Deuteronomy 25:1–4, which limited the number of lashes to forty. This was later reduced by the synagogue to thirty-nine, as Josephus attests: "But for him that acts contrary to this law, let him be beaten with forty stripes, save one, by the public executioner; let him undergo this punishment, which is a most ignominious one for a free man."[78]

From house to house (5:42). Apart from the large gatherings in the temple courts, the thousands of believers in Jerusalem regularly meet in smaller groups in private homes throughout the city. For those who have become Christians, there is a lot to learn—all that Jesus has said and done as well as a fresh perspective on the Hebrew Scriptures in light of their fulfillment in Christ. Apparently the apostles divide up the task of teaching by each going to a set group of homes where believers gathered. The teaching responsibilities for the apostles is enormous (see comments on 2:46).

The good news that Jesus is the Christ (5:42). The heart of the apostles' evangelistic message is that Jesus of Nazareth is indeed the longed-for Messiah of Jewish expectation.

The Neglect of the Greek-Speaking Widows (6:1–7)

A serious problem arises that threatens to undo the unity of the church during a time of great growth. A sharp schism has developed between two social groups within the church. The early characterization of the Christian community as "one in heart and mind" (4:32) has given way to partiality and strife.

This passage describes how the apostles handle this problem and resolve the conflict. They do so by appointing additional leaders for the church. These new leaders possess a strong blend of practical savvy and Spirit-inspired living. By handling this problem effectively, the church continues to grow even more.

Disciples (6:1). The term "disciple" (*mathētēs*) is used regularly in the Gospels to refer to a follower of Jesus of Nazareth. Even though Jesus is now exalted to the right hand of the Father, his followers are still referred to as "disciples." The word itself is surprisingly rare in the Old Testament (only one time; 1 Chron. 25:18), but master-disciple relationships were common in the Old Testament and Judaism, as we see in the relationship between prophets and their students (e.g. 1 Sam. 19:20–24; 2 Kings 4:1, 38) and the rabbis and their students. The common Old Testament way of referring to the relationship is by the term "follow" (*akoloutheō*). In the Greek world, however, the term "disciple" was commonly used. At the time of the New Testament era, it was frequently used in

the sense of an "adherent," such as we might find in the relationships between the philosopher Socrates and his students (or after his death, those who commit their lives to his teaching).[79]

Complained (6:1). The word for complaint (*gongysmos*) is colorful and strong. Luke probably chooses it to recall the griping of the Hebrews when they were in the desert shortly after God provided them a miraculous deliverance through Moses (see Ex. 16:7–9; Num. 11:1).

The Grecian Jews . . . Hebraic Jews (6:1). "Grecian Jews" is a rather imprecise translation of an expression that means "Greek-speaking Jews." The term *hellenistēs* frequently means "Greek-speaking" in a variety of ancient literature.[80] The church father Chrysostom reports that Luke uses the term "Hellenists" for "those speaking Greek."[81] The contrast here is with those who did not speak Greek fluently: "the Hebraic Jews"(*hebraioi*). This latter group is designated as "Hebrews" because they were much more comfortable with Hebrew or Aramaic.

Jews who were raised in Palestine spoke Aramaic as their native tongue. This was a Semitic language that had many similarities to Hebrew. Aramaic was the dominant language of the Near East for centuries before the time of Christ. Many Jews in Palestine, especially in Jerusalem and Judea, continued to use Hebrew (as evidenced for instance in the Dead Sea Scrolls). Most would also probably have learned some measure of Greek—this is now the language of the Roman empire—but certainly would not have felt as comfortable in this language as their native tongue.[82]

Many Jews raised outside of Palestine, such as in North Africa, Egypt, and Asia Minor, would never have learned Hebrew.

Their principal language would have been Greek. When they settled in Jerusalem, these "Hellenists" would have enjoyed meeting together in a synagogue where the Scriptures were read in Greek, prayer was in Greek, and conversation was in Greek.

It is doubtful that there were any serious doctrinal differences between the "Hellenists" and the "Hebrews" at this stage. These "Hellenists" tended to be just as zealous about the temple, the law, and the festivals as any Jew raised in Jerusalem (Saul/Paul is a good case in point).[83] There may have been some cultural differences, however, that further distinguished them from the "Hebrews," such as taste in foods, musical styles, and literature. The "Hebrews," on the other hand, in their efforts not to be tainted by Hellenistic culture, may have been more isolationist and ethnocentric, perhaps going to great lengths to avoid contact with other Jews who did not accept their own outlook and interpretation of purity regulations.[84]

The daily distribution of food (6:1). Many Jews immigrated to Jerusalem to spend their final years in the Holy City and die there. Often the men preceded their wives in death, and the widows were then left with no immediate family to support them and care for their daily needs. There is some evidence that widows even traveled from Diaspora locations to Jerusalem. There is a higher proportion of women's names in Greek ossuary (a burial box for bones) inscriptions.[85]

Jerusalem leaders had put together an organized system of relief for the destitute. Rabbinic literature testifies to the existence of both a daily and a weekly distribution of relief. The daily distribution (*tamhûy*) typically consisted of bread, beans, and fruit. The weekly distribution (*quppāh*) consisted of food and clothing.[86] Although the rabbinic evidence is later than the New Testament, there is little doubt that some sort of organized relief was in place in Jerusalem at this time. The widows in Acts, however, are Christian Jews and are deriving aid from their new Christian community. Presumably the apostles have instituted a similar kind of system of relief to that offered by the temple officials.

Luke does not tell us who is to blame for this discriminatory treatment faced by the Greek-speaking Jewish widows. The apostles, however, do not undertake a blame-finding investigation. They immediately seek a solution to the problem through finding men of integrity to serve as leaders to provide leadership to the relief effort in the church.

To wait on tables (6:2). The verb translated "to wait" is *diakonein* from which is derived *diakonoi* ("deacons"). Consequently, some have assumed that this passage provides the background to the office of "deacon" in the early church.[87]

This is not the case. First of all, the word *diakoneō* was widely used with the simple and non-technical sense of "to serve." Such is the case in Mark 10:45, when Jesus said of himself: "The Son of Man did not come to be served, but to serve, and give his life as a ransom for many." Second, it is unlikely that Luke would tell the story about the origin of the office and never use the term "deacons" (*diakonoi*) for the first office holders.[88] In this situation, an *ad hoc* group of leaders is formed to take care of a pressing matter in the church.

Choose seven men (6:3). There is some precedent in Judaism for choosing seven men to lead. When Josephus took command of Galilee, he appointed seven magistrates in every town of the region.[89] This reflects an implementation of his understanding of Deuteronomy 16:18 ("Appoint judges and officials for each of your tribes in every town"): "Let there be seven men to judge in every city, and these such as have been before most zealous in the exercise of virtue and righteousness."[90] There is also some later rabbinic evidence for the appointment of seven men to carry out various kinds of tasks.[91]

Known to be full of the Spirit and wisdom (6:3). These men need to excel not only in natural abilities to administrate and lead, but they need to demonstrate the presence of the Holy Spirit in their lives. This experience of the life in the Spirit is the mark of the new age and the fulfillment of Old Testament prophecy.

To prayer and the ministry of the word (6:4). The Twelve want to devote more time to prayer. Their time in prayer probably includes but greatly exceeds the typical Jewish practice of praying three times a day. Their "ministry of the word"

REFLECTIONS

THE APOSTLES HAD AN ENORMOUS work load in these early days of the church. They were responsible for teaching and ministering to thousands of people. On top of this, problems often surfaced that required their attention, time, and wisdom. With such a busy schedule, it would have been easy to let their times of prayer slip away. Yet the apostles realize that because of the size and significance of their responsibilities, they needed to spend more time in prayer. They leave a wonderful example to us as we face busy schedules and extensive responsibilities.

would have included both evangelistic proclamation (which, in a Jewish context, would have involved demonstrating that Jesus was the Messiah based on the Old Testament) and teaching the many thousands who recently embraced Jesus as Messiah and joined the Christian community. Integral to this ministry would be passing on the tradition of Jesus—giving accounts of his ministry and faithfully reciting his teaching.

Stephen (6:5). See comments on 6:8.

Philip, Procorus, Nicanor, Timon, Parmenas, and Nicolas (6:5). The surprising twist to this story is that it appears that the people choose seven men who are "Hellenists." That is, they all come from the offended group within the church. Each of the seven men has a Greek name (amply attested by occurrences in Greek inscriptions and literature). The fact that Nicolas is a convert to Judaism and is thus a Gentile indicates that the others are Greek-speaking Jews.

Beyond this passage, nothing further is known about Procorus, Nicanor, Timon, and Parmenas. Some of the church fathers believed that Nicolas is the founder of the heretical sect of the Nicolaitans referred to in Revelation 2:6, 15.[92] There is no evidence to support this assertion. It is more likely that some make an unwarranted connection because of the similarity of names. Philip, as we will see in Acts 8, becomes a zealous ambassador of the gospel in Samaria and later in Caesarea (21:8).

A convert to Judaism (6:5). See comments on 2:11.

Laid their hands on them (6:6). The practice of the laying on of hands in the Old Testament often occurred in the context of sacrifice and symbolized the transfer of sins from the offender to the sacrificial being.[93] The clearest example of this is when Aaron placed his two hands on the head of the scapegoat (Lev. 16:21). But the laying on of hands also took place for the conferral of blessing, as when Jacob blessed each of his sons (Gen. 48:18), and for the conferral of authority on a successor, as when Moses commissioned Joshua (Num. 27:18–23; Deut. 34:9). The latter example became important in rabbinic Judaism as a model for its ordination practice.[94] The laying on of hands in this passage, however, is not a rite of ordination. It represents a conferral of authority and blessing on these seven leaders. They are already full of the Spirit, but now they are commissioned to fulfill a special responsibility in the community.

A large number of priests became obedient to the faith (6:7). It must have been encouraging to the Christian community in Jerusalem to see many priests becoming followers of Jesus. Luke does not specify if some of these individuals are from the high priestly families or whether all come from the order of ordinary priests (like John the Baptist's father Zechariah). The ordinary priests, living throughout Palestine, were organized into twenty-four different rotations, with each group coming and serving a two-week stint (in addition to serving at the three pilgrim festivals). There are many ordinary priests—J. Jeremias estimates eighteen thousand, a number that might even be low[95]—who serve the Jerusalem temple.

It is also possible that among these new converts were Essene priests, with perhaps some from the Qumran community. The original core of this community was of priestly descent. Some Essenes were residents in Jerusalem and may have occupied an area of the city known as the "Essene Quarter."[96]

The Story of Stephen (6:8–15)

Luke now tells the remarkable story of one of these seven men. Although we never see Stephen waiting on tables, we find him doing many of the things the apostles themselves are doing. His bold proclamation of the Word and his success make him a threat to the Jerusalem leaders. He is arrested and interrogated. Like Jesus, he faces false witnesses whose testimony leads to his conviction and death. Whereas earlier, the apostles face imprisonment and flogging for their proclamation of Jesus as Messiah, now the persecution reaches a much higher level.

Stephen (6:8). Luke devotes a significant amount of space to telling the story of this exemplary, Spirit-filled man (6:8–8:2). He has a rather common Greek name that means, "crown" or "wreath." The victor in an athletic contest is crowned with a *stephanos* (see 1 Cor. 9:25). We know nothing of his life prior to his appearance here in Acts. As the others, he is likely a Greek-speaking Jewish settler in Jerusalem originally from somewhere in the empire.

Great wonders and miraculous signs among the people (6:8). Because of his faith and his receptivity to the Spirit's work, God is able to do powerful works through Stephen. These probably include miraculous healings and the casting out of unclean spirits among the unbelieving Jews. Because of these remarkable signs, he is likely gaining a strong and receptive hearing for his proclamation of the gospel.

The Synagogue of the Freedmen (6:9). The term "freedmen" is a translation of the Greek word *Libertinoi*, itself a transliteration of the Latin *Libertini*. This is an expression used to designate emancipated slaves. This particular synagogue thus probably consisted of Jews from Rome who were freed from slavery and migrated back to Jerusalem. They banded

THEODOTUS INSCRIPTION

A first-century inscription attesting to one of the synagogues in Jerusalem.

▼

together and formed their own synagogue where they could worship and praise God in Greek.

During the many battles that took place in Palestine leading up to the conquering of Palestine by the Romans (63 B.C.), many Jews were captured, taken to Rome, and sold as slaves. Philo refers to a Jewish sector of the city of Rome populated mainly by emancipated Jewish slaves who had gained Roman citizenship.[97] The Roman historian Tacitus refers to four thousand Gentile "freedmen" (*libertini*) in Rome who became tainted with the superstitions of the Jewish rites.[98] Many of these assuredly became proselytes.

Jews of Cyrene and Alexandria as well as the provinces of Cilicia and Asia (6:9). The language of the passage in Greek is somewhat ambiguous. There are three possibilities for understanding what Luke is referring to: (1) there is one synagogue—the *Libertinoi*—comprised of Jews from four regions; (2) there are two synagogues—one called the *Libertinoi* consisting of members from Cyrene and Alexandria and another synagogue with members from Cilicia and Asia; or (3) there are five synagogues—the one called *Libertinoi* consisting of emancipated Jews from Rome as well as four other synagogues associated with Jews from each of the other four geographical areas. The evidence slightly favors the third view, in part because the *Libertinoi* most likely refers to emancipated Jews from Rome.[99] We know from Acts 24:12 that there is more than one synagogue in the city. We also know based on other sources that Jews often formed synagogue congregations based on their places of origin.[100]

The synagogue of the Alexandrians is mentioned a number of times in rabbinic literature. A passage in a Jewish Tosephta speaks of a rabbi purchasing the "synagogue of the Alexandrians."[101] Interest-

▶ Archaeological Evidence of a First-Century Jewish Synagogue in Jerusalem

In December 1913, French archaeologist R. Weill discovered a well-preserved Greek dedicatory inscription of a synagogue. The discovery was made on the southeast hill of Old Jerusalem, the hill of Ophel. The inscription has been dated to the first century A.D., sometime in the period prior to the destruction of Jerusalem in A.D. 70. This valuable stone is now housed in the Rockefeller Museum.[A-19] The text of the inscription reads as follows:

> Theodotus, son of Vettenus, priest and archisynagogos [ruler of the synagogue], son of an archisynagogos, grandson of an archisynagogos, constructed the synagogue for the reading of the law and the teaching of the commandments and the guest-room and the (upper?) chambers and the installations of water for a hostelry for those needing (them) from abroad, which was founded by his fathers and the elders and Simonides.[A-20]

In the location where the inscription was discovered, some sparse remains of the synagogue can still be seen. Portions of walls, pavement, stones decorated with rosettes, and the remains of three ritual baths (*miqva'ot*) are all part of the ancient synagogue.[A-21]

The name "Vettenus" is Roman and may suggest that the father of Theodotus had lived in Rome and received Roman citizenship from the *Vettena* family. This and other factors have led many scholars to think that the synagogue of this inscription is, in fact, the "Synagogue of the Freedmen" in Acts 6:9.[A-22]

ingly, the parallel passage in the Babylonian Talmud refers to it as the synagogue of the Tarsians (i.e., Cilicians).[102] There is no direct evidence of a Cyrenian synagogue, but archaeologists have discovered the burial place of a Jewish family from Cyrene in Jerusalem.[103]

Words of blasphemy against Moses (6:11). The first accusation that the witnesses bring is that Stephen is speaking against the Jewish law. There is nothing in Stephen's address to indicate that he attacks the law. The fact that Luke refers to the witnesses as *false*, indicates that he disagrees with their charge.

Sanhedrin (6:12). See "The Sanhedrin" at 4:11.

Speaking against this holy place (6:13). The false witnesses also accuse Stephen of speaking against the temple. The evidence for this charge is the claim that Stephen says that "Jesus of Nazareth will destroy this place." This echoes the false charge brought against Jesus in his trial (Mark 14:57–59). While it is true that Jesus said that the temple would be destroyed and "not one stone will be left on another" (Luke 21:6), this is a long way from saying that Jesus himself would destroy it. Interestingly, the community behind the gnostic *Gospel of Thomas* attributes the destruction of the temple to Jesus.[104]

Stephen Speaks to the Sanhedrin (7:1–53)

In reading through this lengthy address, one may wonder what it has to do with the charges brought against Stephen and why Luke takes the space to record it in all of its details. At first glance it seems merely to be a tedious recounting of the history of Israel.

A closer examination of the speech in light of ancient rhetoric, however, demonstrates that this is a powerful address aimed at refuting the charges leveled against Stephen, namely, that he is blaspheming God, speaking against the law/Moses, and denouncing the temple. Rather than responding to the charges directly and enumerating the reasons why they are false, Stephen responds subtly, yet forcefully, through the indirect route of *insinuation*.[105] He selectively recounts Israelite history in such a way that the audience must infer a correlation between calloused Israel's rejection of Joseph and Moses and their own rejection of Jesus. Stephen begins, however, by establishing common ground with his hearers by reciting their common ancestry in the celebrated patriarch Abraham.

A second crucial theme Stephen develops is that God has not limited the manifestation of his presence and glory to one location, by inference, the temple. God appears to Abraham in Mesopotamia, to Joseph in Egypt, and to Moses in the Sinai Desert. It is therefore inappropriate to claim that the presence of God is isolated to one man-made building. The implication is not that Solomon was wrong in building the temple or that there was something inherently remiss in the whole temple cult, but the attitudes of the Jewish people were wrong if they could not see the glory of God in the person of Jesus, the Messiah. Thus, at the end of his address, Stephen directly and incisively accuses them of obstinately rejecting and opposing God's work in and through Jesus, who has fulfilled the law.

Although the speech is long in comparison to others in Acts, it is not a transcript of what Stephen says. It is more aptly described as a summary, or précis, of the address. It represents a valuable

◀

piece of direct evidence of how the "Hellenists" (the Greek-speaking Jewish Christians) now understood the Old Testament in light of Jesus's coming, his death, and resurrection. In substance, it probably differs little or not at all from what the "Hebraists" or one of the Twelve would have said.

If one wonders how Luke would have known the content of this message, at the end of the chapter Luke points us to someone who was there and witnessed the entire set of proceedings—Saul of Tarsus, his future coworker and traveling companion.

The high priest (7:1). This is Caiaphas, the same high priest who presided over the trial of Jesus. He remained in office until A.D. 36—four or five years after this episode.

The God of glory (7:2). For the people of Israel, the "glory" of God was the visible manifestation of his presence among them. This is exhibited by the cloud that settled on Mount Sinai (Ex. 24:15–18). After the Israelites constructed the tabernacle, the cloud covered it and "the glory of the LORD filled the tabernacle" (Ex. 24:34–35). A special manifestation of the presence of God appeared on the ark of the covenant. When the ark was captured, it was exclaimed, "the glory has

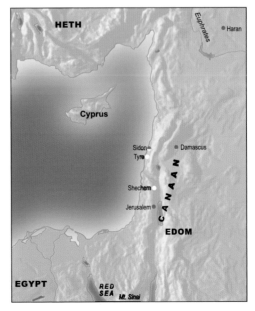

◀

departed from Israel" (1 Sam. 4:21–22). Ultimately, God mediated his presence and glory through the temple in Jerusalem: "When the priests withdrew from the Holy Place, the cloud filled the temple of the LORD. And the priests could not perform their service because of the cloud, for the glory of the LORD filled his temple" (1 Kings 8:10–11). The later Rabbis refer to this manifestation of glory as the *Shekinah*, a word that never appears in the Bible.[106]

For many first-century Jews, the Jerusalem temple was the singular place on earth where God was present in his glory.[107] Throughout his appeal to the Jews, Stephen will demonstrate that both historically and especially now, God regularly manifested his presence outside of the temple. He concludes his address by reporting his own vision of the glory in association with Jesus the Messiah at the right hand of the Father in heaven (Acts 7:56).[108]

The covenant of circumcision (7:8). Circumcision is the removal of the male foreskin. Jews performed this operation as a religious ritual on their children out of obedience to the command of God as it was delivered to Abraham (Gen. 17:2, 10–14). God instituted circumcision as a symbol of his agreement with Israel. Cir-

cumcision came to be understood in Israel as representing their salvation and their ethnic identity as Jews, the chosen people of God. Stephen has nothing disparaging to say about circumcision in his comments. On the basis of his speech, it is impossible to accuse him of speaking against the law (and thus Moses).

Joseph (7:9). Stephen delivers a concise rehearsal of the story of Joseph in verses 9–16. The principal idea that he communicates here is how the patriarchs rejected Joseph, but God was with Joseph and worked through him to save all the descendants of Jacob from the horrible famine afflicting the land.

Their bodies were brought back to Shechem and placed in the tomb that

---

▶ Stephen and the Old Testament

In his recounting of Israel's history, Stephen makes ample use of the Old Testament, quoting portions of at least twenty-two verses from Genesis, Exodus, Deuteronomy, Isaiah, and Amos. A comparison of these citations with the forms of the Old Testament text demonstrate that he is using the Greek version of the Bible, known as the Septuagint (LXX). This is consistent with the fact that Stephen was one of the "Hellenists" (a Greek speaker).

F. F. Bruce aptly comments about Stephen's knowledge and use of the Old Testament: "The speech is no mere catena of quotations, studiously put together; the Old Testament wording is reproduced with a spontaneity which suggest that the author has the narrative at his fingertips and is able to use it with a striking freshness and freedom."[A-23]

Abraham had bought from the sons of Hamor (7:16). Technically, Jacob was buried near Hebron (south of Jerusalem) "in the field of Machpelah near Mamre" (Gen. 23:19), as were the other patriarchs, according to Josephus.[109] Joseph, however, was buried in Shechem (in Samaria) "in the tract of land that Jacob bought for a hundred pieces of silver from the sons of Hamor" (Josh. 24:32).

Moses (7:20). Stephen devotes the greatest portion of his address—twenty-six verses—to telling the story of Moses (7:17–42). This revered deliverer of Israel and the situation he faced are similar to the story of Jesus and the situation he faced with Israel. Both were God's anointed deliverers, but both face rejection by the people of God.

Moses was educated in all the wisdom of the Egyptians (7:22). The Old Testament says nothing about the education of Moses in Egypt. In Exodus 2:1, Pharaoh's daughter took young Moses as her son; in the next verse he is "already grown." There are some statements and traditions in Judaism about Moses' education. Josephus simply says that Moses "was educated with great care."[110] Philo has a lengthy description of the kind of education that Moses received. It is difficult to assess the historical accuracy of Philo's account, although one scholar suggests that he portrays Moses as the "genius, idealised man."[111]

Powerful in speech (7:22). Moses himself claims, "O Lord, I have never been eloquent, neither in the past nor since you have spoken to your servant. I am slow of speech and tongue" (Ex. 4:10). Moses' protest to God should not be taken too seriously. The remainder of the biblical account of his life shows him to be confident and forceful in his addresses to Pharaoh and the Israelites. One Jewish tradition states that "by his words he performed swift miracles" (Sir. 45:3).

Moses thought that his own people would realize that God was using him to rescue them, but they did not (7:25). Stephen explains the response of the Jewish people to Moses in a way that his own hearers' refusal would recognize Jesus of Nazareth as their God-appointed rescuer. Their furious response to his

▶The Education of Moses in Egypt (According to Philo)

Therefore the child being now thought worthy of a royal education and a royal attendance.... And immediately he had all kinds of masters, one after another, some coming of their own accord from the neighbouring countries and the different districts of Egypt, and some being even procured from Greece by the temptation of large presents. But in a short time he surpassed all their knowledge, anticipating all their lessons by the excellent natural endowments of his own genius....

Accordingly he speedily learnt arithmetic, and geometry, and the whole science of rhythm and harmony and metre, and the whole of music, by means of the use of musical instruments, and by lectures on the different arts, and by explanations of each topic; and lessons on these subjects were given him by Egyptian philosophers, who also taught him the philosophy which is contained in symbols, which they exhibit in those sacred characters of hieroglyphics, as they are called, and also that philosophy which is conversant about that respect which they pay to animals which they invest with the honours due to God....

And all the other branches of the encyclical education he learnt from Greeks; and the philosophers from the adjacent countries taught him Assyrian literature and the knowledge of the heavenly bodies so much studied by the Chaldeans. And this knowledge he derived also from the Egyptians, who study mathematics above all things, and he learnt with great accuracy the state of that art among both the Chaldaeans and Egyptians.[A-24]

message indicates that they completely understand his insinuation.

Holy ground (7:33). The remembrance of Moses approaching God on "holy ground" in the Sinai may serve as yet another reminder that the Jerusalem temple is not the only place where God mediates his glory and presence.[112]

He received living words (7:38). Stephen makes no critical remarks about the law, contrary to the false charge leveled against him. In fact here he describes the Torah as "living words (*logia*)" (see Rom. 3:2). A similar thought appears in Psalm 119:50 using the same term: "Your promise (*logia*) gives me life (NRSV)." When Moses gave the law to the people

of Israel, he declared: "Take to heart all the words I have solemnly declared to you this day, so that you may command your children to obey carefully all the words of this law. They are not just idle words for you—they are your life" (Deut. 32:46–47). The rabbis declared regarding the law: "The more study of the Law the more life."[113]

Gave them over (7:42). God was personally involved with Israel throughout their history. They were able to enter the promised land and conquer the enemy tribes because God handed them over (*paradidōmi*) to Israel (Ex. 23:31; Num. 21:2). On the other hand, when his people went their own way and defied him, God gave them over to the sword (Ps. 78:61) or to their enemies (Ps. 106:41). This is in fact what happened when Israel was exiled under Nebuchadnezzar (Jer. 22:25). As judgment and as discipline, God allowed his people to follow the dictates of the power of sin and its consequences excluding them from receiving his enabling grace (see also Rom. 1:24–32; Eph. 4:19).

To the worship of the heavenly bodies (7:42). Stephen's specific accusation is that God handed them over to the "forces of heaven." This refers to evil spirits and wicked angels who tempted Israel to worship the planets, stars, and idols as gods (see Jer. 7:18, 19:13 in the LXX). In the various religions of the neighboring peoples, the planets and stars were thought to be gods.

You have lifted up the shrine of Molech and the star of your god Rephan (7:43). Stephen quotes Amos 5:25–27 in support of his contention that Israel succumbed to idolatry. The Septuagint form of the text that Stephen uses differs somewhat in this passage from the Hebrew Masoretic text. Instead of "Molech" and "Rephan"(the LXX reading), the Hebrew refers to "Sakkuth your king, and Kaiwan your star-god." Both Sakkuth and Kaiwan were Assyrian deities, the latter associated with the planet Saturn (a planet the Romans also worshiped as a god).[114] The variant names may imply an association of the deities. It was common in antiquity for one national group to identify their gods with the similar gods of another nation.

Molech was a prominent Canaanite deity revered as a god of the underworld. Devotees offered children as burnt offerings to the god, probably for some divinatory purpose.[115] In disobedience to the explicit prohibitions in the Torah (Lev. 20:2–5), some of the Israelites worshiped Molech. The Israelite kings Ahaz and Manasseh sacrificed their children by fire to this god.[116] Child sacrifice associated with the worship of Molech was a persistent problem in Israel.[117] Rephan is never mentioned elsewhere in the Old Testament, but the name is an Egyptian form of "Saturn."

Joshua (7:45). The name "Joshua" may here be significant because his namesake is the "Righteous One" of verse 52 whom the Jewish leaders are rejecting. The Hebrew term *Yēšûăᶜ* (the name of Joshua) is translated into Greek in the Septuagint as *Iēsous*.[118] In other words, it is the same Greek term that lies behind the translation of both "Joshua" and "Jesus." Now, a second "Joshua" offers to redeem them and lead them into the kingdom, conquering their (spiritual) enemies. Unfortunately, they have rejected him.

The Most High does not live in houses made by men (7:48). Some scholars have interpreted this sentence to mean that David's desire to build a temple and, consequently, Solomon's work in constructing it were seriously misguided and contrary to God's plan. One commentator goes so far as to say that "Israel's decision was a misguided act in that it made Yahweh like a heathen idol."[119]

This is not the point, however, that Stephen is trying to make. His essential idea, rather, is that God is transcendent and cannot be thought of as limited to a building. The tabernacle, as Stephen asserts, was built according to a divine plan—God sanctioned it. Stephen gives

▶
THE TABERNACLE
A model of the tabernacle and its precincts.

no indication that the construction of the Jerusalem temple was outside the will of God.

When Solomon offered his prayer of dedication for the temple, he recognized that God cannot be confined to it: "But will God really dwell on earth? The heavens, even the highest heaven, cannot contain you. How much less this temple I have built!" (1 Kings 8:27). This point is similarly made in Stephen's quotation of Isaiah 66:1–2. Ben Witherington sums it up well when he concludes: "The point of all three of these verses is not that God's presence can't be found in the temple (clearly Acts 2–4 shows it can), but that God's presence can't be confined there, nor can God be controlled or manipulated by the building of a temple and by the rituals of the temple cultus or the power moves of the temple heirarchy. What is being opposed is a God-in-the-box theology that has magical overtones."[120]

You stiff-necked people (7:51). Stephen uses the language of the Old Testament to describe the intransigence of the Jewish leaders he is addressing. He implicitly compares the leaders of the Sanhedrin to the Israelites in the desert who demanded that Aaron make them a golden calf to worship as their god (Ex. 32). The Lord repeatedly spoke of them to Moses as a "stiff-necked" people worthy of death (Ex. 33:3, 5; 34:9; Deut. 9:6, 13). They refused to recognize their awesome deliverance and God's continued presence with them as well as his leading them to a far better place.

Uncircumcised hearts and ears (7:51). Although these Jewish leaders are physically circumcised in obedience to the law, Stephen accuses them of disobedience to the weightier part of the law that demands a responsive heart to God's revelation. An "uncircumcised heart" is the description in the Torah for those who were disobedient to God and inflated with stubborn pride (Lev. 26:41). The prophet Jeremiah blamed the unresponsiveness of God's people to the call to repent on their "uncircumcised ears" (Jer. 6:10) and spoke repeatedly of the circumcised Israelites as having "uncircumcised hearts" (Jer. 4:4, 9:26).

Was there ever a prophet your fathers did not persecute? (7:52). The Old Testament speaks of numerous prophets that were persecuted and killed by wayward Israelite leaders. Jezebel was accused of "killing off the LORD's prophets" while the prophet Obadiah took a hundred prophets and hid them in caves (1 Kings 18:4). The prophet Elijah told the Lord that he fled to the desert to hide because "the Israelites have rejected your covenant, broken down your altars, and put your prophets to death with the sword. I am the only one left, and now they are trying to kill me too" (1 Kings 19:10). There are other similar complaints in the Old Testament.[121] Jesus himself carried on this protest (Matt. 23:31; Luke 13:34), as did Paul (1 Thess. 2:15) and the author of Hebrews (Heb. 11:32, 36–37).

Jewish tradition contains many stories about the persecution of the prophets. An entire book, *Martyrdom of Isaiah*, purportedly describes the events leading up to and including Isaiah's martyrdom. It portrays Isaiah's martyrdom as follows: "Because of these visions, therefore, Beliar was angry with Isaiah, and he dwelt in the heart of Manasseh, and he sawed Isaiah in half with a wood saw" (*Mart. Isa.* 5:1). The church fathers Justin Martyr and Tertullian also speak of Isaiah being sawed in half.[122]

The Righteous One (7:52). For Luke, this is an important messianic title of Jesus. The most relevant background is Isaiah 53:11: "By his knowledge my righteous servant will justify many, and he will bear their iniquities." Although this title does not figure prominently in the Jewish messianic expectation of the era, Jesus continually referred to himself using the language and imagery of Isaiah 53. This passage also became a key text for the early Christians in understanding the nature of Jesus' messianic mission. For Stephen to assert Jesus' righteousness is a further insult to the leaders of the Sanhedrin since they have aggressively sought Jesus' death.

The law that was put into effect through angels (7:53). Stephen turns the tables on his accusers by charging them with disobeying the law. By rejecting the Messiah, they have rejected the heart and essence of the law itself. This passage refers to angelic involvement in the giv- ing of the law to Moses. The idea first appears in Deuteronomy 33:2, where God is portrayed as accompanied by angels in his appearance on Sinai.[123] The angelic involvement in the giving of the law apparently was a widespread convic- tion among the rabbis.[124] Paul and the author of Hebrews also refer to the par- ticipation of angels in the bestowal of the law (Gal. 3:19; Heb. 2:2). Once again, how can Stephen's opponents accuse him of speaking against the law when he clearly understands it to be an angel- attended revelation of God in accord with Jewish tradition and when he embraces the core of it?

Stephen Is Martyred (7:54–8:1a)

The reaction to Stephen's address is severe. Far from being persuaded and joining the Christian movement, the crowd responds violently. They rush Stephen, drag him out of the city, and stone him to death. This is no official

▶

A PLACE OF STONING

The so-called "Tomb of Absalom" built during the Herodian era in the Kidron Valley near Jerusalem. It may have been a traditional place of stoning.

trial. It has all the marks of a lynching. The scene most likely takes place within two years after the death of Jesus and thus occurs in A.D. 31 or 32.[125]

Stephen becomes the first Christian martyr. He dies as a result of his faith that Jesus of Nazareth is the long-awaited Messiah, that he is risen from the dead and stands at the right hand of the Father. He dies for his bold testimony on behalf of his exalted Lord.

Stephen's speech and the violent response by the Jewish leaders initiates a significant break between the new messianic movement (later to be known as Christianity) and official Judaism. Whereas the early Christians often met in the temple (see 2:46; 3:1), this now will no longer be possible.

Gnashed their teeth (7:54). The grinding of the teeth as an expression of anger and rage was common in Judaism. David says that "the wicked plot against the righteous and gnash their teeth at them."[126] This was his own experience as well: "Like the ungodly they maliciously mocked; they gnashed their teeth at me. O Lord, how long will you look on? Rescue my life from their ravages" (Ps. 35:16–17).

Jesus standing at the right hand of God (7:55). Jesus' present position at the right hand of the Father is strongly attested in early Christianity (see comments on 2:33–34).[127] His exalted place of prominence is seen as the fulfillment of Psalm 110:1: "The LORD says to my Lord: 'Sit at my right hand until I make your enemies a footstool for your feet.'" What is unusual here is that Jesus is portrayed as standing, not sitting. There have been a variety of explanations offered: Jesus stands to welcome Stephen; Jesus rises to make intercession for Stephen; Jesus gets up to come

to Stephen's aid; Jesus stands as a witness in the judgment against Stephen's murderers and as an advocate in Stephen's defense; Jesus is standing to perform his duties as priest in the heavenly temple. We can only speculate as to the precise reason that Jesus is standing, but common to all these is the fact that Jesus is actively watching, involved, and responding to the needs of his people from his exalted position at the Father's side.

It is also significant to recognize how the Jewish leaders respond to his vision. If Stephen is right and Jesus is now standing at the right hand of God, then they must be horribly in error and the Sanhedrin has become God's enemy. In their eyes, this explanation is not only wrong, but must be stopped at all costs.

I see heaven open (7:56). This is the language of visionary experience as well illustrated by the beginning of Ezekiel: "In the thirtieth year, in the fourth month on the fifth day, while I was among the exiles by the Kebar River, the heavens were opened and I saw visions of God" (Ezek. 1:1). In John's Gospel, Jesus saw heaven open "and the angels of God ascending and descending on the Son of Man" (John 1:51). Behind Jesus' vision at the outset of his ministry is the imagery of Jacob's ladder (Gen. 28:12). There is divine commerce between heaven and earth with God revealing himself in a new way through the Son. Now that Jesus has completed his earthly ministry, heaven is open again, but now the Son of Man is in the presence of God watching and involved with his people.

The Son of Man (7:56). This is one of the few times outside of the Gospels that the expression "Son of Man" is used of Jesus (see also Rev. 1:13; 14:14). Within the Gospels, Jesus commonly used the phrase as a Semitic way of referring to himself ("a man such as I") as well as a title associating him with the coming "one like a son of man" (see Dan. 7:13; *1 En.* 46–53; see "Son of Man" at Mark 2:12).[128] In the former usage, Jesus frequently spoke of the suffering he would experience as, for instance, in Mark 8:31: "He then began to teach them that the Son of Man must suffer many things." Here Stephen may have used the expression to emphasize that his vision is of the suffering Son of Man (whom these Jewish leaders conspired to kill), who now stands vindicated at the right hand of God and yet will come as their final judge.

Began to stone him (7:58). The group can tolerate Stephen no longer. Convicted by what he said, but not to repentance, they respond in rash violence. Violating a Roman provincial law requiring the authorization of the Roman governor to prosecute a capital offense (see John 18:31), they seize Stephen and drag him out of the city to stone him. Not even bothering to take a vote on his guilt or innocence, they join in anger to respond to what they perceive to be outrageously blasphemous statements. According to the Old Testament, blasphemy was a capital offense punishable by stoning (Lev. 24:14–16).

The witnesses laid their clothes (7:58). According to rabbinic law, the witnesses were required to take the lead in stoning the condemned person. Here they take off their cloaks to enable them to better carry out the sentence.

A young man named Saul (7:58). With a dramatic twist, Luke here introduces the principal character of the second half of his book. "Saul" is his Hebrew name, a name he shares with one of Israel's illustrious kings, with whom he also shared a common lineage from the tribe of Ben-

---

▶ Rabbinic Regulations For Stoning

Although Stephen's stoning was not the result of a carefully prosecuted trial, some aspects of the rabbinic regulations governing a sentence of stoning are insightful for understanding the scene in Acts 7. The instructions are given in Mishnah, *Sanhedrin* 6:1–4:

> When sentence [of stoning] has been passed they take him forth to stone him. The place of stoning was outside [far away from] the court, as it is written, 'Bring forth him that hath cursed without the camp' (Lev. 24:14). . . .

> When he was about ten cubits from the place of stoning they used to say to him, "Make thy confession," for such is the way of them that have been condemned to death to make confession, for every one that makes his confession has a share in the world to come. . . .

> When a man was four cubits from the place of stoning they stripped off his clothes. A man is kept covered in front and a woman both in front and behind. . . .

> The place of stoning was twice the height of a man. One of the witnesses knocked him down on his loins; if he turned over on his heart the witness turned him over again on his loins. If he straightway died that sufficed; but if not, the second [witness] took the stone and dropped it on his heart. If he straightway died, that sufficed; but if not, he was stoned by all Israel, for it is written, "The hand of the witnesses shall be first upon him to put him to death and afterward the hand of all the people" (Deut. 17:7).

jamin.[129] The name "Paul" (first mentioned in 13:9) is his Roman name (see comments on 13:9).

As a "young man" (*neanias*), Saul is anywhere from twenty-four to forty years of age.[130] This is consistent with the fact that he refers to himself as an "old man" in Philemon 9 (written in the early 60s), a designation that commonly meant over fifty years of age. The most likely inference, then, is that Saul is born sometime in the first decade—A.D. 1–10.[131]

Having been born in Tarsus (in the province of Cilicia), Saul came to Jerusalem for his schooling. He studied with the famous rabbi Gamaliel (see comments on 22:3) and may well have been a part of the Cilician synagogue (see comments on 6:9). It is unlikely that he is an actual member of the Sanhedrin yet—he is too young—but he is certainly associated with its members and on a fast track for becoming a member.

Lord Jesus, receive my spirit (7:59). Echoing the words of Psalm 31:5—"Into your hands I commit my spirit"— Stephen breathes his last breath. He apparently has confidence that he will be ushered immediately into the presence of Jesus. His words also echo those of Jesus on the cross, who utters, "Father, into your hands I commit my spirit" (Luke 23:46). Stephen, however, commits his spirit directly to Jesus, whom he refers to as "Lord"—a title Jesus shares with the Father. This demonstrates his exalted view of Jesus as God.

Lord, do not hold this sin against them (7:60). Stephen follows the example of his Lord who, as he was hanging on the Roman cross, uttered, "Father, forgive them, for they do not know what they are doing" (Luke 23:34).

The Church Faces Persecution (8:1b–3)

Stephen's address to the Jewish leaders serves as a catalyst for a more intense campaign of public persecution against Christians in Jerusalem. Christians are drug from their homes, imprisoned, and possibly even killed. Fearing for their lives, the Christians leave the city and move to towns and villages throughout Judea and Samaria. Ironically, one of the principal antagonists in this persecution is Saul of Tarsus. On the surface, this may appear to be a huge setback for the Jesus movement. But God is using this great evil as a means of spreading the gospel to "all Judea and Samaria" (1:8).

A great persecution (8:1). The body of Jewish leaders who try and kill Stephen—the members of the Sanhedrin as well as leaders from the Hellenistic synagogues—now unleash their hostilities against the entire church, both Hellenists and Hebrews.

All except the apostles were scattered (8:1). The vast majority of Christians flee the city of Jersusalem. Luke informs us earlier that over five thousand men have become believers, not including all of the women and children (4:4). There is thus a sudden departure of five to ten thousand people leaving the city. For the wealthier Christians who are hosting the meetings of the church in their homes, this no doubt meant abandoning their houses and property.

The twelve apostles choose to stay, not because they are any less the objects of attack, but probably because of their commitment to remain as witnesses in the city. Knowing that their lives are in grave danger, the Twelve are nevertheless unconcerned about the possibility of suffering and death for the sake of Christ.

Godly men buried Stephen and mourned deeply for him (8:2). The men probably bury Stephen shortly before the outbreak of persecution and their own flight from the city. Their mourning actually goes against Jewish custom, which disallows open lamentation and only permits silent mourning for a person who is stoned.[132]

Saul began to destroy the church (8:3). One of the principal leaders in this flare-up of persecution is Saul of Tarsus. Later on this man admits in his letters "how intensely I persecuted the church of God and tried to destroy it" (Gal. 1:13; see also Phil. 3:6). Luke uses a rather colorful word that is here translated "destroy" (*lymainomai*). In the literature where it appears, it is often used to describe a person torn up by wild animals, such as lions, wild pigs, leopards, and wolves.[133]

Philip's Ministry in Samaria (8:4–8)

In a few brief verses, Luke tells the story of how the good news of Christ spreads from Jerusalem to Samaria (see 1:8). This happens through the proclamation of another one of the seven leaders chosen to wait tables—Philip.

The Samaritans stood on the fringes of Judaism. They were not Gentiles, but neither were they properly Jews (either in terms of religious convictions or in terms of ethnicity). Incredible tension and downright hatred typically characterized the attitudes of Jews toward Samaritans and vice-versa (see "Samaritains" at 8:5).

For the Samaritans to respond to the gospel and receive the Spirit at the hands of the Jewish-Christian leaders of the church marks a radical step for the church, a step toward fulfilling the vision Jesus had for the church of a people who are not excluded on the basis of race and other human-constructed barriers. On the other hand, it would fan the flames of anger even more on the part of the Jewish leaders in Jerusalem.

Those who had been scattered (8:4). The thousands of Christian Jews who leave Jerusalem travel to cities and villages throughout Judea and Samaria. They simply do not go looking for a safe haven until the persecution subsides; they go with a strong sense of mission proclaiming Jesus as Messiah.

Philip (8:5). Philip is the second of the seven "Hellenists" whose story Luke now tells (see comments on 6:5).[134] How fascinating it would be to hear how God used the other five. We know nothing of Philip's life prior to his choice as one of the seven leaders in Acts 6. God uses him

in amazing ways to reach Samaritans with the gospel as well as a Gentile God-fearer from Africa. Luke reports that Philip eventually settled in Caesarea, where he married and had four daughters, each of whom exercised a prophetic gift (8:40; 21:8–9). According to church tradition, he moved to Hierapolis, which is near Colosse, about a hundred miles due east of Ephesus.[135] The situation for him and his family in Caesarea may have become too dangerous for them as the conflict between Jews and Gentiles grew as a prelude to the Jewish war that began in A.D. 66.[136]

A city in Samaria (8:5). Samaria was a region that contained a number of cities. Luke does not specify which of these cities Philip visits, whether it is Sebaste (the ancient city of Samaria), Gitta, Shechem, Sychar, Neapolis, or even another Samarian city. Least likely is the city of Sebaste, which essentially became a Greek city when it was resettled with Greek (Macedonian) soldiers after Alexander the Great. After the ancient city of Samaria was destroyed by the

Jewish freedom fighter John Hyrcanus and his sons (107 B.C.),[137] it was later rebuilt in the style of a Greek city, and Herod dedicated it to the Roman emperor by renaming it *Sebastos* (a Greek title of respect bestowed on the emperor meaning "venerable" or "august" (cf. the Latin *augustus*).[138]

Proclaimed the Christ there (8:5). Philip goes to a Samaritan city and begins proclaiming that Jesus is the Messiah. Some of the Samaritans may have already heard of Jesus through the woman he had spoken to at the well in a town called Sychar (John 4:1–26). On that occasion, the Samaritan woman confessed to a belief in a coming Messiah that she shared with other Samaritans (John 14:25). Jesus directly told her his identity: "I who speak to you am he."

Not accepting any of the prophetic books, Samaritans based their messianic expectation on one passage—Deuteronomy 18:15—where Moses said, "The LORD your God will raise up for you a prophet like me from among your own brothers." They described him as the

REMAINS AT SAMARIA

(left) The Roman theater in Sebaste.

(right) The Roman forum.

▶Samaritans

The Samaritans[A-25] viewed themselves as Israelites, true remnants of the tribes of Ephraim and Manasseh, who maintained a monotheistic faith and upheld the Torah as holy scripture. They kept the rite of circumcision, regularly observed the Sabbath and the Jewish festivals, and honored Moses as the greatest of the prophets.

The Jews, however, viewed the Samaritans as "half breeds"—descendants of Mesopotamian (Gentile) colonists who settled in the area and intermarried with the Jews remaining there after the Jewish exile by Assyria (2 Kings 17:24–31).[A-26]

At the heart of the schism between Jews and Samaritans in the first century was the fact that Samaritans rejected the Jewish temple worship. Three centuries earlier, they had constructed their own temple on Mount Gerizim. They also rejected all of the Hebrew Bible except the first five books of Moses.

The hostility intensified in the century before Christ when John Hyrcanus destroyed their temple (107 B.C.) and devastated many of their cities. Under the Syrian ruler Antiochus Epiphanes (167 B.C.), they had requested that their temple be dedicated to Zeus Hellenios, thus identifying Zeus with Yahweh.[A-27]

The Jewish rabbi Ben Sira refers to the Samaritans as "the foolish people that live in Shechem."[A-28] Jews regarded Samaritans on the same level as Gentiles in ritual and purity matters. Not only did Jews prohibit intermarriage with Samaritans, but they did not even allow a Samaritan to convert to Judaism.[A-29] The apostle John summarizes the situation well when he says, "Jews do not associate with Samaritans" (John 4:9).

Taheb (an Aramaic term meaning "Returning One"), who would come and restore the true worship on Mount Gerizim.

Evil spirits came out of many (8:7). Just as the twelve apostles cast out evil spirits and healed the sick (see comments on 5:16), Philip continues the same ministry. Luke makes a distinction between the casting out of spirits and physical healing here (see comments on 8:9).

Simon, the Magician (8:9–25)

One episode that stands out in Philip's ministry in Samaria is his encounter with a wonder-working man named Simon. Capable of exhibiting tremendous spiritual power, Simon has garnered a signif-

icant following in Samaria. Yet Luke portrays the power of God working through a disciple of Jesus as vastly superior. In fact, Simon recognizes the greater power at work in and through Philip and wants it for himself, but for the wrong reasons. In this story, Luke demonstrates that the desire to obtain spiritual power—fundamental to magic—is a profoundly inadequate motive for joining the Christian movement. Magic is a poison and imprisons the soul.

A man named Simon (8:9). In terms of extrabiblical evidence, we have little accurate information about Simon. This is due in large measure to a legend that developed in the early church attributing the rise of the Gnostic heresy to Simon.

Luke, however, says absolutely nothing about Simon being a gnostic or as holding any of the worldview assumptions that are typical of Gnosticism. Most scholars today, therefore, regard it as highly unlikely that Simon is the first gnostic. They characterize Simon in terms that do not go beyond Luke's: Simon is a Samaritan who practices magic and has significant influence on people.

Justin, Irenaeus, Origen, Tertullian, and Eusebius are among those church fathers who attribute the beginning of Gnosticism to Simon.[139] It is doubtful, however, that Gnosticism as a religious system of redemption actually came into existence until late into the first century or even into the second century.[140]

Practiced sorcery (8:9). Literally, Luke says Simon practices "magic" (*mageia*; 8:11). In the ancient world, magic was not the art of illusion. Magic was predicated on the reality of spiritual forces (both personal and impersonal) and the belief that they could be coerced and manipulated. A magician was someone who had a deep knowledge of the spirit world and could prescribe the right incantation, formula, or ritual to obtain the desired results. Although no hard examples of first-century Samaritan practices of magic survive today, over 230 papyrus documents have been discovered illustrating the practice of magic generally for the Greco-Roman period.[141]

The divine power known as the Great Power (8:10). Justin Martyr attests to this description of Simon (see "Simon, the Magician" at 8:9). It is not likely that Simon is setting himself up as a rival of

---

▶ The Rise of the Legend of Simon as the Founder of Gnosticism (Justin Martyr)

In his volume defending the Christian faith, Justin Martyr (A.D. 110–165) wrote briefly about Simon. Although aspects of his account may be true, Justin is the first to portray Simon as a gnostic. Justin's account is believed and uncritically passed on by many of the other church fathers. Justin provides the following description of Simon:

> There was a Samaritan, Simon, a native of the village called Gitto, who in the reign of Claudius Caesar, and in our royal city of Rome, did mighty acts of magic, by virtue of the art of the devils operating in him. He was considered a god, and as a god was honoured by you with a statue, which statue was erected on the river Tiber, between the two bridges, and bore this inscription, in the language of Rome: "To Simon the holy God" (*Simoni Deo Sancto*).
>
> And almost all the Samaritans, and a few even of other nations, worship him, and acknowledge him as the first god; and a woman, Helena, who went about with him at that time, and had formerly been a prostitute, they say is the first idea (*ennoia*) generated by him.[A-30]

The portions of Justin's portrayal of Simon that are often regarded as historically plausible are: (1) Simon came from the Samaritan town of Gitta; (2) he was a magician; (3) he attracted a significant following in Samaria; (4) he was worshiped as a god.

The statue that Justin saw has been discovered, but it was not dedicated to Simon, but rather a Roman deity called Semo (*Semoni Sancto Deo*). This false identification may not have originated with Justin.[A-31]

Subsequent writers expand on his consort Helena, whom they identify with the second god of Gnosticism, i.e. *ennoia, sophia,* the "demiurge" or creator god.

Yahweh in the Samaritan cities and thereby attempting to supplant the worship at Mount Gerizim. Simon is simply a magician who is presenting himself as a "Great Power," which in Jewish and Samaritan culture is equal to saying that he is a "Great Angel." In Asia Minor, an inscription set up in honor of the moon-god Men extols him as "the Great Power" of the invisible God.[142]

They were baptized (8:12). Given the great hostility between Jews and Samaritans, it is surprising to see Philip go so far as to baptize them. Baptism is the ritual of incorporation into this new community. The people that Judaism did not allow into their community, the newly constituted people of God, are now embraced on an equal footing.

Simon himself believed and was baptized (8:13). On the surface, it appears that Simon also responds to Philip's preaching, but Luke gives us reason to doubt the sincerity of his convictions in the following verses. Jesus warns about basing one's faith only on signs and wonders: "Now while he was in Jerusalem at the Passover Feast, many people saw the miraculous signs he was doing and be-

lieved in his name. But Jesus would not entrust himself to them, for he knew all men" (John 2:23–24).

They sent Peter and John to them (8:14). Peter and John remain in Jerusalem with the other ten apostles in spite of the terrible threat to their lives. It must come as a shock to them to hear that Samaritans are embracing Jesus as Messiah and entering the community of believers. John, after all, was one of the two disciples who asked Jesus if he should call down fire from heaven on the inhospitable Samaritans who refused to provide lodging for them (Luke 9:52–56). How much more the Sanhedrin and leaders from the Hellenistic synagogues would be upset with Christians when they found that they were now receiving Samaritans into their fellowship!

Peter and John placed their hands on them, and they received the Holy Spirit (8:17). Peter and John journey to Samaria to find out for themselves. Satisfied with the genuineness of their commitment, they lay their hands on these new Samaritan believers and the Holy Spirit comes on them. The intermediate agency of the apostles in this instance raises many ques-

---

▶ **A Magical Spell**

The following text is a portion from a Greek magical papyrus discovered in Egypt and now housed in the British Museum in London. The passage from the papyrus gives some indication of the worldview and technique that stood behind the practice of magic in the time of Jesus and the apostles.

> Come to me, spirit that flies in the air, called with secret codes and unutterable names, at this lamp divination which I perform, and enter into the boy's soul, that he may receive the immortal

form in mighty and incorruptible light, because while chanting, I call, "IAŌ ELŌAI MARMACHADA MENEPHŌ MERMAI IĒOR AIEŌ EREPHIE PHEREPHIŌ CHANDOUCH AMŌN EREPNEU ZŌNŌR AKLEUA MENĒTHŌNI KADALAPEU IŌ PLAITINE RE [an additional seventeen magical names are called upon]."[A-32]

If this is similar to the kind of magic that was being practiced by Simon and others in Samaria, it is not surprising that Philip was casting spirits out of many people.

tions since the Spirit is normally presented as coming at the moment of belief. It is doubtful that this means that the Spirit only comes when the apostles bestow it on new believers (and thus now through ordained clergy who are under the authority of the church in apostolic succession). Nor does this appear to be a special filling of the Spirit for empowerment for witness. The uniqueness of this event can only be appreciated in light of the historical and cultural setting. Because of the longstanding antipathy between the Samaritans and Jews, apostolic participation and confirmation is needed.[143] Peter and John can leave Samaria having no doubts whatsoever about God's inclusion of the Samaritans in this new community of believers joined to Jesus, the Messiah. The conversion of the Samaritans represents the first giant step toward fulfilling Jesus' instructions about witness in Acts 1:8.

He offered them money (8:18). Consistent with his function as a magician (or shaman), Simon wants to purchase the ability to bestow the Spirit on people, presumably so he can charge people for the gift.[144] It is from this situation that the English term "simony" was coined to refer to the buying or selling of a church office.

You are full of bitterness (8:23). The translation of the NIV—"you are full of bitterness"—appears inconsistent with the context. Peter does not see anger and bitterness in Simon: The man is giddy with excitement over the prospect of obtaining this new-found spiritual

power. The literal wording of the phrase, however, is "you are in a gall (poison) of bitterness" (*cholē pikrias*). Peter's language echoes Moses' warnings to the people of Israel when they renewed the covenant with God: "Make sure there is no man or woman, clan or tribe among you today whose heart turns away from the LORD our God to go and worship the gods of those nations; make sure there is no root among you that produces such bitter poison (*cholē kai pikria*)" (Deut. 29:18 LXX). Simon is not bitter; rather, he is full of a bitter poison.[145] This is consistent with the next line that describes him as a "captive to sin." Both expressions suggest that Simon himself has not experienced the redeeming and transforming work of the Spirit.

Peter and John returned to Jerusalem, preaching the gospel in many Samaritan villages (8:25). Peter and John are so utterly convinced of the genuineness of God's work among the Samaritans that they begin proclaiming the gospel of

◀ *center*

SAMARITAN MONEY

Samaritan silver coin dating from the fourth century B.C.

SHECHEM AND MOUNT GERIZIM

▼

Christ to them. We cannot underestimate what a radical shift of thinking this is for them. If word of this reaches the Sanhedrin, the Jewish leaders will be incensed. This is the last mention of the apostle John's activity in Luke's account.

Philip and the Ethiopian Eunuch (8:26–40)

Before his ascension, Jesus said that the disciples would be witnesses to "the ends of the earth" (1:8). The conversion of the Ethiopian marks an enormous stride forward toward the fulfillment of this goal. To Greeks and Romans, Ethiopia was at the ends of the earth. In describing Poseidon's trip to the

ETHIOPIA, GAZA, AND JERUSALEM

Ethiopians, Homer said that they lived "at the world's end."[146] Herodotus claimed that Ethiopia "stretches farthest of the inhabited lands in the direction of the sun's decline."[147]

The conversion of the Ethiopian also represents the inaugural step of the gospel going out to the Gentiles. In many ways, this is a more radical step forward than the conversion of Cornelius and his household. Not only is the Ethiopian a Gentile, but he is from a distant land and in some ways an outcast with respect to Judaism since, as a eunuch, he is regarded as in a constant state of ritual impurity.

For Luke, the mission of the church is out of control—that is, out of the control of the human agents. From beginning to end, this passage shows the work of God in directing every aspect of the outreach.

The desert road—that goes down from Jerusalem to Gaza (8:26). Whether Philip remains and ministers in Samaria or returns with the apostles to Jerusalem, Luke does not tell us. What is important, however, is that Philip is divinely directed to the road leading to southwest Palestine—the area well-known in the Old Testament as the territory of the Philistines. Gaza itself is one of the five cities of the Philistines. Although it had been destroyed by the Jewish ruler Alexander Jannaeus, it had recently been rebuilt by the Roman governor Gabinius.[148]

In 1838, the famous archaeologist E. Robinson suggested that the site of the Ethiopian's baptism is near Tell el-Hesi (about forty miles southwest of Jerusalem and twenty miles northeast of Gaza), and his guess has recently received additional support.[149] Tell el-Hesi is located on a Roman road that led from Jerusalem to Gaza. There is also a

◄

spring at the site that is an important source of water for the area. This proposal can be nothing more than an educated guess, but it does fit the details of the text.

An Ethiopian (8:27). In the Greco-Roman period, "Ethiopia" referred to the land south of Egypt—what is today the Sudan and modern Ethiopia.[150] In Old Testament times, this was the land of Cush (see Est. 1:1; 8:9; Isa. 11:11). The term "Ethiopia" has come to mean the land of the "Burnt-Faced People," indicating their black skin.

The man whom Philip encounters is most likely from the kingdom of Nubia located on the Nile River between Aswan and the Fourth Cataract (a waterfall-like area of rapids). The capital of this region is Meroe.

An important official in charge of all the treasury (8:27). Regardless of his status as a eunuch (which may have been a pre-requisite for his position), this man is a finance minister in a government. As such, he is a man of high social standing, which is consistent with the fact that he travels in style.

Candace, queen of the Ethiopians (8:27). Although "Candace" is a female name in English-speaking circles, it was a title then. *Kandakē* is the transliteration of a Nubian word for "queen."[151]

This man had gone to Jerusalem to worship (8:27). This is an incredible journey for this man and his retinue to undertake. If he covered an average of twenty-five miles per day, the trip to Jerusalem would have taken anywhere from 48–60 days and round trip, 96–120 days. The journey would have taken considerably longer if he stopped for any length of time in the cities along the way. This man is earnestly seeking the God of Israel and spends a great deal of time to go and worship him.

It is unlikely that this man is a prose-lyte (impossible if he is not only castrated but dismembered, because of the requirement for circumcision) since Luke typically points out those who are full proselytes (see 6:5). He may more accurately be described as a "God-fearer" or a "sympathizer."

But how has he become acquainted with Judaism? There is ample evidence of a Jewish presence in Upper (southern) Egypt beginning in the second century B.C. and extending through the second century A.D.[152] One papyrus letter even attests to a synagogue in the city of Thebes.[153] It is unknown if the Jewish Diaspora extended as far south as Nubia and the city of Meroe. If a synagogue was present in Meroe, there is a simple explanation as to how this Ethiopian became a God-fearer. If this man traveled extensively (as it seems he was accustomed to), he may have come into contact with Jews anywhere in Egypt.

As a Gentile God-fearer, he could not have taken part in the temple services in Jerusalem. At the most, he could be admitted into the Court of the Gentiles.

▶ The Social Status of a Eunuch

This Ethiopian is described by Luke as a "eunuch," which most likely means that he had been castrated and possibly even dismembered.[A-33] This is not surprising for a male who holds a high position in the government of a queen or for an official over a king's harem. In the book of Esther, for example, a eunuch named Hegai was in charge of Xerxes's harem (Est. 2:3, 14, 15).

Nevertheless, there was a stigma attached to being a eunuch in ancient societies. Ancient writers speak of the regret that eunuchs felt over their condition as well as occasions of social ostracization.[A-34]

In Judaism, the law excluded eunuchs from public worship: "If a man's testicles are crushed or his penis is cut off, he may not be included in the assembly of the Lord" (Deut. 23:1). Such a man was judged to be physically blemished and in a permanent state of ritual impurity (Lev. 21:20; 22:24).

Josephus reflects the attitudes of some (probably Pharisaic) Jews toward eunuchs:

Let those that have made themselves eunuchs be had in detestation; and do you avoid any conversation with them who have deprived themselves of their manhood, and of that fruit of generation which God has given to men for the increase of their kind; let such be driven away, as if they had killed their children, since they beforehand have lost what should procure them; for evident it is, that while their soul is become effeminate, they have withal transfused that effeminacy to their body also. In like manner to you treat all that is of a monstrous nature when it is looked on; nor is it lawful to geld man or any other animals.[A-35]

By contrast, the prophecy of Isaiah held out hope for eunuchs: "To the eunuchs who keep my Sabbaths, who choose what pleases me and hold fast to my covenant—to them I will give within my temple and its walls a memorial and a name better than sons and daughters; I will give them an everlasting name that will not be cut off. And foreigners who bind themselves to the LORD to serve him, to love the name of the LORD, and to worship him, all who keep the Sabbath without desecrating it and who hold fast to my covenant—these I will bring to my holy mountain and give them joy in my house of prayer. Their burnt offerings and sacrifices will be accepted on my altar; for my house will be called a house of prayer for all nations" (Isa. 56:3–8).

Perhaps the fact that this eunuch was reading this scroll indicated that he was familiar with this passage and found hope in it. Philip can now proclaim its fulfillment.

Perhaps the Ethiopian came for one or more of the three great pilgrim festivals (Passover, Pentecost, or Tabernacles).

Sitting in his chariot (8:28). If the Ethiopian is able to sit and read on his journey, he does not come alone. Whether he comes with one other person or a retinue, Luke is silent. The Greek word translated "chariot" (*harma*) was frequently used for chariots of war, but could also be used of some type of carriage for a long journey (as Joseph used on his trip from Egypt to Hebron to bury his father; Gen. 46:29). We really have no way of knowing what this vehicle really looked like.

Reading the book of Isaiah the prophet (8:28). The fact that the Ethiopian possesses a scroll of Isaiah demonstrates that he is a person of means. Such documents were expensive since they had to be produced by hand. The man is probably reading a Greek version of the text of

◀

CHARIOT

An ancient depiction of a horse-drawn chariot on a coin.

Isaiah since it is doubtful that he knows Hebrew. It was common for people to read aloud in antiquity both because of the way the text was written (there were no word divisions or punctuation) and to aid the memory.

The Spirit told Philip (8:29). From beginning to end of this episode, Luke stresses God's guidance—first by an angel and then by the Holy Spirit. God used a similar pattern in leading Peter to Cornelius (10:3, 19). Philip does exactly what the Spirit led him to do by running to the carriage, initiating a conversation with the man, and then joining him in the carriage.

◀ *left*

ISAIAH SCROLL
FROM QUMRAN

He was led like a sheep to the slaughter (8:32). Of all the passages in the Old Testament that the Ethiopian could have been reading, there is no single chapter more appropriate for explaining the work of Christ than Isaiah 53. Although many Jews thought of their own experience as fulfilling much of the suffering and martyrdom themes of the passage, Philip declares that the passage finds its decisive fulfillment in one person—Jesus. First-century Jews did not interpret the suffering servant of Isaiah 53 as a prophecy about the coming Messiah.[154]

Luke cites only verses 7–8 from the chapter, but assuredly, Philip explains to

the Ethiopian how Jesus has fulfilled every aspect of the entire fourth servant song (Isa. 52:13–53:12). This passage enables Philip to describe Jesus' coming as a humble servant, the fact of his suffering and death, the meaning of his suffering and death ("he was pierced for our transgressions" [v. 5]; the Lord has laid on him the iniquity of us all" [v. 6]), and his resurrection ("after the suffering of his soul, he will see the light of life and be satisfied" [v. 11]).

Who can speak of his descendants? For his life was taken from the earth (8:33). Much of the Isaiah 53:7–8 passage that Luke cites would properly be interpreted as references to the suffering of the Messiah. Philip probably explained the last line ("for his life was taken up from the earth") as a reference to Jesus' resurrection and exaltation (see also Isa. 53:10). The rhetorical question, "Who can speak of his descendants?" thus is not a lament over the fact that the Messiah never marries and has children, but rather that he now has a host of spiritual offspring.[155] This eunuch, who was once deprived of full membership in Judaism, is now to be

THIS PASSAGE PROVIDES SOME helpful guidelines for all believers who seek to share their faith:[A-36]

1. Be sensitive to the prompting of the Spirit.
2. Be prepared to share your faith across cultures.
3. Witnessing is most effective to people whose hearts have already been prepared by God.
4. Start with their questions.
5. The basis for witnessing should be the words of Scripture.
6. The focus of witnessing needs to be the person of Christ.
7. Invite a response.

fully incorporated into the family of the Messiah.

Told him the good news about Jesus (8:35). Philip does not limit himself to the Isaiah passage, which merely serves as the starting point to explain how Jesus of Nazareth has come in fulfillment of Old Testament promises. This constitutes the "good news" or "gospel" (*euangelion*) of the Christian message.

Why shouldn't I be baptized? (8:36). It was the normal practice of the earliest church for baptism to follow immediately after conversion (2:38, 41; 8:12, 13). The fact that the Ethiopian asks for baptism reveals how much Philip has taught this man in a short amount of time. Surely Philip has taught him that baptism is now understood as the rite that represents his identification with the death of Jesus (and, consequently, its atoning significance) and incorporates him into the community of believers. Because the Ethiopian introduces his question with "what hinders me?" he may be alluding to the fact that he has indeed been hindered from becoming a proselyte in Judaism because of his physical blemish.

The Spirit of the Lord suddenly took Philip away (8:39). The word that Luke uses here (*harpazō*) is the same word used by Paul to refer to the Lord Jesus "snatching up" (or rapturing) people to meet him in the air at his second coming (1 Thess. 1:17). Although it is hard for us to imagine the Holy Spirit physically moving Philip from one location to another, this indeed appears to be what happened.[156] This is not without precedent in the Bible. The Spirit of the Lord transported Elijah from one place to another (1 Kings 18:12; 2 Kings 2:16).

Went on his way rejoicing (8:39). Joy is one of the hallmarks and signs of new life in the messianic era (see Luke 2:10; 8:13; Acts 2:46). Rejoicing is anticipated by the prophets (see Isa. 51:11; 55:12). This observation also serves as evidence that the Ethiopian receives the Holy Spirit (see Rom. 14:17). We know nothing more about the Ethiopian but can presume that he returns to his homeland and proclaims Jesus as Messiah to all of the Jews and God-fearers he knows. This may have been the decisive introduction of the gospel into Nubia. Irenaeus (A.D. 120–202) says this much: "This man was also sent into the regions of Ethiopia, to preach what he had himself believed."[157]

Philip, however, appeared at Azotus (8:40). Azotus (Ashdod in the Old Testament) was about twenty miles north of Gaza, twenty miles south of Joppa, and two and a half miles inland from the

◀
━━━━━

AZOTUS AND
CAESAREA

Mediterranean. It was on the "Via Maris," the main coastal road leading from Gaza to Joppa. In the early first century, the city became part of an imperial estate belonging to the empress Livia (the wife of Caesar Augustus).[158] Philip continues to proclaim the gospel in this city as well as in the various coastal towns between Azotus and Caesarea. This includes Jamnia, Antipatris, and possibly the more inland cities of Lydda and Joppa (where Peter later ministered (9:23–43; 10:5–23). This is not the last that we hear of Philip. Luke records a visit that both he (assuming the "we" includes Luke) and Paul had with him twenty years later in Caesarea (21:8).

The Lord Appears to Saul on the Road to Damascus (9:1–9)

After introducing Saul in connection with the death of Stephen and the outbreak of persecution against Christians, Luke now returns to him and describes his dramatic conversion and call to serve. Saul becomes the most important figure in the spread of the gospel to the ends of the earth (1:8).

He went to the high priest and asked him for letters (9:1–2). The high priest in Jerusalem at this time was Caiaphas, the son-in-law of Annas (see John 18:13), who officiated between A.D. 18–37. He is the same high priest who took a leading role in the trial of Jesus, insisting that he was guilty of blasphemy and worthy of death (Matt. 26:57–68). This is also the same high priest who tried Peter and John and sternly warned them about spreading the gospel (Acts 4:1–21, esp. v. 6). Given the history of his antipathy to Jesus and his followers, Caiaphas is more than glad to grant the request of the zealous young persecutor of Christians.

Saul asks the high priest for extradition documents that will authorize him to apprehend Jews who confess Jesus as the Messiah and have fled Jerusalem. This is an extreme measure, but extreme actions have already been taken by the Jerusalem leaders to crush the movement. Rome granted this level of authority to the high priest for dealing with internal matters. The precedent was set by a letter that the Roman proconsul wrote much earlier to the ruler of Egypt: "Therefore if any pestilent men have fled to you from their country, hand them over to Simon the high priest, that he may punish them according to their law" (1 Macc. 15:21). This right was upheld by Julius Caesar and is now applied by the high priest to stop the new pestilence

▶ Damascus

Damascus was located about 135 miles northeast of Jerusalem on the verge of the Syrian Desert.[A-37] It was about sixty miles northeast of the Sea of Galilee and fifty-five miles inland (due east of the coastal town of Sidon). Today the ancient city lies buried beneath the modern city of Damascus, the capital of Syria.

Situated along the banks of the Barada river with fertile soil, the area around the ancient city was a rich agricultural region. The city gained its importance, however, by its function as the major station along the busy trade route connecting Jerusalem to Mesopotamia and the east. All Jews traveling from Babylon to Jerusalem would have passed through this city.

By New Testament times, the city was under Roman control (belonging to the Roman province of Syria) and thoroughly influenced by Greek culture—the streets of the city were laid out in typical Hellenistic fashion (a Hippodamian layout). There was a gymnasium and a theater, and the principal language of the city was Greek. Damascus was, in fact, a principal city of the Decapolis ("ten cities"), a loose federation of Greek cities east of the Jordan river and the Sea of Galilee. Coins from the city demonstrate that the people worshiped Artemis, Athena, Nike, Tyche, Helios, and Dionysus.[A-38]

There was a sizeable Jewish population in the city attested to by Josephus's report that ten to eighteen thousand Jews were killed there at the outbreak of the Jewish revolt (A.D. 66).[A-39]

that has spread all the way to the frontierland of Damascus.

Synagogues in Damascus (9:2). There were many synagogues in the city of Damascus. This was necessary because there was a large Jewish population. We understand the size of this population by a report from the Jewish historian Josephus. He informs us that during the Jewish war of A.D. 66–70 (roughly thirty years later), over eighteen thousand Jews were killed in the city of Damascus.

These synagogues had a strong power of attraction to many in the Gentile populace (especially many women). They were drawn in by the strong ethical standards of the Jews and their claim to be in a covenant relationship with the one true God. Many Gentiles attached themselves to the synagogues by turning their backs to polytheism and embracing the god of Israel. These Gentile God-fearers and proselytes were often among the first to become Christians, accepting the Christian proclamation that Jesus is the awaited Messiah.

Evidently the persecution of Christians in Judea resulted in some of the Greek-speaking Jewish-Christians fleeing to Damascus. Filled with the Holy Spirit and passionate about their conviction that Jesus is the Messiah, they began proclaiming this good news among the synagogues of Damascus. A good number of Jews and probably many Gentile God-fearers were giving their hearts to Christ and committing themselves to this new movement.

The persecution of Christians thus backfired in the face of the chief priest and the Jewish ruling council. It served to spread the messianic movement as far as Damascus. Incensed at what was happening, the Jewish leaders commission Saul to journey to Damascus and extradite the Judean Jews to Jerusalem, where they will stand trial.

DAMASCUS
▼

The Way (9:2). The early Christians often referred to themselves as "the Way." This is derived from the notion that Jesus the Messiah is the way of life or the way of salvation. Jesus, in fact, spoke of himself in these terms: "I am the way and the truth and the life. No one comes to the Father except through me" (John 14:6).

There are no written records of the beginnings of the church in Damascus. It undoubtedly started in the Jewish community. Some speculate that Galileans who heard Jesus and subsequently became Christians traveled to Damascus as the first to proclaim Christ. Jews from Damascus itself may have heard Jesus during his earthly ministry or have been present at the day of Pentecost. The Jews who fled Jerusalem, however, are clearly impacting the city for the cause of Christ.

Take them as prisoners to Jerusalem (9:2). In light of Saul's "murderous threats" (9:1) and the death of Stephen, the lives of these Jewish Christians are in definite danger.

A light from heaven flashed around him (9:3). The light is a special manifestation of the divine presence and glory. No doubt Saul sees himself as a beneficiary of the messianic promise of Isaiah 9:2: "The people walking in darkness have seen a great light; on those living in the land of the shadow of death a light has dawned." For Saul, the more important light is the recognition of Jesus as the Messiah. The fact that the light appears "from heaven" points to Jesus as exalted to the right hand of God.

Saul, Saul, why do you persecute me? (9:4) Jesus directly addresses Saul in Aramaic (*Saoul* is the Aramaic form of his name; *Saulos*, as in 9:1, is the Greek form). Jesus asks Saul a question that he will never forget and that will have a revolutionary impact on every aspect of his life. The question presupposes that Jesus is resurrected and alive (he is not in the grave), that he is in a close relationship with the people who embrace him as Messiah and Lord (he is not a messianic pretender), and that by persecuting Christians, Saul is actually persecuting the Lord and standing in the way of what God is accomplishing in fulfillment of Old Testament promises. What a shattering realization!

The men traveling with Saul (9:7). Although the identity of these men is not explicitly stated, they may have been fellow official representatives of the Sanhedrin. They hear something, but do not know or understand what the Lord says to Saul.

For three days he was blind (9:9). Unable to see after this dramatic encounter, the traveling companions lead Saul by the hand to the city of Damascus. Overwhelmed by what has happened and full of grief at actually opposing the God he is so zealously trying to serve, Saul refuses to eat or drink for three days.

He spends much of this time in prayerful, repentant reflection on the course of his life, the claims of the followers of Jesus, and the messianic texts of Scripture. At some point during these three days, the Lord appears to him again in a vision (cf. 9:12).

Ananias Meets With Saul (9:10–19a)

Following his direct appearance to Saul, the Lord uses one Jewish believer from Damascus to minister to Saul.

Ananias (9:10). He is a Jew living in Damascus who has put his faith in Jesus as the Messiah based on the preaching of Jewish Christians who come to the city prior to Saul. Today in the city of Damascus, there is a chapel bearing the name of Ananias. The tradition that this chapel marks the site of Ananias' home dates back to Byzantine times. Based on the location, the actual house of Ananias may have been situated directly on the wall.[159]

A vision (9:10, 12). In the days that followed Jesus' appearance to Saul in a brilliant light on the road to Damascus, the Lord gives further guidance through two visions. First, he appears to this Damascene believer, Ananias, and gives him specific directions to meet Saul and how to minister to him. Then the Lord again appears to Saul, but this time in a vision, and informs him that someone is coming to meet him and restore his sight. The word that is used for vision (*horama*) indicates something that is actually seen as opposed to something that is purely imaginary. The Lord will once again use a double vision as a means of reaching the Gentile household of Cornelius through the apostle Peter (Acts 10:1–

> ## REFLECTIONS
>
> **ALTHOUGH FEW CHRISTIANS HAVE** experienced a blinding flash of light and a vision of the ascended Christ reaching out to them as a catalyst prompting their conversions, most of us can reflect on people, events, and circumstances that show God's initiative in reaching us with his love in the gospel. Salvation is truly the result of God's initiative. We have done nothing to earn it.

23). It is significant to observe that Saul receives the vision during a period when he has spent considerable time in prayer.

The house of Judas on Straight Street (9:11). Judas is presumably not a Christian, but Paul's Jewish host with whom he has made arrangements prior to leaving Jerusalem. "Straight Street" is actually one of the main roads going through Damascus (the *cardo maximus*), the main east-west route through the city. Part of this street has been discovered by archaeologists. It was colonnaded and was about fifty feet wide. Today it is known as the *Darb el-Moskatim*.[160]

STRAIGHT STREET

The eastern end of the street looking west at the east gate of Damascus. ▼

Tarsus (9:11). Saul was not originally from Jerusalem or even from Palestine. He came from an Asia Minor city in the province of Cilicia called Tarsus (see 22:3). From a grammar school age, however, Saul lived in Jerusalem and there received his education.

Place his hands on him (9:12). In the Old Testament, the laying on of hands is done in connection with a special commission (as Moses did when he conferred the leadership of the nation on Joshua; Num. 27:23) or with the imparting of a blessing (as Jacob did on his sons just before he died; Gen. 48:14). Jesus often laid his hands on people as he healed them: "When the sun was setting, the people brought to Jesus all who had various kinds of sickness, and laying his hands on each one, he healed them" (Luke 4:40). Here the Lord instructs Ananias to confer the divine blessing of healing on Saul by laying his hands on him.

"Lord," Ananias answered, "I have heard many reports" (9:13). Well-informed of Saul's violent persecuting activity against the Jewish Christians, Ananias understandably objects to the instructions. He has not heard that the Lord appeared to Saul on the Damascus road.

Your saints (9:13). This is the first time that this expression is used to refer to Christians. It is here found on the lips of a believer in Damascus. The term reflects the proper understanding that the new covenant people of God have been made holy and pure before God by the forgiveness achieved in Jesus' death on the cross. It also conveys the idea that believers are especially devoted to God.

This man is my chosen instrument (9:15). The Lord overrules all of Ana-

nias's objections and tells him that Saul has been specially chosen as an ambassador of the gospel. God will use Saul to take the gospel particularly to the Gentiles, but also to Jews and even to kings.

How much he must suffer for my name (9:16). The Lord also informs Ananias that this one who has inflicted much suffering on Christians now will experience much suffering himself as he carries out his divinely ordained mission. Saul/Paul himself later enumerates the variety of ways he eventually suffered for the cause of Christ (2 Cor. 11:23–33).

He could see again (9:18). Obeying the Lord Jesus, Ananias locates the house and does exactly as the Lord has told him. Ananias greets Saul and lays hands on him, and Saul regains his sight. Saul's physical blindness has similarities to the spiritual blindness he experienced before his conversion. Saul later reflects, "The god of this age has blinded the minds of unbelievers, so that they cannot see the light of the gospel of the glory of Christ, who is the image of God" (2 Cor. 4:4). The illumination of Christ, however, frees Saul of his spiritual blindness and he wholeheartedly embraces Jesus as the Messiah and Son of God.

Filled with the Holy Spirit . . . and was baptized (9:17–18). At this time, Saul is filled with the Holy Spirit, who will empower this newly commissioned apostle to proclaim the gospel and endure the suffering. Saul is then immediately baptized, presumably by Ananias. In later church tradition, there is a one- to three-year delay for baptism, which follows a long period of instruction. The New Testament pattern appears to be that the rite is performed in a short time after a person professes faith in Christ. It is also important here to observe that Paul experiences the work of the Spirit in his life prior to his baptism.

Saul Immediately Proclaims Jesus in Damascus (9:19b–25)

In one of the greatest reversals in history, the man who once persecutes followers of Jesus now begins proclaiming him as the Son of God and as the long-awaited Messiah among the Jews in the synagogues of Damascus.

At once he began to preach in the synagogues (9:20). Because the first letter of Saul/Paul was written nearly seventeen years later, some have assumed that he spent these years in prayer, study, and reflection before engaging in ministry. But this is not true. Saul begins his preaching almost immediately, only after spending some time with his new brothers and sisters in the Lord.

Oddly enough, some of the Jews in these Damascus synagogues have probably been in contact with members of the Jerusalem Sanhedrin and are anxious for the help Saul will bring in, putting a stop to the encroaching influence of this new movement. Yet now here Saul is passionately advocating the very thing he has come to crush.

Filled with the Spirit and gaining a deeper appreciation day-by-day of the marvelous fulfillment of the Old Testament expectation in Jesus, Saul's presentation of Jesus as the Messiah becomes more and more powerful. Many of the Jews resistant to his preaching have great difficulty providing a credible response to Saul's message. It is possible that it is at this time that he receives the first of his five synagogue beatings mentioned in 2 Corinthians 11:24.

Son of God (9:20). A central part of Saul's teaching is declaring Jesus as the Son of God. This does not mean that Jesus is God's Son in any sort of physical sense. The background of this phrase needs to be understood in its Old Testament context of God's special relationship with the anointed king of Israel. The Lord had a unique relationship with David and promised him that one of his descendants would be king of Israel in the future, that he would have a glorious and eternal reign, and that he would enjoy a relationship of sonship to the Father: "I will establish the throne of his kingdom for ever. I will be his father, and he shall be my son."[161] To announce that Jesus is *the* Son of God is to proclaim the arrival of the anointed king (the "Messiah") who will reign on the throne of David.

[Mission to Arabia (Gal. 1:17)]. If we compare this account to Paul's later own words in Galatians 1, we find that he leaves Damascus shortly after his conversion to journey to "Arabia." This is not to be identified with the Arabian peninsula occupied today by Saudi Arabia, but refers to the vast kingdom of Nabatea (see comments on Gal. 1:17). The Nabateans lived in the land south of Damascus and southeast of Palestine. Today their land is located within parts of southern Syria, Jordan, the Negev of Israel, the Sinai, and the northwestern region of Saudi Arabia. The capital of this vast empire was the city of Petra, about fifty miles south of the Dead Sea.

Because of his commission to reach Gentiles with the gospel, Paul probably spends time in the major cities of Nabatea, such as Petra and Hegra, where there were Jewish synagogues and where he could present the gospel to the Gentile

God-fearers and proselytes. His method for reaching Gentiles throughout his ministry is by first preaching the Messiah in the Jewish synagogues. Here he finds many Gentiles who have already come to believe in the one God of Israel and have gained some familiarity with the Old Testament. He probably spends as much as

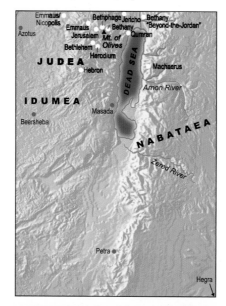

one and a half to two years in this region.[162]

Why does he go to this region? This appears to have been an area where Jewish Christians had not yet taken the gospel after they were scattered from Jerusalem by persecution. In fulfilling the principle of not "building on someone else's foundation" (Rom. 15:20), Saul goes to this neighboring area where Christ has not yet been preached.

After many days had gone by (9:23). Luke chooses not to relate the account of Saul's trip to Arabia, but this is the time it likely occurs. After his one or two years in Nabatea, Saul returns to Damascus for the second phase of his ministry there, where he faces the conspiracy for his death and has to flee.

The Jews conspired to kill him . . . . But his followers took him by night and lowered him in a basket through an opening in the wall (9:23–25). Astonished that their ally from Jerusalem joins this dangerous Messianic sect, the Jewish leaders from the synagogues are so incensed that they begin to make plans to kill Saul. This is not a surprising move on their part since precedent has already been set for killing vocal leaders of this movement (e.g. Stephen; 7:54–8:1). Now they see for themselves Saul's persuasive appeal on behalf of Jesus. Something needs to be done as soon as possible to stop the spread of his influence in their city. He himself describes this incident in 2 Corinthians 11:32:

> In Damascus the governor under King Aretas had the city of the Damscenes guarded in order to arrest me. But I was lowered in a basket from a window in the wall and slipped through his hands.

▶

ARABIA (NABATEA)

PETRA

▼

It is no contradiction that Saul says that the governor under King Aretas is after him and Luke says that the Jews are conspiring against him. The most likely explanation is that both groups are out to get him.[163] Aretas IV was the king of the Nabateans, ruling over them from 9 B.C. to A.D. 40. The "governor" under him was properly an *ethnarch*, that is, a ruler over the Nabateans living in the city of Damascus. Saul's preaching throughout Nabatea evidently stirred up a significant amount of antipathy against him from the Jews living in the area. As happened in other cities during Saul's missionary journeys, they probably complained bitterly to the local officials and represented Saul as a threat. The two groups then—the Jewish leaders and the local Nabatean leaders—collude against Saul in the city of Damascus. His life is in danger and he has to leave the city.

Becoming aware of their plan, Saul's fellow believers hatch a plan to usher him out of the city. They stealthily lower him in a basket through a window under the cover of darkness so he can escape on foot.

Saul Goes to Jerusalem (9:26–31)

To Jerusalem (9:26). Saul immediately departs for Jerusalem. He tells us why in his letter to the Galatians. He wants to become acquainted with Peter (Gal. 1:18)—the most significant leader in the Jerusalem church. Presumably he stays in Peter's home there. These two weeks give them much time to become more personally acquainted.

Saul hears about Peter's three years of accompanying the Lord Jesus in his earthly ministry and many of the details of Jesus' teaching and deeds. Peter, in turn, hears the details of Saul's miraculous conversion and his proclamation of Jesus as Messiah in Damascus and throughout Nabatea (Arabia).

He tried to join the disciples (9:26). Saul soon finds out that there is still much suspicion about the authenticity of his conversion. Knowing all too well the violence Saul has exhibited toward the believers in Jesus, the Christians in Jerusalem are understandably fearful of him. Many consider Saul's conversion a clever ruse to trap them and persecute them. Presumably, he stays with relatives after his arrival into the city before he becomes acquainted with Peter.

More disciples than the twelve apostles are apparently in Jerusalem at this time. Roughly three years has passed since the outbreak of persecution against the church (see Gal. 1:18–20). Apparently the intensity of the persecution has subsided to a sufficient degree that a number have returned to the city.

◀ *left*

A WALL AT THE MODERN CITY OF DAMASCUS

Barnabas took him and brought him to the apostles (9:27). Barnabas, a Jew from Cyprus who became a follower of Christ (see comments on 4:36), intervenes. Believing Saul's story, he takes him to the apostles and explains the details of his conversion. This reduces the cloud of suspicion surrounding Saul. He is then able to meet with groups of Christians and even begins proclaiming Christ in Jerusalem. According to Galatians 1:18, Peter and James (the Lord's brother, not one of the Twelve) are the only apostles Saul meets at this time.

right ▶

JERUSALEM TO TARSUS

Debated with the Grecian Jews (9:29). Saul proclaims Christ particularly among the Jews who are not from Jerusalem but who come from various parts of the Greek-speaking world (see comments on 6:1, 9). For the most part, these zealous Jews outrightly reject Saul's message and are prepared to put him to death—the very thing Saul himself did to such blasphemous people a few years earlier.

Sent him off to Tarsus (9:30). Knowing the reality of the threats from the non-Christian Jews, believers in Jerusalem usher Saul to the coastal city of Caesarea.

This is only a stop-off point for Saul's ultimate destination—Tarsus of Cilicia. To go to Tarsus is to go home for Saul.[164] He may have had family and friends living there since he spent his earliest years there before being sent to Jerusalem for his education. The extensive Jewish population of the area along with the many Gentile sympathizers to Judaism provide an ideal mission field for him to continue fulfilling his divinely given commission. He probably spends between three and four years in Tarsus and the neighboring cities of Cilicia before going to Antioch in 39 or 40 A.D.[165]

TARSUS

(left) A view of the Taurus mountains from the city of Tarsus (looking in the direction of the Cilician gates).

(right) The gate of Cleopatra at Tarsus.

▼

Peter Heals Aeneas and Dorcas (9:32–43)

Luke now shifts his focus away from Saul and back to Peter, partly in preparation to narrate the conversion of the Gentile household of Cornelius. Peter does not remain resident in Jerusalem, but becomes a missionary. After ministering to the new believers in Samaria (8:14–25), he apparently returns to Jerusalem for a period of time (8:25) and then begins traveling to villages in Judea and Samaria. He presumably evangelizes and provides these new converts with apostolic teaching.

Lydda (9:32). Lydda, known as Lod in the Old Testament, was located eleven miles southeast of Joppa (Tel Aviv).[166] The main road from Jerusalem to Joppa passed through this city. Lydda was the chief city over one of the eleven districts (or toparchies) into which Judea was divided.[167] The population was almost exclusively Jewish.[168] Luke does not tell us how this city was evangelized. It may have been reached by the Christians dispersed from Jerusalem following the persecution (8:1, 4) or even by Philip (8:40). Today the ancient city is covered by modern buildings, which have prevented any extensive archaeological work.[169] After the Jewish war, Lydda became an important center for rabbinical learning.

Aeneas (9:33). Luke does not explicitly state whether Aeneas is a believer. His ethnic background is most likely Jewish. Although the name "Aeneas" appears in Palestinian inscriptions, it was also a well-known Greek name.

▶ Tarsus

Tarsus was the principal city of the province of Cilicia located in the southeastern portion of Asia Minor (in modern-day Turkey).[A-40] Ideally situated about ten miles north of the coast of the Mediterranean Sea on the Cydnus River, Tarsus was an important center for commerce. The city served as the nexus point between the interior of Asia Minor and Syria as well as for trade from the Mediterranean. To the north of Tarsus lay the rugged Taurus mountain range with peaks averaging a height of seven thousand feet. There was only one viable pass over the mountains from Tarsus—a narrow gorge called the Cilician Gates.

Stoic philosophy and rhetoric flourished in Tarsus. It was home to four famous Stoic philosophers: Antipater, Archedemus, Athenodorus Cordylion, and Athenodorus of Tarsus. The latter, a friend of Cicero, had even served as the court philosopher for the emperor Caesar Augustus. Strabo said that the Tarsians' zeal for learning surpassed that of Athens or Alexandria.[A-41] In spite of Tarsus' fame for Stoic philosophy, it remains doubtful that Saul had received any formal Stoic education there.

As with any other city of the time, there were an abundance of cults in Tarsus. Most important to the city was the god Sandas, an old Cilician god of war and the weather. He was frequently identified with the Greek hero/god Heracles (in Greek mythology he was born of a human mother and Zeus). There was also a large Jewish population in the province of Cilicia and in the city of Tarsus.

The modern city of Tarsus occupies the ancient site thereby preventing little archaeological work from being undertaken. Excavations conducted a generation ago on the southeastern extremity of the modern city turned up nothing from the Roman period, but archaeologists have recently discovered 250 coins dating as early as the second century B.C.,[A-42] although most date between the third and fifth centuries A.D.[A-43]

Jesus Christ heals you (9:34). Not using any healing formulas, incantations, or rituals, Peter declares that Aeneas will be healed by the power of Jesus Christ. Peter is not a shaman or a magician (like Simon), but is an earthly representative of the living and powerful Christ.

Sharon (9:35). Sharon is a large coastal plain in northern Palestine. Joppa lay at the southern end of this plain that extends north about thirty miles to Caesarea Maritima and inland nearly ten. After the building of Caesarea by Herod and a new network of roads, the population of this area grew considerably.

Joppa (9:36). The seaport where Jonah once boarded a boat to flee from the mission God had called him to (Jonah 1:3), this city became a site for the spread of Christianity and the location where Peter is used by God to raise a woman from the dead.[170] Located about thirty-five miles northwest of Jerusalem and eleven miles northwest of Lydda, Joppa served as the main port for Jerusalem and all of Judea. Ancient Joppa (or Jaffa) was located within the modern city of Tel Aviv. When Herod the Great built his new port at Caesarea Maritima, Joppa became far less significant (although it later regained its

significance when the port at Caesarea deteriorated and fell into disuse in the late Byzantine period). Although many modern buildings cover the ancient site, the modern visitor's center covers the remains of some Roman-era structures.

Joppa was a rather dangerous port because of the rocky breakwater about a hundred yards offshore. Sudden high winds from the north resulted in many ships being dashed against the rocks.[171] The population of Joppa was predominately Jewish. Consequently, it later became a revolutionary center in the Jewish war against the Romans in A.D. 66.[172]

Tabitha (which, when translated, is Dorcas) (9:36). "Tabitha" is an Aramaic name that means "gazelle." "Dorcas" is a Greek translation of the name. The fact that she has a Greek name illustrates the level of Greek influence in Palestine.

Her body was washed (9:37). It was common in the cultures of antiquity to wash and anoint a body in preparation for burial. This was also true in Judaism: "They may make ready on the Sabbath all that is needful for the dead, and anoint it and wash it."[173]

He got down on his knees and prayed (9:40). Peter does not have some inherent power and ability to heal. He calls on God to give him direction on how to respond to this situation and for the ability to do what God wants him to do.

A tanner named Simon (9:43). It is significant that Peter stays with a tanner, since this was viewed as a despised trade in Judaism. One rabbi even exclaimed, "Woe to him who is a tanner."[174] Tanners were suspected of immorality because

LYDDA, SHARON, AND JOPPA

▼

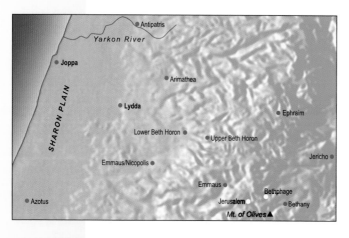

JOPPA

Looking at the modern city of Tel Aviv from the site of Joppa.

women worked in the trade. Many were repulsed by the trade simply because of the stench of working with animal carcases. Jews also had concerns about the ritual purity of tanners because of their contact with dead bodies.[175] At this point, not yet having his vision of unclean animals let down from heaven in a sheet, Peter is still concerned about maintaining Jewish ritual purity.

The Conversion of Cornelius (10:1–48)

The conversion of Cornelius and his household represents the decisive step forward in the spread of Christianity to the Gentiles. Cornelius was not the first Gentile to receive Christ, however. Already a Gentile proselyte (6:5), an Ethiopian Gentile (8:26–39), and some converts of Philip (8:40) have become followers of Christ. But this situation is unique because of the involvement of the apostle Peter (the recognized leader of this new movement) and God's miracu-lous superintending of the events (including God's revelation to Peter that he had declared all foods pure).

This significant event probably occurs sometime between A.D. 39–40. This means it happens roughly ten years after the death and resurrection of Jesus and about seven years after Paul's conversion.

Caesarea (10:1). Caesarea Maritima was a major seaport city about sixty miles northwest of Jerusalem. Politically it functioned as the provincial capital of Judea and was home to the Roman governors.[176] The city had only recently been built by Herod the Great over the former site of a coastal town called Strato's Tower and occupied 235 acres within the perimeter wall.

Herod commissioned an army of workers to begin work on the city and the harbor in 23 B.C. and actually completed the immense undertaking in a decade. He spared no expense in fulfilling his vision of creating a major international port that rivaled Alexandria and

Piraeus (the port of Athens). In creating the first artificial harbor in the ancient world, Herod's engineers made use of a new sophisticated technology. Creating immense wooden forms, the engineers made much of the harbor and breakwater with a type of concrete that hardened underwater.

He patterned the city itself on the style of a Roman provincial capital with

all of the amenities (including temples, theater, market, hippodrome, and an amphitheater). The beautiful four thousand-seat theater was located at the south end of the city with the seats facing the Mediterranean. Archaeologists estimate that the seating capacity around the oval track of the hippodrome was thirty thousand. The city was laid out on the Hellenistic grid model with streets that ran north-south and east-west. The infrastructure of the city included an intricate sewer system and an abundant water supply. Herod's engineers designed an immense aqueduct that brought water from mountain springs (at Shuni) some six miles to the north. Most of the aqueduct was carried on high arches, but part of it is through a quarter of a mile long tunnel, which was bored through a sandstone ridge.

Herod named the city after Caesar Augustus, the reigning emperor. Josephus tells us of the great honor he bestowed on Caesar: "On rising ground opposite the harbour-mouth stood Caesar's temple, of exceptional size and beauty; in it was a colossal statue of Caesar, no whit inferior to the Olympian Zeus which it was intended to resemble, and one of Rome comparable with the Hera of Argos. Herod dedicated the city to the province, the harbour to those who sailed these seas, and the honour of his new creation to Caesar: Caesarea was the name he gave it."[177]

The city had great significance for Christianity not only because of Luke's portrayal of the conversion of the Gentile family of Cornelius, but also as the place where Origen (A.D. 185–254) and Eusebius (A.D. 260–340) lived and taught. For Jews, painful memories were associated with Caesarea. At the outset of the Jewish war in A.D. 66, the Gentile

▶

CAESAREA MARITIMA AND ITS ENVIRONS

▶ ## The City of Caesarea
IMPORTANT FACTS:

- Population: over 50,000
- Prominent Religions: Tyche (Fortuna); Ephesian Artemis (Diana); Apollo; Dionysus; Isis; Serapis; Demeter; Mithras; Ruler cult (Augustus and Roma); Judaism
- The major port city for Palestine
- A city recently constructed by Herod the Great (begun in 23 B.C.)
- Seat of the Roman Government for the Province of Judea

citizens of the city massacred nearly the entire population of Caesarea's Jews.[178]

A man named Cornelius (10:1). Cornelius may have been a descendant of one of the ten thousand slaves freed by the Roman general L. Cornelius Sulla Felix in 82 B.C.[179] It is not uncommon for freedmen to take on the family name (*gens*) of their emancipator. On the other hand, "Cornelius" was a rather common Latin name.

He was a fairly wealthy man of status living in a beautiful city. Evidently he has been stationed in Caesarea for a long period of time because he possesses a home, his family is with him, and he has been there long enough to perform many generous deeds for the Jewish community. It is also possible that he has retired from the military and has chosen to settle in Caesarea. Nothing is known of this man outside of the biblical account.

A centurion (10:1). "The centurions are the principal professional officers in the Roman army."[180] They served as the commanding officers over troops of eighty to a hundred men and are paid well. "The financial attraction of the centurionate,

▶ Archaeology in Caesarea

Caesarea Maritima has been a major focus of archaeological excavation since 1950 by groups from Israel, Italy, and the United States.[A-44] Since 1971 a consortium of nearly two dozen colleges and universities known as the Joint Expedition to Caesarea Maritima (JECM) has been excavating the land site. In 1980, an international consortium was formed to carry out underwater excavations of the ancient harbor. Known as CAHEP—"the Caesarea Ancient Harbour Excavation Project"—and headed by A. Raban (University of Haifa) and R. L. Hohlfelder (University of Colorado)—this group made significant discoveries relating to the ancient harbor. *National Geographic* magazine featured Caesarea Maritima as the cover story of a 1987 issue and produced a video-documentary of the work there.[A-45] Work at Caesarea is now done under the auspices of the Combined Caesarea Expeditions (CCE), a joint initiative of the University of Maryland and the University of Haifa.[A-46]

Among some of the sigificant discoveries on the site of the ancient city were the remains of a synagogue, an underground Mithraeum, and many statues, inscriptions, and coins. The synagogue building dates to the fourth century A.D., but it incorporates walls from a much earlier synagogue structure that dates to the Herodian era. Excavators found the capital of a column engraved with a Jewish menorah. The Mithraeum, an underground structure for performing rituals in honor of the Persian god Mithras, was built in the late first century from a converted subterranean warehouse vault.

In addition to discovering well-preserved statues of Tyche and Artemis, archaeologists found a horde of thirty-seven hundred bronze Roman coins (dating to the mid-fourth century). Of the inscriptions found at the site, three are particularly significant: (1) a Latin stone inscription from the theater that mentions "Pontius Pilate," (2) a Latin inscription on the aqueduct that commemorates the presence of the tenth Roman legion at Caesarea, and (3) fragments of a Hebrew inscription on the mosaic floor of the synagogue that listed the twenty-four priestly courses.

◀

CAPITAL WITH MENORAH FROM CAESAREAN SYNAGOGUE

however, was that the pay was probably some sixteen times that of the basic legionary salary. In short, a centurion had both considerable military and social status and wealth."[181] As a centurion, Cornelius was also a Roman citizen. The historian Polybius (1st cent. B.C.) says of centurions: "They wish centurions not so much to be venturesome and daredevil as natural leaders, of a steady and sedate spirit. They do not desire them so much to be men who will initiate attacks and open the battle, but men who will hold their ground when worsted and hard pressed and be ready to die at their posts."[182]

The Italian Regiment (10:1). This is the earliest reference (c. A.D. 40) to the *Cohors II Italica voluntariorum civium Romanorum* (the "Second Italian Cohort of Roman Citizens"), known from Latin

CAESAREA MARITIMA

(top) Remains of the ancient harbor.

(bottom left) Ruins near the harbor.

(bottom right) The theater. The aqueduct is visible in the top right of the photo.

▶ Josephus's Description of Caesarea

Herod Rebuilds "Strato's Tower": "Herod noticed on the coast a town called Strato's Tower, in a state of decay, but thanks to its admirable situation capable of benefiting by his generosity. He rebuilt it entirely with limestone and adorned it with a most splendid palace. Nowhere did he show more clearly the liveliness of his imagination."

The Creation of the Immense Harbor: "The city lies midway between Dora and Joppa, and hitherto the whole of that shore had been harbourless, so that anyone sailing along the Phoenician coast towards Egypt had to ride the open sea when threatened by the southwest wind; even when this is far from strong, such huge waves are dashed against the rocks that the back-wash makes the sea boil up a long way out. But the king by lavish expenditure and unshakable determination won the battle against nature and constructed a harbour bigger than the Piraeus [the harbor of Athens], with further deep roadsteads in its recesses. The site was as awkward as could be, but he wrestled with the difficulties so triumphantly that on his solid fabric the sea could make no impression, while its beauty gave no hint of the obstacles encountered. He first marked out the area for a harbour of the size mentioned, and then lowered into 20 fathoms of water blocks of stone mostly 50 feet long, 9 deep, and 10 broad, but sometimes even bigger."

The Breakwater: "When the foundations had risen to water-level he built above the surface a mole 200 feet wide; half this width was built out to break the force of the waves and so was called the Breakwater; the rest supported the encircling stone wall. Along this were spaced massive towers, of which the most con-spicuous and most beautiful was called Drusium after Caesar's step-son."

The Situation of the Port; The Colossal Statues and the Towers: "There was a row of arched recesses where newly-arrived crews could land, and in front of these was a circular terrace forming a broad walk for those disembarking. The harbour-mouth faced north, as in that locality the north wind is the gentlest, and on either side rose three colossal statues standing on pillars; those on the left of ships entering were supported by a solid tower, those on the right by two upright stones clamped together, even higher than the tower of the other side."

Houses and Streets: "Adjoining the harbour were houses, also of limestone, and to the harbour led the streets of the town, laid out the same distance apart."

Caesar's Temple and Statue: "On rising ground opposite the harbour-mouth stood Caesar's temple, of exceptional size and beauty; in it was a colossal statue of Caesar, no whit inferior to the Olympian Zeus which it was intended to resemble, and one of Rome comparable with the Hera of Argos. Herod dedicated the city to the province, the harbour to those who sailed these seas, and the honour of his new creation to Caesar: Caesarea was the name he gave it."

Other Public Works and the Games: "The rest of the buildings—theatre, amphitheatre, and market-place—were on a scale worthy of that name. The king also instituted four-yearly games and called them too after Caesar, gracing the first contest—held in the 192d Olympiad—with the personal gift of very valuable prizes, the royal bounty extending not only to the winners but to those who came second and third."[A-47]

Roman Military Command Structure	
Roman Military Title	**Amount of Men**
1. Century	100
2. Maniple	200 (two Centuries)
3. Cohort	600 (three Maniples)
4. Legion	6000 (ten Cohorts)

inscriptions.[183] This cohort was present in Syria during the Jewish revolt (A.D. 66–70) and remained there for an extended period of time following the war. It was likely made up of Roman citizens who were in some sense "Italian." Some of the soldiers were possibly local Syrian recruits or freedmen.[184]

Devout and God-fearing (10:2). Cornelius turns his back to the gods of the military (such as Mithras) and the household gods of Rome and embraces the one true God of Israel as the object of his devotion. He attaches himself to the synagogue (without becoming a full proselyte), sharing his wealth with those in need (in the Jewish community) and praying regularly.

CALIGULA

A marble bust of the renown emperor who reigned A.D. 37–41.

At about three in the afternoon (10:3). This was a set Jewish time of prayer. We can assume that Cornelius is praying at this time and receives the vision in the context of prayer. The time is also further evidence that Cornelius is not simply dreaming.

He had a vision (10:3). Cornelius distinctly sees an angel appear and speak to him by name. Throughout this early period in the spread of Christianity, God frequently uses angels to give direction to his servants.[185]

As a memorial offering before God (10:4). Just as the Old Testament describes the smoke of a burnt offering ascending to the presence of the Lord (see Lev. 2:2), Cornelius's generous giving and his regular and sincere prayers are pleasing to the Lord. This is consistent with the way prayer is described elsewhere in the Old Testament: "May my prayer be set before you like incense; may the lifting up of my hands be like the evening sacrifice" (Ps. 141:2). God receives Cornelius's prayer and giving as acceptable offerings from this Gentile man who responds according to the light of revelation he has received through the synagogue. Now God will give him the full revelation of Jesus Christ.

Send men to Joppa (10:5). Joppa is about thirty miles south of Caesarea.

About noon (10:9). Noon, or "the sixth hour," is not one of the normal Jewish times of prayer (although Daniel sets aside three times a day to pray; see Dan. 6:10). Peter here illustrates the practice of the apostles and the early Christians to pray frequently.

Peter went up on the roof to pray (10:9). Palestinian homes typically had flat roofs with access from an outdoors stairway. It was common for the occupants to climb the stairs to the roof and sit on the top of the house, especially in the summertime, to benefit from a cool breeze. Peter goes to the roof at noon time probably to find a place where he can pray undisturbed.

He fell into a trance (10:10). Whereas Cornelius has a vision (*horama*) in which an angel of the Lord appears to him, Peter falls into a trance (*ekstasis*) and has a vision of heaven opening. The term literally means "to stand outside of yourself" and refers to a state of being brought about by God "in which consciousness is wholly or partially suspended."[186] The same word is used to describe the vision Daniel sees on the banks of the Tigris River after fasting for three weeks and interceding for the people of Israel (Dan. 10:7).

He saw heaven opened (10:11). Stephen experiences the same phenomenon (see comments on 7:56).

Something like a large sheet (10:11). The term *othonē*, translated here as "sheet," refers to a linen cloth. Linen had a variety of applications with a sheet (such as a bed sheet) being just one. The term is used often in ancient literature for the sails of a ship, as in *Martyrdom of Polycarp* 15:2: "like the sail (*othonē*) of a ship filled by the wind." The sheet Peter sees is suspended by its four corners and filled with a large number of animals.

All kinds of four-footed animals, as well as reptiles of the earth and birds of the air (10:12). In this vision, Peter sees all kinds of animals. This description is reminiscent of the summary of animal life at

bottom left

ROOFS

These are homes in the village of Der Samet in the area of Hebron. Inhabitants sleep on the roofs during the hot summer nights.

JOPPA

The modern site of Joppa (or, Jaffa).
▼

the beginning of creation (Gen. 1:24). The Torah, however, prohibited the Israelites from eating certain animals. A detailed set of criteria for determining which animals were clean and which were to be regarded as unclean is given in Leviticus 11. There are four basic criteria:

- Land animals had to both chew the cud and have a split hoof.
- Sea creatures had to have fins and scales.
- Winged insects had to have jointed legs to hop.
- Birds of prey, reptiles, and other crawlers were off limits.

Among those animals the Israelites could not eat were camels, rabbits, pigs, eagles, vultures, owls, weasels, rats, and lizards. Peter sees many of these prohibited (and "unclean") animals in the sheet, presumably mingled together with animals that are ritually pure.

I have never eaten anything impure or unclean (10:14). It is to Peter's credit that he has never eaten any of the pro-

hibited animals. As an observant Jew of his time, Peter exercises great sensitivity not to defile himself with any food that will render him ceremonially impure. God has clearly revealed in the law that he should not eat any of them: "Do not defile yourselves by any of these creatures. Do not make yourselves unclean by means of them or be made unclean by them. I am the LORD your God; consecrate yourselves and be holy, because I am holy" (Lev. 11:43–44). Peter's reaction to the vision and his perplexity are entirely understandable.

"Unclean" (*akathartos*) is the typical description in the law for the prohibited animals; "impure" (*koinos*) never appears. *Koinos* is more often translated as "common." It comes to be used in later Judaism for the foods that Gentiles would eat. "The opposite is that which is sanctified or dedicated *[hagios]* and hence withdrawn from ordinary use."[187]

Jewish literature is filled with examples of people who refused to defile themselves by consuming "common" or unkosher food. Note a few examples from the period around the Maccabean revolt that show the intensity of commitment to avoid unclean foods:

- Antiochus Epiphanes ordered everyone in his kingdom (which included Israel) to give up their ancestral customs "that all should be one people" (1 Macc. 1:41). This included a specific command to "sacrifice swine and unclean (*koina*) animals." The commitment not to defile themselves with impure food was so strong in Israel that many gave their lives to obey it: "But many in Israel stood firm and were resolved in their hearts not to eat unclean food. They chose to die rather than to be

UNCLEAN ANIMALS IN JUDAISM
▼ ▶

defiled by food or to profane the holy covenant; and they did die" (1 Macc. 1:62–63).

- Eleazar, priest during the Maccabean period, was praised for not defiling himself, although he was martyred: "O priest, worthy of the priesthood, you neither defiled your sacred teeth nor profaned your stomach, which had room only for reverence and purity, by eating defiled foods" (4 Macc. 7:6).

The question of *why* God originally designated certain animals as ceremonially unclean is difficult to answer. The Old Testament never explicitly or implicitly tells us. It is inadequate to speculate that God selected a kosher menu as a means of protection for his people from food-borne diseases in an age before refrigeration. It is possible that God originally willed to keep Jews and Gentiles apart in order to unite them in a special way in the messianic age. There was, in fact, a strain of messianic expectation in Judaism that anticipated the declaration of all animals as clean: "All the animals which in this world are declared unclean, God will in the future [that is, in the days of the Messiah] declare clean."[188]

Do not call anything impure that God has made clean (10:15). The full implication of the coming of Christ and the inauguration of the new covenant has not yet dawned on Peter. God is lifting the distinction between clean and unclean foods—a boundary that separates Jews from Gentiles.

The prophets anticipated a time when God would cleanse anyone who worshiped him. The new covenant promise of Ezekiel anticipated a time when God would cleanse his people from impurity and place his Spirit in them: "I will sprinkle clean water on you, and *you will be clean; I will cleanse you from all your impurities* and from all your idols. I will give you a new heart and put a new spirit in you; I will remove from you your heart of stone and give you a heart of flesh. And I will put my Spirit in you and move you to follow my decrees and be careful to keep my laws. You will live in the land I gave your forefathers; you will be my people, and I will be your God" (Ezek. 36:25–28). Zechariah envisioned a day when there would be an abundant source of cleansing in Israel: "On that day a fountain will be opened to the house of David and the inhabitants of Jerusalem, *to cleanse them from sin and impurity*" (Zech. 13:1).

This time has now arrived in the person of Jesus. In fact, Jesus declared all foods to be clean during his ministry: "Don't you see that nothing that enters a man from the outside can make him 'unclean'? For it doesn't go into his heart but into his stomach, and then out of his body. (In saying this, Jesus declared all foods 'clean.')" (Mark 7:15–16). Jesus emphasized that it is actually sinful thoughts and tendencies that defile people rather than what they eat: "He went on: 'What comes out of a man is what makes him "unclean." For from within, out of men's hearts, come evil

TEMPLE TO CAESAR AUGUSTUS

The remains of a temple at Caesarea built by Herod in honor of the namesake of the city.

▼

thoughts, sexual immorality, theft, murder, adultery, greed, malice, deceit, lewdness, envy, slander, arrogance and folly. All these evils come from inside and make a man "unclean"'" (Mark 7:20–25).

God now impresses the reality of this teaching of Jesus on Peter by means of this vision. Of course, this is a critical time. The Gentiles are now to be incorporated into the new people of God.

The Spirit said to him (10:19). From beginning to end, God has been directly involved in orchestrating this entire set of events. The direct guidance of the Spirit is characteristic of ministry in this new covenant era (Joel 2:28; Acts 2:17) and especially of the early Christian mission (see, e.g., Acts 13:2; 16:6).

He is a righteous . . . man (10:22). Cornelius is not "righteous" in the Pauline sense of justified before God. The expression here (*dikaios*) means that he is living as an observant Jew would live at that time by giving heed to and obeying the Mosaic law.[189]

Peter invited the men into the house to be his guests (10:23). Although it was not unlawful for Peter to host Gentile guests in the home, he certainly risks ritual defilement according to Jewish tradition. In general, Jews tried to minimize their contact with Gentiles. This is well illustrated by an exhortation given in the book of *Jubilees:*

> Separate yourself from the gentiles, and do not eat with them, and do not perform deeds like theirs. And do not become associates of theirs. Because their deeds are defiled, and all of their ways are contaminated, and despicable, and abominable (*Jub.* 22:16).

Peter's warm invitation to these men may indicate that he is beginning to understand what the Lord is teaching him about ritual impurity. The much greater test for him, however, will be to enter the home of a Gentile (see 10:25).

Brothers from Joppa went along (10:23). Six fellow Jewish believers from Joppa accompany Peter (see 11:12). This is significant because they will witness the Gentiles receiving the Holy Spirit and will be able to corroborate Peter's story to Jewish believers in Jerusalem.

CAESAREA

(left) Site of the ancient harbor.

(right) The Roman aqueduct.

▼

As Peter entered the house (10:25). In Jewish tradition, entering the home of a Gentile would render one ritually unclean. The Mishnah makes this clear: "The dwelling-places of Gentiles are unclean."[190] The fact that Peter enters the home of this Roman soldier is a big step for Peter and normally would have been an unusual surprise for these Gentiles. Yet God has prepared both Peter and Cornelius for this encounter.

Cornelius met him and fell at his feet in reverence (10:25). In Near Eastern cultures, prostrating oneself before a king or superior is a sign of great respect. The word *proskyneō* is often used "to designate the custom of prostrating oneself before a person and kissing his feet, the hem of his garment, the ground, etc."[191] But because Peter responds by saying, "Stand up, I am only a man," Cornelius probably looks on Peter as a divine messenger, an angel. The apostle John also responds to an angel in this fashion (Rev. 19:10; 22:8–9).

It is against our law for a Jew to associate with a Gentile or visit him (10:28). After being careful all of their lives not to associate with Gentiles in a way that would render them ritually impure, Peter and his six Jewish companions must face a deep inner turmoil. On the one hand, their consciences are sorely troubled by entering into this house and possibly defiling themselves, yet on the other hand, they have a strong awareness that God himself is directing them to do so.

Jews typically did not enter a Gentile home (even that of a God-fearer) because they did not practice the same level of caution as observant Jews did to ensure that only kosher foods were eaten and that they were prepared in the proper way. There was also always the risk that the home may have had a household idol or other trappings of pagan idolatry. The best way for a Jew to be protected was never to enter a Gentile home.[192]

God has shown me that I should not call any man impure or unclean (10:28). The vision demonstrates to Peter that the Torah distinction between clean and unclean animals no longer applies. He can now kill and eat an animal that has previously been regarded as ritually impure. As he has reflected on his vision over the past four days, he has recognized that one of the implications of this new divine decree is that *people* who are previously thought of as ritually defiled because they do not observe Jewish food laws are no longer to be regarded as impure. There is an entirely new situation for Gentiles (and for Jewish attitudes toward Gentiles) made possible by the coming of the Messiah.

Then Peter began to speak (10:34). Verses 34–43 consist of a summary of the message that Peter gives to Cornelius and all those who gathered at his home. In a real sense, the message is the summary of the heart of the preaching of the apostles (what has often been referred to as the *kerygma* ["the proclamation" of the apostles]). It also serves as a general outline to the contents of the four Gospels.

God does not show favoritism (10:34). According to Peter, God has never shown partiality toward one group of people over another. This is not a new idea in Judaism; it has always been in the Torah: "For the LORD your God is God of gods and Lord of lords, the great God, mighty and awesome, who shows no partiality and accepts no bribes" (Deut. 10:17; see also 2 Chron. 19:7). This was a truth that many Jews had lost sight of, including Peter. "Exclusivism as practiced by many first-century Judean Jews was a development of the intertestamental period that had gone beyond the intent of God."[193]

Accepts men from every nation who fear him and do what is right (10:35). The term "accepts" (*dekton*, more properly translated "acceptable") is used frequently in the context of the presentation of sacrifices in the worship of Israel. It was incumbent on worshipers to bring sacrifices that were "acceptable" to the Lord (see Lev. 1:3–4; 19:5). Practicing righteousness in a Jewish context was understood as observing the law, not simply in the sense of being a good person. This passage is clearly not teaching that fearing God and observing the law merits salvation, otherwise Peter's following sermon about the the work of Jesus and receiving forgiveness of sins through his name would be unnecessary. What Peter is expressing is that fearing God and seeking to follow his ways puts a person in an "acceptable state (of repentance) to hear and receive the message of salvation and release from sins."[194] Cornelius still needs salvation.[195]

You know the message God sent (10:36). Cornelius and his guests certainly have heard about Jesus and know something about what he has taught. How fascinating it would be to know what level of contact they may have had with Jesus and what kinds of reports they heard about him.

The good news of peace through Jesus Christ (10:36). The gospel is a message of peace with God, made possible not by achieving ritual purity through observing the law, but by the work of Jesus, the Messiah. This is a fulfillment of Isaiah 57:19, where a day is envisioned when it is declared, "Peace, peace, to those far and near." Peter alluded to this passage in his preaching on the day of Pentecost (see comments on Acts 2:39).

The Old Testament prophets envisioned "peace" (*šālôm*) in the messianic age. Peter's preaching here makes an allusion to the promise of Isaiah 52:7: "How beautiful on the mountains are the feet of those who bring good news, who proclaim peace, who bring good tidings, who proclaim salvation, who say to Zion, 'Your God reigns.'"

The Old Testament notion of peace goes well beyond a cessation of strife and war. It refers to a holistic sense of well-being and fulfillment. This depends on being in a close relationship with God, experiencing his gracious presence, finding strength and encouragement in him, and being free from his judgment and condemnation.[196]

You know what has happened throughout Judea (10:37). A more literal translation would be, "You know the word (or saying) about what has happened throughout Judea." The term *rhēma* ("word") is used here in a similar way to *logos* (which appears in 10:36) to refer to the account of the ministry, death, burial, and resurrection of Jesus. This is a common usage for *rhēma*, which cannot always be pressed to mean a spoken word.

God anointed Jesus of Nazareth (10:38). Peter's words here echo and fulfill Isaiah 61:1–2: "The Spirit of the Sovereign LORD is on me, because the LORD has anointed me to preach good news to the poor. He has sent me to bind up the brokenhearted, to proclaim freedom for the captives and release from darkness for the prisoners." Jesus read these words at the outset of his ministry when he spoke in the synagogue at Nazareth (Luke 4:17–21). The "anointing" occurred when the Spirit came on Jesus at his baptism by John and empowered him to carry out his work as God's deliverer.

Healing all who were under the power of the devil (10:38). The "freedom for the captives" and "release from darkness for the prisoners" referred to in the prophecy of Isaiah 61:1 finds its fulfillment in the exorcisms of Jesus and in his death and resurrection. Both Jews and Gentiles alike have fallen under the sway of the evil one. Not all are demonized and in need of exorcism, but many have been blinded to the revelation of God through the deceiving work of the devil.

Because God was with him (10:38). The source of Jesus' power is not the devil or Beelzebub (as the Pharisees accuse him), nor is he claiming to be a shaman endowed with magical powers. The one true God is at work in and through Jesus of Nazareth.

We are witnesses of everything he did (10:39). This is the unique testimony that Peter (and the other eleven apostles) can provide. For three years they had watched Jesus, heard him speak on repeated occasions, received personal training and instruction from him, and saw him after he rose from the dead. This is why the teaching of the twelve apostles (see 2:42) is so important to the early church.

The country of the Jews (10:39). This refers to the areas of Galilee and Judea.

By hanging him on a tree (10:39). See comments on 5:30.

By us who ate and drank with him after he rose from the dead (10:41). The fact that Jesus took food "proves the physical reality of the body of the risen Jesus."[197] Luke describes this in much more detail at the end of his Gospel (see Luke 24:36–43). Jesus did not appear to the disciples as a bodiless spirit-being (as later Docetism and Gnosticism would teach).

God appointed as judge of the living and the dead (10:42). Jesus is not only the redeemer, but he is also the end-time judge (see also 17:31). Such is the right accorded to the "son of man" figure in

CAESAREA

(left) The south end of the hippodrome.

(right) The theater.
▼

Daniel's prophecy: "He was given authority, glory and sovereign power; all peoples, nations and men of every language worshiped him" (Dan. 7:14).

The Holy Spirit came on all who heard the message (10:44). The Spirit comes on all of these Gentiles with visible and unmistakable signs (the speaking in tongues). In this instance, Peter does not lay his hands on them and ask God to impart the Spirit (as he and John had done for the Samaritans; see comments on 8:15). The Spirit comes spontaneously on them, presumably in response to their faith in the message about Jesus that Peter has just explained to them. Many scholars aptly refer to this event as "the Pentecost of the Gentiles."

The circumcised believers who had come with Peter were astonished (10:45). The Torah-observant Jews recognize the remarkable significance of this event. God is now accepting Gentiles on the same basis that he did the Jews—on the sole basis of believing in Jesus Christ for the forgiveness of sins. These Gentile believers will not be required to be circumcised, offer sacrifices, observe the Jewish festivals, or keep Jewish dietary laws as a means of entering or maintaining their position in the new people of God.

R E F L E C T I O N S

SINCE GOD MAKES NO ETHNIC, CULTURAL, OR SOCIAL distinctions in his new community, we do not have the right to make them either. Unfortunately, the church has had a very difficult time learning this lesson. The church often returns to the boundary-making discrimination that characterized much of Judaism in Jesus' time. Since God shows no favoritism, work hard at breaking down the walls that may exist in your own heart toward others who are different.

Peter Reports to Jerusalem (11:1–18)

When Peter returns to Jerusalem, he is confronted by law-observant Jewish Christians concerned about his involvement with the Gentiles. Peter recounts to them and the Jerusalem church leaders all that happened, emphasizing God's clear direction.

The apostles and the brothers throughout Judea (11:1). Apparently the intensity of the persecution has subsided and some of the Jewish Christians have returned to live and minister in Jerusalem.

The circumcised believers (11:2). On the surface, it seems that this expression refers to all Jewish Christians living in Jerusalem since all male Jews are circumcised on the eighth day after their birth (this is the sense in 10:45). Yet here it appears to imply more. It refers to those Jewish believers in the Jerusalem church who are zealous for the law and want to uphold its requirements for all who believe. This includes the laws regulating purity and uncleanness as well as an insistence on circumcision. The apostle Paul later comes into conflict with this group during his ministry in Antioch of Syria. He describes how Peter succumbs to the influence of "the circumcision group" after some of their members arrive in that city. Paul becomes incensed when Peter begins refusing to eat with the Gentile believers (see Gal. 2:12). At this earlier stage, Peter is less conflicted about eating with Cornelius and his household and never hints that any of them should be circumcised. This may be due in part to Cornelius's sensitivity to have kosher meals prepared for his guests (since he is a God-fearer), but more importantly, it is probably due to the freshness of the vision God gives to Peter, which he now relates to the Jerusalem believers.

Ate with them (11:3). The complaint of these law-conscientious Jews focuses on Peter's entry into a Gentile house and eating with them, something not explicitly said in 10:48 but certainly implied. They cannot understand how Peter, a prominent leader of the church, could so flagrantly violate the law. Of course, they have not been given the vision Peter received nor have they been in Caesarea to witness the Gentiles' experience of the Spirit coming on them after they put their faith in Christ.

Peter began and explained everything to them (11:4). In verses 4–17, Luke summarizes the entire Cornelius episode that he has narrated in Acts 10. Repetition is a technique used by ancient writers to emphasize the importance of key events (see comments on Acts 10).

All your household will be saved (11:14). The Roman *familia* often consist of three generations living together. Cornelius may have had his parents and possibly even grandparents living with him in addition to his own children. The slaves are also considered an integral part of the household.[198]

You will be baptized with the Holy Spirit (11:16). John the Baptist proclaimed that Jesus would baptize his followers with the Holy Spirit (Luke 3:16), and Jesus himself reiterated this shortly before he ascended to heaven (Acts 1:5). This was fulfilled on the day of Pentecost for the Jewish believers. The episode of the Spirit's coming on the household of Cornelius—"as he had come on us at the beginning" (11:15)—stresses that Jews and Gentiles now have equal access to the new covenant blessing of the Spirit solely on the basis of faith in Jesus Christ.

They had no further objections (11:18). After Peter carefully explains to them all that has happened and how God himself superintended these events, the rest of the apostles and possibly many from the circumcision group are satisfied. This only lasts for a time. A few years later, the circumcision group asserts the indispensibility of circumcision for salvation (see 15:1).

God has granted even the Gentiles repentance unto life (11:18). The Jerusalem leaders recognize that the events surrounding Cornelius are not an isolated exception. This event has wide-ranging implications that extend to the Gentiles as a class of people.

The Establishment of the Church in Antioch (11:19–30)

Luke now tells the story of the first major turning of Gentiles to the Christian faith. This takes place in Antioch, the capital city of the Roman province of Syria.

NIGHT IN MODERN JERUSALEM

Those who had been scattered by the persecution (11:19). Luke told us earlier about this persecution (8:1, 4), which apparently led to thousands of Christians leaving Jerusalem. Some apparently traveled much further than Judea and Samaria.

Traveled as far as Phoenicia (11:19). Phoenicia was a stretch of land along the Mediterranean coast west of Damascus and belonging to the Roman province of Syria. Much of ancient Phoenicia today lies within the borders of Lebanon. The principal cities of Phoenicia were Acco, Aradus, Berytus, Byblos, Dora, Heliopolis, Ptolemais, Tyre, and Sidon. There is inscriptional evidence of Jewish settlements in a number of the Phoenician cities.[199] In a letter King Agrippa I wrote to the emperor Claudius, he referred to the presence of Jewish colonies in the land of Phoenicia and on the island of Crete.[200] The southern portion of Phoenica lay seventy-five miles northwest of Jerusalem. The northern region of Phoenicia was about a hundred miles south of Antioch, Syria.

Cyprus (11:19). See comments on 13:4.

Men from Cyprus and Cyrene (11:20). Among the Jewish Christians in Jerusalem who were scattered by the persecution are some who originally came from the island of Cyprus and northern Africa. Roman Cyrenaica was due south of Greece across the Mediterranean Sea on the African continent. Luke is probably referring here to the Roman province of Cyrenaica rather than the city of Cyrene.

Began to speak to Greeks (11:20). These Greek-speaking Jewish Christians from the Diaspora make their way to the city of Antioch and take a bold step. Based on the

PHOENICIA
▼

▶ Antioch on the Orontes

Nearly three hundred miles north of Jerusalem in the province of Syria was a city—Antioch on the Orontes—that became a major center for Christianity as it spread to the Gentile world.[A-48] Antioch was the third largest city in the Roman empire with a population between a quarter and a half-million people.[A-49] The city also had a sizeable Jewish population, estimated between thirty and fifty thousand.[A-50]

The city lay in a fertile plain near the foot of Mount Silpius with the Orontes river flowing through it and continuing on a distance of fifteen miles to the sea. Antioch was a major junction for roads coming from the east (Aleppo), the south (the Lebanon, Damascus, and Palestine), and the north (Tarsus and the whole of Anatolia). At the mouth of the river, it was served by its port city, Seleucia Pieria.

About five miles south of the city at the natural springs supplying water to the city was a famous park called Daphne where there was a sanctuary dedicated to the god Apollo. A variety of ecstatic rites were held there in the name of this deity.

There was a period of significant hostility against the Jews in the summer of A.D. 38. Many Jews were killed and their synagogues were burned. In response, the Jewish high priest in Jerusalem (Phineas) retaliated by sending thirty thousand men to Antioch attacking and killing many Gentiles in the city. The trouble only ended once the emperor intervened.[A-51]

Antioch had a bad reputation for its morality. A passage in Juvenal bemoans the influence Antioch had on Rome: "The waters of Syrian Orontes flowed into the Tiber." Yet it was through this city that God worked to spread the good news of salvation throughout the empire.

precedent set by Peter, which they have undoubtedly heard about, they begin to proclaim the gospel directly to the non-Jewish Greek-speakers of Antioch.

Luke does not tell us if these Gentiles are predominantly God-fearers linked to the synagogues of the sizeable Jewish population in Antioch or if they are Gentiles with virtually no exposure to Judaism and still adherents of the local religions. If they preach primarily to Gentile God-fearers, it is only a matter of time until more Gentiles—friends, family members, and neighbors of the initial wave—respond to the gospel. Most of these people turn to Christ from adherence to Apollo, Artemis, Zeus, Tyche, or the Syrian cults of Baal and the mother goddess—some of the popular deities of the city. We can safely assume that a good number of the Jews in the city also turn to Christ during this period.

The Lord's hand was with them (11:21). "The hand of the Lord" is a common Old Testament metaphor for the manifestation of God's presence and power. The "hand of the LORD" was on Elijah (1 Kings 18:46) and Elisha (2 Kings 3:15), enabling them to do amazing feats. Ezra experienced the power and blessing of "the hand of the LORD" on his life. Luke says that "the hand of the Lord" was with John the Baptist (Luke 1:66). Clearly to Luke the outreach efforts of these Hellenistic Jewish Christians cannot be explained in any way other than God's being with them and blessing their efforts.

They sent Barnabas to Antioch (11:22). When news of the conversion of these Gentiles reaches Jerusalem, they send Barnabas both to investigate what they are hearing and to facilitate the work there. Luke does not tell us why Peter does not travel to Antioch. The apostles

have a great amount of confidence in Barnabas. Like some of the Jewish-Christian evangelists that go to Antioch, Barnabas is also originally from Cyprus (see comments on 4:36). The fact that the apostles send Barnabas indicates that, at least to some degree, they feel a responsibility to exercise a level of leadership for the movement, especially to ensure the ongoing unity of the church. Upon arriving, Barnabas finds ample evidence that God has been powerfully at work

REFLECTIONS

CHURCH LEADERS OFTEN SPEND a great deal of time and effort searching for new strategies for doing effective outreach in their communities. Books, conferences, and seminars present a variety of models for reaching a neighborhood with the gospel. Luke reminds us here that it is not so much the strategy that is most important, but the work of God. In doing outreach, our greatest concern should be, "Is the hand of the Lord with us?"

bringing these Gentiles to himself. There is no hint that Barnabas criticizes any facet of the work there. Rather, he rejoices and joins with the brothers in proclaiming the gospel and teaching the new Gentile believers.

Barnabas went to Tarsus to look for Saul (11:25). As numerous people begin turning to Christ and as Barnabas sees the potential for continued effective outreach, his thoughts turn to Saul. Here is a man who was trained as a rabbi and extremely competent in the Scripture, who was able to argue effectively and proclaim the gospel in Greek, and most importantly, who had received a commission from the Lord to reach the Gentiles. Barnabas was one of the first Jerusalem disciples to believe in the authenticity of Saul's conversion and confidently introduced him to the apostles (9:27). Because of the danger to his life in Jerusalem, Saul's fellow believers helped him leave the city safely so he could go to Tarsus in Cilicia. There he remained proclaiming Christ in his home region.

With Tarsus being over a hundred miles away, Barnabas's trip takes many days. The difficulty is compounded by the fact that he does not know precisely where Saul is. The word translated "to look for" (*anazēteō*) implies the search entails some difficulty. It is often used in the context of hunting for criminals or fugitive slaves.[201] But Barnabas successfully locates Saul and is able to convince him to join him in the work at Antioch.

For a whole year Barnabas and Saul met with the church (11:26). This may mean that Barnabas and Saul work together for a year in the church before they travel to Jerusalem on their famine relief visit (c. A.D. 44–45). It is more likely, however, that Barnabas had Saul come to Antioch much earlier (c. A.D. 39). In this case, they spend a year working intensively with believers in Antioch and then Paul or both of them journey to other cities in Syria where they proclaim the gospel and plant churches,

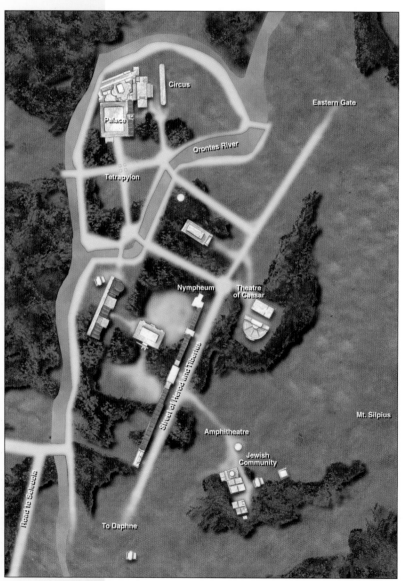

Circus

Eastern Gate

Palace

Orontes River

Tetrapylon

Nympheum

Theatre of Caesar

Mt. Silpius

Street of Herod and Tiberius

Amphitheatre

Jewish Community

Road to Seleucia

To Daphne

while maintaining their involvement with Antioch. They most likely reach the principal Syrian cities of Seleucia Pieria, Apameia, and Laodicea as well as other towns and villages in the province.[202]

The disciples were called Christians first at Antioch (11:26). Disciples, believers, servants of Christ, those who are "in Christ," saints, and followers of "the Way" are some of the ways Christians refer to themselves in this early period. It appears that the term "Christians" (*christianoi*) was created by non-Christians in Antioch as a way of distinguishing them from Jews (and possibly other religious groups). In the only other places in the New Testament where the term is used, it is used by non-Christians referring to the followers of Jesus (26:28; 1 Peter 4:16). The name itself is formed on the analogy of "Herodians" (*herodiani*—the adherents and clients of the house of Herod; see Matt. 22:16) and *caesariani* (the servants of Caesar). For these new believers in Antioch, however, the new designation reveals their allegiance to the Messiah (*christos*), Jesus of Nazareth. The very fact that the local population coins a name for this new movement attests to its growth in the city. The new name for believers apparently becomes a popular self-designation only in the period after the New Testament attests, interestingly, by Ignatius, a famous church leader from Antioch.

Prophets came down from Jerusalem to Antioch (11:27). The gift of prophecy was commonly practiced in the early church. Luke specifically names Agabus (11:28; 21:10), Judas and Silas (15:32), the four daughters of Philip (21:8–9),

---

▶ **The City of Antioch**
IMPORTANT FACTS:

- Population: about 300,000 (the third largest city in the Roman empire)
- Religions: Apollo, Artemis, Isis, Zeus, Tyche, the Syrian cults of Baal, the mother goddess, Judaism, the emperor cult (in addition to many other gods and goddesses)
- Commercial Importance: agriculture (esp. grain, olives, and grapes), trade between East and West
- Political Importance: a free city, but under Roman rule, capital of the Roman province of Syria
- Cultural Importance: became the center for the spread of Christianity to non-Jews

---

▶ **How Long Was Saul in Tarsus and Then in Antioch?**

An accurate chronology of Saul's first seventeen years as a believer (c. A.D. 33–49) is difficult to construct. He does not write any letters during this period and only makes a handful of references to this time in his later letters (especially in Gal. 1–2). Luke gives only a few details that can help. Fortunately, we are on much firmer ground for putting together an accurate chronology for the period following the Jerusalem council until his imprisonment in Rome (A.D. 49–62).

Estimates for how long Saul was in Tarsus range from three years (A.D. 36–39) to ten years (A.D. 37–47). Similarly, estimates for how long he ministered in Antioch and in Syria range from ten years (A.D. 39–49) to one to two years (A.D. 47–49).[A-52]

If the mission of the Hellenistic Jewish Christians to Antioch began early (c. A.D. 36 or 37) and Barnabas went there a short time later, it is more convincing to think of Barnabas looking for Paul's help within a year after his arrival.

▶ The Anti-Jewish Upheaval in A.D. 38–41

During the infant years of the church at Antioch (which began in A.D. 36 or 37), a horrible tempest of hostility toward Jews raged in Alexandria and spilled over into Palestine and Syria. In the autumn of A.D. 38, mobs of citizens in Alexandria, Egypt, took part in a bloody rampage against the Jewish inhabitants of that city. Many Jews were tortured and killed, synagogues, homes, and businesses were destroyed, and numerous other atrocities were perpetrated against the Jews. Much of the crisis was sparked by the emperor Gaius Caligula's insistence that he be worshiped as a god.[A-53]

The conflict spread to Judea in late A.D. 39 when Caligula arrogantly ordered the Syrian governor P. Petronius to set up his image in the Jerusalem temple. The Jews were horrified and threatened all-out war against the Roman forces if the abominable act was carried out. Fortunately, Petronius defied Caligula's orders and, before the emperor could respond, the emperor was assassinated.[A-54]

In Antioch at roughly the same time (A.D. 39–40), Gentile hostility toward Jews boiled over into violence. Many Jews were killed and their synagogues burned down. According to the *Chronicle* of Malalas, when news of this reached Jerusalem, the high priest Phineas dispatched an army of thirty thousand Jews who traveled to Antioch and attacked and killed many Gentiles in the city. The emperor then intervened and had Phineas beheaded.[A-55]

Nevertheless, in spite of this uproar, the church at Antioch—consisting of Jews and Gentiles in one unified community—continued to grow significantly. It was during this period that the apostle Paul came and began to serve the church with Barnabas.

and leaders of the church at Antioch (13:1). Paul speaks extensively about prophecy in 1 Corinthians 14 and teaches that prophets, together with the apostles, have laid the foundation of the early church (Eph. 2:20). Two early Christian writings have much to say about how to discern a false prophet.[203] Among the criteria mentioned are: Does he exibit the Lord's ways? Does he ask for money? Is his life inconsistent with his prophecies? Is he gentle, quiet, and humble? Does he refrain from evil? Hermas warns that the false prophet is actually inspired by a spirit from the devil.[204]

Agabus (11:28). Luke singles out one of the prophets and mentions him by name, possibly because of his accurate predictions. He not only prophesies the impending famine, but thirteen years later in Caesarea prophesies Paul's arrest in Jerusalem (21:10–11). Because he appears in one of the "we" sections of Acts, Luke meets him personally. We know nothing else about this important figure in the early church.

Through the Spirit predicted (11:28). Luke clearly sees that one important aspect of prophecy is prediction. Receiving inspiration from the Holy Spirit of God, the prophet simply declares what he hears. The New Testament prophet did not need to descend into an oracle chamber, invoke the deity with any kind of formula or incantation, go into an ecstatic

trance, observe a period of taboos, or go through any preparatory ritual.

A severe famine would spread over the entire Roman world (11:28). There is abundant ancient evidence attesting food shortages and greatly inflated food prices during the reign of Claudius (see below).[205] The word translated "famine" in this verse (*limos*) can also mean "death" or "severe shortage."[206] Obviously Antioch is not affected as badly as Jerusalem and Judea, otherwise they would not have been able to provide substantial help.

Rome began to experience a scarcity of food in the winter of A.D. 40–41, the beginning of Claudius's reign. This general disruption in the food supply is attributed to declines in the production of grain in Egypt, the principal grain supplier for Rome and much of the Mediterranean region. Crop failures in Egypt grew particularly severe in the period of A.D. 45–47.[207] One writer indicates that the crisis was felt in all of Syria in A.D. 44.[208]

But Jerusalem and Judea were the hardest hit of all during this time. This was exacerbated by still other factors. When the emperor Gaius Caligula ordered

his statue to be erected in the Jerusalem temple in late A.D. 39, the Jews refused to plant their crops.[209] Indeed, they were ready to die rather than allow their temple to be profaned. The next year was a sabbatical year, which kept their ground out of production and intensified the food shortage. Just three years later, in A.D. 44–45, Judea strongly felt the adverse effects of the more general food shortage and the resultant exorbitant prices for grain that was in short supply and in high demand.

Of course the Jewish Christians in Jerusalem, ostracized from the temple and any official relief efforts tied to the temple, were especially vulnerable. Now more than ever they needed to depend on the generosity and true fellowship of the larger Christian community.

This happened during the reign of Claudius (11:28). Claudius reigned from January 15, A.D. 41 to October 13, A.D. 54, assuming power at the age of fifty immediately after the assassination of Caligula. His full name is Tiberius Claudius Nero Germanicus. Suetonius says of Claudius that, "nearly the whole of his childhood and youth was so troubled by various diseases that he grew dull-witted and had little physical strength; and on reaching the age at which he should have won a magistracy or chosen a private career, was considered by his family incapable of doing either."[210] He was made emperor by the Roman army against his will in a comical series of events. He ruled

BUST OF THE
EMPEROR
CLAUDIUS

Roman Emperors	
Emperor	**Date of Reign**
Octavian "Augustus"	31 B.C.–A.D. 14
Tiberius	14–37
Gaius "Caligula"	37–41
Claudius	41–54
Nero	54–68

▶ Ancient Testimony About the Great Famine

Among the ancient accounts of food shortages during the reign of Claudius, two are rather striking. The first, by the Roman historian Suetonius, illustrates the severity of the food shortage in Rome: "Once, after a series of droughts had caused a scarcity of grain, a mob stopped Claudius in the Forum and pelted him so hard with curses and stale crusts that he had difficulty in regaining the Palace by a side-door; as a result he took all possible steps to import grain, even during the winter months—insuring merchants against the loss of their ships in stormy weather."[A-56]

In the second account, the Jewish historian Josephus tells of how Queen Helena of Adiabene (a small kingdom in north Mesopotamia) came to the aid of Jews in Jerusalem in A.D. 44. Helena and her son, King Izates, had just converted to Judaism. This passage shows that some food was available for those who had the money to purchase it: "Now her coming was of very great advantage to the people of Jerusalem; for whereas a famine did oppress them at that time, and many people died for want of what was necessary to procure food withal, Queen Helena sent some of her servants to Alexandria with money to buy a great quantity of corn, and others of them to Cyprus, to bring a cargo of dried figs; and as soon as they were come back, and brought those provisions, which was done very quickly, she distributed food to those that were in want of it, and left a most excellent memorial behind her of this benefaction, which she bestowed on our whole nation; and when her son Izates was informed of this famine, he sent great sums of money to the principal men in Jerusalem."[A-57]

for many years, however, and was the emperor responsible for the expulsion of Jews from Rome in A.D. 49.

Each according to his ability, decided to provide help (11:29). The way the community responded to the need is similar to the way Paul encouraged the church in Corinth to give for a subsequent collection.[211]

To the elders (11:30). One might expect the funds from Antioch to be taken to Jerusalem and laid at the feet of the apostles (4:35, 37; 5:2). In the decade that has elapsed since the beginning of the Jerusalem church, a leadership structure emerges that worked in conjunction with the unique authority of the twelve apos-

tles. Following the pattern of the local synagogues, the early Christians identified leaders for their household groups and retained the name "elders" (*presbyteroi*). They probably retained many facets of the role and function of elders in the synagogue structure. Luke does not tell us how the elders related to the apostles or the seven, nor does he indicate whether there was a higher group of elders serving as leaders of the entire collection of churches in Jerusalem and Judea. This latter idea could follow from the fact that there were elders over the Jewish people in the Holy Land (see 4:5, 8, 23). By this time, many of the apostles may have already left Jerusalem to proclaim Jesus as the Messiah in distant cities.

Chronology of the Early Years of Saul of Tarsus		
Year	**Event**	**Location of Saul**
33	• conversion of Saul	
34	• Saul in Damascus and Arabia (36–39?)	Saul in Damascus and Arabia
35	• conversion of Cornelius (?)	
36	• Saul visits Peter in Jerusalem	
	• Jewish-Christian mission to Antioch	Saul in Tarsus and Cilicia
37		
38	• Barnabas goes to Antioch	
39	• Barnabas gets Saul	Saul in Antioch and Syria
40		
41		
42		
43	• Death of James, the apostle	
44	• Death of Agrippa I	
45		
46	• Jerusalem collection visit	
47	• 1st Missionary Journey	1st Missionary Journey
48		
49	• Council at Jerusalem	

Sending their gift . . . by Barnabas and Saul (11:30). This is the second time Saul travels to Jerusalem after his conversion. The previous time was three years after his conversion for the purpose of becoming acquainted with Peter (see comments on Acts 9:26 and Gal. 1:18). Now, between eight and ten years later, he goes again as an emissary of the church at Antioch to bring relief.

There is much discussion among Bible scholars as to whether this is the visit that Saul/Paul refers to in Galatians 2:1–10 or whether the Galatian passage describes his next visit for the Jerusalem council. The weightier arguments are in favor of identifying this famine-relief visit with the details Paul describes in Galatians 2:1–10,

not least because the results of the council decision are not communicated in Galatians. This reconstruction also fits better with the overall sequence of events Paul describes in Galatians 1–2.[212]

If this is the case, Paul uses this same time to "set before [the authorities in Jerusalem] the gospel that I preach among the Gentiles" (Gal. 2:2). Apparently some dissension has already surfaced with a handful of law-observant Jewish Christians who have gone to Antioch to investigate how faithful Paul and the Antioch believers are to the law, presumably circumcision, purity regulations, and observance of Jewish festivals and rites (Gal. 2:4). Paul raises this issue with the leadership of the Jerusalem church in an informal way, and they reaffirm Paul and Barnabas in their work among the Gentiles (Gal. 2:9).

Herod Agrippa I Persecutes the Church (12:1–25)

This chapter dramatically portrays the power of God working to ensure the success of the church and its mission despite violent opposition. God directly intervenes by sending an angel to free the apostle Peter from his imprisonment and stems the persecution by striking down the king of the land. Herod the Great murdered the innocent children of Bethlehem to oppose God's work; now his descendant embarks on a murderous tirade against the leaders of the church.

King Herod (12:1). This is not Herod the Great who ruled Israel at the time of the birth of Jesus. This is his grandson, Herod Agrippa I.[213] Agrippa's father is Aristobulus, son of Mariamne, the favorite of Herod the Great's many wives. Born in 10 B.C., Agrippa's father was killed when Agrippa was three years

The House of Herod	
Herod the Great	• ruled Palestine from 37 B.C.–4 B.C.
Herod Archelaus	• son of Herod the Great and Malthace • ruled Judea from 4 B.C.–A.D. 6; following his oppressive reign, Roman governors ruled Judea
Herod Antipas	• son of Herod the Great and Malthace • ruled Galilee and Perea as a "tetrarch" from 4 B.C.–A.D. 39
Herod Philip	• son of Herod the Great and Cleopatra of Jerusalem; half-brother of Antipas • ruled the northern portion of Herod the Great's domain (Gaulanitis, Auranitis, Batanea, Trachonitis, Paneas, and Iturea) from 4 B.C.–A.D. 34
Herod Agrippa I	• grandson of Herod the Great • grew up in Rome with future emperor Claudius • ruled Palestine from A.D. 41–44
Agrippa II	• son of Agrippa I and Cypros • ruled Palestine from A.D. 50 through the Jewish War (A.D. 66–70) • because he sided with the Romans during the war, the emperor Vespasian bestowed on him rulership over all his previous realm (A.D. 75–100) • his death ended the Herodian family

old because of the irrational suspicions of Herod the Great. Agrippa was raised in Rome where he grew up with Claudius, the future emperor, and Drusus, son of the emperor Tiberius. His imperial connections served him well later in life. Because of lavish spending, he returned to Palestine as a poor man and held no significant position of power until Gaius Caligula became emperor in A.D. 37. Because Agrippa earlier endeared himself to Caligula, the new emperor gave him the title "king" and put him in charge of territory in northern Palestine. After the death of Herod Antipas in A.D. 39, Caligula added Galilee and Perea to his domain. When his childhood friend Claudius became emperor in A.D. 41, Agrippa's kingdom was extended to include Judea and Samaria. He ruled as a client king over Israel for a little over three years (A.D. 41–44).

The Pharisees appreciated Agrippa both because he was a descendant of the Hasmoneans (through his mother) and because he scrupulously kept Jewish customs. Josephus says, "He loved to live continually at Jerusalem, and was exactly careful in the observance of the laws of his country. He therefore kept himself entirely pure: nor did any day pass over his head without its appointed sacrifice."[214]

Arrested some who belonged to the church, intending to persecute them (12:1). What motivates Agrippa to take

violent action against the church is not clear. Verse 3 may indicate that he is sensitive to the denunciation of the messianic sect by his fellow Jews and seeks to please them by his actions. The most effective way of dealing with this new group is through robbing it of its leaders.

He had James, the brother of John, put to death with the sword (12:2). This is James, the son of Zebedee, one of the twelve apostles. He is the first of the Twelve to die for the cause of Christ. This is the last time John is mentioned in the book of Acts. According to church tradition, the apostle John at some point moved to the capital city of Asia Minor, Ephesus, where he served the church for many years and from where he wrote his three letters and his Gospel.[215] "With the sword" probably indicates that James is beheaded. This was the tradition in church history.[216] It was a common Roman form of execution.[217] It also illustrates the extent of authority Agrippa had been granted by Rome, that is, to use "the law of the sword" (*ius gladii*).[218] It is important to recall that Jesus told James and John that they would share his "cup" and share his "baptism" (referring to his martyr's death) when they quarreled over

Four "James" in the Early Church	
James, the father of Judas	• his son, Judas, was one of the twelve apostles (Luke 6:16; Acts 1:13)
James, the son of Alphaeus	• one of the twelve apostles (Luke 6:15; Acts 1:13)
James, the brother of John	• the son of Zebedee (Luke 5:10; 9:28, 54) • one of the twelve apostles (Acts 1:13) • killed by Herod Agrippa (Acts 12:2)
James, the brother of the Lord	• half-brother of the Lord Jesus; son of Mary and Joseph (Acts 12:17; 15:13; 21:18; 1 Cor. 15:7; Gal. 1:19; 2:9, 12; James 1:1; Jude 1)

who would sit at Jesus' right hand and his left (Mark 10:39). Jesus' words are now fulfilled for James.

This pleased the Jews (12:3). The Sanhedrin, the elders of the people, and many Jews living in Jerusalem and Judea continue in their hostile attitudes toward the followers of Jesus. This encourages Agrippa to follow through with his violent intentions toward the church.

The Feast of Unleavened Bread (12:3). This is one of the great pilgrim festivals of Judaism that swelled the population of Jerusalem from a hundred thousand upward to a million people.[219] The Feast of Unleavened Bread occurred in conjunction with the celebration of Passover. Commemorating the Exodus from Egypt and the miraculous deliverance of the first-born Israelite children, Passover was celebrated every spring beginning on the thirteenth day of Nisan with the slaughter of the lamb and the taking of the Passover meal (on the evening of the fourteenth day). The Feast of Unleavened Bread began on the next day and was celebrated for seven consecutive days (see Ex. 12–13). During this period, leaven (or yeast) was avoided altogether as a reminder of the haste with which God's people fled Egypt.

Four squads of four soldiers each (12:4). Luke relates the high level of security placed on Peter. This is not suprising since stories of the arrest and previous escape of the apostles are probably known to Agrippa (see comments on 5:17–42). These are most likely Roman soldiers and not the temple guard. It was common Roman procedure to have four squads of soldiers keep watch in succession throughout the night. One Roman writer explains, "And because it used to seem impossible for sentries to maintain successful watches, the watches therefore were divided into four parts by the waterclock, so that it not be necessary to

stand watch for more than three night-time hours."[220]

Herod intended to bring him out for public trial after the Passover (12:4). The text literally says, "To bring him up to the people after the Passover." There has been some debate as to whether this implies a trial or simply a public execution. Regardless of whether Agrippa plans some half-hearted attempt at a public hearing or not, the intent is clear based on how he handles James: Peter's life will end immediately after Passover. Significantly, it is Passover some ten years previously that Jesus faced a farce of a trial and his death (see Luke 22:1–2).

Peter was kept in prison (12:5). Although Luke does not explicitly state what prison, most scholars think it was probably in the Fortress of Antonia.

The church was earnestly praying to God for him (12:5). News of the imprisonment of Christians, the death of James, and now the impending execution of Peter grips believers throughout Jerusalem and Judea. They respond by meeting in homes and praying fervently and passionately for one of their beloved leaders.

Between two soldiers, bound with two chains (12:6). There is variation in the manner of chaining prisoners, but at night, as Lucian reports, the prisoner "had to be fully secured by his bonds."[221] On the last night prior to his execution, God intervenes in a dramatic and unmistakable way: An angel enters the prison and releases Peter.

He struck Peter on the side (12:7). Deep in sleep, Peter is not roused by the illumination of the cell caused by the presence of the angel of the Lord. The angel does more than nudge Peter to wake him; the word for "struck" (*patassō*) suggests a strong blow. The word is often used in contexts where one is struck in a fight, such as when Moses struck down the Egyptian (Ex. 2:12).

The iron gate leading to the city (12:10). One exit of the Antonia Fortress led to the temple; the other led into the city. An addition in the manuscript tradition inserts, "They went down seven steps" (Codex D). Most scholars agree that this likely reflects an authentic historical reminiscence, but since the Antonia Fortress was totally destroyed in the Jewish war, it is difficult to verify this information.

From everything the Jewish people were anticipating (12:11). Shortly after Pentecost, the Christians in Jerusalem are "enjoying the favor of all the people"

REFLECTIONS

IT IS DIFFICULT TO UNDERSTAND WHY GOD MIR-aculously intervened to save Peter, but did not do so to rescue James from the murderous hands of Agrippa. Luke makes no direct attempt to address this question here, yet it is a question that we ask from time to time when a loved one is taken from this world. Part of the answer lies in perspective. This life is only a temporary and partial experience of what God has in store. There is another place, far better, where Jesus himself has gone after he suffered an excruciatingly painful death (Acts 1:11). Stephen received a glimpse of this new existence when "heaven was opened," and he saw Jesus just prior to his own unjust murder (Acts 7:55–56). Peter was given an additional thirty years to live. For him, these years were dedicated to serving his Lord in flareups of suffering, but with the anticipation of "an inheritance that can never perish, spoil or fade—kept in heaven for you" (1 Peter 1:4).

(2:47). Over the last decade, the tide of opinion has changed dramatically.

He went to the house of Mary (12:12). This is the first and only reference in the New Testament to this Mary, the mother of John Mark. It is noteworthy that no mention is made of her husband. Perhaps he has died or possibly has not become a Christian.[222] Mary must be one of the wealthier members of the church. The passage suggests that she owns a sizeable home—it was large enough to host a considerable gathering of people to pray and it had an outer courtyard with a gate (see "The 'Cenacle'" at 1:13).[223] The forecourt is reminiscent of the high priest's house (Matt. 26:71).

This is further evidence that the Jerusalem church met in a network of homes throughout the city. The entire church of Jerusalem was clearly not present since Peter later instructs those present to tell James and the brothers about his miraculous release (12:17). How many believers are still in Jerusalem at this time is difficult to know. At one point there are thousands (see Acts 2:41; 4:4), but then the violent persecution hits that forced virtually all but the apostles to leave the city (Acts 8:2–3). Apparently many have returned.

John, also called Mark (12:12). Luke here introduces a young man who will become a significant figure in the book of Acts and early Christianity. Like Saul/Paul, he has both a Jewish name (John) and a Roman name (Mark). Paul identifies him as the cousin of Barnabas (Col. 4:10). After returning from Jerusalem to Antioch with Paul and Barnabas, he became one of their missionary traveling companions (Acts 12:25; 13:5). For some unstated reason, he left them in the middle of their journey and returned to Jerusalem (13:13). This led to a sharp disagreement between Paul and Barnabas over Mark's suitability for ongoing missionary service—an irresolvable dis-

---

▶John Mark in Later Church History

Among other achievements, Mark is credited with writing the second Gospel and preaching the gospel in Egypt.

Regarding the Gospel, Eusebius says: "When, at Rome, Peter had openly preached the word and by the spirit had proclaimed the gospel, the large audience urged Mark, who had followed him for a long time and remembered what had been said, to write it all down. This he did, making his Gospel available to all who wanted it."[A-58] Papias, a church leader in Hierapolis (Asia Minor), reaffirms this tradition and describes Mark as "Peter's interpreter" who "wrote down accurately everything he remembered, though not in order, of the things either said or done by Christ."[A-59]

According to Eusebius, after Mark writes his Gospel, he travels to Rome where he proclaims the gospel and is "the first to establish churches in Alexandria."[A-60] It is highly unlikely that Mark is the first to establish churches there. As with Rome, Christianity probably gains its initial foothold in Egypt shortly after the outpouring of the Spirit in Jerusalem on the day of Pentecost. The widespread character of the tradition that Mark ministers in Egypt, however, lends to its credibility.[A-61]

agreement that led to each of these leaders going separate ways (15:37–41). Whatever misgivings Paul has about Mark later evaporated, for Paul instructed Timothy to "get Mark and bring him with you, because he is helpful to me in my ministry" (2 Tim. 4:11).

A servant girl named Rhoda (12:13). Her name means "rose." It is a name that is well-attested in Greek, found in inscriptions naming women from Athens, Miletus, Mysia (Asia Minor), and Antioch.[224] It is doubtful that she is a literal slave. The term *paidiskē*, here translated "servant," can mean a "young woman."[225]

It must be his angel (12:15). When those in the prayer meeting hear Rhoda's exclamation of who is at the door, they do not believe her and some think it is Peter's angel. Many Jews believed in the notion of an angel who was closely associated with a person and could even take on that person's appearance. Note the book of Tobit, where the angel Raphael took on the disguise of Azarias (a relative of Tobit's) and became a guide for Tobit's son, Tobias (Tobit 5:4–16). Jesus himself spoke of angels associated with children: "See that you do not look down on one of these little ones. For I tell you that their angels in heaven always see the face of my Father in heaven" (Matt. 18:10). This led to a belief in the church about angels assigned to people for their lifetimes and who from time to time intervene on their behalf.[226]

Tell James (12:17). James, the son of Zebedee, has been executed by Agrippa. This refers to James, the brother of the Lord. The Gospels say little about this James. In fact, together with the rest of his siblings, he exhibits concern about Jesus' activities and teaching at the outset of his ministry—"he is out of his mind" (Mark 3:21). Apparently after Jesus' death and resurrection, James has a massive change of heart, perhaps triggered by Jesus' personal appearance to him (1 Cor. 15:7). At the beginning of Acts, he and his brothers are portrayed as joining together with the apostles in prayer as they await the promised outpouring of the Holy Spirit (Acts 1:14). Throughout the early years of the church, James stayed in Jerusalem and became a significant leader in the church. He helped the church navigate its way through the difficult issues handled in the Jerusalem council.[227] The Jewish historian Josephus refers to James in one passage: "James, the brother of Jesus, who was called the Christ."[228]

Then he left for another place (12:17). Luke is deliberately vague about where Peter goes. This is a signal in the narrative that Peter's story, though unfinished, will no longer occupy Luke's attention in the development of his account of the spread of the gospel.[229] The most pressing concern for Peter (and for the church) is for Peter to escape to a place where Herod cannot harm him.

Ordered that they be executed (12:19). According to the Code of Justinian, guards faced the same punishment that the escaped prisoner was sentenced to receive.[230]

To Caesarea (12:19). On Caesarea, see comments on 10:1.

He had been quarreling with the people of Tyre and Sidon (12:20). This is the only ancient account of this conflict. Josephus is silent about it. Presumably it had something to do with the food supply to the cities.

Tyre and Sidon were the principal cities in the territory of Phoenicia and, in the Roman era, were under the jurisdiction of the Roman governor of Syria. Both were coastal cities. Tyre was a little over fifty miles north of Caesarea, whereas Sidon was about twenty miles north of Tyre.

Blastus, a trusted personal servant of the king (12:20). Blastus is otherwise unknown in any accounts of Herod Agrippa.

They depended on the king's country for their food supply (12:20). Phoenicia

relied heavily on Galilee for its supply of food. This was true a thousand years earlier when Solomon supplied Hiram, king of Tyre, with wheat and olive oil year after year (2 Kings 5:9–12; see also Ezek. 27:17). Because of the famine afflicting Judea, the need in Tyre and Sidon was particularly acute.

Herod, wearing his royal robes (12:21). Josephus provides a much fuller and par-

▶The Missionary Travels of Peter

Based on other passages in the New Testament letters, it appears that Peter began a period of widespread missionary activity. Where he went immediately, we do not know, but he was back in Jerusalem for a brief period in A.D. 46, where he met with Saul during the famine relief visit (Gal. 2:9). He was in Antioch of Syria not much later where he ran into conflict with Paul (Gal. 2:11–15) and was back in Jerusalem in A.D. 49 for the Jerusalem council. Some have suggested that he may have even visited Corinth sometime between A.D. 52–55 on the basis of a faction in Corinth that claimed they were "of Cephas" (1 Cor. 1:12). The origin of this group, however, could be explained on other grounds.

According to 1 Corinthians 9:5 (written in A.D. 54/55), Peter had a wife who accompanied him in his missionary travels. He must have spent considerable time in northern and central Asia Minor (the provinces of Pontus, Galatia, Cap-

padocia, Asia, and Bithynia) since he addressed two letters to believers in these regions (1 and 2 Peter). It is doubtful that Peter ministered in Rome for any extended period of time in the 40s or 50s (although we cannot completely rule out a brief visit). When Paul wrote to the Roman church he never mentions Peter or alludes to any foundation-laying work that he had done there (see Rom. 15:20).[A-62] In A.D. 60–61, when Paul wrote his so-called captivity letters, there is no mention of Peter or inclusion of any greetings from Peter.

At some point, probably in the early 60s, Peter did journey to Rome and it was from there that he wrote his two letters. He cryptically refers to Rome in the first letter as "Babylon" (1 Peter 5:13). Eusebius reports that Peter and Paul were in Rome at the same time during this period and eventually lost their lives as martyrs under the Neronian persecution.[A-63]

allel account of the death of Agrippa I (see "Josephus's Account of the Death of Agrippa I"). According to Josephus, Herod appeared in front of the people early on a sunny morning wearing an unusual robe made entirely of silver. As the bright morning sun shone on the robe and reflected brightly off of it, Herod gleamed in dazzling splendor. The effect on the people was precisely as Herod intended. They acclaimed him as a god. This is certainly not unusual for the time. Emperors were often honored as gods after their deaths. Gaius Caligula, however, was at this time insisting that people worship him as a god during his reign. Herod sought no less an honor.

This is the voice of a god, not of a man (12:22). The gathered crowd (the *dēmos*)—the citizens of Caesarea and possibly also including the delegations from Tyre and Sidon—begins to acclaim Agrippa as a divine being. Ironically, hun-

dreds of years earlier, the ruler of Tyre dared to consider himself a god. God warned him through the prophet Ezekiel that his insolence would lead to his sudden demise and death: "This is what the Sovereign LORD says: 'In the pride of your heart you say, "I am a god; I sit on the throne of a god in the heart of the seas." But you are a man and not a god, though you think you are as wise as a god. . . . Because you think you are wise, as wise as a god I am going to bring foreigners against you, the most ruthless of nations; they will draw their swords against your beauty and wisdom and pierce your shining splendor. They will bring you down to the pit, and you will die a violent death'" (Ezek. 28:2, 6–8). Many Jewish and Christian interpreters see in this prophetic oracle a deeper reference to the fall of Satan himself.

He was eaten by worms and died (12:23). Herod dies a gruesome and painful death. Josephus claims that he suffered five days before he died. The one and only true God utterly humiliates this arrogant earthly ruler, who has not only opposed the work of God on earth, but also dared to put himself in the place of God. There has been a variety of suggestions based on known afflictions involving worms to explain the nature of Herod's death. Luke's point, however, is that an angel strikes him down.

According to Josephus, Herod Agrippa dies three full years after the accession of Claudius.[231] This puts his death in A.D. 44.

But the word of God continued to increase and spread (12:24). The early church is facing incredible opposition. There is a severe famine in Judea, the Sanhedrin and Jewish leaders persecute believers and chase them out of Jerusalem, and now, the king of Palestine himself executes a principal leader of the movement and threatens more. Nevertheless, nothing will stop the spread of the Word of God. God himself intervenes in history to guide and protect his people as they carry out their divinely appointed task.

When Barnabas and Saul had finished their mission, they returned (12:25). This verse draws to conclusion Luke's brief account of the famine relief visit of Saul and Barnabas to Jerusalem (11:27–30). They return to Antioch taking John Mark with them.

Saul and Barnabas Are Commissioned (13:1–3)

As the church at Antioch is worshiping and seeking the Lord, the Holy Spirit clearly directs them to send two of their gifted leaders on an evangelistic mission.

▸ Josephus's Account of the Death of Agrippa I

Now, when Agrippa had reigned three years over all Judea, he came to the city Caesarea, which was formerly called Strato's Tower; and there he exhibited shows in honor of Caesar, upon his being informed that there was a certain festival celebrated to make vows for his safety. At which festival, a great multitude was gotten together of the principal persons, and such as were of dignity through his province.

On the second day of which shows he put on a garment made wholly of silver, and of a contexture truly wonderful, and came into the theatre early in the morning; at which time the silver of his garment being illuminated by the fresh reflection of the sun's rays upon it, shone out after a surprising manner, and was so resplendent as to spread a horror over those that looked intently upon him; and presently his flatterers cried out, one from one place, and another from another (though not for his good), that he was a god; and they added, "Be thou merciful to us; for although we have hitherto reverenced thee only as a man, yet shall we henceforth own thee as superior to mortal nature."

Upon this the king did neither rebuke them, nor reject their impious flattery. But, as he presently afterwards looked up, he saw an owl sitting on a certain rope over his head, and immediately understood that this bird was the messenger of ill tidings, as it had once been the messenger of good tidings to him; and fell into the deepest sorrow. A severe pain also arose in his belly, and began in a most violent manner.

He therefore looked upon his friends, and said, "I whom you call a god, am commanded presently to depart this life; while Providence thus reproves the lying words you just now said to me; and I, who was by you called immortal, am immediately to be hurried away by death. But I am bound to accept of what Providence allots as it pleases God; for we have by no means lived ill, but in a splendid and happy manner."

When he said this, his pain was become violent. Accordingly he was carried into the palace; and the rumor went abroad everywhere, that he would certainly die in a little time.

But the multitude presently sat in sackcloth, with their wives and children, after the law of their country, and besought God for the king's recovery. All places were also full of mourning and lamentation. Now the king rested in a high chamber, and as he saw them below lying prostrate on the ground, he could not himself forbear weeping. And when he had been quite worn out by the pain in his belly for five days, he departed this life, being in the fifty-fourth year of his age, and in the seventh year of his reign.[A-64]

This excursion takes about two years—A.D. 47–48.

There were prophets and teachers (13:1). This group of five apparently are the leaders of the church at Antioch. Luke describes them here in terms of their ministry function rather than simply "elders" (*presbyteroi*; see 11:30) or "overseers" (*episkopoi*; see 20:28). As teachers, they pass on the teachings of Jesus, tell the stories of his deeds and explain them, and teach and interpret the Old Testament in light of what has taken place in the ministry and work of Christ on the cross.

What is most notable about these five is their racial, cultural, and social diversity. Two are from northern Africa, one is from Cyprus, and the other is from Cilicia (Tarsus). Only one is from the Holy Land and not one is from Antioch or Syria. One is clearly from the upper class society of Palestine, while the others are from the Hellenistic Diaspora.

Barnabas (13:1). See comments on 4:6 and 11:22.

Simeon called Niger (13:1). *Niger* is the Latin term for "black" (the Greek term, not used here, is *melas*). This clearly implies that Simeon's complexion is darker than most Syrians. He probably comes from somewhere in northern Africa.

Lucius of Cyrene (13:1). The team of leaders in the church at Antioch includes another individual from northern Africa. Lucius is most likely one of the Hellenistic Jews, originally from Cyrene, who fled Jerusalem at the outbreak of the persecution and went to Antioch to proclaim the gospel to Gentiles (see 11:20). Although some think he may be the same Lucius that Paul refers to as his relative in Romans 16:21, there is no evidence to support this identification.

Manaen (who had been brought up with Herod the tetrarch) (13:1). Although Luke does not tell us where Manaen is from, he refers to his high social status. Manaen was raised as a foster-brother (*syntrophos*) of Herod Antipas, son of Herod the Great and Malthace, who ruled Galilee from 4 B.C. to A.D. 34. Luke is the only source for this information; Josephus never mentions Manaen. Did Manaen ever hear Jesus when he taught in Galilee? When did he become a follower of Christ? Did Manaen ever try to reach his childhood friend with the gospel of Christ? These are intriguing questions for which we have no answers. Manaen is undoubtedly an important source of information for Luke.

While they were worshiping the Lord and fasting (13:2). What is significant to notice here is that the choosing of Saul and Barnabas is not due to the church's careful planning and strategizing. The Holy Spirit directly leads the church to send these two men out on an important mission. The context for receiving this special guidance of the Spirit is the community's gathering for worship. The fact

REFLECTIONS

IN MANY WAYS, THE CHURCH AT ANTIOCH IS A "MODEL church"—the kind of example our churches should strive to emulate. It is a church with a plurality of gifted leaders who zealously and selflessly serve the Lord. It is a multi-ethnic church reflecting the fact that the gospel is not for just one particular group. And it is a church of people who worship the Lord with sincere hearts, sensitive to the leading of the Spirit, and obedient to the Lord's directives.

that they are also fasting may imply that they are earnestly seeking the Lord's guidance. In Judaism, fasting sometimes accompanied a period of deep and sincere waiting on the Lord (see Neh. 1:4; Luke 2:37). The specific words from the Spirit probably come to them in the form of a prophecy.[232]

They placed their hands on them (13:3). See comments on 6:6.

The Mission to the Island of Cyprus (13:4–12)

The men decide to go to the island of Cyprus for their first outreach into Gentile territories. This is a logical place to start since Barnabas originally came from this island.

CYPRUS

▼

Seleucia (13:4). Seleucia Pieria, near the mouth of the Orontes river, was the port city for Antioch. The Syrian capital was located fifteen miles upriver from Seleucia. The city was also the home port for a fleet of Roman imperial naval vessels. The city was founded and named after Seleucus I Nicator in

300 B.C., one of Alexander the Great's generals.[233] The upper city was built on the slope of Mount Pierius and was a well fortified acropolis.

Sailed from there to Cyprus (13:4). It is about a seventy-five mile boat trip from Seleucia to Salamis, Cyprus.

Salamis (13:5). Salamis is the largest city on the island. It is located on the east coast and is the natural entry point for anyone traveling from Syria. Among the Roman-era archaeological discoveries on the ancient site are a gymnasium, a theater, an aqueduct, and a large temple complex of Zeus.[234]

In the Jewish synagogues (13:5). Apparently the Jewish population in the city is large enough to support more than one synagogue. It is here that the missionary team begins in their efforts to reach the island with the good news of Jesus Christ.

The apostle to the Gentiles inaugurates his missionary work by proclaiming the gospel in Jewish synagogues. There are two reasons Paul has for this practice. First, he maintains the conviction that

▶ The Island of Cyprus

Cyprus is the third largest island in the Mediterranean following Sicily and Sardinia.[A-65] At its widest and longest points, it measures 138 miles long and sixty miles wide.

The island has a long and rich history that can be traced back as far as 6000 B.C. to neolithic era settlements. It features prominently in Greek and Roman era literature. In 22 B.C. it came into the possession of the Roman empire and was governed by Roman proconsuls who lived in the city of Paphos.

Jewish settlers migrated to Cyprus from the time of Alexander the Great onward. There is ample evidence of substantial Jewish presence on the island throughout the period leading up to the New Testament era.[A-66] In the early part of the second century in the reign of Trajan (A.D. 98–117), Jews on the island took up arms against the rest of the population and massacred thousands of Gentiles.[A-67]

Cyprus was home to Barnabas (see Acts 4:36). He would therefore have known the territory, the synagogues, and many of the people there.

the gospel should first be presented to the Jews and then to the Gentiles (Rom. 1:16). The second reason is more pragmatic. The easiest way of reaching the Gentile community is by presenting the gospel to the Gentile proselytes and God-fearers who gathered regularly in the synagogues. These Gentiles have already turned from their idols and are seeking the one true God. All that they need to hear is that the promises for them have now been fulfilled in Jesus, the Messiah. The conversion of these Gentiles, in turn, provides a natural segue for reaching the larger Gentile community. This is a principle that had been effective in Antioch.

John was with them as their helper (13:5). As the cousin of the Cypriot Barnabas, John Mark also has some knowledge of the island and its population. The term "helper" (*hypēretēs*) is used of any kind of subordinate assistant. His help includes assisting Barnabas and Paul with the daily needs, but also probably extending to involvement in preaching and teaching (see the use of the word in Luke 1:2 and Acts 26:16).[235]

They came to Paphos (13:6). After proclaiming the word in Salamis (for which Luke provides no report as to their success), they journey roughly 106 miles (115 Roman miles) westward to the other side of the island to the city of Paphos.[236] It is entirely possible that they stop in cities and villages along the way—

such as Tremithus, Citium, Amathus, Curium, and Palaipaphos—and proclaim the gospel in these places. Luke's account is abbreviated at this point; his intent is to set the stage for telling the story about Elymas and Sergius Paulus.

Paphos was the capital city of Cyprus and seat of the Roman provincial procurator. This *Nea Paphos* ("New Paphos") is to be distinguished from the *Palaipaphos* ("Old Paphos"), which was located about ten miles southeast. The old city was a famous sanctuary of the goddess Aphrodite. *Nea Paphos* was the principal port city for the western side of the island and the seat of the provincial administration. Archaeologists have discovered the remains of three enormous Roman villas, two temples, a theater, and an amphitheater in the city.[237]

A Jewish sorcerer and false prophet (13:6). This man is not a member of the Persian priestly caste (a common usage of *magos*). He is a popular magician, or shaman, who in many respects is similar to the Samaritan Simon (see 8:9–25; also Sceva in 19:14) in his beliefs and techniques. The fact that he is known as a magician indicates that he has been reputed as having extensive esoteric knowledge about spirit forces and how to manipulate them through incantations, rituals, and formulas. Luke's reference to him as a "false prophet" may indicate that he practices revelatory magic or divination as a means of fortune telling. Luke here draws on the Old Testament traditions about lying prophets (see Jer. 23:9–32) as a means of characterizing this man.[238] The fact that he is Jewish is not a surprise. Many Jews engaged in various forms of magical practices in the Greco-Roman era. In fact, Jewish magic was famous in antiquity.[239] Josephus gives an account of the Roman procurator Felix securing the services of a Jewish magician from Cyprus to use spells in his quest to secure the attraction of Drusilla, with whom he fell madly in love.[240]

Bar-Jesus (13:6). The name of this person is "the son of Jesus (or Joshua)." *Bar-* is an Aramaic expression meaning "son of." It is unlikely that this magician has taken the same name as Jesus of Nazareth. "Jesus/Joshua" was a common Hebrew name (see Col. 4:11) and is the name of the father of Elymas.

An attendant of the proconsul (13:7). It was not unusual for Roman leaders to

▶ A Spell For Divining the Future

Among the many Greek magical papyri that have been discovered, some contain examples of revelatory magic, or divination. This particular text illustrates how this was done and connects it with prophecy:

> Whenever you seek divinations, be dressed in the garb of a prophet, shod with fibers of the doum palm and your head crowned with a spray from an olive tree—but the spray should have a single-shooted garlic tied around the middle. Clasp a pebble numbered 3663 to your breasts, and in this way make your invocation ... [an invocation follows] ... "Stay allied, lord, and listen to me through the charm that produces direct vision which I do today, and reveal to me concerning those things I ask you through the lamp divination for direct vision which I do today, I, [name of the conjurer], ΙΥ ΕΥΕ ΟΟ ΑΕΕ ΙΑΕΕ ΑΙΑΕ Ε ΑΙ ΕΥ ΕΙΕ ΟΟΟΟΟ ΕΥ ΕΟ ΙΑΟΑΙ." [A-68]

have "spiritual advisors" who were astrologers and magicians. Caesar Augustus frequently consulted soothsayers and magicians.[241] The emperor Tiberius retained the services of an astrologer from Alexandria named Claudius Thrasyllus, whom he made a member of his household and whose many predictions he trusted.[242] Emperor Nero also employed the services of astrologers, including Balbillus (the son of Thrasyllus), who predicted the future for him.[243] Nero also followed the advice of a magician named Tiridates, who led him to perform a ritual of initiation.[244]

Sergius Paulus (13:7). A Latin inscription discovered in Rome makes explicit mention of this man. His full name is given as "Lucius Sergius Paullus." He is listed along with four other men as a director of water management for the Tiber river in Rome.[245] The men were responsible for managing the flow of the river to prevent the disastrous flooding that sometimes occurred in the city. The inscription explicitly mentions that he served in this capacity during the reign of Claudius. Since the title "censor" is not used in the inscription of Claudius (a title he gained in A.D. 47), the inscription can be dated to the early period of Claudius's reign, A.D. 41–47. The dating suggests that Sergius Paulus served as proconsul of Cyprus either just before his position in Rome or just after.[246]

He and his son, who bare the same name, are mentioned on yet another inscription. In the 1912 excavation of the city of Pisidian Antioch, Sir William Ramsay discovered an inscription (dated in the

JEWISH MAGICAL AMULETS

These medieval amulets were intended to protect people from evil spirits.

▼

sionary team goes directly from Cyprus to Pisidian Antioch may have something to do with the proconsul's family connections in that city.[249]

period A.D. 60–100) that read: "To Lucius Sergius Paullus the younger, son of Lucius, one of the four commissioners in charge of the Roman streets, tribune of the soldiers of the sixth legion styled Ferrata, quaestor." Apparently the son of the proconsul of Cyprus became an important Roman official in Pisidian Antioch, the very place the apostle Paul and his companions travel to next.[247] It is possible that the Sergii Paulli family, although ultimately of Italian origin, were native to Pisidian Antioch.[248] The fact that the mis-

Elymas the sorcerer (for that is what his name means) (13:8). There are two possibilities for understanding the origin of the name "Elymas." It may be derived from the Aramaic word *haloma*, meaning "one who dreams" (in the sense of receiving visions). Or it may come from a Semitic word related to the Arabic *'alim*, which means "wise man." In this sense it would have much in common with our translation of *magoi* from the East as "wise men" in the birth narrative of Jesus (Matt. 2:1).[250]

Saul, who was also called Paul (13:9). Up to this point, Luke only refers to the apostle by his Hebrew name, "Saul." Now, as the apostle begins his mission to the Gentiles, Luke will refer to him as

Roman Names				
PRAENOMEN	**NOMEN GENTILE**	**COGNOMEN**	**SUPERNOMEN**	
(an individual's name identifying the person within the family—similar to our first name)[A-69]	(family name— similar to our surname)	(additional family name designating a branch of the family—used as the ordinary personal name)	Signa (Nickname)	Hebrew Name
Lucius	Annaeus	**Seneca**		
Marcus	Tullius	**Cicero**		
Gaius	**Julius**	**Caesar Germanicus**	Caligula ("little boots")	
Gaius	Octavius	**Caesar** ("**Augustus**" a title)		
Tiberius	Julius	Caesar Augustus		
Tiberius	**Claudius**	Nero Germanicus		
Nero	Claudius	Caesar		
(Lucius)	Sergius	Paullus		
?	?	**Paullus**		**Saul**

"Paul." The change probably reflects the historical reality that Paul himself begins using his Roman name as he ventures into Gentile territory with the gospel. In addition, it may be that Paul wants to avoid using his Hebrew name since, in Greek, *Saulos* is an adjective that refers to "the loose, wanton gait of courtesans or Bacchantes."[251]

It was common for Roman citizens to have three names: the praenomen, nomen, and cognomen (see the chart below). "Paul" is the apostle's Roman cognomen. Since Paul gained his citizenship at birth (see 22:26–29), it is a matter of speculation to determine how his parents or grandparents received their citizenship. Scholars suggest two different ways that Paul's ancestors may have gained their prized Roman citizenship. (1) F. F. Bruce suggests that it may have been bestowed on Paul's father or grandfather by one of the Roman generals (Pompey or Antony) known to have been in control of the province of Cilicia in the first century B.C. and for whom his relative rendered some outstanding service to the Roman cause. Bruce suggests that if the citizenship was bestowed by Mark Antony, Paul's full name would have been: Marcus Antonius Paullus.[252] (2) Alternatively, Paul's ancestors may have gained their citizenship after being freed as enslaved prisoners of war (perhaps enslaved during the Roman general Varus's campaign against Jews in Galilee in 4 B.C. or even in earlier Roman excursions into Palestine).[253]

You are a child of the devil (13:10). By trying to turn the proconsul away from the faith and opposing the missionary group, Elymas shows his true colors. Far from being a "son of Jesus" (the savior) he is a "son of the devil" (the enemy). The language here is reminiscent of what Jesus told the Jewish leaders who opposed him and sought to kill him: "You belong to your father, the devil, and you want to carry out your father's desire" (John 8:44). Paul also recognizes that the devil is source of the spiritual power behind the magic and divination that Elymas practices.

The hand of the Lord (13:11). It is not by counter-magic or personal vindictiveness that Elymas is struck blind. God himself intervenes in this situation to thwart this opponent of the gospel (see comments on 4:28).

For a time you will be unable to see (13:11). A temporary blindness came on Saul when he was confronted by the Lord (9:9). "For a time" may imply that the blindness will be removed if and when Elymas turns to the Lord in repentance.

He believed (13:12). The mission to Cyprus is a success. The Roman proconsul of the entire island puts his faith in Jesus. We know nothing more about the subsequent history of Sergius Paulus, Elymas, or the others who become believers on Cyprus at that time. This would certainly be an exciting series of stories.

The Mission to Antioch of Pisidia (13:13–52)

Paul and Barnabas continue the mission to the Gentiles in south-central Asia Minor. This is a natural westward extension of Paul's previous work in the nearby province of Cilicia (where his home city of Tarsus was located). In this section, Luke records a lengthy summary of one of Paul's messages that he delivers in a local synagogue.

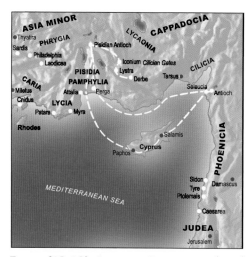

**PERGA IN
PAMPHYLIA**

(left) Remains of
the Hellenistic-era
towers marking the
beginning of the
colonnaded street.

(right) The remains
of the main
street through
this port city.

▼

Perga (13:13). Leaving Cyprus, Paul and his two companions journey over 150 miles by boat to the south coast of Asia Minor. Coming to the Cestrus river, they travel five miles up the river to the port of Perga.[254] Luke does not tell us how long they stay in the city or whether they proclaim the gospel there at this time. On the return trip, they share the gospel in the city.

Perga was one of the leading cities of Asia Minor. It had a sizeable population evidenced in part by its fourteen thousand-seat theater. It also boasted a large stadium, many Roman baths, a large gymnasium, and three aqueducts sup-

plying water to the city. The principal deity of the city was Artemis (associated with the Ephesian Artemis), also known as the Queen of Perga. The remains of her famous temple in Perga have not yet been discovered. There were presumably many Jews in the city and a synagogue. Philo speaks of a colony of Jews in the province (*Embassy* 281) and Jews from Pamphylia were present in Jerusalem on the day of Pentecost (Acts 2:10).

In Pamphylia (13:13). Pamphylia is a small Roman senatorial province located west of the province of Cilicia (where Paul was from). In A.D. 43, Pamphylia combined with Lycia (a province to the west) to form a joint Roman province. It was enclosed by the Mediterranean Sea to the south and the territory of Pisidia to the north.

John left them to return to Jerusalem (13:13). Luke gives no indication as to why John Mark leaves, but Paul regards it as desertion and it becomes an issue that divides Paul and Barnabas later (see 15:37–39). There are numerous suggestions as to why John Mark leaves, many relating to his youthful inexperience: He

is homesick; he is having difficulty living and ministering in a strange culture; or, he is unwilling to take the rugged hundred-mile journey northward to Antioch. Some assume there are other reasons for the departure: He resents the fact that Paul is assuming more of the leadership over his cousin Barnabas; he thinks the plan is to stay in Pamphylia and resents the sudden decision to go to Antioch; or, he feels increasingly uncomfortable with the nature of this mission to Gentiles. We will never know for sure.

Pisidian Antioch (13:14). Pisidian Antioch technically lay in the territory of Phrygia but was called "Antioch towards Pisidia" to distinguish it from another Antioch in Phrygia that was on the bank of the Maeander river. Today the site lies just north of the modern city of Yalvaç. Pisidia was a mountainous region in southern Asia Minor stretching some 120 miles east to west and fifty miles north to south. The mountains would have made it a difficult journey for Paul and Barnabas and may be one of the reasons why he was ill

▶ Antioch (Near Pisidia)

Antioch was a prosperous city in central Asia Minor in the ancient territory of Phrygia, but now the Roman province of Galatia.[A-70] It was regarded as the most important Roman colony in Asia Minor. The city lay just west of the rugged Taurus mountain range. This colony was a miniature Rome in the midst of Asia Minor and was even organized into seven districts.[A-71] Antioch was second in importance in Galatia only to Ancyra, the capital city of the Roman province.

In addition to a large population of local indigenous Anatolian peoples, Antioch also had many Roman citizens. It was home to many Roman senators and equestrians. Sometime after Paul's visit, Sergius Paulus, the proconsul of Cyprus, took up residence there. The city had a large imperial sanctuary constructed to serve the emperor cult. Other surviving Roman structures from the New Testament period include a large bathhouse, an aqueduct, the remains of a street system and a decorated city gate. Paul's visit would have occurred at the climax of an era of building and development in the city. One expert on the city notes, "Antioch would have appeared to Paul as a model of the capital itself."[A-72]

The principal deity of the city was the moon-god Mên, called Mên Askaênos. Remains of the second-century B.C. sanctuary can still be seen on the hill called Karakuyu, about an hour's climb above the city (2.5 miles southeast). Inscriptions also attest to the worship of Jupiter (*Iuppiter Optimus Maximus*), Dionysus, and Asklepios in the city. There was also a strong Jewish presence in the city most of whom came c. 200 B.C. when two thousand Jewish families (perhaps more than ten thousand people) were forcibly resettled in Phrygia and Lydia from Babylon.[A-73]

The ruler cult was of paramount importance in the city. Construction of the imperial temple in honor of the city's founder, Caesar Augustus, began during the reign of Tiberius. A triumphal arch celebrating Augustus's Pisidian victories was completed in A.D. 50, just after Paul's initial visit. An expert on the Roman site notes: "There is no doubt that the imperial temple and the associated buildings provided the main focus for the public and religious life of the colony." [A-74]

Since 1991, the site has been excavated by teams led by Turkish archaeologist Mehmet Taschalan. Excavations have focused on a bathhouse, the imperial sanctuary, the theater, and the east section of the main road (the *decumanus maximus*). Taschalan's team has also discovered a stadium (measuring 208 yds. by 33 yds.) in a valley west of the city.[A-75]

when he first preached the gospel to them (see Gal. 4:12). The territory of Pisidia was now included in the large Roman province of Galatia.[255] In fact, "the region around Derbe, Lystra, Iconium, and Antioch was all part of the province of Galatia in the mid-first century A.D."[256]

They entered the synagogue and sat down (13:14). There would have been significant variety in synagogue architecture in the first century throughout the Mediterranean world. In general, however, most would have had stone benches built along two or three of the walls and rows of wooden benches in the middle of the structure.[257] The seating was segregated according to men and women. There is also evidence of a hierarchical seating order with more distinguished members sitting in the front and younger and less distinguished members seated in rows behind them.[258] Archaeologists have not yet discovered the synagogue remains in the city.

After the reading from the Law and the Prophets (13:15). According to the

PISIDIAN ANTIOCH

The Roman road through the middle of the city.

▼

Mishnah, the synagogue service includes a recitation of the *Shema* and the *Shemoneh ʿEsreh* (the Eighteen Benedictions), a reading from the Torah and the Prophets, and the "lifting up of the hands" (the blessing of the priests).[259] Philo stresses the importance of the message that follows the reading of the Scriptures: "Accordingly, on the seventh day there are spread before the people in every city innumerable lessons of prudence, and temperance, and courage, and justice, and all other virtues; during the giving of which the common people sit down, keeping silence and pricking up their ears, with all possible attention, from their thirst for wholesome instruction; but some of those who are very learned explain to them what is of great importance and use, lessons by which the whole of their lives may be improved."[260]

A message of encouragement (13:15). This is a technical expression for a synagogue sermon following the reading of the Scriptures.[261]

Please speak (13:15). It is not surprising that the synagogue officials would invite Paul to speak. Here in their midst is a rabbi who was trained under Gamaliel in Jerusalem.

Standing up, Paul motioned with his hand and said (13:16). Standing and motioning is what one expected of a good orator delivering a synagogue sermon.

You Gentiles who worship God (13:16). The synagogue in Antioch already has attracted many Gentiles sympathetic to the worship of the one God of Israel (see comments on 2:11).

The God of the people of Israel chose our fathers (13:17). Paul begins his message with a historical retrospect touching on the exodus, the conquest, the period of the judges, and the monarchy of David. Luke probably gives us merely an outline of what Paul says in his address. This sketch of the history of Israel establishes common ground with his synagogue audience and lays the foundation for what he will soon say about Jesus as the messianic descendant of David.

He overthrew seven nations in Canaan (13:19). These seven nations are "the Hittites, Girgashites, Amorites, Canaanites, Perizzites, Hivites and Jebusites, seven nations larger and stronger than you" (Deut. 7:1).

All this took about 450 years (13:20). This 450 years would represent four hundred years in Egypt (Gen. 15:13), forty years in the desert (Num. 14:33–34), and ten years conquering the land (Josh. 14:1–5).

I have found David son of Jesse a man after my own heart (13:22). This verse represents a combination of portions

◀

PISIDIAN ANTIOCH

Overview of the excavation of the Byzantine church recently identified as the previous site of the Roman-era Jewish synagogue.

▶ The Organization of a Synagogue

There was no "pastor" of a synagogue as we would have in a contemporary church. The reading of the scriptures, the preaching, and public prayers were given by members of the assembly. Most synagogues would have had the following leadership structure:[A-76]

- *Archontes* ("leaders") or *Presbyteroi* ("elders")— These were the chief leaders of the synagogue in charge of its direction and oversight. It appears that this position was held for a year at a time. Although both titles are attested in the inscriptions, *archontes* was used far more often to denote these leaders.

- *Archisynagōgos* ("ruler of the synagogue")— This officer had the special responsibility of organizing the public worship for each Sabbath and for all of the additional meetings of the synagogue. This leader was selected from among the *archontes*. Usually there was one person who held this office, but on occasion, as here, there were two.

from two Old Testament passages about David: Psalm 89:20 ("I have found David") and 1 Samuel 13:14 ("a man after his own heart").

From this man's descendants (13:23). The Old Testament is clear that the coming Messiah would be a descendant of David (2 Sam. 7:12–16; Ps. 89). The prophet Jeremiah revealed: "'The days are coming,' declares the LORD, 'when I will raise up to David a righteous Branch, a King who will reign wisely and do what is just and right in the land. In his days Judah will be saved and Israel will live in safety. This is the name by which he will be called: The LORD Our Righteousness'" (Jer. 23:5–6; see comments on 2:14–36).

The Savior Jesus (13:23). See comments on 5:31.

Whose sandals I am not worthy to untie (13:25). Rabbi Joshua ben Levi teaches that "all manner of service that a slave must render to his master, the pupil must render to his teacher—except that of taking off his shoe."[262] By contrast, because of Jesus' infinite superiority, John did not feel he was even worthy to perform a task that was considered too menial for most disciples to perform for their masters.

The people of Jerusalem and their rulers did not recognize Jesus (13:27). Both the crowds and the leaders of the Jewish people in Jerusalem—the members of the Sanhedrin, the chief priests, the elders, and the scribes—bore guilt for inciting the death of Jesus at the hands of the Romans. They refused to believe the claims of Jesus and did not recognize that he was the anticipated Messiah of Israel. Paul's hope is that his audience in Antioch does not make the same mistake as their compatriots in Jerusalem.

Executed . . . laid him in a tomb . . . raised him from the dead . . . was seen (13:28–31). Paul presents the heart of the gospel message in these four verses. This is the essence of the *kerygma*, the early Christian preaching (see 1 Cor. 15:3–4).

The tree (13:29). The cross is often referred to as "the tree" by the early Christians. This reflects a connection with Deuteronomy 21:22–23: "If a man guilty of a capital offense is put to death and his body is hung on a tree, you must not leave his body on the tree overnight. Be sure to bury him that same day, because anyone who is hung on a tree is under God's curse." In his letter to these people (and probably also in his preaching), Paul clarifies that Christ redeems us from the curse pronounced by the law on our human sinfulness by himself becoming a curse for us by dying on a tree (Gal. 3:14).

For many days he was seen (13:31). Paul stresses the role of Jesus' many post-resurrection witnesses. They can vouch for the authenticity and reliability of the message Paul is proclaiming.

PISIDIAN ANTIOCH

The Roman aqueduct bringing water to the city.

▼

What God promised our fathers he has fulfilled for us (13:32–33). Paul insists that Jesus of Nazareth fulfills the promises of the Old Testament recorded in Psalm 2:7; 16:10; and Isaiah 55:3 (see comments on Acts 2:27–31).

Everyone who believes is justified (13:39). In his first sermon recorded in Acts, Paul proclaims his well-known doctrine of justification (*dikaioō*) by faith (see Rom. 3:28; 5:1; Gal. 2:16). There is a judicial (or forensic) background to this important theological concept that is well-illustrated in Deuteronomy 25:1: "When men have a dispute, they are to take it to court and the judges will decide the case, acquitting (*dikaioō*) the innocent and condemning the guilty." Applied to people who put their faith in Christ, "justification" means that they have been acquitted of all their guilt before God. This acquittal is tantamount to having all of one's sins forgiven.

From everything you could not be justified from by the law of Moses (13:39). On the surface it appears that Paul implies that the Mosaic law is capable of justifying people in spite of certain sins, but not others. This is not at all what Paul is saying. Paul makes it clear in his letters that the Mosaic law is unable to bring ultimate acquittal for any of the sins they have committed.

Take care that what the prophets have said does not happen to you (13:40). Concerned that the members of the synagogue in Antioch may scoff at his message and reject it, Paul uses the words of Habakkuk 1:5 to warn them about the dire consequences of dismissing what he has to say. In that context, the prophet derided the people of Israel for not recognizing that the impending invasion of Babylon was God's own doing—it was an act of judgment against his people. Paul echoes the words of this passage to warn these people that it is once again a dangerous proposition to ignore what God is doing, but in this instance through Jesus of Nazareth, who has come as Messiah and Savior. The common thread between the two situations is that God acts in surprising ways.

◀

PISIDIAN ANTIOCH

The ruins of the temple of Augustus.

On the next Sabbath almost the whole city gathered (13:44). The initial response to Paul's message is excellent. Many Jews and Gentile proselytes show keen enthusiasm. Invited to speak again on the following Sabbath, Paul and Barnabas are astounded that the synagogue is overflowing with Gentiles who want to hear the gospel. This event illustrates the effectiveness of Paul's strategy of reaching Gentiles through the synagogue. These believing Gentiles can immediately go and reach family, friends, neighbors, and coworkers.

They were filled with jealousy (13:45). The leading members of the synagogue who disagree with Paul's message are provoked by his success in attracting Gentiles to their synagogue. This may stem from their own inability to attract as many or possibly from a concern about their synagogue being defiled by impure Gentile sinners. The latter concern may also be connected to their perception of Paul's relaxed attitude about the Jewish law in his explanation of the Scriptures, especially as it relates to the Gentiles.

Light for the Gentiles (13:47). Paul declares his focus on the Gentiles as fulfilling the divine directive as related in Isaiah 49:6 that God calls his servant to be a light to the Gentiles. Jesus himself alluded to the wording of this passage in Acts 1:8 by stating that the gospel goes to the far reaches of the inhabited world.

All who were appointed for eternal life believed (13:48). This is one of the clearest statements affirming absolute predestination found anywhere in the New Testament.[263] Jews commonly believed that God enrolled his people in a book of life. This is attested in the Torah itself: "The LORD replied to Moses, 'Whoever has sinned against me I will blot out of my book'" (Ex. 32:33). The prophet Daniel spoke of a future deliverance for "everyone whose name is found written in the book" (Dan. 12:1).[264] The expression "eternal life" can literally be rendered "life in the age (to come)." This new age has dawned in the life and work of Jesus.

The word of the Lord spread . . . they stirred up persecution (13:49–50). The Jews and Gentiles who believe do not keep the good news to themselves, but begin telling others throughout the south Galatian region. By contrast, the unbelieving Jewish leaders harden in their opposition and do all they can to get Paul and Barnabas out of the area.

The God-fearing women of high standing (13:50). These are probably Roman (Italian) women from the colonial families settled there by Augustus—aristocratic provincial elite who become Jewish sympathizers.[265] Similarly, the leading men are most likely Roman officials.

They shook the dust from their feet in protest (13:51). Jesus commended this action to the Twelve and the seventy when he sent them out on their respective missions as a symbolic protest against those who rejected their message (Luke 9:5; 10:11). The symbol was expressed in first-century Judaism as a means of ridding oneself of the impurities of walking through Gentile lands.[266] For Jesus and the apostles, the Gentiles were not intrinsically impure—only those who refused to receive the gospel of the Messiah's saving work (see comments on Acts 18:6).

The Evangelization of Iconium (14:1–7)

After their mixed reception at Antioch, the missionary partners travel nearly a hundred miles to Iconium where they receive a similar response to their preaching.

Went as usual into the Jewish synagogue (14:1). Paul begins his outreach in Iconium at the Jewish synagogue in spite of the fact that he angrily turns to the Jewish leaders in Antioch of Pisidia and

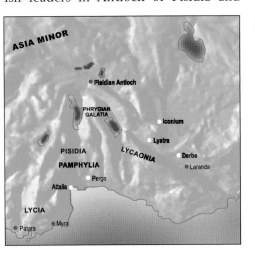

exclaims, "We turn now to the Gentiles" (13:46). Because of the presence of Gentile God-fearers, the synagogue is the best place to begin his witness to the Gentiles.

The Jews who refused to believe stirred up the Gentiles (14:2). This is precisely the response he encounters in Antioch (14:46, 50) and will later experience in Thessalonica (17:5) and elsewhere. Many Jews as well as Gentiles respond to the gospel.

Miraculous signs and wonders (14:3). The people of the city see miraculous things happen as Paul and Barnabas minister here. These signs and wonders no doubt include healings and exorcisms. As at other times in the outreach of the early church, God intervenes in these dramatic ways to demonstrate the authenticity of the message about his grace that these two missionaries are proclaiming. These miracles serve as background to a comment Paul later makes to the Galatian believers in his letter: "Does God give you his Spirit and work miracles among

◀ *left*

SOUTH GALATIA

▶ Iconium

The city of Iconium lay about ninety miles east southeast of Antioch and roughly 150 miles due south of Ancyra (modern Ankara, the capital city of Turkey).[A-77] It was part of the Roman province of Galatia, but for many years was regarded as the easternmost city of the ethnic territory of Phrygia. The Phrygian dialect was still spoken there as inscriptions dating as late as the second century A.D. attest.[A-78]

The city was friendly to Rome and was honored by the emperor Claudius sometime shortly before Paul's visit. Iconium was situated on a major trade route (the *Via Sebaste*),[A-79] which linked the Syrian east to Ephesus and served as an important commercial city for the area. Numismatic evidence attests to the establishment of a Roman colony (*Colonia Iulia Augusta Iconiensum*) in the city during the reign of Vespasian (A.D. 69–79).[A-80] Agriculture flourished in the fertile plateau area encompassing Iconium and water was plentiful. The city was, therefore, prosperous and growing.

There is evidence that the population worshiped the Asia Minor mother goddess Cybele, Herakles (Hercules), Zeus Megistos (Jupiter Optimus Maximus), as well as Apollo.[A-81] From Luke, we know that there was a Jewish community and a synagogue in the city. Numerous inscriptions attest to the fact that Christianity became deeply rooted in this city.

you because you observe the law, or because you believe what you heard?" (Gal. 3:5).

With the apostles (14:4). Luke here explicitly labels Paul and Barnabas "apostles," as he does again in verse 14. Apparently, Luke uses the title in two different ways: someone who travels with Jesus in his earthly ministry, has seen him risen from the dead, and constitutes one of "the Twelve"; and someone set apart by the Holy Spirit for an evangelistic mission and then commissioned and "sent out" by the local church.[267]

The Lycaonian cities (14:6). In A.D. 25, the "Lycaonian cities" of Lystra and Derbe were incorporated into the Roman province of Galatia. Luke, however, demonstrates his knowledge of the former territorial divisions, to which the local populace was still sensitive. The territory of Lycaonia reached northeast nearly as far as Iconium and bordered Cilicia on the south, Cappadocia to the east, Phrygia and the former ethnic territory of Galatia to the north, and Pisidia and Isauria to the west.[268] Another of the principal cities of Lycaonia was Laranda, located about twenty miles east southeast of Derbe in the direction of Tarsus.

The Evangelization of Lystra (14:8–21a)

Undaunted by the threats of stoning and persecution, Paul and Barnabas travel on to the cities of Lystra and Derbe. An unusual situation surfaces at Lystra where the two are mistaken to be gods.

Lame from birth and had never walked (14:8). Luke's statement about the severity of the handicap highlights the "wonder" (see 14:3) of this healing. For the man to walk and jump, God has to restore bone mass and a significant amount of muscle.

In the Lycaonian language (14:11). While these people know Latin and Greek, they still retain facility in their

▶ **Lystra**

The city of Lystra had a fairly recent history, having been established by Augustus in 26 B.C. and made a Roman colony (*Colonia Iulia Felix Gemina Lustra*) in A.D. 6, the southernmost colony in this portion of Asia Minor.[A-82] It was located roughly twenty miles south of Iconium, but a day's journey off the main road, the *via Sebaste*. It was never an important city in this portion of Asia Minor.

The Roman influence in this city is seen by the predominance of Latin inscriptions. The raising of livestock (especially sheep) and agriculture were the principal occupations in this region. This is consistent with the discovery of a coin in Lystra from the time of Augustus depicting the Ceres, the goddess of vegetation.[A-83]

native Anatolian dialect, which Luke refers to as *Lykaonisti*. Usage of this dialect in the area around Lystra persisted until as late as the fifth century A.D. and beyond.[269] There is evidence that two Christian monasteries in Constantinople (Byzantium) founded in the sixth century used the Lycaonian language in their liturgy.[270] Inscriptions in the dialects of other nearby Anatolian languages also survive (namely, Carian, Sidetic, and Pisidian).

The gods have come down to us in human form (14:11). The famous first-century Roman poet Ovid tells a story about Zeus and Hermes taking mortal form and visiting an elderly couple in their humble Phrygian countryside home. Leading up to this, Zeus and Hermes visited a thousand homes seeking shelter and rest but were repeatedly spurned, their true identities being concealed. It was not until they came to the home of Philemon and Baucis that they found hospitality. The old couple welcomed the two visitors, fed them well, and prepared for them a place to rest. Not knowing that they were entertaining gods "in the guise of human beings," the old couple finally learned the identity of their heavenly visitors. The gods then led Philemon and Baucis to the top of a hill and mercifully spared them from a devastating flood sent in judgment on the inhospitable inhabitants of the region. Their humble home was miraculously transformed into a marble temple.[271] If this local legend was known to the inhabitants of Lystra, it may help to explain their identification of the missionaries as Zeus and Hermes and their eagerness to honor them.

There is also inscriptional evidence from Lystra attesting the local worship of Zeus and Hermes. A stone relief found at Kavak (in the territory of Lystra) depicts Hermes accompanied by the eagle of Zeus. In the city of Lystra, a stone was discovered that portrays Hermes and a second god (possibly the earth-god *Gē* or Zeus *Epēkoos*).[272]

Barnabas they called Zeus, and Paul they called Hermes (14:12). Although Zeus (Jupiter) is the head of the pantheon of gods, it is not surprising that Paul is associated with Hermes (Mercury) instead of

Zeus. Hermes was widely regarded as the messenger of Zeus. One ancient writer describes Hermes as the god "who is the leader in speaking."[273]

The priest of Zeus (14:13). Another group of manuscripts uses the plural, "the priests of Zeus," which more accurately reflects the historical situation. It was common for such temples to have a college of priests.[274]

Whose temple was just outside the city (14:13). The temple has not yet been discovered. Archaeologists, however, have found many statues and inscriptions attesting the worship of Zeus and Hermes in this region. None of these, however, dates any earlier than the third century A.D.[275]

Brought bulls and wreaths to the city gates (14:13). The bulls are brought to be sacrificed. Such animals were typically adorned with garlands on their way to be slaughtered.[276]

They tore their clothes (14:14). In Jewish culture, extreme grief is often expressed by tearing one's clothes. It was an outward expression of what the person was feeling inwardly. "The destructive action reveals the sudden and sharp emotion that overshadows all ordinary concerns, such as care for appearance and possessions."[277] Reuben and Jacob both tore their clothes when they thought Joseph had been killed (Gen. 37:29, 34). Many of Israel's leaders tore their clothes when God's honor was impugned.[278] When the Sanhedrin heard an account of blasphemy against God, the judges "stand up on their feet and rend their garments, and they may not mend them again."[279] This is what the high priest did at the trial of Jesus (see Matt. 26:65; Mark 14:63).

Men, why are you doing this? (14:15). This question marks the beginning of a short address that Paul gives to the crowd, wherein he appeals to them to desist in their acclaiming of him and Barnabas as gods, and points them to the one true God. What Luke records in the span of these three verses is a brief summary of what is likely a longer address. This is not exactly an evangelistic message, at least from what we know of it, because it makes no mention of Jesus or the elements of the *kerygma*—the message of the death, resurrection, and exaltation of Christ, drawing the implications of this event for the forgiveness of sins and a relationship with God.

There are similarities between this address and his message to the Greeks on the Areopagus in Athens (see 17:22–30). These are the only two occasions where Luke records Paul's preaching to non-Jews. In both instances Paul contextualizes his message to people who do not know the Scriptures. The apostle stresses natural revelation (focusing on God as Creator and the providential sustainer of

BULLS AND WREATHS

The altar of Domitian in the Ephesos museum in Selçuk.

▼

the world) and the emptiness of idolatry while avoiding a recounting of Israel's history or how Jesus fulfills Jewish prophecies about a coming Messiah.

From these worthless things (14:15). Jews typically regarded idolatry as "empty" (*mataios*). One Jewish writer writes, "For just as one's dish is useless when it is broken, so are the gods of the heathen, when they have been set up in the temples."[280] Another Jewish writer asserts that "men themselves are much more powerful than the gods whom they vainly worship."[281]

The living God (14:15). Frequently throughout the Old Testament, the one God of Israel is described as "the living God." Joshua tells the people of Israel as they enter the promised land that "the living God is among you."[282] A popular story is told in Palestinian Judaism shortly before the birth of Christ about Daniel challenging the Persian king about his worship of the statue of Bel, the patron deity of Babylon: "The king revered it and went every day to worship it. But Daniel worshiped his own God. So the king said to him, 'Why do you not worship Bel?' He answered, 'Because I do not revere idols made with hands, but the living God, who created heaven and earth and has dominion over all living creatures.'"[283] This story well depicts the Jewish attitude toward idols.

Paul's comments are offensive to these Gentile worshipers of Zeus. The implication of what Paul says is that other gods, including Zeus and Hermes, are not alive.

Who made heaven and earth and sea and everything in them (14:15). This line repeats the same words we find used in support of the fourth commandment enjoining Israel to keep the Sabbath holy: "For in six days the LORD made the heavens and the earth, the sea, and all that is in them, but he rested on the seventh day" (Ex. 20:11). But God is also extolled as Creator in these words in other Old Testament and Jewish contexts.[284]

In the past, he let all nations go their own way (14:16). Throughout the history of Israel, God directly and repeatedly intervened by revealing himself to them, making them his own people, redeeming them from slavery, guiding and leading them, bestowing on them his law, speaking to them through the prophets, and giving them promises of a bright future. God did not respond to the Gentile nations in the same way, but he did not leave them without a witness. Paul's comments here echo what he says elsewhere to the Greeks on the Areopagus (17:30) and to the Romans in his letter (Rom. 1:28).

He has shown kindness by giving you rain from heaven (14:17). God's witness to the Gentile nations is not through

> ## REFLECTIONS
>
> **PAUL'S COMMENTS ABOUT OTHER RELIGIONS WOULD** solicit a hostile reaction today in the contemporary climate of pluralism. To infer that worshipers of other gods are devoted to "empty" things and neglect the living and true God would be viewed today as intolerant and inflammatory. It is important to realize that Paul was no angry man who said these things out of an unstable or uncharitable personality. He came to these people in love earnestly desiring for them to recognize and acknowledge the one true God. In Paul's understanding, there were not many paths that led to the same ultimate reality. There was one path and many deceptive counterfeits.

their religions, which Paul has characterized as "worthless." The living God's providential care for the nations by providing them with land, rain, crops, and the enjoyment of life is a sufficient testimony to point these people to a greater reality. A Jewish rabbi said that if a person sees "mountains, hills, seas, rivers and deserts he should say, 'Blessed is the author of creation,'" and "for rain and good tidings he should say, 'Blessed is he, the good and the doer of good.'"[285]

Paul's remarks here may have functioned as a direct polemic against the local cult religions. Zeus was popularly worshiped as the god of weather and the one who provided vegetation.[286]

Some Jews came from Antioch and Iconium (14:19). It is surprising that Paul's Jewish opponents from Antioch (near Pisidia) travel a hundred miles to oppose him in Lystra. Do they receive word from Jews living in Lystra about what is transpiring there? Contact between the cities of Antioch and Lystra, in spite of the distance, is evidenced in part by a statue of Concordia that the people of Lystra erected in the city of Antioch.[287]

They stoned Paul and dragged him outside the city (14:19). There is great irony in the fact that the apostle goes from being venerated as a god to an object of derision whom the people try to kill. Luke does not say why they do not attempt to stone Barnabas as well. It may point to the role Paul is playing in the events—especially in the speaking. Since stoning was a distinctively Jewish form of punishment, we can assume that these Jewish opponents from Antioch and Iconium threw the rocks while the Gentile crowd from Lystra looked on.

But after the disciples had gathered around him, he got up and went back into the city (14:20). Since the crowd supposes that Paul is dead, the apostle probably is seriously injured—at least stoned in the head and knocked unconscious. Some interpreters have thought that God works a miracle in raising Paul up in response to the prayers of these who "had gathered around him." This may be the case.

They preached the good news in that city (14:21). Luke says nothing about any of

▶ **Derbe**

Very little is known about the ancient city of Derbe either from literary evidence or from archaeology. The site was only positively identified in the late 1950s when two inscriptions were discovered on the site that mentioned the city (although Sir William Ramsay had erroneously identified a different site as Derbe in the late 1800s). One of the inscriptions, the shaft of a large statue base and weighing nearly a ton, reads: "The Council and the People of Claudio-

Derbe...." The other inscription, dating to the fourth or fifth century, also gives evidence of Christianity in the city: "The most God-loving Michael, bishop of Derbe."

The site of Derbe is located about sixty-five miles southeast of Iconium (thirty miles east of the area originally suggested by Ramsay) at modern Devri Scehri. The mound where the city is situated, Kerti Hüyük, still has not been excavated.[A-84]

the events surrounding the ministry of Paul and Barnabas in Derbe. Yet he does say that many people there become followers of Christ.

Revisiting and Strengthening the New Galatian Churches (14:21b–23)

Then they returned to Lystra, Iconium and Antioch (14:21). After being expelled from Antioch, plotted against in Iconium, and nearly stoned to death in Lystra, it is a tribute to God's power in their lives that Paul and Barnabas even consider stepping foot in those cities again. They are willing to risk their lives for the sake of the gospel, however, and their love and concern for the well-being of these new converts drive them to take incredible risks.

Appointed elders for them in each church (14:23). Knowing that these fledgling communities need leadership to facilitate their continuing growth in the Lord, Paul and Barnabas appoint *presbyteroi*. The plural suggests that a group of gifted men is selected for each church and share equally in the task of leading the respective congregations.[288] Paul's model for this form of leadership comes from the synagogue pattern and from how he sees the network of house churches structured in Jerusalem (see comments on 11:30).

Returning to Antioch, Syria (14:24–28)

Rather than continuing to other cities in Asia Minor to proclaim the gospel, the two decide to return to their sending church in Antioch of Syria. Luke does not state why they decide to return at this juncture, but it may have had to do

◀

with a sense of accomplishment of their work in south Galatia and a desire to solicit further support for a more extensive future trip.

They went down to Attalia (14:25). Attalia served as the harbor for Perga, the capital of the Roman province of Pamphylia. Although Luke does not explicitly tell us that Paul's boat came into Attalia when they first arrived in this region (see 13:13), this was probably his point of entry. This time, however, Paul and Barnabas spend some time preaching the gospel in Perga (five miles upriver from Attalia), although we have no report of the response.

▼

They sailed back to Antioch (14:26). The journey has now come full-circle, and these two emissaries return to the church in Syria that sent them out.

The door of faith to the Gentiles (14:27). The missionary report alludes to the language of Jesus, who described himself as "the door" to salvation (John 10:9). At the heart of Paul's preaching is the presentation of faith as the means by which one enters the door and receives justification and forgiveness of sins (see Acts 13:39).

They stayed there a long time (14:28). It is impossible to know exactly how long the two stay in Antioch and resume their ministry to the many believers there. It is certainly less than a year and may have been just a few months. It is during this time and prior to the Jerusalem Council that Paul receives word that a group of Jewish believers zealous for the law visits the new believers in south Galatia and begin to subvert his teaching. In response, Paul writes his first letter—Galatians.

The Jerusalem Council (15:1–29)

For many years, the Jewish people welcomed Gentiles into their covenant community provided that they turned from their idols to the one true God and

adhered to the Jewish law— most notably by being circumcised. Now that the Messiah of Israel has come and an ingathering of Gentiles into the newly con-stituted people of God is happening, a number of law-observant Jews are wondering why Paul and the church at Antioch are not insisting that the Gentile converts keep the law. This issue becomes divisive and threatens to split the movement. The wisest course of action is to convene a meeting with the leaders of the Jerusalem church and reach a mutual understanding that will govern the movement as more and more Gentiles put their faith in Jesus Christ.

Some men came down from Judea to Antioch (15:1). A faction within the Jerusalem church consisting of believers who have been Pharisees (see 15:5) are disturbed about the way Gentiles are being admitted into the church. They are upset that Gentile believers are not being circumcised as commanded by the law. To make sure that the Antioch church is not lax in its fidelity to God's law, a group of them make the three hundred-mile journey to Syria to press this issue. Verse 24 makes it clear that they are not authorized by the leaders of the Jerusalem church.

Unless you are circumcised, according to the custom taught by Moses, you cannot be saved (15:1). These Jewish believers, committed to the law of God, make it clear to the leaders of the church at Antioch that circumcision is essential to salvation. They are not excluding Gentiles from becoming authentic members of the people of God; they are simply insisting that they be circumcised.

Sharp dispute (15:2). The apostle Paul is equally convinced that circumcision is *not* necessary as a sign of the covenant for the newly constituted people of God. For Paul, this is not an issue on which the two

▶ The Perspective of a Pharisaic Jewish Believer on Circumcision

Circumcision was a sign and seal of the covenant relationship between God and his people. It began with God's covenant to Abraham and was thought to continue forever: "You are to undergo circumcision, and it will be the sign of the covenant between me and you . . . my covenant in your flesh is to be an everlasting covenant. . . . Any uncircumcised male, who has not been circumcised in the flesh, will be cut off from his people; he has broken my covenant" (Gen. 17:10, 13–14).

In the two centuries leading up to the time of Christ, circumcision became a hallmark of Israel's distinctiveness in relationship to the Gentile nations. The Syrian rulers had tried to forbid circumcision to the men of Israel. The Maccabean freedom fighters, in turn, reasserted the indispensability of circumcision and fought to retain this rite. Circumcision became the principal symbol of being a Jew. This attitude is well illustrated in the book of *Jubilees* (c. 180–170 B.C.): "Anyone who is born whose own flesh is not circumcised on the eighth day is not from the sons of the covenant which the Lord made for Abraham since he is from the children of destruction. And there is therefore no sign upon him so that he might belong to the Lord because he is destined to be destroyed and annihilated from the earth and to be uprooted from the earth

because he has broken the covenant of the Lord our God."[A-85]

When the Maccabees successfully revolted against the Syrians, they would not permit any Gentiles to remain in the country unless they were circumcised: "Hyrcanus . . . permitted them to stay in that country, if they would circumcise their genitals, and make use of the laws of the Jews; and they . . . submitted to the use of circumcision, and the rest of the Jewish ways of living; at which time therefore this befell them, that they were hereafter no other than Jews."[A-86]

Circumcision thus became the principal rite for Gentile proselytes to perform. The book of Judith (2d cent. B.C.) tells of a Gentile (an Ammonite) who joined the covenant people of God: "And when Achior saw all that the God of Israel had done, he believed firmly in God, and was circumcised, and joined the house of Israel, remaining so to this day."[A-87]

For these Pharisaic Jewish Christians, there was no clear indication that Jesus had abolished circumcision. Gentiles should enter the family of God not only by putting their faith in Jesus of Nazareth as the Messiah, but also by accepting the law, just as Gentiles had done historically. How, then, could the most important sign of the covenant be neglected?

▶ Gentile Attitudes About Circumcision

Gentiles were culturally predisposed to avoid circumcision. Although public nudity was acceptable in the context of the baths, gymnasia, and athletic events, circumcision was viewed as repugnant. "Circumcision became the target of horror, contempt, scorn, and ridicule."[A-88] Antiochus IV Epiphanes (c. 160 B.C.) outlawed circumcision with a penalty of death: Mothers with their circumcised babies were killed.[A-89] Philo writes that Jews were often ridiculed because of circumcision.[A-90]

One scholar observes: "Cultural pressure against circumcision manifested itself in several ways. Since Jews were widely known to be circumcised, they were frequently ridiculed and ostracized. The Greek gymnasium or the Roman bath, both favorite institutions of those who could afford them, presupposed public nudity. The severe social stigma against circumcision discouraged Jews from participating."[A-91]

parties should amiably "agree to differ." This is central to the gospel and needs to be settled by the principal leaders of the church—the apostles and elders in Jerusalem.

They traveled through Phoenicia and Samaria (15:3). This three hundred-mile journey is not an overnight ride. It takes a minimum of twenty days and probably takes them a month, given their stops along the way. The fruit of the evangelism of those Jerusalem believers scattered by the persecution is now seen (see 11:19). Communities of believers have been established not only in the territory of Phoenicia, but also in Samaria (see 8:5–25). Paul and Barnabas stop and fellowship with a number of these groups of believers. They encourage them by telling them the story of numerous Gentile conversions in Antioch, on the island of Cyprus, and in the regions of Cilicia and southern Galatia.

Believers who belonged to the party of the Pharisees (15:5). Not surprisingly, those who are the most vocal opponents of Paul's position were Pharisees prior to their conversion. In accepting Jesus as the Messiah of Israel, they have not changed their distinctive views about the law.

And required to obey the law of Moses (15:5). Here we find that the issue actually involves more than circumcision. The Pharisaic believers want the Gentiles to observe the entire law of Moses as a condition of membership in the people of God. This includes especially the laws regulating ritual purity, Sabbath observance, and the celebration of the key Jewish festivals. In the letter he writes to the Galatians just prior to the council, Paul explains the implications of the Pharisaic believers' view: "Again I declare to every man who lets himself be circumcised that he is obligated to obey the whole law" (Gal. 5:3).

The apostles and elders met to consider this question (15:6). Of the Twelve, Luke only explicitly mentions Peter, but presumably at least some of the others are present (see comments on 11:30). The fact that leaders from the church at Antioch travel to Jerusalem and meet with the leaders there shows the ongoing oversight for the entire movement exerted by the Jerusalem church and the commitment of both churches to be unified in the essential aspects of the gospel.

SAMARIA

The place of sacrifice on Mount Gerizim.

PHOENICIA

The modern city of Sidon.

Some time ago God made a choice (15:7). Peter, the principal leader among the Twelve, stands up and addresses the entire group. He begins by calling them to reflect back on the beginning of the Christian movement when God sovereignly chooses him to explain the gospel to Cornelius and his household some ten years ago.

He accepted them by giving the Holy Spirit to them (15:8). Peter does not take a "middle of the road" position on the issue. He presents a case firmly on the side of Paul and opposed to the Pharisaic believers. His argument is that God poured out his Spirit on Cornelius and his household before they received circumcision (and actually even before they received water baptism). For Peter, this signified God's sovereign decision to incorporate Gentiles into the one people of God solely on the basis of faith apart from a requirement of circumcision or law obedience.

He purified their hearts by faith (15:9). "Purification" and cleansing (*katharisas*) from sin no longer comes from the blood of the sacrifices, but by putting one's trust in the Messiah, who has poured out his blood to make purification for sin.[289]

You try to test God (15:10). Whether they do so wittingly or unwittingly, Peter accuses his Pharisaic brothers of putting God to the test by requiring circumcision and law-obedience of Gentile believers. Testing God is tantamount to unbelief. The Israelites repeatedly tested God in the desert by distrusting him and grumbling against what he was doing among them.[290] God himself has decided to free Christians (Jewish and Gentile) from the former obligations of circumcision and law-observance. To insist on these rites

and practices now, in light of the significance of the cross and resurrection of Christ, is to ignore the significance of what God has done and to blatantly provoke him.

Putting on the necks of the disciples a yoke (15:10). A yoke is a harness put around the neck and front quarters of a large animal enabling it to pull a farm implement or a wagon. It comes to represent any kind of burden someone endures and, in some instances, an image of bondage. Sin, for instance, is a yoke around a person's neck (Lam. 1:14). Jews referred to the law of Moses as a yoke, but one that protected them from the dangers of this world. The Mishnah says, "He that takes upon himself the yoke of the Law, from him shall be taken away the yoke of the kingdom [that is, the troubles that come from the earthly rulers] and the yoke of worldly care; but he that throws off the yoke of the Law, upon him shall be laid the yoke of the kingdom and the yoke of worldly care."[291] Peter, however, takes a much more negative view of the law—especially in terms of the numerous rituals, purity regulations, and various observances—viewing it as an inappropriate

YOKE

The man is plowing his field in the Nile Valley with a pair of bulls harnessed to a wooden yoke.

burden to place on Gentiles as a condition for their salvation.

Neither we nor our fathers have been able to bear (15:10). The law, taken together with the protective "fence" of traditions and regulations the Pharisees have built around it, is beyond human ability to keep. In this, Peter reflects the teaching of his master, who said to the Pharisees, "You load people down with burdens they can hardly carry, and you yourselves will not lift one finger to help them" (Luke 11:46).

We believe it is through the grace of our Lord Jesus that we are saved (15:11). The main point of Peter's argument is not how difficult the law is to keep, but rather its irrelevance now for salvation. Peter states unequivocally that salvation—for Jews as well as for Gentiles—is through grace and not by successfully completing the various requirements of the law. In this he is perfectly in line with Paul, who also stresses that salvation was a gift of God's grace (Eph. 2:8–9; Gal. 2:15–16). For Peter, the case of Cornelius and his household is paradigmatic. Their reception of the Spirit upon exercising faith in the Lord Jesus is sufficient evidence to convince him that God now receives Gentiles as his new covenant people solely on the basis of faith.

The whole assembly became silent (15:12). The silence of the crowd of believers may imply that the majority are

▶ The Jerusalem Council and Galatians

There has long been a debate in biblical scholarship over the relationship between Acts 15 and Galatians 2:1–10. On the surface, the correspondence between the two chapters suggests that Galatians 2 represents Paul's report about the conference to the Galatian Christians: It speaks of Paul and Barnabas going up to Jerusalem; a meeting with James, Peter, and John; a discussion about the Gentile mission and the role of circumcision; and an agreement reached by all the parties involved. This means that Galatians is written well after the Jerusalem council. Many who take this view see the letter written to Christians in the northern ethnic territory of Galatia, especially in the cities of Ankyra, Tavium, and Pessinus (places not mentioned by Luke in Acts).

A closer examination of the two texts, however, leads to the conclusion that the two passages are not referring to the same events. First, Acts 15 speaks of a meeting with the apostles, elders, and the entire church; the meeting in Galatians 2 is held privately with the "pillars" of the church. Second,

Galatians says nothing about the so-called "Apostolic Decree." Third, Paul's dispute with Peter (Gal. 2:11–21) is less likely to occur after the Jerusalem Council than before. Fourth, Luke speaks of three visits that Paul makes to Jerusalem: first (Acts 9:26–29), second (Acts 11:27–30; 12:25), and third (Acts 15). Paul refers to the events of Gal 2:1–10 as occurring on his second visit (Gal 2:1), i.e. the famine relief visit, not the Jerusalem Council visit.

In light of this evidence, it is best to see the events spoken of in Galatians 2 as having taken place on Paul's previous trip to Jerusalem recorded in Acts 11:30 and 12:25. This is the time when Paul and Barnabas take a relief gift to Christians in Jerusalem on behalf of the church at Antioch. It is a time conducive to a private meeting with James, Peter, and John to discuss the outreach to the Gentiles. This view is then understood as Paul writing Galatians just after his mission to Antioch, Iconium, Lystra, and Derbe (the southern part of the Roman province of Galatia) just prior to the Jerusalem Council.[A-92]

convinced by Peter and agree with him.[292] It must be remembered, however, that Luke does not give us a full account of the proceedings in Jerusalem, an account that would have taken many pages. Now the group listens to Paul and Barnabas describe the ways God has been at work through them in reaching Gentiles. The "signs and wonders" give further evidence of God's own sovereign inclusion of Gentiles on the basis of faith and not through fulfilling the requirements of the law.

James spoke up (15:13). On James, see comments on 12:17. He appears to have become one of the most significant leaders in the Jerusalem church. Like Peter, he does not lend his support to the position of the Pharisaic believers. He agrees with Paul and Barnabas in affirming that circumcision and law-obedience are not essential for obtaining salvation.

Simon (15:14). James refers to Peter by his Hebrew name (see 2 Peter 1:1).

Taking from the Gentiles a people for himself (15:14). God originally chose Israel, not the Gentiles (*ethnē*), to be his special people: "For you are a people holy to the LORD your God. Out of all the peoples (*ethnē*) on the face of the earth, the LORD has chosen you to be his treasured possession" (Deut. 14:2). James recognizes that there has been a fundamental change in the way God constitutes his people. Yet this change is not unanticipated, since Zechariah 2:11 predicted a future period when "many nations [*ethnē*] will be joined with the LORD in that day and will become my people." Once again, the conversion of Cornelius and his household is seen to mark this development in the plan of God.

I will return and rebuild David's fallen tent (15:16). James appeals to Amos 9:11–12 to provide further support for what Peter has said and what actually happened in the case of Cornelius and the many other Gentiles who believed the gospel and received the Spirit. This prophecy anticipates Gentiles becoming a part of God's people when the house of David is restored. The royal line of David reigning over Israel came to an end when Jehoiachin and Zedekiah were exiled to Babylon (2 Kings 24:15–25:7). This prophecy anticipates a reestablishment of David's kingdom. The Qumran community also understood this passage in a messianic sense.[293]

The coming of Jesus marks the restoration of "David's fallen tent." The conviction that Jesus of Nazareth is David's descendant who assumes the throne is at the heart of the gospel message (see Acts 2:29–36; 13:22–23).

That the remnant of men may seek the Lord, and all the Gentiles who bear my name (15:17). With the coming of Jesus as the Davidic Messiah, the extension of his reign over the Gentiles has now taken place. They enter the covenant people of God not by "becoming Jews," however, but as Gentiles by putting their faith in Jesus. The "remnant" is more properly translated "all other peoples"— that is, all the various ethnic groups comprising the Gentiles. There are many Old Testament prophecies that speak of the conversion of the nations in the messianic age.[294]

We should not make it difficult for the Gentiles (15:19). James comes down squarely on the side of Peter, Paul, and Barnabas. Because of his relationship with Peter as one of the "pillars" of the Jerusalem church (Gal. 2:7), it is doubtful that this decision reflects a change in his thinking from a position similar to the Pharisaic brothers. This meeting in Jerusalem appears to be the catalyst for formalizing a conviction that the Jerusalem leadership already holds, but that significantly challenges the Jewish believers who belong to the Pharisaic party.

The term translated "make it difficult" (*parenochleō*) is a strong, colorful, and somewhat pejorative term only appearing here in the New Testament. It is used in the Old Testament to describe what the lions could have done to Daniel (Dan. 6:19, 24 LXX) and to portray Delilah's nagging of Sampson (Judg. 16:16).

Telling them to abstain from (15:20). The focus of the debate now shifts away from the question of what is essential for salvation to one of how to help Gentile believers break away from their idolatrous pre-Christian practices. Each of these four instructions relates to dangers associated with involvement in idolatry. James wants to make sure that these Gentiles make a clean break with their past when they embrace the living and true God. The instructions are, therefore, guidelines to assist their growth as believers, knowing full well that the Gentiles will continue to face significant cultural and spiritual pressures stemming from their past immersion in idolatry and ongoing association with family, friends, and coworkers still involved with it. These guidelines are a practical help in the spiritual and moral battle these Gentiles will face.

Later, in a similar vein, Peter wrote a letter to Gentiles in the northern portion of Asia Minor, encouraging them to abstain from certain practices: "Dear friends, I urge you, as aliens and strangers in the world, to abstain from sinful desires, which war against your soul" (1 Peter 2:11). The apostle John abruptly ended his first letter with the warning, "Dear children, keep yourselves from idols" (1 John 5:21).

It is important that we do not view the so-called "Apostolic Decree" as a compromising effort of the Jewish leaders to get the Gentiles to obey at least some of the Jewish law. The decree is not at all a matter of law-obedience for the sake of obtaining salvation. Nor is the decree a concession to the law-oriented consciences of Jews who want the Gentiles to meet them halfway as a means of expressing cultural sensitivity and thereby promoting unified table fellowship. The latter view cannot explain why these four specific prohibitions are selected as opposed to others. In other words, why didn't the council restrict Gentiles from eating pork in the presence of Jewish believers?

Food polluted by idols (15:20). The Greek word *alisgēma* should not be limited to food, but should be understood as referring to any kind of contact with idolatrous practices. The church father Gregory of Nyssa describes well what James is referring to: "The pollution around the idols, the disgusting smell and smoke of sacrifices, the defiling gore about the altars, and the taint of blood from the offerings."[295] In his revelation on Sinai, the Lord explicitly prohibited the worship of other gods in the first two of the Ten Commandments (Ex. 20:2–6) and forbade offering sacrifices to idols (Lev. 17:7). This is one aspect of the law that is never repealed.

From sexual immorality (15:20). The term *porneia* is used in Judaism to refer to any kind of sexual activity outside the bond of marriage.[296] *Porneia* is roundly condemned throughout the New Testament.[297] The sexual mores of the Greek and Roman world were much more lax than what was expected and practiced in Judaism and early Christianity. This was certainly one area where new Gentile believers needed admonishment. But illicit sexual activity also occurred in connection with the worship of other gods.[298] Growing as a disciple of Christ meant leaving the sensual delights associated with idolatry.

From the meat of strangled animals and from blood (15:20). These prohibitions are often interpreted in light of Leviticus 17:10–16. In this context, both Israelites and resident Gentile aliens were commanded not to eat blood or any animal from which the blood had not been drained. But this view does not do justice to the precise wording of this text.

"The meat of strangled animals" is an interpretive translation of the Greek word *pnikton*, which simply means "choked" or "strangled." The term neither appears in Leviticus 17 nor anywhere else in the Old Testament, but is known and used in connection with pagan idolatry.[299] Both Jews and the early Christians are convinced that demonic spirits were involved in idolatry. When writing to the Corinthians, the apostle Paul wrote, "The sacrifices of pagans are offered to demons, not to God, and I do not want you to be participants with demons" (1 Cor. 10:20). In commenting on this passage, the church father Origen observes that demons especially like blood and sacrificial animals that have been strangled:

> As to things strangled, we are forbidden by Scripture to partake of them, because the blood is still in them; and blood, especially the odour arising from blood, is said to be the food of demons. Perhaps, then, if we were to eat of strangled animals, we might have such spirits feeding along with us.[300]

Similarly, Basil the Great, explains how demons savor the smell of burning blood from the burnt offering of a strangled animal:

> The demon sits in the idol, to which sacrifices are brought, and partakes of a part of the blood that has evaporated into the air as well as of the steam rising from the fat and from the rest of the burnt-offering.[301]

The so-called decree from the Jerusalem church may, therefore, best be understood as a set of guidelines to protect new Gentile believers from the many dangers of idolatry.[302] The intent of

◀ *left*

AN IDOL

Statue of the goddess Aphrodite.

these latter two prohibitions may help these Gentile believers avoid demonic influence that could arise after consuming sacrificial food.

For Moses has been preached in every city from the earliest times (15:21). James concludes his address by pointing out that the law of Moses is read in the synagogues on a regular basis in all the cities of the Mediterranean world where there are Jewish communities, which is certainly all major cities. Philo observes that "each seventh day there stand wide open in every city thousands of schools [viz., synagogues]" where anyone can come and hear the law of Moses being taught.[303]

The literal translation of this clause is, "Moses has those who are preaching him." Perhaps James concludes in this way to provide a contrast: There will continue to be those who proclaim Moses in the synagogues throughout the empire, burdening the Gentiles with the requirements of the law for salvation (Acts 15:19), but we will preach a message of grace based on faith in the work of Christ (15:11). James is not trying to reassure the Pharisaic Christians that the Gentile converts will learn the law of Moses in all of their respective cities. This wrongly assumes that these Gentiles will be attending the synagogue services every Sabbath.

They chose Judas (called Barsabbas) (15:22). What Peter and James say appears to gain the consensus of the Jerusalem church. They then choose two representatives from the church to travel to Antioch with Paul and Barnabas to communicate to the Gentile believers what has happened in the proceedings and to pass on the letter. Of Judas, also called Barsabbas (as was Joseph in 1:23), nothing else is known in the New Testament or later church history.

Silas (15:22). Silas is the shortened form of the name "Silvanus." He is here identified as a leader (*hēgoumenos*) in the Jerusalem church, which probably implies that he was an "elder" (*presbyteros*). It is not known whether he was from a Pharisaic background. Paul gains a great deal of confidence in this leader as they spend time together in Jerusalem and Antioch. Silas becomes a fellow missionary with Paul and helps to plant the churches in Philippi, Thessalonica, and Corinth (see the references to him in 16:19–18:5). He is mentioned by Paul in three of the letters.[304] He is not mentioned again after Paul leaves Corinth for Ephesus and then Jerusalem (unless the "Silas" Peter refers to in 1 Peter 5:12 is the same person). Luke comes into contact with Silas at Troas and journeys with the team to Philippi (see Acts 16:10–12). Silas may have been an important source of information for Luke about the early years of the Jerusalem church and the Jerusalem Council.

Some went out from us without our authorization and disturbed you (15:24). Luke now reveals that "the men who came down from Judea to Antioch" did so without the blessing and approval of the apostles and elders of the Jerusalem church. Some interpreters suggest that the Jerusalem church sent them on a "fact-finding" mission, but that they drastically overstepped their authority by insisting on circumcision and law observance.[305] The arrival of this law-oriented delegation in Antioch corresponds with the arrival of a similar delegation in the churches of Galatia (Gal. 1:7). Both had the same disruptive impact.

It seemed good to the Holy Spirit (15:28). There was a widespread conviction among the leaders of the Jerusalem church that the Holy Spirit led them in making these decisions. Given the gravity of this decision and its implications for the future direction of the church, it is especially significant to have this unanimity on discerning how the Spirit is directing them.

The Church at Antioch Receives the News (15:30–33)

They gathered the church together and delivered the letter (15:30). Letters are typically read aloud to groups in antiquity. They are not duplicated and distributed.

Glad for its encouraging message (15:31). Their worst fears—that the Pharisaic Christian delegation represent the convictions of the Jerusalem congregation—are alleviated. The Gentile Christians in Antioch now rejoice in a reaffirmation of the genuine unity with the Jerusalem church. They are probably also encouraged by the letter giving wise

> ### REFLECTIONS
>
> **THE SAME SPIRIT WHO LED THE**
> first century church indwells the lives of
> godly leaders in the church today. Contro-
> versy and passionate debate over sub-
> stantive issues are inevitable. But are we
> truly submitting the issues to the Lord and
> asking for the guidance of his Spirit? Are
> we examining our motives to see if there
> are other less godly pressures inclining us
> to a certain view on a matter?

guidance to stimulate their growth in the faith.

Who themselves were prophets, said much to encourage and strengthen the brothers (15:32). Luke now informs us that Judas and Silas are prophets. Although Christians often think of prophecy primarily in terms of revelatory insight into future events, there is a strong edificatory function in prophecy, as exhibited here (see 1 Cor. 14:3).

Paul Returns to South Galatia (15:36–40)

Let us go back and visit the brothers in all the towns (15:36). Paul's proposal to Barnabas is to return and visit all of the new believers from their recent trip across the island of Cyprus as well as Antioch, Iconium, Lystra, and Derbe in the southern part of the Roman province of Galatia.

They had such a sharp disagreement that they parted company (15:39). Apparently Paul is still upset about John Mark's sudden departure during their initial journey to Asia Minor (see 13:13). He does not see John Mark as a suitable coworker for the kind of rigorous mission work they will be engaging in. The word translated "sharp disagreement" (*paroxysmos*) is a rare and colorful word. It is used only twice in the Greek Old Testament—in both instances to express "the furious anger" of God.[306] Whatever it is that so exasperated Paul about John Mark was overcome in the next few years and the two are completely reconciled. He was with Paul ten years later during his Roman imprisonment (Col. 4:10; Philem. 24), and Paul asked for him during his subsequent imprisonment in terms expressing his high esteem: "Get Mark and bring him with you, because he is helpful to me in my ministry" (2 Tim. 4:11).

Barnabas took Mark and sailed for Cyprus (15:39). Accompanied by Mark, Barnabas returns to his native island to continue the evangelization of the cities and villages that he began with Paul. This is the last that we hear of Barnabas in the biblical record.

Paul chose Silas and left (15:40). Not wanting to travel alone and aware of the significant giftedness of Silas, Paul contacts him (he is presumably still in Jerusalem) and asks him to be his coworker in the mission. Because of Silas's prominent role as a leader in the Jerusalem church, he is an important voice for the churches in Galatia disturbed by the Pharisaic Christians insisting on circumcision and law observance.

He went through Syria and Cilicia (15:40). Rather than taking a boat from Seleucia to Attalia, Paul decides to take an overland route. This enables him to visit and encourage churches that he and others had previously established in these regions, including his hometown of Tarsus (see 9:30; 11:25). This rugged route takes him through a narrow mountainous pass called the "Cilician Gates."

Revisiting the Galatian Churches (Acts 16:1–5)

A disciple named Timothy (16:1). During Paul's initial visit to Lystra, members of three generations of one family come to faith in Jesus Christ—a grandmother (Lois), a mother (Eunice), and a son (Timothy) (see 2 Tim. 1:5). This young man, Timothy, has taken root and grown so much in his faith and the knowledge of the Lord that Paul now wants him to accompany him and Silas in their missionary efforts.

Timothy becomes Paul's most valuable coworker over the span of the next fifteen years. He works alongside Paul in the evangelization of Philippi, Thessalonica, Berea (Acts 17:14–15), Corinth (18:5; 2 Cor. 1:19), and Ephesus (Acts 19:22). During Paul's Ephesian ministry, Timothy serves as Paul's emissary to the Corinthian church for handling some of the problems that surface there (1 Cor. 4:17; 16:10). In a similar way, he serves the Philippian church (Phil. 2:19) and

right ▶

ANTIOCH OF SYRIA TO SOUTH GALATIA

the Thessalonian church (1 Thess. 3:2, 6). He is also named as a cowriter of Paul's second letter to the Corinthians (2 Cor. 1:1; Phil. 1:1) as well as his letters to the Thessalonians (1 Thess. 1:1; 2 Thess. 1:1), the Colossians (Col. 1:1), and to Philemon (Philem. 1). Shortly before the end of his life, Paul writes Timothy two personal letters: One gives a variety of instructions for exercising leadership in the church at Ephesus (1 Tim.) and the other offers significant advice and encouragement to the young coworker as Paul awaits death in a Roman prison (2 Tim.). Paul's affection for him is summed up well in a remark he makes to the Philippian church: "As a son with his father he has served with me in the work of the gospel" (Phil. 2:22).

It appears that Timothy is known to the writer of Hebrews. The reference to him in that book refers to his recent release from prison (Heb. 13:23).

Whose mother was a Jewess and a believer, but whose father was a Greek (16:1). The fact that Timothy has a Greek father and has not been circumcised suggests that he was not brought up in a strictly observant Jewish household. Such a mixed marriage between a Jew and a Greek was illegal in Jewish law.[307] According to rabbinic texts, descent is reckoned from the mother's line in the event of an illegal marriage, which means that Timothy is regarded as a Jew by the Jewish community.[308] It was not uncommon to find mixed marriages in the Diaspora. The tense of the verb in the passage suggests that Timothy's father has died.

He circumcised him because of the Jews who lived in that area (16:3). Some think Paul is grossly inconsistent in this action. After all, he comes from the Jerusalem Council, where circumcision and law

obedience are deemed unnecessary. But it must be recognized that Paul's purpose in circumcising Timothy is not to ensure him or others of the fact that he is now saved; Timothy is already a vibrant believer. His purpose is strategic. The Jews who live in the area know that Timothy is a Jew, but they would regard him

◀

DERBE

The countryside south of Derbe from on top of the ancient site.

LYSTRA INSCRIPTION

The name "Lystra" appears in this inscription at the Konya museum.

▼

as an apostate since he is not circumcised. If Paul wants to continue to have access to the synagogues, here and elsewhere, as a part of his evangelistic strategy, he needs to make Timothy acceptable to Jews. This action accords well with what Paul says elsewhere about the overriding concerns of the gospel: "Though I am free and belong to no man, I make myself a slave to everyone, to win as many as possible. To the Jews I became like a Jew, to win the Jews. To those under the law I became like one under the law (though I myself am not under the law), so as to win those under the law" (1 Cor. 9:19–20). There was nothing inherently evil now in circumcision. It is a matter of indifference as long as it is not mistakenly taken as essential to salvation (1 Cor. 7:19).

They delivered the decisions (16:4). Paul by no means ignores the outcome of the Council's decisions. He faithfully passes these on to the churches in every city. In this regard, Silas fills a vital role in confirming and explaining the Jerusalem church's decisions to Jewish Christians. As a leader of the Jerusalem church, he commands a great deal of respect. Four cities were evangelized in Paul's first visit to this area. It is possible that these new believers shared their faith in other

towns and villages in south Galatia since then, resulting in communities of believers in other places.

Paul's Vision of a Man in Macedonia (Acts 16:6–10)

The region of Phrygia and Galatia (16:6). This expression is better translated "the region of Phrygian Galatia" (also known as Phrygia Paroreius). Phrygia here serves as an adjective modifying Galatia.[309] When the Romans created the political province of Galatia in 25 B.C., they incorporated a portion of the ethnic territory of Phrygia. The rest of Phrygia was included in the Roman province of Asia.[310] In 16:1, Luke tells us that Paul came to Lystra and Derbe (not in Phrygian Galatia). Now Paul continues his journey through Phrygian Galatia (this includes the cities of Iconium and Antioch). This interpretation of the phrase stands in contrast to the view of some other interpreters who do not take Phrygia as an adjective here and interpret Galatia as a reference to the northern ethnic territory of Galatia. They would then see this as a highly abbreviated reference to Paul evangelizing the cities of Ancyra, Tavium, and Pessinus.[311] But this is unlikely since this region of north Galatia lies over 125 miles northeast of any route between Lystra and the region of Mysia.[312]

Kept by the Holy Spirit from preaching the word in the province of Asia (16:6). Paul apparently follows the principal Roman road called the *Via Sebaste* from Lystra to Antioch. From there, he probably intends to take the road that runs due west through Apamea, Colossae, and Laodicea to the Asia Minor capital of Ephesus.

ASIA MINOR

This map shows the region of "Phrygian Galatia."

They came to the border of Mysia (16:7). Paul now journeys northwest from Antioch along the major road to either Cotiaeum or further north to Dorylaeum. Both of these cities are close to the ancient territories of Mysia and Bithynia. Mysia is part of the Roman province of Asia Minor and is bordered by Lydia to the south, Phrygia to the east, and Bithynia to the north. Two of the principal cities of Mysia are Adramytium and Pergamum.

They tried to enter Bithynia (16:7). Bithynia is a territory in northern Asia Minor that forms a dual Roman province with Pontus.[313] Because Ephesus is closed to him, it is not surprising that Paul wants to enter this region since the city of Byzantium (later to become Constantinople) is located here as well as other important cities such as Nicomedia (the seat of the Roman government), Nicaea, and Prusa. Although Paul never has the opportunity to preach the gospel in this region, the apostle Peter later spends time evangelizing in Bithynia and Pontus (see 1 Peter 1:1).

Paul had a vision of a man of Macedonia (16:9). When Paul reaches Troas, he cannot go any farther west by land and the Lord has directed him not to go north or south. Is he to stay in Troas? Where is he to go? In the midst of this quandary, the Lord gives him a night vision that

▶Alexandria Troas

Paul and his companions come to Troas after the Holy Spirit prevents them from going north to Bithynia or south to Mysia or Ephesus. Paul also spends some time there after his Ephesian ministry (Acts 20:5–6).

Troas was properly called "Alexandria Troas" or "Alexandria" of the Troad.[A-93] It was believed that the Troad was the area originally under Trojan rule during the time of Homer. The city was originally called Antigoneia, but was renamed in honor of Alexander the Great. The city was located on the west coast of Asia Minor about ten miles south of the ancient city of Troy (Ilium) and was the major seaport for northwest Asia Minor because of its artificial harbor.

Augustus made the city a Roman colony, the only one he established in western Asia Minor. By Paul's time Strabo spoke of Troas as "one of the famous cities of the world."[A-94] The city had a temple dedicated to the god Smintheus, a god of healing and associated with Asclepios.

The ruins are located on a site called Eski Stamboul and remain unexcavated. Recently, however, E. Schwertheim and C. Özgünel have jointly inaugurated an expedition to conduct a thorough site survey.[A-95]

provides him with clear direction. There have been some creative guesses as to the identity of this man of Macedonia, ranging from Luke to Alexander the Great. It is unlikely that the Lord gives him a vision of any particular person other than the fact that the man is clearly identifiable as a Macedonian.

We got ready (16:10). Luke's narrative now abruptly changes from the third person ("he" and "they") to the first person ("we"). The best explanation for this is that Luke, the author of Acts, now joins the team of Paul, Silas, and Timothy. It is possible that Troas was Luke's home although there is a strong historical tradition that Luke is from Antioch of Syria.[314] Some speculate that Luke lives in Philippi and that, as an itinerant doctor, he travels between Philippi and Troas.[315] Wherever he is from, Luke is already a believer and an ardent supporter of this missionary outreach to the Gentiles. He travels with the team to Philippi and apparently remains there after the other three leave (this is where the "we" passages end for a time).

The Evangelization of Philippi (Acts 16:11–40)

Luke tells the exciting and dramatic story of the creation of the church in Philippi by giving three vignettes involving people who come in contact with the gospel. One is a prominent, wealthy, Gentile businesswoman who is already a Jewish sympathizer and attached to the local synagogue. The second is a low-status slave girl who is being exploited for spirit-inspired divination abilities. Luke never says that she puts her faith in Christ, but the account of Paul's encounter with her demonstrates the power of Christ over the realm of the demonic. The final episode involves a Roman official charged with keeping Paul and Silas in custody. He is ready to commit suicide until the missionaries intervene and give him hope rooted in Jesus Christ.

▶ Macedonia

The region of Macedonia had an illustrious history as the homeland of Philip II of Macedon and his son, Alexander the Great. From Philip's time on, Macedonia was a leading center and purveyor of Greek culture. The territory lay between the Balkans and the Greek peninsula.[A-96] In spite of its distinctiveness, Macedonia was often considered to have been a part of Greece.

Caesar Augustus (Octavian) made Macedonia a Roman senatorial province in 27 B.C., but this was later combined into one large province with Achaia by Tiberius. In A.D. 44, six years before Paul's visit, the emperor Claudius once again separated Macedonia into a distinct senatorial province. Macedonia was divided into four separate districts with the cities Amphipolis, Thessalonica, Pella, and Pelagonia as the administrative centers of each. Augustus established four cities in the province as Roman colonies: Philippi, Kassandreia, Dion, and Pella.

Numerous gods and goddesses were worshiped throughout this province, including Zeus, Apollo, Artemis, Bendis (goddess of the forests and fertility), the Cabiri, *Theos Hypsistos* ("God most high"), Herakles, Dionysus, the Egyptian deities Serapis and Isis, and *Dea Syria* (Atargatis).[A-97] The emperor cult and the cult of *Roma* (the deified personification of Rome) were also well established. The New Testament is the most important witness for a Jewish presence in Macedonia.

◀

Sailed straight for Samothrace (16:11). Samothrace is a small island (sixty-nine square miles) in the northern Aegean sea lying twenty-five miles south of the Thracian coast. The name reveals the island's historical connection with Thrace—it is the "Samos" ("height" or "mountain") of Thrace. This reflects the fact that a mountainous peak rises to a height of 5250 feet on the island. The mountain makes the island visible for boats passing through the Hellespont and provides a safe anchorage on the north side of the island. On the way to Macedonia, Paul's boat apparently spends the night at this port. The island is best known as the center of worship for the cult of the Cabiri.

The next day on to Neapolis (16:11). Neapolis (modern Kavála) is the principal port city for this district of Macedonia and serves its main city, Philippi, which is located nine miles inland. After landing here, Paul most likely takes the

famous Roman highway called the *Egnatian Way* to Philippi. The road continues west from Philippi through Amphipolis and Thessalonica and on to the Adriatic sea. One scholar rightly notes, "The mention of the seaport and the island of Samothrace are unnecessary detail in the account of the trip to the main destination of Philippi . . . but it is detail that is understandable in an alleged eyewitness account."[316]

NEAPOLIS

The modern harbor
at Kavala, the site
of ancient Neapolis.

▼

PHILIPPI

Ruins of the
ancient city.
▼ ▶

A Roman colony (16:12). Augustus created the Roman colony of Philippi expressly for the purpose of making homes for his military veterans. He was also motivated by a desire to establish a military presence in this strategic area and to further the cultural and political Romanization of Macedonia. Philippi had a sizeable population of Latin-speak-

▶ Philippi

Properly known as *Colonia Julia Augusta Philippensis,* Philippi was famous in antiquity as the place commemorating the victory of Octavian (later called Caesar Augustus) over the murderers of Julius Caesar, Brutus, and Cassius in 42 B.C.[A-98] Following the battle, Augustus made Philippi a Roman colony and renamed it after his daughter.

The city was founded nearly four hundred years earlier and called *Krenides* because of the springs in the area. It was located not far from the base of Mt. Pangaion, where there were a number of productive gold mines. Shortly after it was established, the town was taken over by the rising Greek leader, Philip of Macedon (father of Alexander the Great), who renamed it after himself.

The Roman colony occupied a vast portion of the plain of Datos. It was a wealthy city because of the mines, its relationship to Rome, and its commer-

cial importance on the *Via Egnatia.* The population would have consisted of a mixture of Greeks, Romans, native Thracians, and foreigners.

Emperor worship thrived in the city, but so did the worship of Greek, Roman, Thracian, Egyptian, and Asia Minor deities. Among the most prominent were Dionysus, Bendis (a local Thracian deity), Artemis, Apollo Comaeus, Isis, Liber Pater, Hercules, the Thracian Horseman, and the cult of the emperors (Augustus, Livia, and Claudius).

Among the remains of Philippi visible today is a theater (built in the 4th cent. B.C. and altered by the Romans in the third cent. A.D.), two Byzantine era churches (Basilica A = c. A.D. 500; Basilica B = c. A.D. 560), some scant remains of the ancient forum, and the foundations of the sanctuary dedicated to the Egyptian deities.

ing Roman citizens. Colonies were often initially established with between two and five thousand men.[317] The citizens were probably extended the privilege of the *ius Italicum*, giving them the same rights as colonies in Italy and *immunitas* (exemption from direct taxation).

The leading city of that district of Macedonia (16:12). Politically, Philippi was not the leading city. Thessalonica was the seat of the Roman procounsul for the entirety of Macedonia and Amphipolis the center of Roman administration for this one of the four districts of Macedonia. By this expression "first city" (*prōtē polis*), Luke accurately conveys the local sense of pride in Philippi as the "leading city"—even over the regional capital.

We went outside the city gate to the river (16:13). The "river" (*potamos*) refers either to the River Gangites or to a stream that flows a short distance away from the city's west gate.[318]

A place of prayer (16:13). Many commentators assume that there was no synagogue in Philippi and that there was simply an area by the river Gangites that the Jews had agreed to meet each Sabbath. But there may have been a synagogue building there. The Greek term *proseuchē* can mean "prayer," but in Jewish circles it was also a common term for "a house of prayer," that is, a synagogue. By referring to the Philippian synagogue as a *proseuchē*, Luke simply reflects what they likely called it, similar to the usage of Jews in Palestine and Egypt.[319] Jews commonly built syn-

agogues outside of cities near the sea or by rivers to facilitate their ritual washings. A recently discovered grave stele from the western cemetery of Philippi mentions the presence of a synagogue in the city: "Nikostratos Aurelios Oxycholios himself furnished this flat tomb and if someone lays down on it a dead body of others, he will give a fine to the synagogue."[320] The inscription, however, dates to a time later than Paul's ministry in the city—probably to the early third century.

right ▶

PURPLE DYE

Shellfish from which a purple fluid was extracted and used in the production of dye.

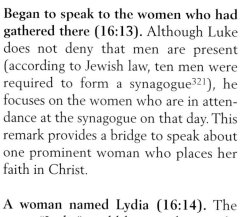

Began to speak to the women who had gathered there (16:13). Although Luke does not deny that men are present (according to Jewish law, ten men were required to form a synagogue[321]), he focuses on the women who are in attendance at the synagogue on that day. This remark provides a bridge to speak about one prominent woman who places her faith in Christ.

A woman named Lydia (16:14). The name "Lydia" could be an ethnic nickname for this woman—Lydia was the ethnic territory in western Asia Minor where the city of Thyatira was located. There are inscriptions, however, that attest to Lydia as a proper name in Asia Minor, such as one referring to Julia Lydia Laterane of Ephesus, "high priestess and daughter of Asia."[322]

A dealer in purple cloth from the city of Thyatira (16:14). The dyeing of fabrics in the city of Thyatira was well known in the ancient world, which included a long history. Homer speaks of purple-dyeing taking place in the regions of Lydia and Caria as early as his time.[323] Pliny notes that the practice was invented by the Lydians in the city of Sardis.[324] Seven

inscriptions have now been discovered that attest to a guild of dyers in Thyatira.[325] One inscription even speaks of the guild of purple dyers in Thessalonica honoring one of their members who was Thyatiran.[326] Two inscriptions discovered in Philippi mention "sellers of purple."[327] Purple dye was commonly made from a marine shellfish called a *Murex*, but there is also evidence that dyers from this area used the root from a madder plant.

It is not surprising to find a woman undertaking such business in Macedonia or in Asia Minor. Women had begun taking on significant business and civic roles in these areas. Evidently, Lydia had moved to Philippi and set up a business of selling dyed fabrics to Romans in the colony. Her business was apparently doing well if she owned a house large enough to accommodate Paul and his team in addition to the members of her household.

A worshiper of God (16:14). Lydia is not a Jew, but she becomes exposed to the God of Israel through the local synagogue and places her faith in him. Many more women were God-fearers in the

ancient world than men. Of all the Jewish inscriptions discovered thus far that mention God-fearers, about 80 percent are women.[328]

She and the members of her household were baptized (16:15). After listening to Paul's teaching about Jesus as the Messiah, Lydia and her entire household believe the gospel and are immediately baptized. Her household includes any of her children still living at home and her domestic servants. It is most likely that she has been widowed, although we cannot rule out the possibility that she is divorced (keeping in mind that divorce was less common than it is now).

Come and stay at my house (16:15). Just as Peter stayed at the house of the Gentile Cornelius, Paul, Silas, Timothy, and Luke now stay at the home of a single Gentile businesswoman. For Silas, as an elder from the Jerusalem church, this is undoubtedly a difficult step to take in light of his former Jewish scruples about Gentile impurity.

A slave girl who had a spirit by which she predicted the future (16:16). This young girl receives her inspiration from what Luke literally calls a "python spirit" (*pneuma pythōn*). The Python dragon or serpent was associated with the oracle sanctuary at Delphi, about eighty miles northwest of Athens. In the story of the origin of the cult, Apollo killed this large snake that was guarding the entrance to the oracle cave. Apollo then became the guardian and patron of this sanctuary, which was an entrance to the underworld. During the Greco-Roman era, people came from all over the Mediterranean world to consult the priestesses of Apollo (called *pythia*) for advice. The Pythia descended into the oracle grotto to seek inspiration from the god by allowing herself to be possessed by a spirit. She then arose and uttered the god's instructions to the inquirer—first in an ecstatic, gibberish speech and then typically in the form of Greek verse.[329] The first-century writer Plutarch, himself a priest of the Delphic god, refers to the priestesses as *engastrimythoi* ("belly talkers") because of

bottom left

STATUE OF THE GOD APOLLO

APOLLO TEMPLE AT DELPHI

The *omphalos* stone (the "navel of the earth") at Apollo's famous sanctuary in Greece.

▼

the sound of their voices as the god or spirit spoke through them.[330]

These men are servants of the Most High God (16:17). "Most High" is a title given to God in the Old Testament emphasizing his sovereignty. The LXX often translates ʾelyôn with *hypsistos*, as in Deuteronomy 32:8, "when the Most High (ʾelyôn/hypsistos) gave the nations their inheritance. . . ."[331] Some scholars suggest that the young girl is referring not to the God of Israel, but to a deity known in the Greco-Roman world as *Theos Hypsistos*. This is, at least, how Philippian Gentiles who hear the girl's screams might understand her.[332] The worship of such a deity, sometimes associated with Zeus, is well attested in inscriptions. It is more likely, however, that the indwelling python spirit rightly recognizes the connection of Paul and his companions to the one true God. This explains, in part, the reason why the slave girl harasses the missionaries. This is also consistent with the way one of the spirits manifesting in the Gerasene demoniac responds to Jesus with the exclamation: "What do you want with me, Jesus,

Son of the Most High (*theos hypsistos*) God" (Luke 8:28; Mark 5:7).

In the name of Jesus Christ I command you to come out of her! (16:18). Paul discerns in this slave girl an evil spirit, or demon, that enables her to practice divination. Following the example of Jesus and based on the authority of his name, Paul firmly commands the demon to leave, and it promptly obeys.

REFLECTIONS

EVIL SPIRITS HAVE NOT DISAP-peared since Jesus' day; nor have they turned into psychological pathologies. They continue to exist and do all they can to oppose the redemptive work of God in the world. In the same way that Paul dealt with these spirits, we can effectively deal with them as well. Overcoming them has nothing to do with our own strength, but the power and authority of acting in the name of Jesus by virtue of our close relationship with him.

PHILIPPI

(left) Small temples cut into the rock hillside near the theater in honor of Artemis and Silvanus.

(right) Temple ruins.

Paul's method leaves an impression of awe and curiosity on many who witness the event. His method differs sharply from other exorcists, who performed rituals (often involving animal viscera and blood), used various substances, uttered strings of unintelligible sounds, and invoked a number of deities and helper spirits (they frequently included Hekate, the goddess of the underworld). It also was unusual for any other pagan shaman/exorcist to seek to remove a "python spirit," which was thought to be a good and helpful spirit, not a malevolent one. Of course for Paul, this is part of the deception of idolatry. This attitude toward a Python spirit is consistent with his Jewish background, which taught that a person who has a Python and "speaks from his armpits" has "a familiar spirit."[333]

In the subsequent history of the church, "python spirits" are seen as evil and are subject to exorcism. Origen speaks of some who "have been under the influence of the demon called Python, i.e. the ventriloquial spirit, from the commencement of their existence."[334] Another early church leader observes, "For pythons prophesy, yet they are cast out by us as demons and put to flight."[335]

Realized that their hope of making money was gone (16:19). The passage literally reads, "their hope of making money had gone out of her," which highlights the fact that her fortune telling was not a gimmick, but was dependent on the python spirit that lived within her. This poor girl was doubly exploited—by the spirit and by those who owned her.

Dragged them into the marketplace to face the authorities (16:19). The missionaries are taken to the *agora*, or, as the Romans called it, the *forum*. There they are accused before the *stratēgoi*, the equivalent of the Latin *duoviri* (lit., "the two men")—the two principal city officials in any Roman colony. They are responsible for judging cases and wielding the power to inflict punishment. Helmut Koester comments that the use of this term here "reveals Luke's good knowledge of the local situation."[336]

These men are Jews . . . advocating customs unlawful for us Romans to accept or practice (16:20). Luke previously explained the real motive of the accusers was that they were furious about their loss of potential income. When they now bring their case to the judges, however, they begin their case with racial comments. This is not surprising since anti-Jewish feelings were common among the Romans.[337] Tacitus goes so far as to denounce the Jews by saying that "they have a hostile hatred of all men."[338]

▶ An Example of a Roman Beating

Cicero gives an account of a man named Gaius Servilius who suffered an official beating from Roman *rhabdychoi* (Latin = *lictors*): He was beaten "till finally the senior lictor Sextius . . . took the butt end of his stick, and began to strike the poor man violently across the eyes, so that he fell helpless to the ground, his face and eyes streaming with blood. Even then his assailants continued to rain blows on his prostrate body. . . . Such was the treatment he then received; and having been carried off for dead at the time, very soon afterwards he died."[A-99]

The principal charge, however, is not exactly a fabrication. Roman law prohibited the adoption of foreign cults: "No one shall have gods for himself, either new or foreign gods, unless they are officially recognized."³³⁹ In practice, this law was typically overlooked, but it was a convenient and effective charge for the owners of the slave girl.

Stripped and beaten . . . thrown into prison (16:22–23). Paul and Silas receive a severe punishment. They are handed over to the *rhabdychoi* ("rod bearers") and shackled in the city prison. It appears that Timothy and Luke somehow escape this punishment, possibly because they are not as actively engaged in the preaching and in the exorcism as their companions, or possibly because they are not Jews. It is curious why Paul and Silas do not invoke their Roman citizenship at this point to avoid this painful and degrading punishment. It is worth remembering, however, that Paul's principal allegiance is to Christ, not to Rome. Paul knows that if a church is successfully established in Philippi, these new believers will assuredly face hostile opposition from the local populace (as indeed was the case not only here, but in Thessalonica and elsewhere). Not all of these people would be protected from punishment by Roman citizenship. His suffering demonstrates that the gospel is for all people, not just Roman citizens, and that it is worth suffering for (see Phil. 3:20). This is only one of three occasions in which Paul faced this kind of beating (2 Cor. 11:25).

He put them in the inner cell and fastened their feet in the stocks (16:24). The inner cell was typically reserved for those who committed serious crimes and for those of low social status. The magistrates intended to demoralize and humiliate the two men.³⁴⁰

A set of Roman leg stocks was found in the Gladiators Barracks at Pompeii, Italy, and illustrate the kind of mechanism securing Paul and Silas. It was a long metal comb with spaces between each of the teeth for the legs of a number of prisoners to be placed. A metal rod was inserted into the holes in the top of each tooth and anchored to the floor. The bar pressed tightly on the legs and made it impossible for the prisoners to shift positions to avoid discomfort. Sleep was only possible

PHILIPPIAN JAIL

(left) Ruins of the structure that is traditionally identified as the prison where Paul stayed.

(right) An inner cell.
▼

through laying or sitting on the floor. The stocks were not only a security measure, but were also a form of torture.[341]

Singing hymns to God (16:25). In spite of the indignity, shame, and physical pain they suffer, both from the severe beating as well as from the leg stocks and the repulsive conditions of the inner cell, Paul and Silas find joy in their Lord. This is as much a demonstration of the power of the Spirit as the exorcism they have just performed. Among the hymns they sing are probably not only some of the Old Testament Psalms, but also new compositions in honor and praise of Christ (Col. 3:16).

A violent earthquake (16:26). There is nothing surprising about an earthquake rocking this region. It was prone to more severe earthquakes than it is today. What is surprising, though, is the timing of the quake and its impact on the prison; that is, it loosens the leg stocks from the floor of the prison.

Sirs, what must I do to be saved? (16:30). The potential escape of all of the prisoners causes the jailer to fear for his own life as a penalty for the escape of any of his wards while he is on duty. Faced with the ultimate question of life—"What happens when I die?"—the jailer asks Paul and Silas. Most likely the jailer has heard some of the hymns Paul and Silas sang and possibly overheard them sharing the gospel with other prisoners. So, at his moment of crisis, he has heard enough to know that these two men have the answers.

He was filled with joy (16:34). Rejoicing is a common response for those who believe the gospel (e.g., the new believers in Jerusalem, 2:46; the Ethiopian, 8:39;

the Gentiles at Pisidian Antioch, 13:48, 52) and a sign of the presence of the Holy Spirit.[342]

When it was daylight (16:35). The hours between midnight and 7:00 A.M. are eventful for Paul and Silas: a major earthquake (and presumably a number of aftershocks), preventing a suicide, leading the jailer to Christ, having their wounds treated, sharing the gospel with the jailer's family, baptizing them, and enjoying a meal with this family of new believers. The weary and wounded missionaries now have another big day in front of them.

Release those men (16:35). Perhaps the magistrates originally only desired to hold the men overnight as a deterrent to their activities. But they may also have now connected the earthquake with the two men and want them out of town as soon as possible.[343] Greeks and Romans often saw natural phenomena, such as earthquakes, as omens and signs from the gods.

Even though we are Roman citizens (16:37). Roman law prohibited Roman citizens from receiving the kind of treatment Paul and Silas suffered. The Roman historian Livy writes, "The Porcian law alone seems to have been passed to protect

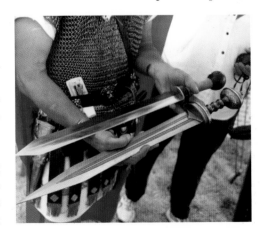

ROMAN SWORDS

Models of ancient Roman swords.

the persons of the citizens, imposing, as it did, a heavy penalty if anyone should scourge or put to death a Roman citizen."[344] The later Julian laws upheld the Porcian laws: "Also liable under the *Lex Julia* on public violence is anyone who, while holding *imperium* or office, puts to death or flogs a Roman citizen contrary to his [right of] appeal."[345] It is not surprising, then, that the magistrates are greatly alarmed.

Then they left (16:40). Luke apparently remains in Philippi since he does not here say, "then *we* left." Because he is not Jewish and not at the center of the controversy, Luke is not likely under the same pressure to leave. It is also possible that he is already known in the city as a medical doctor. The circumstances provide him with the opportunity to stay and help these new believers grow in the faith. Luke reappears in the narrative in 20:5–6 some six or seven years later. He is still in Philippi, but joins Paul for his trip to Jerusalem at the conclusion of the so-called third missionary journey.

Reaching Thessalonica (Acts 17:1–9)

Taking the famous Egnatian Way—the road leading west from Byzantium to the Adriatic sea—Paul, Silas, and Timothy travel a hundred miles from Philippi to Thessalonica. The party decides to spend no time in the cities of Amphipolis and Apollonia (except for a possible stayover of a night in each city). Amphipolis is situated on a hill surrounded on three sides by the river Strymon. As beautiful and significant as these cities are, Paul desires to go to the strategic center for the province—Thessalonica. From there, the entire province can hear the gospel message, as in fact happened (see 1 Thess. 1:8).

Thessalonica (17:1). The city was named after the half-sister of Alexander the Great when it was founded in 315 B.C. by her husband Cassander. It became the seat for the Roman governor and the capital for the entire province of Macedonia. Possessing a fine harbor, Thessalonica

▶ The Gods and Goddesses Worshiped at Thessalonica

Just like any other city in the Mediterranean world, Thessalonica had an array of cults.[A-100] The Greek deities Zeus, Asclepius, Aphrodite, and Demeter were popular among the people. Archaeologists have discovered the remains of a sanctuary in the sacred cult area of the city devoted to the Egyptian god Sarapis. This deity was worshiped as one who healed the sick, worked miracles, broke the powers of astral fate, and could speak to his followers in dreams. Many of the inscriptions found at this site also point to the worship of the Egyptian goddess Isis.

By far the most popular cult of the city was the cult of the Cabirus. Not well known, this cult had a wild, bloody, and sexually perverse set of features. The central myth of this cult involved two brothers killing a third, decapitating the body, and burying the head at Mount Olympus. One of the key symbols of the cult was the male genitals. In a similar way, the cult of Dionysus gave prominence to phallic symbolism in addition to the drunken revelry that went along with the celebrations of the god. These two cults certainly had a powerfully negative impact on the social ethics of the city. Converts from these cults had a long way to go in appropriating a distinctively Christian lifestyle.

In addition to these traditional deities, the Thessalonians also revered the Roman rulers as divine. During the reign of Caesar Augustus, a temple was built for the ruler cult to honor Augustus and his successors.

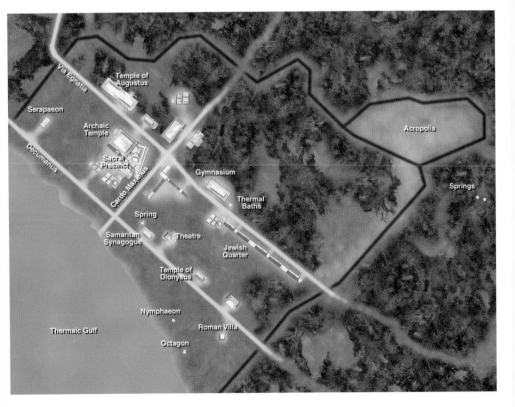

became the chief seaport of Macedonia. Although we do not have precise figures about the population of the city, Strabo notes that it was the most populous city in Macedonia.[346] The modern city of Salonica (or Thessaloniki) occupies the site of the ancient city and thereby hinders the undertaking of any extensive archaeological work. With a population of over a half-million, the modern city is the second largest city of Greece.[347]

Jewish synagogue (17:1). Archaeologists still have not discovered the remains of the synagogue. A few Jewish inscriptions, however, have been discovered in the city. An inscription published in 1994 that dates to the third century A.D. actually points to the existence of a number of synagogues in the city. The inscription on a sarcophagus (a stone coffin) warns intruders that if anyone places another body in it, they will be liable for a fine of seventy-five thousand denarii "to the synagogues."[348]

Three Sabbath days (17:2). The total length of Paul's stay in Thessalonica may actually have been longer than three weeks; this is merely how long his welcome lasts in the synagogue. We know that he stays long enough to receive a monetary gift from the Philippians (Phil. 4:16) and that he spends time working in the city to earn his support (1 Thess. 2:9).

◀
___
MACEDONIA AND THESSALONICA

◀
___
THESSALONICA

His stay in the city, however, lasts no more than a couple of months.

This Jesus I am proclaiming to you is the Christ (17:3). Over the course of three Sabbaths, Paul attempts to persuade the Thessalonian Jews that Jesus of Nazareth, who was put to death under Pontius Pilate, is indeed the Messiah that they were anticipating. This is particularly difficult since most Jews expected a Messiah that came with power and broke the chains of Roman rule. It is thus necessary for Paul to explain to them where the Old Testament teaches that the Messiah must suffer and die. The key text is the fourth servant song, Isaiah 52:13–53:12.

God-fearing Greeks (17:4). These are Gentiles who have already turned from their gods and goddesses and embraced the one true God. Now, together with some of the Jews, they respond to the gospel.

Prominent women (17:4). These women are probably both Jew and Gentile. Inscriptional evidence points to women participating in all levels of society (although not to the same degree as men) and conducting business in the province.

Jason (17:6). Paul's host may have been a Jew converted during Paul's preaching in the synagogue. His name is a Greek equiv-

REFLECTIONS

PAUL'S CHURCH PLANTING EXPE-rience in Thessalonica was not ideal from our perspective. What would we think of a church planter who stayed for only a few weeks and provoked the wrath of the city officials and numerous people? Although the persecution forced Paul to leave (in large measure out of concern for the safety of the small nucleus of Thessalonian Christians), God remained powerfully at work. A few months later Paul writes a letter to them rejoicing because of their faith, hope, love, and active proclamation of the gospel—and that in a context of ongoing persecution. We are not alone in the work of the ministry.

▶

THE HARBOR AT MODERN THESSALONICA

alent to the Hebrew names Joshua or Jeshua.[349] Jason's home probably becomes a meeting place for a house church.

Caesar's decrees (17:7). The Roman Caesars issued decrees (*dogma*) warning anyone about predicting a change of ruler over the empire. Caesar Augustus issued an edict in A.D. 11 explicitly forbidding the use of astrology to predict his or anyone else's day of death.[350] The emperor Tiberius reaffirmed this decree (*dogma*) by putting to death foreigners who ignored it.[351]

In response to these decrees, some cities pledged their commitment to the Caesar by offering oaths of loyalty. A good example of such an oath comes from the city of Paphlagonia in Asia Minor (dated to 3 B.C.):

> I swear . . . that I will support Caesar Augustus, his children and descendants, throughout my life, in word, deed and thought . . . that in whatsoever concerns them I will spare neither body nor soul nor life nor children . . . that whenever I see or hear of anything being said, planned or done against them I will report it . . . and whomsoever they regard as enemies I will attack and pursue with arms and the sword by land and by sea. . . .[352]

These oaths help us see how violence toward Paul and his companions could easily be formed.

Another king, one called Jesus (17:7). Because Paul's preaching about Jesus includes references to him as "Lord," the fact that he has a "kingdom," and that he is coming again in judgment, it is easy to

◄

———

POLITARCHAI INSCRIPTION

▶ The City Officials

Luke uses a rather uncommon word to refer to the civic officials—the term *politarchai*. Earlier generations of critical scholars argued that the choice of this term by the author of Acts demonstrates his unreliability as a historian. They observed that *politarchai* does not appear in the Greek inscriptions of the first century (or before), whereas it does appear in second century and later literary documents. This is taken as evidence that "Luke" is writing well into the second century and using terminology familiar to him from his own setting.

Archaeology has dramatically vindicated Luke's reliability on this issue. A total of seventy inscriptions have now been discovered that make use of this term. Over three quarters of these are from Macedonia and over half of those are from the city of Thessalonica. Some of these inscriptions date to the first century and a few date as early as the third century B.C.[A-101]

The term appears to have been used primarily in Macedonia as the title for the chief magistrates in the cities. Thus, Luke not only chooses an appropriate term to refer to the local officials at Thessalonica, but appears to have carefully selected the precise title that the Thessalonians are using.

right ▶

**PHILIPPI,
THESSALONICA,
AND BEREA**

see how Paul's words can be turned against him as a threat to the Roman Caesar. Furthermore, Paul's proclamation about the Day of the Lord and the impending return of Christ (the *parousia*) easily signals to those who hear that he is predicting a change of ruler in direct defiance of the decrees of Caesar.

Thrown into turmoil (17:8). The mob creates an uproar in the city that has big implications for the ongoing life of this infant church. First, Jason and others from his household come under legal trouble and presumably ongoing scrutiny. Second, Paul's life is now in danger and his presence possibly places the lives of the other Christians in jeopardy as long as he remains in the city. This makes it impossible for him to return. Third, the evidence of Paul's letter to the Thessalonians suggests that some of these new believers do, in fact, lose their lives as a result of this local persecution (see 1 Thess. 4:13).

In Berea (17:10–15)

Leaving the Via Egnatia, which goes west to the Adriatic, Paul's friends take him to

Berea, about forty-seven miles southwest of Thessalonica on the road to Athens. Some scholars think that Paul may have originally intended to take the Egnatian Way to the west coast and from there to take a boat to Italy and on to Rome. The fact that Emperor Claudius has recently expelled the Jews from Rome (in A.D. 49) may also contribute to the decision to go south.

Berea (17:10). Lying twenty-five miles inland from the Aegean coast, Berea is situated at the foot of Mount Bemius (Mount Vermion; 6614 feet) and on a tributary of the Haliacmon River at an elevation of 591 feet. The site is occupied by the modern city of Veria. Nevertheless, there have been many archaeological discoveries, including the remains of houses, public buildings, roads, graves, statuary, and inscriptions.[353] Archaeological evidence points to the worship of Zeus Hypsistos, Hermes, Asclepius, and Herakles in this city.[354]

▶

BEREA

The site of the ancient city.

They went to the Jewish synagogue (17:10). As with Thessalonica, no synagogue remains have yet been discovered. A couple of Jewish inscriptions have been found, but these date much later than the time of Paul.

More noble character (17:11). Luke contrasts the response of the Bereans to that of the Thessalonians. He commends the fact that they check Paul's preaching against the testimony of Scripture and are eager to learn. The term he chooses only appears here in the New Testament and is the comparative form of *eugenos*, which can mean "one of noble birth" or simply "noble" or "excellent." An eagerness to learn about God, to discern how he is working, and to evaluate it in light of written revelation is a more excellent path than an emotive response based on faulty knowledge and cultural bias.

Many of the Jews believed (17:12). Paul's preaching once again generates a good response, but this time especially with the Jews. Word quickly reaches the Thessalonian Jews who oppose Paul, and they travel to Berea to try their same methods of stopping him that worked in their own city. Unfortunately, they find success, and Paul is forced to leave the city. He is escorted to the coast by some concerned Christian brothers and from there departs to Athens. There are many possible ports along the coast that Paul may use to catch a boat—Dion, Methone, Makragialos (Pydna), or Aliki.

Luke gives no indication of the amount of time Paul spends in Berea. The circumstances of his stay and the overall chronology of this time suggests no more than a month or two. Although we have no record of Pauline correspondence to this city, we do know that he gains a valuable companion from one of his converts, a man named Sopater (see 20:4).

In Athens (17:16–21)

Athens (17:16). After disembarking at the harbor of Piraeus, Paul walks to

◀

ATHENS

The modern harbor of Piraeus.

Athens and enters the famous city through one of the northwest gates. The size of Athens can be appreciated by the fact that the wall that surrounded the city had a circumference of five to six miles.

As Paul journeys into the heart of the city, he feels a sense of awe at the impressive architecture and grandeur of the immense buildings from this center of Hellenistic culture. What he only heard about previously, he now sees firsthand. Entering the city, the Hephaesteum first comes into view. This is a beautiful Doric style temple dedicated to the god Hephaestus and the goddess Athena built between 449–444 B.C. Just across from this is the Stoa of Attalus, a two-storied colonnaded building gifted to the city c. 150 A.D. by Attalus, King of Pergamum.

Towering above all, however, is the magnificent Parthenon, a Doric temple dedicated to Athena Polias (447–438 B.C.) and sitting atop the Acropolis as a crown. The rectangular temple measures 228 feet by 101 feet (23,000 square feet) and includes Doric columns that stand thirty-four feet high with a diameter at the base of six feet. The columns support a roof made of richly ornamented slabs of

ATHENS

(top left) The temple of Athena Nike.

(top right) Tower of the Winds.

(bottom left) The Parthenon.

(bottom right) A column capital of the Temple of Hephaestus with the agora in the background.
▼ ▶

marble depicting a variety of scenes. Inside the temple stands a thirty-nine-foot high statue of Athena.

The Acropolis itself, a large limestone plateau measuring 1050 feet by 512 feet and rising 512 feet high, stands impressively at the center of the city. The sides of this rocky crag are steep on every side but the west. Also on the Acropolis is the Erechtheum (built 421–405 B.C.) for the worship of Athena and Poseidon, the temple of Athena Nike ("Athena who brings victory") built 427–424 B.C., and the Propylaea (built 437–432 B.C.)—a monumental roofed gateway on the west side of the Acropolis.

As Paul takes in all of these grand sights, he first passes through the Greek Agora ("market place") and then the Roman Agora. Standing prominently in the Roman market is a forty-foot octagonal structure housing a waterclock and sundials known as the Horologion. It is also called "The Tower of the Winds" because it contains carved representations of the eight wind gods below the cornice.

The city was full of idols (17:16). Every building in the city and, indeed, every-where Paul turns have a representation of some god or goddess. The fact of idolatry is nothing new to Paul. He saw it on the streets of Tarsus as a young child; it was present in Damascus, Antioch, and all the cities where he planted churches. There is something about the pervasiveness of it in Athens that causes him to grieve deeply. The spiritual darkness of this city is a tremendous obstacle to the gospel.

The synagogue (17:17). In the midst of such an idolatrous city is a Jewish community that met to worship the one true God. Many Jewish burial inscriptions have been discovered in Athens that

> ▶ **The City of Athens IMPORTANT FACTS:**
> - Religion: pluralistic, with many gods and god-desses
> - Political Importance: free city, but under Roman rule
> - Cultural Importance: the historic cradle of Greek civilization and culture, the premier "university town" of the empire

◀

THE ACROPOLIS

attest to the Jewish presence. They range in date from the second century B.C. to the third century A.D., but a high proportion of them date to the first century A.D.[355]

God-fearing Greeks (17:17). Even in Athens, there are Gentiles who have forsaken their deities and turned to God. These Gentiles now hear Paul contend that Jesus is the fulfillment of Israel's messianic hope. In contrast to his accounts of Thessalonica and Berea, Luke does not tell us the response Paul receives about his preaching in the synagogue at Athens.

The marketplace (17:17). The Greek agora had once served Athens as the center for democratic assemblies. Now as a city under Roman imperial rule, democratic rule is a relic of the classic past. The Greek agora is now filled with altars, statues, and temples. Paul probably spends time presenting the gospel in the Roman agora, the area used for buying and selling and other commercial purposes.[356] There is no shortage of people to talk to in this busy place.

Epicurean and Stoic philosophers (17:18). At some point during Paul's brief stay in Athens, he encounters adherents of two of the most popular philosophical schools.[357] Intrigued by what Paul is saying, these philosophers invite him to address a larger gathering of people.

The Stoics derived their name from the *stoa poikilē* (the "painted colonnade") in the Greek agora. Their founder Zeno

▶ The "Idols" of Athens

There were numerous gods and goddesses worshiped at Athens—more than will be named here. Listed are a few that can be attested by archaeological evidence or because they are mentioned in ancient literature describing Athens.[A-102]

Greek: Athena, the patron goddess of Athens, was probably the most popular with temples and edifices dedicated to her. Certainly every deity of the Greek pantheon was worshiped here. These included Zeus, Hera, Apollo, Ares, Artemis, Aphrodite, Asclepius, Athena Nike, Athena Polias, Castor and Pollux, Demeter, Dionysus, the Erinyes, Eros, Ge, the Graces, Hades (Pluto), Hephaestus (Vulcan), Hekate, Heracles, Hermes, Hestia, Pan, Persephone, and Poseidon. A vast number of images of Hermes could be found all over the city and particularly in the agora. Numerous images of lesser deities and heroes are also found throughout the city.

Asia Minor: Cybele.

Roman: The Romans identified the gods and goddesses in their pantheon with similar deities in the Greek pantheon. Thus, Jupiter is identified with Zeus, Mars with Ares, etc. Thus, the counterparts of the Roman deities were worshiped in Athens.

Ruler Cult: In 27 B.C., the cult of "Roma" (the divinization of Rome) and the cult of Caesar were established in Athens.

(340–265 B.C.) is from the island of Cyprus. Stoicism is an influential school of thought that was prevalent in the first century and focused on a moral earnestness.

The Epicureans, named after their founder Epicurus (340–270 B.C.), are an often misunderstood group today. While it is true that they say, "Pleasure is the beginning and end of living happily," their understanding of pleasure was not that of unrestrained lust and a party mentality. Their understanding of pleasure chiefly involved "living in accord with nature"; for them, this involved a fairly disciplined and ordered lifestyle. Diogenes Laertius clarifies the Epicurean understanding of "pleasure":

> When, therefore, we maintain that pleasure is the end, we do not mean the pleasures of profligates and those that consist in sensuality, as is supposed by some who are either ignorant or disagree with us or who do not understand, but freedom from pain in the body and from trouble in the mind. For it is not continuous drinkings and revellings, nor the satisfaction of lusts, nor the enjoyment of fish and other luxuries of the wealthy table, which produce a pleasant life, but sober reasoning, searching out the motives for all choice and avoidance, and banishing mere opinions.[358]

The Epicurean philosophy did not attract many adherents among the common people. Most Epicureans were wealthy and educated, that is, from the upper classes of life.

This babbler (17:18). The philosophers use a colorful word to describe Paul from typical Athenian slang, the term *spermologos*.[359] This word was commonly used to describe a person who went around the market picking up scraps. Some philosophers used it when referring to a person who picked up scraps of learning here and there.

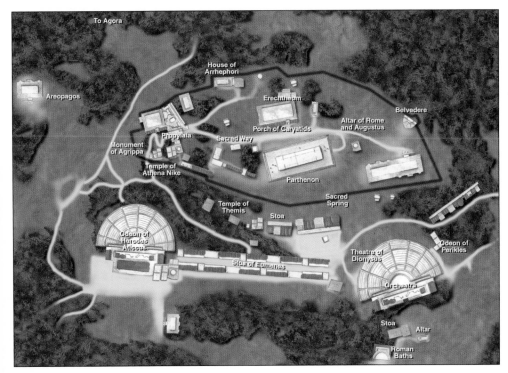

Foreign gods . . . Jesus and the resurrection (17:18). Although they view Paul demeaningly, these philosophers are curious about the non-Greek Eastern deities he is proclaiming. This interest is nothing new for Greeks and Romans. They embraced many of the gods and goddesses coming from the Orient, including Persian, Anatolian, Egyptian, and Syrian deities.

The philosophers misunderstand Paul to be proclaiming two gods. The wording of Luke's text can be interpreted to mean that they think Paul is teaching about a god named "Jesus" and a goddess named "Anastasis" (the Greek word meaning "resurrection"). The idea of a bodily resurrection from the dead is a strange idea to a Greek during this time.

The term that is used here for foreign gods is the Greek word *daimonia*, elsewhere translated "demons," with the meaning "evil spirits." The Greeks, however, used the word in a neutral sense to refer to the gods.

The Areopagus (17:19). The name means "hill of Ares" (the Greek god of war). The Romans identified Ares with their god of war, Mars, which resulted in the alternative translation, "Mars Hill." The hill was adjacent to the Acropolis with only a ravine separating the two. Standing 378 feet high, this rocky hill

---

▶ Stoic Beliefs

Creation: The world has been created out of fire, the foundational element. From fire came air, from air water, and from water earth. The balance achieved by these elements is attributed to *logos,* the impersonal forces that create and hold together.

God: The Stoics are pantheistic materialists (god is in everything). They may refer to the supreme god as Zeus, but they can also equate him with fate, nature, *logos,* and the "world soul" (with the universe understood as a living organism). The gods of the popular religions exist, but their mythologies are only a crude expression of the truth.

Soul: The soul is corporeal, similar to the human body. The closest comparison to the soul is warm breath of a human.

◀
_____

ZENO

The founder of Stoicism.

Sin: There is no concept of sin. Error is nothing more than the failure of attaining the ideal, or acting contrary to the laws of nature. There is no concept of offending the will of an all-holy, righteous being.

Fate: We all live in the grip of the relentless pull of fate. Although we have no control over destiny, we do have the power to control our selves and our wills.

Ethics: The pursuit of virtue is the primary good. To be virtuous is to live in harmony with reason (logos) and to be at one with nature.

Afterlife: The Stoics believe in a limited survival after death, but not in the sense of a personal, individual existence. Individual human souls will ultimately be absorbed into the basic elements in periodic cosmic conflagrations. Seneca says, "We whose souls are blessed and who have shared in eternity . . . will be changed into our former elements."[A-103]

Hell: There is no underworld or place of torture for those who die.

was once the foundation for the supreme court of ancient Athens, but now no buildings remain on the site.[360]

Originally, the Areopagus was the ruling council for the city of Athens. As a democratic form of government progressively came into prominence, the powers of the council began to wane (around the 6th cent. B.C.). When Roman power became dominant in Greece, the Areopagus was reinstated as the governing body of the city. There is some question as to whether this council met on the hill or at a different location in the city (such as the Royal Stoa, the *Stoa Basileios*).[361] It is not likely, however, that Paul is standing before this governing body in an official trial. Paul appears informally before a group of people—including Stoics, Epicureans, and other philosophers—who evidently meet on the hill to dialogue and debate on various issues.

Talking about and listening to the latest ideas (17:21). Luke's comment about the Athenians passing their days away discussing the latest ideas is culturally appropriate; this is what some Greek writers said about them. The Greek historian Thucydides records an observer reproaching the Athenians by saying: "You are the best people at being deceived by something new that is said."[362]

Paul Addresses the Areopagus (17:22–34)

Taking advantage of a unique opportunity to proclaim the gospel, Paul

▶ Epicurean Beliefs

Creation: The world developed out of a collection of atoms in space that operate according to natural laws. There is not a divine creation. Epicureanism is an essentially materialist worldview.

God: Gods exist, but they live outside the world in interstellar spaces. They do not intervene in the affairs of humanity, so there is no place for providence or prayer. Nor is there any reason to fear them. Because they are superior beings, they are worthy of worship and honor. Because so little attention is paid to the gods, the Epicureans are called "atheists" by their contemporaries.

Soul: The soul is like the body in that it is composed of atoms. It is thus corporeal. According to Lucretius, once it separates from the body, it has no existence.[A-104]

EPICURUS

Sin: There is no concept of sin. The avoidance of actions that produce pain is a major objective of the Epicurean.

Ethics: The chief goal of human existence is to live in accord with nature. This involves understanding the physical laws of the universe and living in a consistent manner with these. Pleasure is in accord with nature and instructs us how to live in harmony with her. Pleasure represents the absence of pain.

Community: Friendship in community is a primary source of pleasure.

Afterlife: There is no life after death. When the body dies, the soul also disintegrates. According to Epicurus, "Death is nothing to us; for the body, when it has been resolved into its elements, has no feeling, and that which has no feeling is nothing to us."[A-105] Epicureans do not accept the idea of a bodily resurrection.

Hell: There is no underworld or place of torture for those who die.

addresses a large gathering of people at the Areopagus.[363] Luke provides us with an apt summary of what Paul says. This message is of great importance because it gives us insight into how the apostle communicates the gospel to non-Jews—in this instance, Greek philosophers and people who worship a variety of other gods.

The thrust of his address is in response to the observation of the Epi-

AREOPAGUS (MARS HILL)

(right) A bronze plaque with the text of Paul's speech on the hillside.

(bottom) The location of the ancient Areopagus.

cureans and Stoics that "he seems to be advocating foreign gods" (17:18). Paul tactfully yet firmly declares that he is proclaiming the one true God.

It is striking to see the ways that Paul tailors his message to communicate to these people. This message contrasts considerably with what Paul said when he spoke in the synagogue at Antioch of Pisidia (13:16–41). There he recounted Israel's history and peppered his sermon with quotations from the Old Testament.

Here he employs an entirely different strategy. Recalling the numerous statues, temples, and altars he has seen in his walks through the agora and around the city, he finds an entrée with the people by referring to the altar "TO AN UNKNOWN GOD." He thereby capitalizes on their concession of at least some ignorance of ultimate reality.

When Paul says, "Now what you worship as something unknown I am going to proclaim to you" (17:23), he does not imply by this statement that they are already unconsciously worshiping the one true God. This merely serves as a means to raise for them the most basic question of life: Who is God?[364]

In the first part of his message, he confidently states that the God he proclaims is indeed the supreme God who is Creator, Lord of all, and the source of life. Up to this point, many of his listeners are inclined to believe what he is saying (except, of course, the Epicureans). Paul then reveals that this God is not aloof from his creation, but has established it in a way that humanity seeks after him. To support his denial of the utter transcendence of God, Paul cites lines from two Greek poets, Epimenides and Aratus (see below).

Lest we think that Paul has watered down his gospel by adapting it so readily to his Greek audience, we need to take a deeper look at what he actually says. Apart from the lines he quotes from the two Greek poets, the language, imagery, and concepts in his sermon are derived from the Old Testament. His entire message is thoroughly rooted in a biblical worldview and not in a Greek polytheistic, pantheistic, or dualistic worldview. The following chart shows the Old Testament references to many of Paul's statements.

What Paul says about the one true God is, by implication, a biting critique of idol worship. On this, many of the Epicureans and some of the Stoics agreed. But the larger part of the people, who are immersed in the worship of the various gods and goddesses, find what Paul says hard to accept.

Very religious (17:22). The word that Paul uses here—the comparative form of *deisidaimonia*—can be translated "superstitious" in the sense that they revere many gods and fear the possibility of offending them. This may be the sense that Paul intends because he calls attention to the altar dedicated to an "unknown god." It is possible, however, that Paul means nothing more than that they are devoted to many gods. This comment shows that Paul's audience includes many people who are not Stoics or Epicureans since the remark is not

Paul's Dependence on the Old Testament in the Areopagus Address	
Statement	**Old Testament Reference**
God made the world and everything in it (v. 24)	Gen. 1–2; Isa. 42:5; Jer. 10:12, 16
Lord of heaven and earth (v. 24)	Ex. 20:11; Isa. 42:5 (see also Matt. 11:25)
God does not live in temples built by hands (v. 24)	1 Kings 8:27 (see also 2 Cor. 5:1)
God does not need anything from the people he has created (v. 25)	1 Chron. 29:14; Ps. 50:7–15
God as the source of "breath" (v. 25)	Gen. 2:7; Isa. 42:5
God appointed the eras for the successive nations (v. 26)	Deut. 32:8; Dan. 2:36–45 (see also Luke 21:24)
God established national boundaries (v. 26)	Deut. 32:8; Ps. 74:17
God desires that people would seek him (v. 27)	Ps. 14:2; Prov. 8:17; Isa. 55:6; 65:1; Jer. 29:13
God is not far away (v. 27)	Ps. 145:18; Jer. 23:23–24
God is not like an image made out of gold, silver, or stone (v. 29)	Deut. 5:8; Ps. 115:2–8; Isa. 37:19; 44:9–20
God has overlooked such ignorance (v. 30)	(see Rom. 3:25)
God calls men now to repent (v. 30)	Isa. 59:20; Jer. 15:19; Ezek. 14:6; 18:30, 32; (see also Matt. 3:2; 4:17; Acts 2:38; 3:19)
God will judge the world (v. 31)	Ps. 9:8; 96:13; 98:9; Isa. 66:16; Jer. 25:31 (see also Matt. 11:22, 24; 12:36)
God has appointed a man who will judge (v. 31)	(see John 5:22, 27, 30)

typical of either school of thought. In fact, the Epicureans speak demeaningly of people who are "superstitious."

An altar with this inscription: TO AN UNKNOWN GOD (17:23). Although archaeologists have still to discover an altar with this inscription, ancient writers clearly attest to the existence of such altars:

> *Pausanias* (2d cent. A.D.): "The Athenians have another harbor at Mounychia with a temple of Mounychian Artemis, and one at Phaleron, as I said, with Demeter's sanctuary beside it. The temple of Athena Skiras is also here, and one of Zeus further off, *and altars of the 'Unknown gods,'* and of heroes, and the children of Theseus and Phaleros."[365]

> *Philostratus* (late 2d cent. A.D.): Athens is a place "where altars are set up in honor even of unknown gods."[366]

> *Diogenes Laertius* (3d cent. A.D.): This Epicurean author reports that "nameless altars" (*anōnymous bōmous*) can be found in different parts of Athens. These were set up in honor of gods whose names had been forgotten or

local deities whose names were unknown. Epimenides had ostensibly appeased these unknown gods to avert a plague afflicting Athens.[367]

People living during this time were afraid of what might happen if they did not properly honor a local deity. They could bring sickness or misfortune on their household or city by not giving the god or goddess the proper veneration. On the other hand, by honoring the deity, one might experience benevolence and blessings from the deity. By setting up altars even to unknown gods, people could be sure that they were not unwittingly neglecting to honor one of the gods.

He determined the times (17:26). By establishing the providence of God over the course of history, Paul clearly distinguishes his view of a personal God from the fatalism of the Stoics and the impersonal view of the Epicureans. These comments also show God to be more concerned about his creation than what is popularly thought to be true about the Greek gods.

For in him we live and move and have our being (17:28). This appears to be a citation from a poem attributed to Epimenides (c. 600 B.C.):

> They fashioned a tomb for thee,
>   O holy and high one—
> The Cretans, always liars, evil beasts,
>   idle bellies!—
> But thou art not dead; thou livest and
>   abidest for ever,
> For in thee we live and move and
>   have our being.[368]

Epimenides was originally from the island of Crete, but came to Athens and taught about the gods and allegedly per-

formed many wonders. By quoting this line, Paul seems to give tacit approval to a pantheistic conception of God (such as held by the Stoics). This is not the case, however. This pagan concept of God is correct only up to a certain point. The God Paul proclaims is not so immanent in humanity (as salt infuses water) that individuals are in fact divine. Otherwise his comments about the impending judgment and the resurrection of the dead make no sense. The line also bolsters his argument against idolatry in that idols lack life, they cannot move, and they have no real existence.

We are his offspring (17:28). Paul's next quotation is from a Stoic philosopher who is originally from the city of Soli in Cilicia (not far from Tarsus). Aratus (315–240 B.C.) also traveled to Athens where he learned his Stoicism from Zeno, the founder of the philosophy. In an astronomical poem, entitled *Phaenomena*, Aratus speaks of Zeus:

> *Let us begin with Zeus. Never,*
> *O men, let us leave him*
> *unmentioned.*
> *All the ways are full of Zeus, and all*
> *the market-places of human*
> *beings.*
> *The sea is full of him; so are the*
> *harbors.*
> *In every way we have all to do with*
> *Zeus, for we are truly his*
> *offspring.*[369]

Once again, Paul cites a pagan philosopher and agrees with his conception of divinity up to a point. Yet, as we already noted, Paul is not a pantheist. He conceives of men and women as created in the image of God, but not actually participating in the divine nature. If people bear this divine likeness, it is inconsistent to create inanimate objects as represen-

tations of the gods. Paul then uses these two quotations to bolster his criticism of the idolatry that vexes his soul.

He commands all people everywhere to repent ... he will judge the world (17:30–31). Paul does not soft-pedal the demands of the gospel. Repentance for these people involves above all turning from their gods to serve the living and true God (see the pattern of the Thessalonians that Paul commends; 1 Thess. 1:9). The God Paul proclaims will bring history to a conclusion and there will be a time of judgment by the resurrected Jesus.

A few men became followers of Paul and believed (17:34). Paul's overall response is discouraging. Only "a few" believe. Perhaps this is enough for the beginnings of one house church (although we have no other indications that a church is started at this time). Because of the increasing tendency in Greek thought toward a rigorously dualistic view of the person—a strong separation between the material and immaterial—the notion of a reanimation of the physical body is considered repugnant. Why be joined again with that which is inferior and base? Consequently, this idea is rejected.

Dionysius, a member of the Areopagus (17:34). Luke's comment about Dionysius makes it clear that at least some official members of the ruling council are present when Paul speaks. In his history of the church, Eusebius records a tradition stemming from another Dionysus from Corinth (c. 170 A.D.). He further informs us that Dionysius the Areopagite who, as related in the Acts, was converted to the faith by the Apostle Paul, was the first to be appointed Bishop of Athens.[370]

In Corinth (18:1–17)

Although not forced to leave Athens, Paul wants to get to Corinth—the strategic center of the province of Achaia. He stays in this city for eighteen months, longer than he has spent in any other place during his mission. Many people, both Jews and Gentiles, turn to Christ during this important ministry. Following a period of intense opposition to the gospel from certain Jews, the Roman ruler over the province of Achaia makes a critical decision imposing a bearing on the legal freedom of Christianity for the next decade.

Corinth (18:1). The city of Corinth had a rather tumultuous history leading up to the time of the apostle Paul.[371] The orig-

inal (Greek) city of Corinth was wiped off the map by the Roman general L. Mummius and his troops in 146 B.C. because the city was part of a confederacy aligned against Rome. The city was not rebuilt immediately and the site lay largely unoccupied for a century. Due to its strategic location overlooking the isthmus connecting the Peloponnesus to central Greece, Julius Caesar city rebuilt the city and established it as a Roman colony in 44 B.C. The city rapidly grew and acquired a distinctively Roman character.

By the time of Paul's arrival, Corinth is serving as the capital of the Roman province of Achaia (which encompasses Athens). The province includes the whole of the Peloponnese as well as territories on the other side of the isthmus (such as Epirus, Aetolia, and Thessaly). The city is also a thriving commercial center because it controls the important trade route between east and west as well as the land route between northern Greece (and Macedonia) and the Peloponnese.

Corinth was served by two ports— five miles to the east was Cenchrea on the Saronic Gulf with access to the Aegean Sea and two miles to the north was Lechaeum on the Gulf of Corinth leading to the Adriatic Sea.

The immorality in the city was renowned in antiquity and often associated with the cult of Aphrodite. The first-century historian Strabo claims that the temple owned a thousand prostitutes:

> And the temple of Aphrodite was so rich that it owned more than a thousand temple-slaves, courtesans, whom both men and women had dedicated to the goddess. And therefore it was also on account of these women that the city was crowded with people and grew rich; for instance, the ship-captains freely

▶ The City of Corinth
IMPORTANT FACTS:

- Population: 80,000–100,000[A-106]
- Prominent Religions: Apollo, Athena, Isis, Serapis, Asclepius, Aphrodite, Demeter and Kore; Tyche (Fortuna); the Ruler Cult; Judaism
- Roman Colony
- Seat of the Roman Government for the Province of Achaia

CORINTH

An aerial view of the ancient city of Corinth from the top of the Acrocorinth.

▶ Archaeological Remains in Corinth

The site of ancient Corinth is unoccupied and there are extensive remains. Since 1896, the American School of Classical Studies has been the principal entity conducting excavations at Corinth.

The foundation and columns of a sixth century Doric temple (possibly for Apollo) is the most noticeable structure one sees today in arriving at the site. Just east of the temple is the well-preserved Lechaeum Road that leads from the forum to the harbor (about two miles away). On the east side of this road, just before reaching the forum, is the fountain of Peirene, the collection and distribution point of the city's water supply. The large rectangular forum had two stoas (colonnades)—one on the northwest and another on the south running the entire length of the forum. A large square stone platform stands on the south side of the forum that has been identified as the *rostra* (or *bēma*), the speaker's platform from where an official announcement might be made or a civic official might address an assembly.[A-107]

The remains of temples and shops line each of the sides of the forum. Some remains on the west side of the forum of the temple have been provisionally identified as belonging to Aphrodite (Venus), the Clarian Apollo, Tyche (Fortuna), and Hercules. Still further west are the scant remains of a large temple constructed during the reign of Claudius that was probably the site of the imperial cult temple.

Archaeologists have recently focused their efforts on the sanctuary of Demeter and Kore, which is located just south of the city on the slope leading to the ascent to the Acrocorinth. Some thirty-six dining halls have been identified at the sanctuary along with the discovery of much cookware. Recently, archaeologists discovered eighteen curse tablets in one of the rooms of the sanctuary that date to the first or second century A.D.

In the far north part of the city (a half mile north of the forum), archaeologists have found the remains of a sanctuary of the healing god Asclepius. This structure would have pre-dated the Roman colony, but was probably still in use as an Asclepion during Paul's time. Excavators have found many terra-cotta replicas of human body parts (such as arms, legs, eyes, ears, breasts, and genitals) apparently donated to the temple as expressions of gratitude for the god's healing. More recently, they have unearthed about four thousand oil lamps in the fountain adjacent to the Asclepion (the Fountain of Laerna). The lamps appear to date substantially later than the New Testament era. Some of the lamps are inscribed with the line: "Angels who dwell on these waters."[A-108]

squandered their money, and hence the proverb, "Not for every man is the voyage to Corinth."[372]

Although the relevance of Strabo's claim for the New Testament period has sometimes been disputed by modern scholars, his testimony likely reflects accurately on the social situation of Corinth at the time of Paul.[373] The women of Aphrodite extended their lascivious trade not only in the temple on the Acrocorinth (the 1900-foot mountain just south of the city), but throughout the city as well. In the pre-Roman era of Corinth, there were a series of expressions people used in the Greek-speaking world built on the word Corinth to refer to various kinds of sexual activities: "to act the Corinthian" (*korinthiazomai*) means practicing fornication; "Corinthian companions" (*korinthiai hetairai*) and "Corinthian girls" (*korinthiai korai*) were prostitutes.[374]

Aquila . . . with his wife Priscilla (18:2). Not long after arriving in the city, Paul develops a close friendship and ultimately a life-long partnership with a Christian couple who have recently arrived from Rome.[375] They work with Paul for the duration of his stay at Corinth, accompany him to Ephesus, and later return to Rome after the death of Emperor Claudius. Aquila is originally

CORINTH

(top) The Lechaeon Road leading into the Roman city with the Acrocorinth in the background.

(bottom left) Columns from the ancient temple of Apollo.

(bottom right) The Corinthian canal, which was dug across the isthmus in modern times.

▼ ▶

from Pontus, a region of northern Asia Minor along the coast of the Black Sea. The name Priscilla is a diminutive and familiar form of Prisca.

Claudius had ordered all the Jews to leave Rome (18:2). Aquila and Priscilla had no choice about departing from Rome. The Roman emperor actually took the radical step of ordering every Jew to leave Rome immediately. This was nothing new for the Jews. A similar expulsion occurred twenty years earlier under the reign of Tiberius.[376] There were also significant ethnic tensions between the Jews and Gentiles in Alexandria and other cities in the empire.

From the first year of his reign (A.D. 41), Claudius looked with suspicion on the Jews. The Roman historian Dio Cassius notes this when he writes:

> When the Jews had again multiplied to a point where their numbers made it difficult to expel them from the city without a riot, he did not directly banish them, but forbade

them to gather together in accordance with their ancestral way of life.[377]

Eight years later (A.D. 49), Claudius was no longer tolerant and decided to rid the city of the Jews altogether. In his biography of Claudius, Suetonius corroborates Luke's account by verifying this expulsion: "Because the Jews at

REFLECTIONS

RACISM IS NOTHING NEW. THE Jews living in the Mediterranean world in the first century knew a lot about it. Priscilla and Aquila were the victims of racism. Although what they suffered was unjust and discouraging, God worked in a powerful way through these evil circumstances. Had they not left Rome, they would not have met Paul and had a vital partnership role in planting the churches in Corinth and Ephesus.

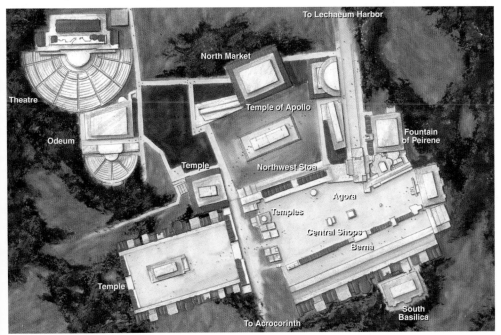

To Lechaeum Harbor

North Market

Theatre

Temple of Apollo

Odeum

Fountain of Peirene

Temple

Northwest Stoa

Agora

Temples

Central Shops

Berna

Temple

South Basilica

To Acrocorinth

Rome caused continuous disturbances at the instigation of Chrestus, he expelled them from the city."[378] The identity of "Chrestus" is most likely "(Jesus) Christ." This suggests that there were heated debates among the Jews in the synagogues in Rome with the Jewish Christians who contended that Jesus is the Messiah (*Christos*), which did not go unnoticed by the Roman authorities.

Tentmaker (18:3). Paul discovers that Aquila and Priscilla also work in the same trade, so they join forces. "Tentmaking" is the literal translation of the Greek word *skēnopoios* and involves working with leather as the primary material from which tents are made, [379] although there is some evidence that the word implies that Paul works with various kinds of fabrics.[380] The work also includes the making and repair of a large range of leather and woven goods. Tents were needed for the many travelers staying in the city and for the sailors who usually lived in tents while their boats were docked. People also needed skilled workers to repair their torn or broken tents. One scholar suggests that since the Isthmian Games were held in the spring of A.D. 51, the trio probably had plenty of demand for their products.[381]

Paul most likely learned his trade skills in his preparation to be a rabbi. These teachers were expected to support themselves by some form of labor. According to Rabbi Gamaliel III, "An excellent thing is the study of Torah combined with some secular occupation, for the labor by them both puts sin out of one's mind. All study of the Torah which is not combined with work will ultimately be futile and lead to sin."[382]

The synagogue (18:4). In the early part of this century, archaeologists discovered an inscription preserved on a block of white marble that probably served as the lintel over a doorway. The inscription simply read: "The Synagogue of the Hebrews." It is possible that the inscription dates to the time of Paul, but it could date as late as the second century. Archaeologists have also uncovered seven other inscriptions from Corinth confirming the Jewish presence in the city. Among these inscriptions, some being in Hebrew, one contains an engraving of the seven-branched menorah and one has the title, "ruler of the synagogue" (*archisynagōgos*).[383]

Silas and Timothy came from Macedonia (18:5). Silas and Timothy remained in Macedonia (with the churches of Philippi, Thessalonica, and Berea) while Paul continued on to Athens and then to Corinth. Now they return and bring Paul good news about how all the new believers in this area are doing in their walk with the Lord in spite of the most trying of cir-

SYMBOLS OF JEWISH PRESENCE IN CORINTH

(top) Three menorahs adorn a column from a fourth-century A.D. synagogue.

(bottom) "The Synagogue of the Hebrews" inscription.

▼ ▶

cumstances. Paul also receives at this time a substantial monetary gift from the new church at Philippi that enables him to leave his tentmaking and devote all of his energies to proclaiming the gospel (see 2 Cor. 11:9; Phil. 4:16).

He shook out his clothes in protest (18:6). As he experienced elsewhere, his regular proclamation of Jesus as Messiah in the synagogue met with a positive response from a few Jews and God-fearing Gentiles, but a hostile reaction on the part of other Jews within the synagogue. When some of the opposition become abusive and make blasphemous statements (presumably about the Lord Jesus Christ), Paul leaves the synagogue, departing with a dramatic gesture of shaking the dust off his garments. This symbolic act has precedent in the Old Testament (see Neh. 5:13) and in Judaism as a way of distancing oneself from the sinful and rebellious actions of a people. Jesus himself advised the Twelve on their mission to "shake the dust off your feet" when a home or a town did not receive them (see Matt. 10:14).

Your blood be on your own heads! I am clear of my responsibility (18:6). Paul's action here needs to be seen in close connection with his words of condemnation that echo the language of the prophet Ezekiel (see Ezek. 33:5).

Titius Justus, a worshiper of God (18:7). After Paul leaves the synagogue, the core of new believers begins meeting next door at the home of a Gentile God-fearer. These probably are times of considerable tension as members of the two groups pass each other on the street.

In Romans 16:23, Paul speaks of the church as meeting in the home of a man named Gaius. This may be the same per-

son as Titius Justus and means that Luke only refers to him by his Roman *nomen* (Titius) and *cognomen* (Justus), not by his *praenomen* (Gaius). Paul says that Gaius is one of the Corinthian converts that he baptized himself.

Crispus (18:8). In spite of the initial resistance of many synagogue members, there is a dramatic reversal. The synagogue ruler himself embraces Jesus as Messiah along with his entire household. Apparently many other Corinthians also become believers at this time, which probably includes many of the Jews from the synagogue. This is certainly a major blow to the Jewish opposition and probably helps to precipitate even more hostility. In 1 Corinthians 1:14, Paul tells us that he personally baptized Crispus.

A vision (18:9). The Lord grants Paul an encouraging vision, directing him to stay in the city. The apostle remains in Corinth for a period of eighteen months.

While Gallio was proconsul of Achaia (18:12). Much is known about this man from literature outside the Bible including the writings of Tacitus, Pliny, Dio Cassius, and Seneca.[384] L. Iunius Gallio Annaeanus, his full Roman name, was actually the brother of the famous Stoic

◄

THE GALLIO INSCRIPTION

philosopher Seneca, who spoke of him with admiration and love. He was a well-known jurist and had important connections with the Roman emperor and others in power.

Gallio served as the Roman proconsul (*anthypatos*) of the province of Achaia. Consequently, any decision he made would have more widely ranging implications than a decision made by a local civic official (such as the *politarchēs* at Thessalonica).

In the early part of this century, an important inscription explicitly naming Gallio was discovered in the Greek city of Delphi.[385] This inscription has been the single most important piece of evidence enabling us to date Paul's stay in Corinth with accuracy. The inscription itself is dated, which thereby enables us to fix a precise date on Gallio's proconsulship in Corinth, and thereby also the

time of Paul's eighteen-month ministry in the city. The inscription reads:

> Tiberius [Claudius] Caesar Augustus Germanicus, [Pontifex maximus, in his tribunician] power [year 12, acclaimed Emperor for] the 26th time, father of the country, [consul for the 5th time, censor, sends greeting to the city of Delphi.] I have for long been zealous for the city of Delphi [and favorable to it from the] beginning, and I have always observed the cult of the [Pythian] Apollo, [but with regard to] the present stories, and those quarrels of the citizens of which [a report has been made by *Lucius] Junius Gallio* my friend and [pro]consul [of Achaia].[386]

We know from other sources that the 26th acclamation of Claudius took place during the first half of his twelfth year as

CORINTH

The Roman *bema*
(judgment seat).
▼

emperor. His accession occurred on January 25 in A.D. 41, which means that this inscription would be dated somewhere in the period of January 25 to July 31, A.D. 52. Thus, Gallio was serving in Corinth during this time. He probably became proconsul in the spring of A.D. 51 (the season when proconsuls typically took office) and served in this capacity for about a year. Because Paul stayed in Corinth "for some time" (18:18) after this incident, it probably occurred within the first few months of his ministry there.

The Jews made a united attack on Paul (18:12). Jewish opposition to Paul's preaching continues to grow in Corinth. At one point, a group from the synagogue forcefully apprehend Paul and take him before the Roman proconsul, where they charge him with violating their own law (the Torah). The real essence of their complaint before Gallio is the Jews' contention that the Jesus movement is not a legitimate form of Judaism and, therefore, should not come under the same legal protection under Roman law.

I will not be a judge of such things (18:15). Gallio, however, sees things differently and interprets their complaints against Paul as a matter of intramural debate. Annoyed that they bring this issue before him, Gallio summarily dismisses them and instructs them to settle the matter themselves. This decision constitutes an important precedent for the legal freedom of the early Christians, at least until midway into Nero's reign, when matters grew exceedingly worse for the church. At this point Christianity is judged to be a sect within Judaism and, therefore, a legal religion (*religio licita*) by a Roman governor with expertise as a jurist.[387]

They all turned on Sosthenes the synagogue ruler and beat him (18:17). Sosthenes, possibly the successor to Crispus as ruler of the synagogue, is among the Jews who seized Paul and brought him before Gallio. When matters did not go in their favor before Gallio and they are ordered to leave, Sosthenes becomes the brunt of a fierce attack by a group of Corinthian Gentiles. Such flare-ups of anti-Jewish sentiment were not uncommon in the cities of the empire. Furthermore, Gallio may have given tacit approval to this hostility toward the Jews as an action consistent with the emperor's anti-Semitism.[388] This is a tragic turn of events for the Jewish community.

Paul's Initial Ministry In Ephesus (18:18–23)

In the early spring of A.D. 52, Paul decides to leave Corinth and return to the Roman province of Syria. Here he visits his "home church," the church at Antioch, and journeys to Jerusalem, possibly for the festivals of Passover and Pentecost. Paul is also

THE END OF THE SECOND MISSIONARY JOURNEY ▼

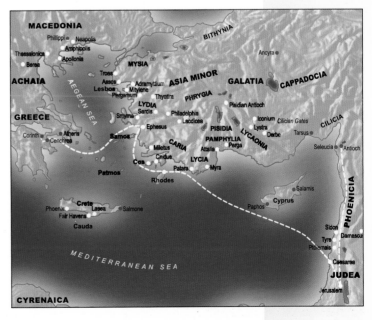

motivated to go to Jerusalem so that he can properly conclude a Nazirite vow he has taken. His shorn hair is an offering he takes to the temple.

Departing from Corinth's eastern port, he is accompanied by his coworkers Aquila and Priscilla. Evidently they make plans to begin working in Ephesus, the capital city of Asia Minor, which Paul had tried to reach previously (16:6). Silas and Timothy presumably remain in Corinth to continue giving leadership and help to the fledgling church.

He had his hair cut off . . . because of a vow (18:18). Paul has apparently initiated a Nazirite vow; the period of this special consecration has now come to a conclusion. The roots of the Jewish tradition of the Nazirite vow are explained in Numbers 6:1–21 and elaborated on in the rabbinic literature.[389] It was common in Judaism for a person to take a Nazirite vow for a fixed period of time, such as thirty days. This kind of vow involved abstaining from wine, avoiding impurity (such as contact with the dead), and leaving one's hair uncut. When the period of the vow was finished, the hair was shaved and brought to the Jerusalem temple as an offering, where the person would also make a sacrifice.

Luke does not explain why Paul has taken this vow. It may have been an expression of faith and commitment to the Lord for the challenge of the new circumstances of proclaiming the gospel in Corinth in the midst of heavy opposition. It may also have been a way for Paul to express his thanksgiving to God for his hand of blessing on the Corinthian ministry and for keeping him safe, just as God had promised to do in the vision. The passage clearly shows that Paul does not abandon Jewish traditions altogether. He finds this form helpful to express his devotion and commitment to the Lord.

Cenchrea (18:18). At some point during Paul's ministry a church was planted in this eastern port city of Corinth. Phoebe, a deaconess of the church, carried the letter Paul later wrote to the Roman Christians (Rom. 16:1). The site of Cenchrea has been found and excavated to a limited extent. The artificial breakwaters for the harbor are still visible in addition to many of the harbor buildings. These include a variety of warehouses and several temples. One has been identified as a sanctuary of the Egyptian goddess Isis.

They arrived at Ephesus, where Paul left Priscilla and Aquila (18:19). After arriving in Ephesus, Paul immediately begins preaching in the Jewish synagogue. He is met with a favorable reception, so much so that the people beg him to return to the city after his trip to Syria. This provides a good opening for Aquila and Priscilla, who settle in the city, secure a home, start a business, and begin ministering the gospel of Jesus Christ to the people in the synagogue. This couple has a solid and fruitful ministry in the city in

CENCHREA

Harbor remains at the ancient port city.
▼

Traveled from place to place throughout the region of Galatia and Phrygia (18:23). On his return trip to Ephesus, Paul opts to take an overland route rather than sail so he can visit the many churches he had a hand in starting throughout Asia Minor. At Galatia, he most likely revisits the churches at Antioch, Iconium, Lystra, and Derbe.

◄ *left*

THE REGION OF
GALATIA AND
PHRYGIA

the intervening months until Paul returns. It is likely that a number of people turn to Christ as a result of their ministry, and they begin hosting a church in their home.

When he landed at Caesarea, he went up and greeted the church and then went down to Antioch (18:22). Paul lands at the beautiful seaport of Caesarea Maritima (see comments on 10:1). Paul travels from there to Jerusalem (this is the meaning of "he went up and greeted the church") and then makes the long trek to the city of Antioch. In one concise statement, Luke condenses a lengthy and probably eventful journey. In fact, Paul's travels recorded in 18:22–23 (Corinth to Ephesus to Caesarea to Jerusalem to Antioch and then to Ephesus) span a distance of about fifteen hundred miles.

During his visit to Jerusalem, Paul hears about and sees the conditions resulting from a famine that ravages the country. When he returns to the churches he plants, it is with a sense of urgency for mounting a relief collection for helping the Jerusalem and Judean believers in their dire need. Luke himself gives us no details about Paul's visits to Jerusalem and Antioch. From the time he drops off Aquila and Priscilla until he rejoins them in Ephesus may have been as much as a year.

The Ministry of Apollos in Ephesus (18:24–28)

During Aquila and Priscilla's ministry in Ephesus while Paul is in Syria, a Jewish man from Egypt named Apollos[390] (short for Apollonius) comes and speaks in the synagogue. He is an incredibly capable speaker, but more importantly, he believes that Jesus is the Messiah. Oddly, however, he has not heard the full extent of Jesus' teaching, and probably has not heard about Jesus' resurrection, nor has he experienced the empowering of the Holy Spirit in his life.

Learned man (18:24). Apollos knows the Old Testament well, probably in the

ALEXANDRIA,
EGYPT
▼

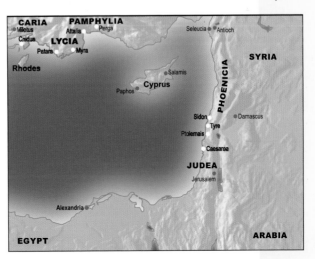

Greek version known as the Septuagint. The word *logios* can also mean "eloquent," and this is also a characteristic of his speaking. Apollos has been trained in the art of rhetoric and may have functioned as a Jewish sophist—an itinerant teacher. He most likely comes to Ephesus as a businessman, like many other Egyptians.

Explained to him the way of God more adequately (18:26). Seeing his openness to Jesus, Aquila and Priscilla invite Apollos into their home and give him a complete account of the cross, resurrection, and Pentecost events. This also includes a clear explanation of the nature of Jesus' atoning sacrifice. Evidently, Apollos responds with enthusiasm and delight and thus enters into a new understanding of the nature of God's salvation and the experience of the new covenant blessing of the promised Holy Spirit.

Wanted to go to Achaia (18:27). As Apollos becomes more acquainted with Priscilla and Aquila, they presumably tell him of their ministry in Corinth and the struggles they have there with unbelieving Jews. Apollos most likely takes this as a challenge and makes plans to travel to Achaia to proclaim the gospel. Upon

right ▶

EPHESUS AND WESTERN ASIA MINOR

▶ Alexandria

Founded by Alexander the Great in 331 B.C., the city of Alexandria subsequently became the capital of Egypt and eventually eclipsed Athens as the cultural and educational center of the Hellenistic world.[A-109] Alexandria was the second largest city of the Roman empire with a population of over a half million people. Located in lower Egypt on the Mediterranean Sea, Alexandria's port was the connection point for shipping between India and Rome. The enormous lighthouse (328 feet high) on the small island of Pharos at the opening of Alexandria's two artificial harbors was acclaimed by early writers as one of the Seven Wonders of the ancient world.

There was a large Jewish community in Alexandria—possibly numbering in excess of a hundred thousand—and many synagogues. The Jews were accorded special privileges in the city, but there were occasional flare-ups of intense anti-Jewish sentiment. The most serious of these happened in A.D. 38, under the Roman prefect Flaccus, when there was severe rioting against the Jews that resulted in the destruction of synagogues and property as well as the loss of life.

It was at Alexandria where the Hebrew Scriptures were translated into Greek. [A-110] This was also home for the famous Jewish writer Philo, whose writings combined Old Testament ideas with Greek philosophy.

There is no written record recounting the story of how Christianity began in Egypt and in Alexandria. Undoubtedly it started early, perhaps shortly after Pentecost. The earliest papyrus fragments of our New Testament were discovered in Egypt. Unfortunately, Alexandria became a major center for Gnosticism in the second century.

arriving there, he uses his rhetorical skills and knowledge of the Scripture to persuade the Jews that Jesus is the promised Messiah. Apollos's ministry has a deep impact on the Corinthian church, as we can see from Paul's first letter to the Corinthians. After Paul returns to Ephesus, Apollos comes and ministers alongside the apostle (see 1 Cor. 16:12).

Paul and the Disciples of John the Baptist in Ephesus (19:1–7)

Because of the city's strategic importance to the spread of the gospel in Asia Minor, Paul earnestly desires to minister for an extended period of time in Ephesus. As it turns out, he stays in Ephesus for about three years, twice as long as he spent in any other place in his apostolic travel. The apostle comes to the city by traveling an overland route from Antioch. This takes him across Asia Minor to this beautiful coastal city.

Ephesus (19:1). Numerous inscriptions refer to Ephesus as "the first and greatest metropolis of Asia." This is not an empty boast. Ephesus was clearly the leading city of the most prosperous region of the Roman empire. With a population of a quarter million, Ephesus ranked only behind Rome, Alexandria (Egypt), and Antioch (Syria) in size.[391]

For about 150 years, Ephesus served as the seat of the Roman administration for Asia Minor. As the Romans built their famous network of roads throughout the province, they numbered their milestone markers from Ephesus. Economically, one ancient writer calls Ephesus "the greatest commercial center in Asia this side of the Taurus river."[392] Another speaks of Ephesus as the most prosperous commercial center of the time, con-

trolling the financial affairs of western Asia Minor.[393] The location of Ephesus on a natural port helped the city achieve its prominence in commerce and flourish during the days of the Roman empire.

There he found some disciples (19:1). Immediately upon his arrival in Ephesus, Paul faces a unique situation. He discovers a group of men who claim to be followers of Jesus, but they are familiar only with what John the Baptist announced and possibly a small amount of independent information about him. They have put their faith in Jesus, but apparently do

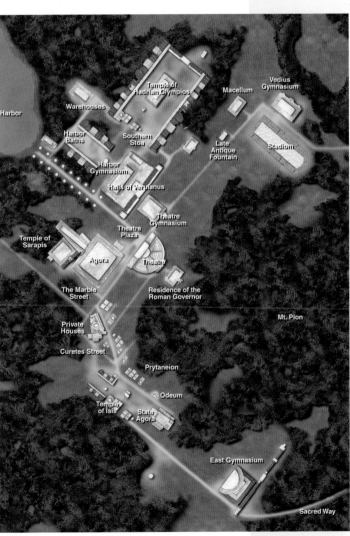

not know about his death, resurrection, and the outpouring of the Holy Spirit.

This is an incredible circumstance since over twenty years has passed since John the Baptist announced the coming of Jesus. If these men are Jews, it is unlikely they have traveled to Jerusalem for one of the pilgrimage feasts in the intervening years, where they could have inquired further and received more information about Jesus Christ.

Nevertheless, these men have acted on the limited information they heard and believe in Jesus. Luke does not tell us whether they worship in the synagogue or if they have created their own group. They lack, however, the new covenant experience of the Holy Spirit in their lives. Without the Spirit's presence, one is not a true Christian.[394]

The Holy Spirit came on them (19:6). Paul teaches these men, and after their response, he baptizes them into the Lord Jesus Christ. They receive the Holy Spirit, which immediately manifests his presence by enabling them to speak in tongues and prophesy.

This is the only situation we find in the New Testament or early Christian literature of a group of people who are aware of Jesus only through John the Baptist's teaching (though see 18:25). It

▶ The City of Ephesus
IMPORTANT FACTS:

- Population: about 250,000
- Religion: official covenant with the Ephesian Artemis, up to fifty other gods and goddesses worshiped
- Port City
- Seat of the Roman Government for Asia Minor
- Location of the Temple of Artemis—one of the Seven Wonders of the Ancient World

▶ Archaeology In Ephesus

Archaeologists have been working at the site of ancient Ephesus for well over a hundred years. Excavation of the city first began in 1863 under the directorship of J. T. Wood, who had been commissioned by the British Museum to find the ancient temple of the Ephesian Artemis. Since 1895, the Austrian Archaeological Institute in Vienna has assumed primary responsibility for the systematic exploration of the site and has sent teams every year. They publish their discoveries annually in a journal sponsored by the Institute.[A-111]

In recent years, teams have been excavating and working to preserve a set of terraced dwellings near the city center. These were thought to be the homes of wealthy citizens. Most of these lavish houses had three floors, which surrounded a columned open area in the center. The rooms were decorated with frescoed walls and mosaic floors depicting a variety of scenes from the Greek classics.

Over thirty-five hundred inscriptions have been discovered in the city. During the 1980s they were combined into a seven-volume anthology called *Die Inschriften von Ephesos* ("The Inscriptions of Ephesus").[A-112] Most of these inscriptions date from the Roman period and provide much helpful insight into the political, social, religious, and cultural life of the city.

The foundations and walls of numerous buildings have now been identified. These include temples of various gods and goddesses, two marketplaces, gymnasiums, bathhouses, a library, and fountains. Since Ephesus has been an uninhabited site for centuries, much has been preserved.

is important to see that their partial knowledge is not enough for a genuine Christian experience and the reception of the Spirit. In the gracious providence of God, however, they gain the opportunity to hear the complete story and enter into a relationship with the Spirit of God.

Preaching in the Synagogue and the Hall of Tyrannus (19:8–10)

As is his custom, Paul begins teaching in the Jewish synagogue. He uses it as a strategic starting point in fulfilling his commission from the Lord to take the gospel to the Gentiles in Ephesus. Every synagogue has a number of Gentiles already attracted to the one true God of Israel.

The synagogue (19:8). The synagogue at Ephesus has not yet been discovered by archaeologists. This is due in part to the fact that the section of the city where most Jews likely lived has not yet been excavated. Archaeologists, however, have discovered a few inscriptions that confirm the presence of a Jewish synagogue in the city:

- There is a fragment of a stone block (possibly from a synagogue at Ephesus) that is inscribed with a menorah and bears the inscription, "the altar."[395]
- Another inscription reads: "May the years of the rulers of the synagogue (*archisynagogoi*) and of the elders (*presbyteroi*) be many!"[396]

The Jewish historian Josephus confirms that there was a Jewish presence in the city. In fact, he claims that the Ephesian Jews were granted citizenship in the city.[397] Josephus also records many documents granting Jews in Ephesus certain privileges, such as exempting them from certain duties because of their Sabbath-keeping obligations.[398] Three tomb inscriptions have also been discovered that come from the Jewish community in Ephesus, one of them honoring a Jew who had been a "chief doctor" in the city.[399] All the available evidence suggests that the Jews in Ephesus were well integrated into the civic and social life of the city and did not experience the same level of hostility toward them that Jews faced in other cities (such as Alexandria).[400] Luke tells us that Paul spoke in the synagogue for three months, "arguing persuasively about the kingdom of God."

The lecture hall of Tyrannus (19:9). After opposition to his teaching grows too intense in the synagogue, Paul is able to secure the use of a lecture hall in the city for his teaching. Although a variety of buildings have been discovered by archaeologists, we have yet to find one with the name of "Tyrannus" attached to it. One ancient tradition (the Western text of Acts) explains that Paul teaches "from the fifth hour to the tenth," that is, from 11:00 A.M. until 4:00 P.M.

THE HARBOR OF EPHESUS

Only an outline of the harbor is visible today since the Cayster River has filled it with silt.
▼

If this tradition is true, we can surmise that Paul spends the mornings plying his leatherworking trade in the workshops (see Acts 18:3). Then he engages in a daily period of intense teaching in this public hall at a time that is normally reserved for a meal and rest. During the evening he returns to work or spends time meeting with people house to house.

All the Jews and Greeks who lived in the province of Asia heard the word of the Lord (19:10). By teaching in this fashion in a public place, Paul is able to touch the lives of many people who are curious about his message. In fact, because so many people travel to Ephesus on business, the gospel message spreads all over the province. Presumably at this time, groups of people begin meeting in homes on the Lord's Day to worship Christ, learn about him, and fellowship together. Most likely Epaphras is one of those who hears, becomes a Christian, and proclaims the gospel in his hometown of Colosse. Similarly, others from such Asia Minor cities as Pergamum, Sardis, and Philadelphia hear Paul's preaching and return to their cities to plant churches. What an exciting time to see the spread of the gospel. Luke could have filled a whole volume with stories about Paul's ministry in Ephesus.

God Does Extraordinary Miracles Through Paul (19:11–12)

Luke continues to tell us what a remarkable time of ministry this was. Paul heals the sick and casts out demons—apparently on a regular basis (the imperfect tense of the verb "did" underlines this). The power does not come from Paul,

however; it comes from God. Luke emphasizes that God is performing these extraordinary works of spiritual power "through Paul."

Handkerchiefs and aprons (19:12). Some of the sick people never come into direct contact with Paul. Their caregivers merely bring them handkerchiefs and aprons that Paul has touched, and the people are healed. The word for "handkerchief"(*soudarion*) probably refers to a face cloth for wiping perspiration, and the word translated "apron" (*simikinthion*) generally means a belt, but can refer to any article of clothing that has been in contact with the apostle's skin.[401] This practice looks "magical" in orientation, such that an object is charged with a power (like electricity) and released when it comes into contact with a sick person. Indeed, this view was prevalent in the common belief of the day and in the local occultism. Various kinds of objects were thought to be spiritually charged, and other objects could be empowered for use in a variety of purposes. What is important to see here is that (1) this method does not come from the initiative of Paul; it appears that the people assume things would work this way; and, (2) God chooses to manifest his healing power in spite of this deficient understanding of spiritual power. As we will see below, God dramatically teaches the Ephesian Christians about the futility of their magical practices and assumptions.

The evil spirits left them (19:12). As in the teaching of Jesus, we see here an assumption that the demonic realm is real and that there is a close association of demonic presence with certain illnesses. We do not know, however, whether Paul is here ministering to people who turn to Christ or to those who have yet to believe. Clearly the power of God is superior to the power of the enemy, who can be summoned to depart.

A Failed Exorcism and the Public Renunciation of Magic (19:13–20)

Ephesus was the hot place of ministry for a number of itinerant Jewish exorcists. This may correspond to the fact that this city had a reputation for being a center for magical and occult practices (see below). These men apparently developed special ability in effectively dealing with evil spirits. In this instance, however, their techniques are woefully inadequate.

Tried to invoke the name of the Lord Jesus (19:13). People who practiced magical incantations invoked any name thought to be laden with spiritual power. Because of the reputation surrounding Jesus as a mighty exorcist, it is of little surprise to find someone adding his name to their repertoire of names in the formula. We know of at least one magical incantation text that illustrates this tendency. This passage is from an Egyptian magical papyrus that dates to the late Roman period. Note the use of various kinds of rituals, the strings of magical names, and the way the name of Jesus is thrown into the mix:

> A tested charm of Pibechis [a legendary magician from Egypt] for those possessed by daimons: Take oil of unripe olives with the herb mastigia and the fruit pulp of the lotus, and boil them with colorless marjoram while saying, "IOEL OS SARTHIOMI EMORI THEOCHIPSOITH SITHEMEOCH SOTHE IOE MIMIPSOTHIOOPH PHERSOTHI AEEIOYO IOE EO

▶ Jewish Magic in Antiquity

Among many Gentiles, Jewish magic was famous in antiquity.[A-113] Certain Jews had a reputation for having power to manipulate evil spirits. Jewish magic is well illustrated in many different sources.

Jewish amulets. There are numerous magical amulets that are of a distinctively Jewish character. Many invoke Jewish angels and have various kinds of Jewish symbolism engraved on them. Most of these are made to protect people against the attacks of demonic powers.

Incantations and exorcism techniques associated with Solomon. There are many accounts of Jewish belief that Solomon's unsurpassed wisdom applied to dealing with evil spirits. Josephus notes of Solomon: "Now so great was the prudence and wisdom which God granted Solomon that he surpassed the ancients, and even the Egyptians.... And God granted him knowledge of the art used against

demons for the benefit and healing of men. He also composed incantations by which illnesses are relieved, and left behind forms of exorcisms with which those possessed by demons drive them out, never to return."[A-114]

Many of these incantations and exorcism formulas are compiled into a document that becomes known as *The Testament of Solomon*.[A-115] The *Testament* purports to explain how Solomon manipulated evil spirits to force them to do the work of building the temple. Imbedded in this plot are many loosely related formulas, recipes, and incantations for dealing with evil spirits when they caused all kinds of physical infirmities and perpetrated other evils.

Jewish involvement in magical practices continued through the centuries and is well attested in the "Kabbalistic" and "Hekhaloth" texts.

CHARI PHTHA [Ptah is the Egyptian creator god], come out from (the name of the victim). The phylactery: On a time lamella write "IAEO ABRAOTH IOCH PHTHA MESENPSIN IAO PHEOCH IAEO CHARSOK," and hang it on the patient. It is terrifying to every daimon, a thing he fears. After placing the patient opposite to you, conjure. This is the conjuration: "I conjure you by the god of the Hebrews, Jesus, IABA IAE ABRAOTH AIA THOTH ELE ELO AEO EOY IIIBAECH ABARMAS IABARAOU ABEL-BEL LONA ABRA MAROIA BRAKION, who appears in fire, who is in the midst of land, snow, and fog, TAN-NETIS; let your angel, the implacable, descend and let him assign the daimon flying around this form, which god formed in his holy paradise, because I pray to the holy god, calling upon AMMON IPSENTANCHO."[402]

Sceva, a Jewish chief priest (19:14). We know of this person only from Luke. Whether he is recognized by leaders in the local synagogue is unknown.

He gave them such a beating (19:16). The itinerants working with the demonized man in Ephesus face unbelievably powerful resistance from the victim. The demon taunts them by saying through the man, "Jesus I know, and I know about Paul, but who are you?" He then physically assaults the exorcists and they flee. The account clearly shows that it is not adequate merely to rely on formulas and names thought to be full of supernatural power. These exorcists have no relationship to Jesus. As Paul reiterates in his letters on many occasions, it is not out of his own personal power that he ministers, but out of the empowering presence of the Lord Jesus Christ working through him. For Paul, spiritual power is found in solidarity or union with Christ.

This became known to the Jews and Greeks living in Ephesus (19:17). Word of this dramatic situation spreads rapidly to people living in the city. Folks regard the name of Jesus with great respect and even fear. Surely people feel a sense of vulnerability if these Jewish exorcists were injured by this demonized man. Yet, what a stark contrast Paul provides in his regular ministry of exorcism. Certainly many people realize that nothing like this ever happens to him.

Many of those who believed (19:18). Even the Christians of Ephesus are moved to fear by this episode involving Sceva. Many of these believers come forward and openly confess their wicked deeds. This statement demonstrates that there are many who did not make a clean break with the past. They continued to be involved in occult arts in spite of their belief in Christ.

Sorcery (19:19). Many Christians in Paul's day are still wearing amulets, reciting magical invocations, and possessing papyrus scrolls of magical formulas and recipes. In the ancient world, "magic" (*mageia*) or "sorcery" (*perierga*) was a way of controlling various sorts of spirits. By knowing the right names, performing the appropriate rituals, or saying the appropriate incantations, one could command spirits to manifest themselves, to provide protection from other malicious spirits, to provide success, to compel the attraction of the opposite sex, or to effect a curse.

Brought their scrolls together and burned them publicly (19:19). Having never renounced their involvement in the occult arts, God brings conviction on the hearts of many of these new Christians. They go to their homes and gather together all of their papyrus scrolls of magical formulas (and presumably all other paraphernalia associated with magical practices), and burn them in front of a large assembly of believers.

Fifty thousand drachmas (19:19). Some of the people apparently sit down and calculate the value of the scrolls accord-

ing to their current market rate. The amount comes to fifty thousand drachmas, roughly the equivalent of fifty thousand days' wages. Another way of looking at this is that it would require over 150 people working a full year to equal the financial value of these scrolls. This strongly suggests that *many* Christians bring *many* scrolls out to the burning. Certainly they could have sold these documents and provided ample funds for the fledgling Christian community; however, it is worth no amount of money to these Christians to allow these scrolls to continue in circulation.

In this way the word of the Lord spread widely and grew in power (19:20). Luke ends this account on a triumphal note. These events in Ephesus demonstrate that the power of God is mightier than any other power. Writing to Christians in this area five to eight years later, Paul says of Christ that God exalted him to a position "far above all rule and authority, power and dominion, and every title that can be given" (Eph. 1:21). No spirit,

◀ *left*

A LEAF FROM A MAGICAL PAPYRUS

This is identified as *PGM* LXX and is housed at the University of Michigan.

▶ Magic and the Occult In Ephesus

Ephesus was renown as being something of a center for magical practices in the Mediterranean world.[A-116] The practice of magic was everywhere—it was part of the fabric of common "folk belief"—but Ephesus acquired a significant reputation for it.

This reputation was perpetuated, in part, by the so-called "Ephesian Letters" (*Ephesia Grammata*). These were actually six names—*askion, kataskion, lix, tetrax, damnameneus,* and *aisia*—thought to be laden with protective power for warding off evil demons. One ancient writer says that the "magi" instructed people possessed by evil spirits to repeat to themselves the magic words in order to drive the demons out.[A-117] There was a story that circulated

about an Ephesian wrestler who traveled to Olympia to compete in the games. This wrestler wore the "Ephesian Letters" on an ankle bracelet while he competed and was winning every match. Finally an opponent from Miletus discovered the bracelet and protested, whereupon the item was removed by the officials. The Ephesian wrestler then fell to three successive defeats by his Milesian opponent.

No magical papyri have been discovered in Ephesus. But this has more to do with the fact that the climate of this area is not conducive to the preservation of papyri. Nevertheless, a variety of magical amulets, gems, and inscriptions have been discovered in the city.

demon, god, goddess, or any other supernatural agent that anyone cares to name can come close to rivaling the Lord Jesus Christ.

REFLECTIONS

OUR FAMILIES, FRIENDS, COMMUNITY, culture, and pre-Christian religious beliefs have an amazing staying power over our lives. An important part of the discipleship process is confronting and replacing the ungodly aspects of what we believe and how we live. Whether it is trafficking in magic or the idolatry of greed, it is essential that we repudiate the evil and replace it with a pure commitment to Christ and his ways.

Paul's Plans (19:21–22)

To Jerusalem (19:21). Paul now makes plans to return to Jerusalem. Luke does not tell us why he intends to go there, but based on Paul's letters we know that he initiates a collection from among the churches for the relief of impoverished Christians there.[403]

Through Macedonia and Achaia (19:21). These are the Roman provinces in Greece where Paul planted churches—in Philippi, Thessalonica, Berea, and Corinth. All of these churches are participating in the famine relief collection.

Rome (19:21). We know from the end of Acts that Paul finally arrives at Rome. Even at this early stage, Paul has a strong

▶The Problem of Christian Magic and Syncretism

The Ephesian Christians provide us with a marvelous example of forsaking everything to gain Christ and hold firmly to him. We cannot underestimate, however, how difficult this sort of renunciation was for people who had grown up with household gods and magical formulas and spells. Surely the apostle Paul taught the importance of leaving behind these idolatrous objects and devoting oneself to Christ alone. Yet no amount of preaching appears to have convinced these Ephesians in the earliest stage of their walk with the Lord. God used a dramatic event to help them see the futility and danger of holding on to their occult practices.

Not all Christians in the early history of the church followed the example of the Ephesians. Many continued to worship their idols alongside Jesus and to call on other spiritual powers in magical invocations. This is probably what was happening at Colosse when Paul denounced their practice of invoking angels (Col. 2:18).

In recent years, more papyrus documents have been discovered that may aptly be called "Christian magic." Most of these papyrus texts have been discovered in Egypt and are written either in Greek or Coptic (an Egyptian language). Many have now been translated into English in a volume titled, *Ancient Christian Magic*.[A-118] The texts are highly syncretistic—that is, they blend Christianity with occultism and various other religious practices and beliefs. What is striking in these texts is how the name of Jesus is invoked in a formula alongside angels and pagan deities. For example, one text calls upon: "Hor, Hor, Phor, Eloei, Adonai, Iao, Sabaoth, Michael, Jesus Christ. Help us and this household. Amen."

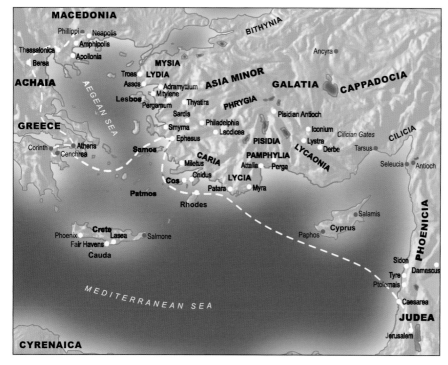

MACEDONIA
Phillipi • Neapolis
Amphipolis
Thessalonica
Apollonia
Berea
MYSIA
Troas • LYDIA
ACHAIA
Assos • Adramyttium • ASIA MINOR
Lesbos • Mitylene
Pergamum • Thyatira
Sardis
GREECE
Smyrna • Philadelphia
Ephesus • Laodicea
Corinth • Athens
Cenchrea
Samos
Miletus • CARIA
Cnidus
Cos • Patara
Patmos
Rhodes
Phoenix • Crete • Lasea
Fair Havens • Salmone
Cauda
MEDITERRANEAN SEA
CYRENAICA

BITHYNIA
Ancyra •
GALATIA • CAPPADOCIA
PHRYGIA
Pisidian Antioch
Iconium
PISIDIA • Lystra • Cilician Gates • CILICIA
PAMPHYLIA • Derbe • Tarsus
Attalia • Perga • LYCAONIA
LYCIA • Seleucia • Antioch
Myra

Salamis
Cyprus
Paphos
PHOENICIA
Sidon • Damascus
Tyre
Ptolemais
Caesarea
JUDEA
Jerusalem

197

Acts

◀

PAUL'S INTENDED
JOURNEYS

Macedonia to
Achaia to
Jerusalem.

---

desire to go to the capital city to minister the gospel. He has no idea what lies before him.

Timothy and Erastus (19:22). Anticipating an imminent departure, Paul sends two members of his ministry team ahead of him to the churches at Philippi and Thessalonica. Although it is easy to think of Paul as working alone, we must remember that he has a strong team concept of ministry. This is the only mention of Timothy in connection with Paul's ministry at Ephesus. From his correspondence to Corinth (he writes 1 Corinthians while he is in Ephesus), we learn that the apostle uses Timothy as an emissary in continuing ministry to the Corinthians while he is in Ephesus. Timothy travels there at least once to help the church deal with certain issues (see 1 Cor. 4:17; 16:10–11). Paul's other companion, Erastus, is probably a different person from the Erastus mentioned in Romans 16:23 as the city treasurer of Corinth.

Opposition From the Cult of the Ephesian Artemis (19:23–41)

Shortly after Paul decides to leave Ephesus, he faces the most heated opposition to his ministry in the city yet.[404] A huge mob forms at the instigation of some local businessmen and they begin shouting their adherence to the local patron goddess of the city, Artemis of Ephesus. The success of Paul's ministry and the growth of the church is now seen as a significant threat to this famous cult.

A silversmith named Demetrius (19:24). In the late 1800s an inscription found in Ephesus and dated to the mid-first century was published by a British scholar. The inscription honored a group of men who had served as "temple wardens" (*neopoios*). One of those honored was a man from Ephesus named "Demetrius, son of Menophilos, and grandson of Tryphon." While some scholars have argued for a positive identification

▶ The Cult of the Ephesian Artemis

Artemis of Ephesus, known to the Romans as Diana of Ephesus, was the principal deity of the huge metropolis of Ephesus and popular throughout the Mediterranean world. In fact, the Greek writer Pausanias notes that she was worshiped more widely than any other deity he knew.[A-119] She was worshiped as the great "mother goddess" and was thereby closely related to the main mother goddess of Asia Minor, Cybele (also called "the great mother" [magna matēr or ma]).

As a mother goddess Artemis possessed fertility and reproductive power that caused the earth to blossom with life of all kinds. She was the goddess of childbirth and a nourishing mother to all. Animals and wildlife were also a part of her domain and under her control.

Her grand temple in Ephesus was lauded by ancient writers as one of the Seven Wonders of the World. The structure of the cult was integrally interwoven into the fabric of daily life and culture. The temple actually functioned as the banking and financial center for the province. Large amounts of money were deposited and borrowed from the Artemision. The cult also owned substantial amounts of property in the area. One of the twelve calendar months was named after her—the month of Artemision—and during this month an annual festival was held in her honor.

The worshipers of Artemis regarded her as supreme among all the gods and goddesses. They honored her as "first among thrones," "savior," "Lord," "Queen of the World," and "the heavenly goddess."

Her cultic image is richly ornamented in the oriental style.[A-120] The first thing one notices is the rows of bulbous objects on her chest. Although some have interpreted these as numerous female breasts, the shape does not suggest this; others have suggested ostrich eggs, steer testicles, grapes, nuts, and acorns. Whatever they are supposed to be, they probably represent in some way her role as a goddess of fertility. The ferocious lions on her arms depict her mighty power.

The skirt of Artemis is adorned with a series of frightful-looking creatures that appear to be in a posture of surrender to the goddess. These probably represent more than her dominion over wildlife in nature. These animals may be understood as representing the harmful spirits of nature over which Artemis wielded authority.

Although the Ephesian Artemis was not widely known as a goddess of magic, she does appear to have a close association with the magical practices of the time. As a supremely powerful deity, she could exercise her power for the benefit of her adherents who faced attacks from opposing powers and spirits. In the magical papyri, she is virtually identified with Hekate (the goddess of witchcraft) and Selene (the moon goddess) and ascribed with power over the spirits of the underworld. Many magical amulets have been discovered bearing the image of the Ephesian Artemis.

Her power extended also to the stars, which were widely believed to be animated by spirit powers and tied to a person's fate. In fact, the symbols of the Zodiac were prominently depicted on the cultic image of Artemis as a necklace.

Those who worshiped Artemis believed they were devoted to an awesome, unrivaled deity, who could not only help them in the daily affairs of life but could also provide them with protection from evil powers and break the bonds of fate.

between this Demetrius and the one mentioned in Acts, it is impossible to be certain. The text here could be referring to another person of the same name, since Demetrius was a popular name. Nevertheless, the possibility remains that this is indeed the same person.

Silver shrines (19:24). These were not simply statuettes of the goddess, but depictions of her sitting on her throne in the center of the temple. Archaeologists have not yet discovered any of these sil-ver shrines. Presumably, most of them were melted down and the silver reused as they were discovered over the centuries. These shrines were probably sold to people to use primarily as dedicatory offerings. They would have been brought to the temple and offered to the goddess.

Workmen in related trades (19:25). Inscriptions found at Ephesus have brought to light the existence of numerous trade guilds in the city. Presumably there are also craftsmen who make less

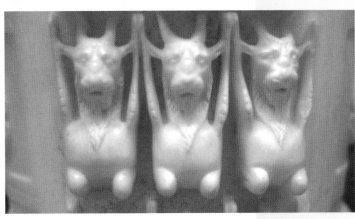

THE EPHESIAN ARTEMIS

(left) A beautiful marble statue of the goddess found under the town council building at Ephesus.

(right) The image depicts lions on her arms and the Zodiac on her chest.

(bottom) Ghoulish creatures are represented on her cultic vestment.

 ◀ ▼

▶Archaeological Discovery: An Inscription Attesting the Guild of Silversmiths

A Greek inscription discovered at Ephesus dating to the time of the emperor Claudius in the mid-first century gives solid evidence for the existence of silver shrine makers and a whole guild of silversmiths (*argyrokopoi*).

> This tomb and the area around it and the subterranean vault belong to M. Antonius Hermeia, silversmith, shrine-maker (*neopoios*)⚹ and Claudia daughter of Erotion, his wife. No one is to be put in this tomb except the aforementioned. If anyone does dare to put in a corpse or excise this text, he shall pay to the silversmiths at Ephesus 1000 denarii. Responsibil-

ity for this tomb rests with the association of silversmiths, and Erotion dedicated 50,000 denarii. The legacy was provided in the 6th month, on the appointed day.[A-121]

In addition to this text, at least seven other inscriptions have now been discovered making some reference to silversmiths. One of these texts (inscribed on a column) suggests that the shops of the silversmiths were located on the Arcadiane Street—the street that ran from the theater to the harbor.[A-122] Another reads, "may the guild of the silversmiths flourish!"[A-123]

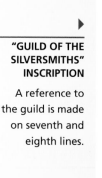

expensive shrines of Artemis out of terra cotta and marble.

A good income from this business (19:25). It is interesting to note that the catalyst for the great disturbance can be traced back to an economic incentive. These businessmen are losing money and feel they can turn things around by changing public opinion.

Paul has convinced and led astray large numbers of people (19:26). This is an insight into the tremendous success of the gospel in penetrating this strategic city. The loss of business to these shrine-makers is also an indication that many of the new Christians are people who turn to God directly from idols.

Worshiped throughout the province of Asia and the world (19:27). This is no exaggeration on the part of Demetrius. The Ephesian Artemis was worshiped throughout the Mediterranean world.

Great is Artemis of the Ephesians (19:28). Demetrius' speech to the trade workers of the city has its intended effect. The people are furious and begin chanting their support for the goddess. What starts as a meeting of trade workers quickly attracts numerous others from the city, who join in the chorus of protest.

The theater (19:29). The crowd assembles at the theater, though we do not know if this is where the meeting originates. The central location of the theater and the numerous people shouting in concert would certainly attract others. The theater, which overlooked the harbor, could hold up to twenty-four thousand people. There is no way of determining the approximate number of people who are involved in this uproar, but it is not inconceivable that it is numbered in the thousands. This is underlined by Luke's comment that, "soon the whole city was in an uproar."

The officials of the province (19:31). When Paul wants to speak to the assembled mob in the theater, some fellow believers and friends of his who are civic officials prevent him. The expression

"officials of the province" (NIV) is an interpretive translation of the Greek word *Asiarchēs* (a combination of the Greek words for "Asia" and "ruler"). Over a hundred references to Asiarchs have now been counted in the many inscriptions found on the west coast of Asia Minor.[405] These people were wealthy, aristocratic Roman citizens who held this high provincial Roman office for an indeterminate period of time. Some of the Ephesian Asiarchs were important benefactors of the city, providing money for public works, setting up honorary statutes of civic and Roman officials, and subsidizing embassies to Rome on the city's behalf. Although we do not know the exact duties of their official service, they were people of great influence who had often served in a variety of important public offices. Because there was no separation of religion and state, they probably bore some responsibilities regarding the cult of the Ephesian Artemis.

The fact that some of the Asiarchs are friends of Paul suggest that they may be Christians. It is possible that the house churches of Ephesus met in the larger homes of these people. It is also possible that Paul becomes acquainted with some of them as his customers in his tent-making business.

The Jews pushed Alexander to the front (19:33). In the beginning, many Gentiles view Christianity as a form of Judaism. In fact, most Christians viewed themselves as a form of Judaism. But the non-Christian Jews of the city want to dissociate themselves from this Christian movement. The Jewish effort to have the assembly hear from one of their representatives is unsuccessful, however. This fiasco results in a furthered frenzied response by the crowd, who continue shouting "Great is Artemis of the Ephesians" for two hours.

The city clerk (19:35). The "city clerk" (*grammateus*) is the elected head of the city council. He functions much like a mayor to the city. Recognizing the danger the citizens are putting the city in with respect to the Roman authorities, the city clerk appeals to the noisy crowd for calm and advises a more cautious approach to the burgeoning Christian movement. By doing so, he exemplifies the duty of an excellent civic official. The Roman historian Dio Chrysostom, addressing leaders in Tarsus, describes the ideal ruler of a city:

> But I say that the counsellor who is a good counsellor and fit to be leader of a city should be prepared to withstand absolutely all those things which are considered difficult or vexatious, and especially the vilifications and anger of the mob. Like the promontories that form our harbours, which receive the full violence of the sea but keep the inner waters calm

---

ASIARCH INSCRIPTION

This inscription makes reference to an *Asiarch* and speaks of a man named Salutaris as a "lover of Artemis."

▼

and peaceful, so he too should stand out against the violence of the people, whether they are inclined to burst into a rage or abuse him or take any measure whatever, and he should be wholly unaffected by such outbursts.[406]

The people listen to him, and the tension of the volatile setting is defused. When he finishes speaking, he simply dismisses the assembly.

Paul Travels to Macedonia and Greece (20:1–6)

The next six verses are a highly abbreviated summary of nearly two years of activities by Paul. He pours his efforts into visiting many of the churches he has established to encourage them and help them in their growth and development.

After encouraging them, said good-by (20:1). After nearly three years of ministry in Ephesus, Paul decides to leave. This is not a sudden or forced departure. He tells the Corinthians that he has planned to stay in Ephesus through Pentecost (1 Cor. 16:8), which in the year 55

falls on May 25.[407] Now he wants to revisit his churches and begins gathering a collection for the impoverished Christians in Jerusalem.

After leaving Ephesus, he apparently travels first to Troas, a fact that we learn from 2 Corinthians, which he writes a short time later in Macedonia: "Now when I went to Troas to preach the gospel of Christ and found that the Lord had opened a door for me, I still had no peace of mind, because I did not find my brother Titus there. So I said good-by to them and went on to Macedonia" (2 Cor. 2:12–13). Before leaving Ephesus, Paul sends Titus to Corinth to deal with a difficult situation. Paul himself has just visited Corinth and faces a hostile response. He writes them what he terms a "sorrowful letter" (2 Cor. 2:3–9), which is now lost. At this point, Paul is anxious about the situation in Corinth and awaits news from Titus (2 Cor. 7:5–7).

Set out for Macedonia. He traveled through that area (20:1–2). During this time, he revisits the churches in Philippi, Thessalonica, Berea, and presumably others that were established on the basis of their witness in the region. It may have been during this period that Paul travels to the west coast and proclaims the gospel in Illyricum (Rom. 15:19), a Roman province on in the northwest portion of the Balkan peninsula along the Adriatic sea. Paul writes 2 Corinthians while he is in Macedonia.

Arrived in Greece, where he stayed three months (20:2–3). This probably refers to Corinth rather than Athens (or any other Greek city). While in Corinth, he is able to deal personally with the deep concerns that he writes about in 2 Corinthians and to gather the final portions of his collection for the Jerusalem church. It is also during this time that he writes his substantive letter to the church at Rome. In it, he expresses his plans to visit them shortly as he anticipates a journey to Spain.

The Jews made a plot against him (20:3). We know nothing about this plot. It may have involved not only plans to kill him, but also to take the large amount of money Paul is carrying with him. Apparently Paul wants to first visit the church in Antioch (Syria) before going on to Jerusalem. Now his plans take an abrupt change, and he returns overland to Philippi.

He was accompanied by (20:4). For his trip to Jerusalem with the collection, Paul takes with him seven delegates from churches in Macedonia, Asia, and south Galatia. Two of the companions he names here, Sopater and Secundus (we know nothing else about them, unless Sopater is the same person as Sosipater in Rom. 16:21). Luke later joins Paul in

Philippi and accompanies him to Rome. It is not known whether Silas is still in Corinth (Acts 18:5) or whether he has left and journeyed elsewhere. On Timothy, see comments on 16:1. These delegates go ahead of Paul to Troas and wait for him there.

Aristarchus (20:4). A convert from Paul's ministry at Thessalonica (or possibly as a product of the early Thessalonian Christians' evangelization), Aristarchus joins Paul in his Ephesian ministry, as also has Gaius from Derbe (19:29). He also later visited Paul during his Caesarean imprisonment and accompanied him on his eventful voyage to Rome (27:2). Evidently, he was imprisoned with Paul in Rome and was with him when he wrote to the Colossians (Col. 4:10) and to Philemon (Philem. 24).

Tychicus (20:4). Tychicus, an Ephesian believer, later ministers to Paul during his Roman imprisonment. He was with Paul when he wrote his letters to the Ephesians and to the Colossians and carried those letters to the churches (Eph. 6:21; Col. 4:7). He remained faithful to Paul and was an important emissary for him (2 Tim. 4:12; Tit. 3:12).

Trophimus (20:4). The only other time we hear about this Ephesian is when Paul was accused of taking him into the temple precincts (21:29).

We sailed from Philippi ... joined the others at Troas (20:6). Paul now leaves Macedonia with Luke (note the "we") and joins the other delegates in the northern Asia Minor city of Troas. It is now early spring (April of A.D. 57),[408] which Luke dates by reference to the Feast of Unleavened Bread.

TROAS

Archaeological remains at Alexandria Troas with the Aegean Sea in the background.
▼

REFLECTIONS

THE APOSTLE PAUL DOES NOT
work alone. He is a team player and team developer. He is constantly investing himself into the lives of other people who will share the work of the ministry with him and continue it in his absence. This same priority and method should characterize the work of Christian leaders today.

Eutychus Falls and Is Healed (20:7–16)

As a direct result of his preaching after Paul left Ephesus (2 Cor. 2:12–13), a community of believers had been established in Troas (on Troas, see Acts 16:7). Paul feels an obligation to visit them and encourage them before he travels on to Jerusalem. During his short stay, God works an amazing miracle through the hands of the apostle.

On the first day of the week we came together to break bread (20:7). This is a clear reference to the fact that the early Christians began meeting on the first day of the week to worship (Sunday), rather than on the Sabbath day (Saturday). A similar reference occurs in 1 Corinthians 16:12, where Paul encourages the believers in Corinth to set aside some money when they gather on the first day of every week. "Breaking bread" refers to the early Christian practice of sharing a meal together followed by a time of worship when those gathered remember the significance of the death of Jesus by partaking of bread and wine (see comments on Acts 2:42).

Kept on talking until midnight (20:7). This does not imply that the believers have met throughout the day and into the night. Slaves and artisans may not have been free from their work-related responsibilities to meet until the evening, so they may not have gathered together until this time. This is a unique opportunity for Paul and for the Christians of this city, and they want to make the most of their brief time together.

The upstairs room ... the third story (20:8–9). Luke's description suggests that the meeting is held in the third floor room of a Roman *insula*. This was typically a three-story building that had apartments on the top two floors and shops at the street level. Most of the population of the major cities lived in these multi-storeyed tenement blocks.[409] This so-called "house church" is actually an "apartment church."

Eutychus (20:9). This young man, whose name means "fortunate," succumbs to his body's weariness

MACEDONIA

Phillippi • • Neapolis
Thessalonica • • Amphipolis
• Berea • Apollonia
ACHAIA
MYSIA
Troas •
Assos • Adramyttium ASIA MINOR
Lesbos • Mitylene
Pergamum • Thyatira
LYDIA PHRYGIA
GREECE
Chios • Sardis • • Philadelphia
Smyrna • • Laodicea
Ephesus •
Corinth • Athens
Cenchrea • Samos • CARIA
• Miletus
AEGEAN SEA
Cos • Cnidus LYCIA
Patmos • Patara • Myra
Rhodes

after a day of work and the late hour of the night.

Was picked up dead (20:9). Luke clearly states that he is dead, not that he "appeared to be dead" (see 14:19).

Threw himself on the young man (20:10). Similar to Peter when he raised Tabitha (9:36–41), Paul brings this young man back to life. The essence of this story is also similar to Elijah's raising of the widow of Zarephath's son (1 Kings 17:17–24) and Elisha's restoring the life of the Shunammite woman's son (2 Kings 4:33–36). In both instances, the prophets lay on the young men they were attempting to bring back to life. We may assume that Paul calls out to God in a way similar to Elijah: "O LORD my God, let this boy's life return to him!" (1 Kings 17:21).

Sailed for Assos (20:13). The group of eight men (the seven mentioned in 20:4 plus Luke) board their ship at the port while Paul stays behind to squeeze as much time out of his visit as possible. He knows an overland shortcut that enables him to get to the next port of call before the ship leaves from there. The port city of Assos is twenty miles south of Troas. Aristotle once lived in this city and it is also the birthplace of the Stoic philosopher Cleanthes.

Mitylene . . . Kios . . . Samos (20:14–15). The ship leaves the port of Assos and sails to Mitylene, about thirty miles south of Assos and only ten miles off the Asia

Minor mainland. Mitylene is the capital and port city of the island of Lesbos, the third largest Aegean island (629 square miles) after Crete and Euboea. Leaving there, the boat sails south skirting the coastline and "right through" (*antikrys*) the passage separating the island of Kios from the mainland. Contrary to the NIV translation, the boat probably does not dock at Kios. At the narrowest point, Kios is only five miles from the mainland of Asia Minor. The boat passes by Ephesus and eventually comes to the island of Samos. The island is only a mile from the mainland. Leaving the port city of Samos, the boat then makes its way roughly twenty miles to the city of Miletus.

In a hurry to reach Jerusalem, if possible, by the day of Pentecost (20:16). Having spent nearly three years in Ephesus, it is extraordinarily difficult for Paul to visit without spending significant time meeting with people and dealing with problems and issues. In A.D. 57, Pentecost falls on May 29.[410] It has been nearly twenty-five years since the outpouring of the Holy Spirit on that important Pentecost after Jesus' resurrection. The offering Paul is carrying and the Gentile delegates that accompany him will be a significant symbol of God's work in reaching Gentiles.

Paul Speaks to the Ephesian Elders (20:17–38)

Paul takes advantage of his stay in Miletus to meet with the Ephesian elders to encourage them and advise them in their important ministry. As with the other addresses that Luke records in Acts, this is merely a précis of a much longer talk that Paul gives. Luke provides us with the highlights and central points of Paul's talk. This is the only occasion thus far in Acts where Luke himself is actually present at one of the messages that he records and can thereby now write as an eyewitness to the event and from memory (and possibly notes) on what Paul says.

This message is also unique in being the only speech given by Paul in Acts that

MILETUS

Ancient ruins at the site of Miletus.
▼

▶ Miletus

The city of Miletus was located just thirty miles due south of Ephesus.[A-124] Miletus was also a harbor city and, during the pre-Roman era, was a more significant city in Asia Minor than Ephesus. Situated on a small peninsula, Miletus actually had three harbors.

There is a well-preserved theater in the city that was capable of accomodating fifteen thousand people. Both Josephus and archaeology confirm a strong Jewish presence in the city.[A-125] On the fifth row of the theater, an inscription was discovered that reads, "the place of the Jews and the God-fearers (*theosebion*)." The inscription suggests that Jews and God-fearers were viewed as two distinct but related groups who were held in high esteem by the city. The theater management granted to them the privilege of a special section of seats.[A-126]

is addressed explicitly to Christians. The Miletus address is thus much more comparable to Paul's letters, all of which are addressed to Christians. It is not surprising, then, that there are numerous themes in this speech that amply parallel similar statements and themes in the letters.[411]

Paul sent to Ephesus for the elders of the church (20:17). Paul does not neglect the Ephesian church in this fortuitous few days he would be in Miletus. He decides to gather the leadership of the church and meet solely with them. It would take one to two days to get the message to Ephesus and at least two days for them to get to Ephesus. On "elders" (*presbyteroi*), see 11:30.

I served the Lord with great humilty and with tears (20:19). It is sometimes easy to think of Paul as a thick-skinned, cognitively-oriented, driven personality. This statement gives a unique perspective on the tender side of Paul. In verse 31, he repeats the fact that he serves them with many tears. Paul has a huge capacity to love and embrace those who came into the body of Christ. Paul invariably develops a great deal of affection for these new believers and is deeply grieved when they lapse morally or are taken in by some kind of false teaching.

"Humility" was not a virtue that is emulated in the Greco-Roman world and was often thought of as a sign of weakness in an individual. Paul seeks to embody a servant model of leadership that he learns from the Lord Jesus.[412]

Severely tested by the plots of the Jews (20:19). Luke reveals nothing about any Jewish plots against Paul in Ephesus, although it would be surprising if he does not face opposition from the zealous members of the synagogue there. Fresh on Paul's mind is the fact that he is not able to take a boat directly from the port of Corinth (Cenchrea) to Syria precisely because of a plot on his life (20:3). He has also faced many other violent outbursts against him in most of the cities where he has proclaimed the gospel.

Publicly and from house to house (20:20). The Ephesians have fond memories of the hours they spent learning from Paul in the Hall of Tyrannus. But this passage makes it clear that Paul exercises his teaching ministry also "from house to house." This also reveals something of the organization of the Ephesian church as a network of house churches.

Compelled by the Spirit, I am going to Jerusalem (20:22). Paul here uses the imagery of being chained or tied up like a prisoner, but in this instance by the Holy Spirit. This is the same word used to describe Paul's binding in chains when he is later taken into custody by the Romans in Jerusalem (22:29) or the chains with which people try to shackle the Gerasene demoniac (Mark 5:3). The metaphor underlines Paul's conviction that he is under a divine imperative to get to Jerusalem.

In every city the Holy Spirit warns me (20:23). The Judean prophet Agabus soon warns Paul that he will be bound and arrested if he goes to Jersusalem (21:10–11). Prophets in Tyre warn of the same fate awaiting Paul (21:4). Presumably, the Spirit speaks similarly through prophets in Corinth, Troas, Philippi, and elsewhere to the same effect.

I am innocent of the blood of all men (20:26). Paul's words here echo the image of the watchman in Ezekiel: "Son of man, speak to your countrymen and say to them: 'When I bring the sword against a land, and the people of the land choose one of their men and make him their watchman, and he sees the sword coming against the land and blows the trumpet to warn the people, then if anyone hears the trumpet but does not take warning and the sword comes and takes his life, his blood will be on his own head."[413] Like the faithful watchman in Ezekiel, in proclaiming the kingdom of God, Paul has warned the people in the cities where he ministers about the impending judgment.

The flock . . . be shepherds (20:28). The concept of a flock of sheep as an image of the community of God's people has deep Old Testament roots. Israel is God's special "flock" and the sheep of his pasture (Ezek. 34). God gave stern warnings to the shepherds who tended his flock through the prophets Jeremiah and Ezekiel (Jer. 23:1–4; Ezek. 34:1–31). The main concern in Ezekiel is that the shepherds have become so concerned about feeding themselves that their sheep have not been well fed, have roamed the hillsides unprotected, and have become prey for the wild animals. Because of this dreadful situation, God himself becomes the shepherd for his sheep. God's role as the shepherd of his people is beautifully expressed in Psalm 23. Jesus claims to have fulfilled this distinctive role as "the good shepherd" (John 10:1–18). Peter, as a representative of all Christian leaders, is three times enjoined by Jesus to "take care of my sheep" (John 21:15, 16, 17).

Of which the Holy Spirit has made you overseers (20:28). The apostle Paul may appoint leaders in the churches (14:23), but ultimately the decisions for leaders are based on the prior appointment by the Holy Spirit. Luke does not tell us how Paul discerned this decision of the Spirit—whether through prophecy, a strong inner leading of the Spirit both in himself and in those who are to be appointed, or by a recognition of the Spirit's work in their lives granting giftedness and abilities that are clear leadership qualities.

Overseers (20:28). The leaders of the church at Ephesus are first called "elders" (20:17) and now referred to as "overseers." This verse demonstrates that "elders" (*presbyteroi*) and "overseers" (*episkopoi*) are not two distinguishable groups of leaders in the first-century church. The function and role of these leaders is intimately associated with the meaning attached to the image of "shepherd." The term *episkopos* was widely used in the ancient Greco-Roman world. There are instances of it used of people who managed buildings or cargo on a boat.[414] There were also market overseers who judged between fair and shady dealings.[415] Inscriptional evidence points to the use of *episkopoi* as a designation for community officials in Rhodes.[416] The

term is also used in the Greek Old Testament and Judaism for various kinds of leaders of the people (e.g., Neh. 11:9, 14, 22). Philo even refers to Moses as an *episkopos* who keeps watch over the condition of the soul.[417]

Savage wolves will come (20:29). The prophet Ezekiel complains that the rulers of Jerusalem are "like wolves tearing their prey" (Ezek. 22:27). Similarly, Zephaniah pronounces woe over Jerusalem's rulers because they "are evening wolves, who leave nothing for the morning" (Zeph. 3:3). Jesus warns his disciples about the coming of false prophets who "come to you in sheep's clothing, but inwardly they are ferocious wolves" (Mark 7:15). Jesus also stresses the protection the shepherd provides since a "hired hand" runs away when he sees a wolf coming leaving the sheep vulnerable to the wolf's attack (John 10:12–13).

▶

"SAVAGE WOLVES WILL COME"

Even from your own number men will arise and distort the truth (20:30). Paul may be speaking prophetically here—the Spirit has revealed to him that a struggle for the truth will ensue within the Ephesian church. If not, perhaps Paul sees some tendencies within members of the church that disturb him. His prediction indeed proves to be correct. Less than ten years later, an unhealthy teaching

emerged in the Ephesian church that he instructed Timothy to deal with.[418] Toward the end of the first century, the Ephesian church struggled with an outbreak of docetic teaching that the apostle John fought against in his letters (see esp. 1 John 2:19; 2 John 7).

So be on your guard! (20:31). A good shepherd will keep the flock secure from all dangers. This command reaffirms the need for the Ephesian *presbyteroi/episkopoi/*shepherds to be vigilant over the large community of believers in their care. The word used in this context literally means to "watch" (*grēgoreō*). After Nehemiah built the walls of Jerusalem, he stationed men on the walls and on the gates to "watch" (Neh. 7:3). During the Jewish revolt in the second century B.C., the Jewish commander Jonathan learned that the enemies from Syria were preparing to attack and so "commanded his men to be alert [*grēgoreō*] and to keep their arms at hand so as to be ready all night for battle" (1 Macc. 12:27). Jesus repeatedly instructed his disciples to "watchfulness" (Mark 13:34, 35, 37).

These hands of mine have supplied my own needs and the needs of my companions (20:34). Paul did not avail himself of his apostolic right to be financially supported in his ministry, although financial gifts were sent to him from time to time (2 Cor. 11:8; Phil. 4:14–18). He worked hard in a trade to support himself, not only during his Ephesian ministry, but also in other places that he ministered.[419] This is the one place we learn that his work helped support others on his team. Paul was sensitive to the potential danger of being compared with other kinds of itinerants (such as the Cynics) who exploited people financially.

We must help the weak (20:35). Generosity with money, food, and material possessions is a hallmark of the early church and a virtue that Paul enjoins his congregations to practice (see also Eph. 4:28). "The weak" probably refers to those in the church who are not able to entirely support themselves. Paul is elsewhere clear that able-bodied people must work so they have adequate resources to purchase food and shelter (2 Thess. 3:6–15). Nevertheless, there are some in the church who cannot survive without substantive help from their brothers and sisters in the community of believers.

Remembering the words the Lord Jesus himself said (20:35). Jesus' teaching, "It is more blessed to give than to receive," is not present in any of the four Gospels. Paul is apparently here quoting a saying of Jesus that is only known in oral tradition or in a written source that is not preserved. There are a variety of similar statements made by other people in Jewish, Greek, and early Christian literature.[420] A principle of reciprocity is deeply ingrained in Greco-Roman culture, that is, one must give in equal measure to what one has received. Paul's exhortation strikes out at this idea and encourages believers to give to those who cannot give in return.[421]

They would never see his face again (20:38). Paul intends to visit Jerusalem and travel from there to Rome and on to Spain in his efforts to reach Gentiles with the gospel of the Lord Jesus Christ (Rom. 15:24–29). At this point, Paul does not know that he will travel to Italy in Roman custody and face trial in the capital city of the empire. If the Pastoral Epistles are to be dated to shortly after

this imprisonment, it appears that Paul does, in fact, have the opportunity to see the Ephesians again (1 Tim. 1:3).

The Journey From Asia Minor to Jerusalem (21:1–16)

After the tearful good-bye, Paul departs with his eight companions on a boat and travels to Jerusalem. Luke describes some of the stops along the way. Paul is able to meet with believers in a variety of locales, but he is also served twice with prophetic warnings that he will face suffering in Jerusalem.

We had torn ourselves away from them (21:1). The verb expresses the difficulty and anguish both groups experienced in having to be separated. It is comparable to the weaning of a child from his mother's breast (see Isa. 28:9 where the passive construction of the same verb is used).

Cos (21:1). The group boards a vessel that skirts the coastline and takes them as far as the southern Asia Minor coastal city of Patara, from where they board a larger boat that takes them to Palestine.

Cos is a small island in the Aegean (112 square miles: twenty-seven miles long and between one and seven miles wide) that is part of the Sporades group

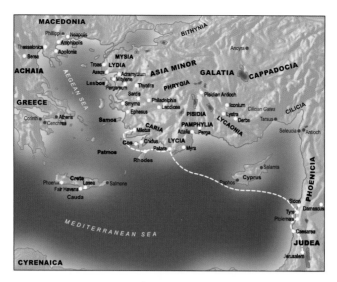

▶

MILETUS TO JERUSALEM

RHODES

"St. Paul's Bay" at Lindos, Rhodes.

▼

of the ancient world. However, the Colossus was later destroyed by an earthquake in the third century B.C.

Patara (21:1). Patara is one of the principal cities of the Roman province of Lycia and the seat of the Roman proconsul. The port was an important shipping port for the Alexandrian grain vessels.[423] It was located on the mouth of the Xanthus River a few miles south of the city of Xanthus. At this port, Paul finds a cargo ship that is scheduled to make a non-stop ocean crossing to Phoenicia. The four hundred-mile voyage would have taken between three and five days depending on the wind.

We landed at Tyre (21:3). On Tyre, see comments on 12:20. On Phoenicia, see comments on 11:20.

Finding the disciples there (21:4). The verb Luke uses here suggests that Paul searches for the believers. These people most likely received the gospel from the Jerusalem Christians who traveled to Phoenicia after the outbreak of persecution (11:19).

Through the Spirit they urged Paul not to go on to Jerusalem (21:4). Paul has told the Ephesian elders that he is "compelled by the Spirit" to go to Jerusalem. There is probably no contradiction here. It appears that the Spirit is telling prophets in a variety of places that Paul will face suffering and imprisonment in Jerusalem. The prophets conclude, out of their natural human concern, that Paul should not go to Jerusalem in order to

of islands. At the narrowest point, it is less than five miles from the Asia Minor mainland and the city of Halicarnassus. Cos may be best known for being the location of the school of medicine founded by Hippocrates in the fifth century B.C.[422]

Rhodes (21:1). After spending the night in Cos, they travel another sixty miles to the island of Rhodes. This is the largest island (540 square miles) of the Sporades and the fourth largest island currently belonging to Greece. Rhodes lies twenty miles off the coast of Asia Minor. The harbor of Rhodes was the site of the great "Colossus" (a hundred-foot statue of the sun god Helios), one of the Seven Wonders

avoid the persecution.[424] Paul, however, is thoroughly convinced that the Spirit is leading him to go. He is willing to suffer anything for the sake of Christ.

And their wives and children accompanied us out of the city (21:5). This is a touching observation that demonstrates how Paul endears himself to entire families of believers.

Landed at Ptolemais (21:7). Paul and his companions reboard their ship and sail south down the coastline to Ptolemais, the southernmost Phoenician port.[425] This city, located about eight miles north of Haifa, was known as Acco in the Old Testament era (Judg. 1:31); Ptolemy II Philadelphus (282–246 B.C.) later renamed it after himself. During the Roman era, Acco-Ptolemais came under the direct control of the Roman proconsul of Syria. Emperor Claudius refounded the city, improved its port, and settled many veterans there. Josephus regarded the city as the western boundary of Galilee.[426] Under Nero, the city became a Roman colony. The Gentile population of the city was consistently hostile to the Jews. This reached a boiling point roughly nine years later at the outbreak of the Jewish war when the inhabitants of this city massacred two thousand Jews.[427] As at Tyre, Paul is able to locate a group of believers and spend time with them.

We reached Caesarea (21:8). Staying only one day at Ptolemais, the party then makes the thirty-mile trip (probably by boat) to the beautiful port city of Caesarea (see comments on 10:1).

Stayed at the house of Philip the evangelist (21:8). Luke refers to Philip here as an "evangelist," the only time he uses the word in the book of Acts (see comments on 8:5; see also Eph. 4:11; 2 Tim. 4:5). No doubt part of the reason for this designation is based on the astonishing ways God used him to reach many Samaritans (8:4–25) and the Ethiopian official (8:26–40). Following his ministry to the Ethiopian and evangelistic work in Azotus, Philip traveled to Caesarea (8:40). Apparently he settled in the city, married (if he was not married earlier), and raised a family. Perhaps many in the city of Caesarea have come to know Christ as a result of Philip's ministry. Whatever his means of generating income, it has been adequate for him to purchase a home that is large enough to host this group of nine men. In the spirit of Christian hospitality, Philip opens his home to this group. Philip probably proves to be an important source of information to Luke about the early days of the church in Jerusalem.

Four unmarried daughters who prophesied (21:9). The church historian Eusebius, quoting an Ephesian church leader from the second century, reports that Philip later moved with his daughters to Hierapolis in Asia Minor (near Colosse

PTOLEMAIS (ACCO)

Ancient ruins at this important port city.

and Laodicea). Two of the daughters never married and remained in Hierapolis until their deaths; another daughter "lived in the Holy Spirit and rests in Ephesus."[428] The fact that Philip's daughters prophesy further demonstrates the fulfillment of Joel 2:28 ("your sons and your daughters will prophesy") that Peter quoted in his message on the day of Pentecost nearly twenty-five years earlier. Women continued to exercise prophetic gifts, as seen in the church at Corinth (1 Cor. 11:5).

A prophet named Agabus came down from Judea (21:10). The Jerusalem prophet, Agabus, now meets with Paul a second time. Whereas in the first instance, he predicted the coming of a severe famine (11:27–28), this time he predicts Paul's arrest in Jerusalem.

He took Paul's belt (21:11). Agabus acts out what he believes the Spirit to be telling him about Paul's impending arrest and custody. The way he does this is reminiscent of how Old Testament prophets sometimes delivered their messages, as, for example, Isaiah did when he went around stripped and barefoot for three years as a sign of what Assyria would do to the Egyptian and Cushite captives.[429]

And will hand him over to the Gentiles (21:11). The words were not fulfilled precisely as they are recorded here. When the Jews seized Paul, the Romans actually intervened and took him into their custody. Ultimately, however, the Jewish leaders were responsible for Paul's Roman custody, and in this way the prophecy was fulfilled.

Breaking my heart (21:13). The Caesarean Christians are deeply upset that Paul will shortly be facing persecution in Jerusalem and do their best to dissuade him from going to the capital city. Although compelled by the Spirit and determined to go, despite the threat of suffering, Paul is affected by their pleas. The word used here is found in the context of women pounding on clothes with stones as they wash them to get them clean.[430] Nevertheless, he remains obedient to the leading of the Spirit of God.

We got ready and went up to Jerusalem (21:15). The term used for getting ready (*episkeuazō*) is used by some ancient authors for saddling and packing horses for a trip.[431] It may imply that the group made the sixty-four-mile journey to Jerusalem on horseback.

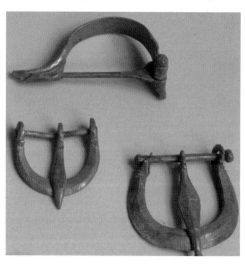

▶

ANCIENT BELT BUCKLES

These Roman-era buckles were discovered in the excavations at Masada.

The home of Mnason (21:16). The group travels to the home of an apparently wealthy Jerusalem believer named Mnason, who has a house sufficiently large to accommodate Paul's entourage of nine plus some from Caesarea.[432] Mnason came from the island of Cyprus (like Barnabas) and is most assuredly a Jew. He is strong enough in his faith not to worry about opening his home up to Gentiles from Macedonia and Asia Minor and face the dangers of ritual impurity (from a Jewish perspective). His commitment to Christ has given him a new perspective on Gentiles. It is possible that his name is a shortened and Grecized form of the Jewish name Menaham or Manasseh.[433]

One of the early disciples (21:16). This can be viewed one of three ways: (1) He is one of the disciples of Jesus during his earthly ministry and may have been one of the 120 in 1:15; (2) he is one of the early converts of the preaching of the apostles in Jerusalem; or (3) he is one of the converts of Paul and Barnabas in their missionary journey to Cyprus. One of the first two options is most likely. As one who has been a foundational member of the Jerusalem church, Mnason proves to be an important source of information to Luke for his writing during this visit. This value is all the greater for Luke's first volume if Mnason had been a disciple of Jesus.

Paul Meets With the Jerusalem Church (21:17–26)

Paul and the delegates presumably make it to Jerusalem in time for the Pentecost celebration of A.D. 57. But the celebration of this festival is far less significant to Luke than the warm and supportive reception Paul receives by the Jerusalem church and the deliberations about how to handle the problem of negative perceptions about Paul and his ministry by many Jewish believers in Jerusalem.

The brothers received us warmly (21:17). In light of the turmoil that will follow, Luke stresses the fact that Paul and his eight Gentile companions receive a warm reception by their fellow Christians in Jerusalem. Certainly not all Jerusalem Christians are opposed to Paul.

Went to see James, and all the elders were present (21:18). Absent is mention of any of the twelve apostles. Apparently Peter and John are away from Jerusalem in other places of service as are the other apostles. James has surfaced as the most prominent leader of the Jerusalem church (on James, see comments on 12:17; on elders, see comments on 11:30). Some have suggested that James is now functioning as a president over a kind of Christian "sanhedrin" with as many as seventy elders, but this is speculative.[434]

Paul and his group probably present to the leaders the collection of funds for the relief of the poor and suffering Jerusalem Christians.[435] What Paul hopes

MODERN JERUSALEM

The Muslim Dome of the Rock is in the foreground.

to be the high point of his visit to Jerusalem is quickly overshadowed by the controversy brewing about him and his attitude toward the Jewish law.

When they heard this, they praised God (21:20). The leadership of the Jerusalem church is solidly in support of Paul and the ministry he has among the Gentiles. This is not a begrudging support; they genuinely give thanks to God for the many Gentiles who have become Christians and for the numerous communities of believers that have been established throughout Asia Minor, Macedonia, and Achaia.

How many thousands of Jews have believed (21:20). God has not only been powerfully at work through Paul, but also through the Jerusalem believers. Evangelistic efforts have resulted in thousands of Jews embracing Jesus as the Messiah. This is certainly fantastic news for Paul, who a year or so earlier had told the Romans, "Brothers, my heart's desire and prayer to God for the Israelites is that they may be saved" (Rom. 10:1) and that he could wish himself cut off from Christ if it would lead to the people of Israel turning their hearts to Jesus (Rom. 9:3). Paul no doubt "praised God" for this encouraging result.

All of them are zealous for the law (21:20). These new believers have not yet matured in their faith to the point that they share the same outlook as their leaders on the law. The difficulty is compounded further by the ongoing presence of the Pharisaic Jewish believers who had already troubled the churches at Antioch and south Galatia some eight to ten years earlier. These "Judaizers," no doubt, had made efforts to orient the new believers toward their position in the "battle for the law" being waged within Judean Christianity. The position of James and the elders was also increasingly difficult in light of the fervency about fidelity to the law in prevailing Jewish culture.

You teach all the Jews . . . to turn away from Moses (21:21). The principal charge is that Paul is literally teaching "apostasy from Moses." Of the specific charges that are levelled, there is no indication in Paul's letters that Jewish Christian parents should no longer circumcise their children nor is there any indication that Paul is actively teaching that Jewish Christians should altogether cease being Torah-observant. As long as circumcision is not performed as a rite that is essential for salvation, Paul has no difficulty with Jews continuing to practice this procedure. Paul, of course, has actually been the one responsible for Timothy's circumcision—and Timothy is present in the delegation (16:3).

These Jerusalem Jewish Christians apparently are living by the conviction that when people receive Jesus as the Messiah and are indwelt by the Spirit, they need to continue (if Jews) or take on (if Gentiles) the Jewish law with its rites and observances. Their position is not as extreme as the "Judaizers" who contend that obedience to the law, especially circumcision, is essential for salvation (15:1, 5).

These Jewish believers have heard that Paul is radically opposed to what they regard as a fundamental part of their Christian life. Their assumptions regarding Paul are only partly, not entirely, wrong. Paul probably does not *insist* on Torah observance for converted Jews in the Gentile cities and, no doubt, some begin to live on a principle of freedom from the law.

What shall we do? (21:22). James and the Jerusalem elders are in a difficult situation. On the one hand, they are in agreement with Paul theologically and want to affirm his work among the Gentiles. On the other, they want to continue to reach Jerusalem and Judean Jews with the gospel of Christ and not give a cause for deeper division within the Jerusalem church.

Four men with us who have made a vow . . . . pay their expenses (21:23–24). James and the elders come up with a plan that they think will demonstrate to the Jewish Christian believers in Jerusalem that Paul is at least to some degree law-observant and certainly not opposed to the law in ways that they assume. The plan involves supporting four Jewish-Christian men in the fulfillment of their Nazirite vows (see Num. 6:2–21; *m. Naz.*).

The purpose of the Nazirite vow was to dedicate oneself to the Lord for a set period of time. A Jewish man took a Nazirite vow typically for a thirty-day period, but sometimes longer (as in the case of Samson) or shorter periods (such as seven days) were also possible. During this time the Nazirite abstained from wine (or anything from the vine), scrupulously avoided any contact with a corpse, and left his hair uncut. At the end of the period of his special consecration to the Lord, he shaved off his dedicated hair and offered it at the temple. He was also required to present an offering of a year-old male lamb, a year-old ewe lamb, a ram, a basket of bread, and various grain and drink offerings (see Num. 6:14–17). These offerings resulted in a considerable expense to the Nazirite. Paul apparently helped subsidize the cost of these sacrifices. This kind of participation in the

▶ Jerusalem: Nine Years Before the War

Nine years after the events of Acts 21, a massive Jewish revolt against Rome broke out in Galilee and Judea (A.D. 66). It culminated with the legions of Titus laying seige to the holy city and killing thousands upon thousands of Jews, tearing down the walls of the city, and utterly destroying the massive temple complex.

Many Jews had grown weary of Roman rule in Palestine and despised their ongoing presence. The Roman procurator Felix (A.D. 52–59) had been a rather inept ruler and showed little sensitivity to Jewish concerns, especially in his massacre of many Jews when the Egyptian false prophet led thousands astray. There were many other less severe confrontations with the Romans that struck the flames of antipathy toward them. One such incident occurred when a Roman soldier found a copy of the Jewish law, tore it in two, and threw it on a fire during the procuratorship of Cumanus (A.D. 48–52).

Josephus's remarks about this incident reveal the fervor for the law that characterized this period: "The Jews, as if their whole country was in flames, assembled in frantic haste, religious fervour drawing them together irresistibly."[A-127]

Apocalyptic hopes were high that God would mightily intervene with his Messiah and crush these Gentile sinners who had little or no respect for the Jewish law. These hopes led to many false messiahs and assorted revolutionaries appearing on the scene. It is during this time that a group called the *Sicarii* (see "Terrorists" at Acts 21:37) surreptitiously plunged their knives into those who did not measure up to their zeal for the law.

Such was the atmosphere in Jerusalem during the time when many Jews were coming to faith in Jesus as Messiah. In spite of receiving Jesus, they would have felt tremendous pressure to maintain their fidelity to the law.

expenses was not without precedent. Herod Agrippa I at one time paid the expenses of a group of poor Nazirites.[436]

Join in their purification rites (21:24). In addition to paying the expenses of the four Nazirites, James urges Paul to join in their purification rites. This probably does not mean that Paul is also completing a Nazirite vow at this time, but that he is completing a special purification ritual (see, e.g., Num. 8:21; 19:12; 31:19). Paul's seven-day purification rite, with washings on the third and seventh days, is consistent with a Jewish understanding that a Jew who took a trip outside of the Holy Land and into Gentile territories would become ritually impure.[437] Such a cleansing was essential for Paul, according to Jewish tradition, since he would be entering the temple to assist with the Nazirite ceremony. He apparently times the final sprinkling on the seventh day of his purification so that it would coincide with the completion of the Nazirite vows of the four men. Paul's willingness to support the Nazirites and to undertake the purification rites himself illustrates his principle of becoming "all things to all men" for the sake of the gospel (1 Cor. 9:22–23).

As for the Gentile believers, we have written to them our decision (21:25). James once again reiterates that he and the elders of the Jerusalem church stand by their previous decision. What they have recommended to Paul is a practical maneuver, not a reassertion of the importance of the law for salvation. James reiterates the elements of the so-called decree, which the leadership of the Jerusalem church still affirm as essential for Gentile believers to facilitate their growth in the faith by ensuring that they have made a decisive break with idolatry and all that is associated with it.

Jews From Ephesus Provoke Hostility Against Paul (21:27–40)

The prophecy of Agabus is now to be fulfilled. Paul is bound and taken into Roman custody after he is nearly killed by a mob of Jews who wrongly think he has defiled the temple. Luke does not report on what happened to the delegates who accompany Paul. They do not appear to have been arrested; they probably return to their homes after they realize that Paul will be in custody for some time. Luke may have remained in Palestine for the next two years (A.D. 57–59), possibly gathering information for his two-volume work. He is with Paul in Caesarea (27:1) and will accompany him on his voyage to Rome.

Jews from the province of Asia (21:27). These are no doubt Jews from the city of Ephesus who have rejected Jesus as Messiah and are resentful of the influence Paul has exerted on the Jewish community of their city. It is ironic that they, not Jerusalem Jews, are the main instigators of the commotion that followed.

▶ The Boundary Warnings to Gentiles in the Temple

There was a stone wall that separated the court of the Gentiles from the inner courts of the temple (such as the holy area, the women's court, the court of the Israelites, and the court of the priests). Warning signs were posted along this wall prohibiting the Gentiles from entering. Josephus describes the stone wall and these notices:

> Anyone passing through this towards the second court found it enclosed within a stone balustrade 4 1/2 feet high, a perfect specimen of craftsmanship. In this at equal intervals stood slabs announcing the law of purification, some in Greek and some in Roman characters. No foreigner was to enter the holy area—this was the name given to the second court.[A-128]

Two of these stone warning tablets have been discovered by archaeologists. One complete tablet written in Greek is on display in the Archaeological Museum in Istanbul, Turkey. Half of another is housed in the Rockefeller Museum in Jerusalem. The inscription reads: "No foreigner is to enter within the forecourt and the balustrade around the sanctuary. Whoever is caught will have himself to blame for his subsequent death."[A-129]

Defiled this holy place (21:28). The Jews from Asia Minor stir up all the other Jews in the temple precincts. They claim that Paul has led Trophimus, a Gentile believer from Ephesus, from the court of the Gentiles into the inner courts of the temple, which was prohibited to Gentiles. Paul certainly has not done this, but the charge is believable to the masses.

They dragged him from the temple, and immediately the gates were shut (21:30). Paul is apparently seized by the temple police, dragged out of the Court of Women into the Court of the Gentiles, and has the doors shut behind him.[438] One cannot help but notice the irony of God's ordained messenger to bring light to the Gentiles now being shut out of the most holy place of Judaism—the place where God mediated his grace to his people for centuries. In Paul's view as well as Luke's, the temple is no longer the place to receive God's grace; God's grace is now supremely manifested and available in the Lord Jesus Christ.

They were trying to kill him (21:31). The Jews are ostensibly within their legal rights to have Paul executed for the crime they are convinced he is guilty of, although there is no evidence in Josephus or elsewhere for anyone being killed for

▶
FORTRESS OF ANTONIA

A model of the fortress, which stood in the northwest corner of the temple grounds.

this offense. The Romans, however, do not look favorably on this frenzied mob justice.

The commander of the Roman troops (21:31). The commander, a *chiliarch* named Claudius Lysias (cf. 23:26), is in charge of a thousand Roman soldiers. Josephus informs us that a Roman cohort was always stationed at the fortress of Antonia "and at the festivals they extended along the colonnades fully armed and watched for any sign of popular discontent."[439] A cohort typically consisted of 760 infantry troops and 240 cavalry.

He at once took some officers and soldiers and ran down to the crowd (21:32). The fortress of Antonia was located just outside the northwest corner of the temple precincts. The structure rose sixty feet high with three towers reaching seventy-five feet high and a fourth, just over a hundred feet. It gave the Romans a vantage point to watch over all that happened in the temple courts. Josephus notes: "Where

▶ Josephus's Account of the Egyptian Rebel

The exploits of the Egyptian revolutionary, whom the Roman *chiliarch* refers to, is described in detail by Josephus.

A greater blow than this was inflicted on the Jews by the Egyptian false prophet. Arriving in the country this man, a fraud who posed as a seer, collected about 30,000 dupes, led them round from the desert to the Mount of Olives, and from there was ready to force an entry into Jerusalem, overwhelm the Roman garrison, and seize supreme power with his fellow-raiders as bodyguard. But Felix anticipated his attempt by

meeting him with the Roman heavy infantry, the whole population rallying to the defence, so that when the clash occurred, the Egyptian fled with a handful of men and most of his followers were killed or captured; the rest of the mob scattered and stole away to their respective homes.[A-130]

There is a discrepancy in the two stories over the numbers involved. Most scholars think that Luke's figure of four thousand as more reliable given Josephus's tendency to exaggerate numbers.[A-131] This occurred when Felix was procurator of Judea (A.D. 52–59).

▶ "Terrorists"

The "terrorists" led by the Egyptian pseudo-Messiah (Acts 21:38) were a loosely organized political extremist group that surfaced in Palestine during the procuratorship of Felix. "Terrorist" is the NIV translation of the Greek word *sikarios,* which is a loanword from Latin (*sicarius*). In Latin, a *sica* is a dagger, and thus, the Sicarii were "dagger men."[A-132] Josephus provides us with an informative description of this violent group:

> Another type of bandit sprang up in Jerusalem, known as 'Sicarii.' These men committed numerous murders in broad daylight and in the middle of

the City. Their favourite trick was to mingle with festival crowds, concealing under their garments small daggers with which they stabbed their opponents. When their victims fell, the assassins melted into the indignant crowd, and through their plausibity entirely defied detection. The first to have his throat cut by them was Jonathan the high priest, and after him many were murdered every day. More terrible than the crimes themselves was the fear they aroused, every man hourly expecting death, as in war.[A-133]

it joined the Temple colonnades stairs led down to both, and by these the guards descended."[440]

Bound with two chains (21:33). Paul's wrists are secured with manacles and he is bound to two soldiers.[441]

He ordered that Paul be taken into the barracks (21:34). Paul is taken up the stairs and into the fortress of Antonia.

Kept shouting, "Away with him!" (21:36). The crowd means more than merely "Get him out of here"; they desire him to be led away to his death. Paul is experiencing the same response from the crowd that Jesus faced (see Luke 23:18; John 19:15).

Do you speak Greek? (21:37). The Roman official appears surprised when Paul addresses him in Greek. It was not astonishing to him that a Jew from Palestine would know Greek. Most Jews have probably learned at least some Greek. In

listening to Paul, the tribune most likely discerns that Paul knows the language as well as any native Greek speaker. This may lead the tribune to conclude that Paul is not a local Judean revolutionary.

From Tarsus in Cilicia (21:39). On Tarsus, see comments on 9:30.

A citizen of no ordinary city (21:39). On the surface, it seems astonishing that Paul would reveal his Tarsian citizenship to the Roman official before disclosing his Roman citizenship. Yet in the ancient world, there was significant status attached to citizenship in an important city, such as Tarsus. Mention of his civic citizenship would have increased the esteem with which the tribune held him and perhaps incline the official to accede to Paul's request to address the people.

◀

ROMAN MILITARY DAGGER

A model of a dagger similar to what the Sicarii may have used.

Had Paul mentioned his Roman citizenship at this juncture and this were announced to the assembled crowd, it would only have inflamed their passions against him even more.[442] Yet there was a strong Jewish community in Tarsus which, at one point, even sent legates to help provoke the Jewish rebellion against Rome.[443]

He said to them in Aramaic (21:40). "Aramaic" is the NIV translation of the Greek expression *hebrais dialektos*. This can be interpreted to mean that Paul speaks to the crowd in (Mishnaic) Hebrew,[444] but it more likely means that he addresses them in the closely related Aramaic language. Aramaic is a Semitic language closely related to the Hebrew, which was widely spoken throughout ancient Palestine, Nabatea, Syria, Persia, and Parthia. It would have been the mother-tongue of Jews living in the Holy Land. Not all the crowd knows Hebrew and, if Paul were to address them in Greek, it would be a serious insult given their concerns that Paul is much too friendly with Gentiles.

Paul's Address to the Crowd in Jerusalem (22:1–21)

This is the second of three accounts of Paul's conversion in the book of Acts.

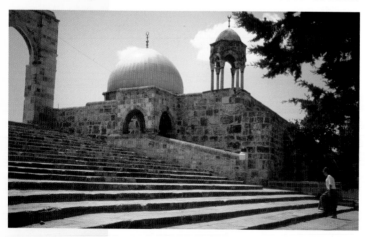

Only the new features supplementing what is said before will be commented on (see comments on 9:1–31; see also 26:1–23). The setting of this address before a hostile crowd of Jews in Jerusalem needs to be carefully considered in the reading of what Paul says. He tailors his comments appropriately to communicate the reality of his conversion to this group. Paul's address is effective in communicating the events surrounding his conversion, but it does not have the desired impact on this crowd. Rather than hundreds turning their hearts to Christ, they are enraged and want him flogged.

In Aramaic (22:2). See comments on 21:40. The fact that this nonnative Palestinian who is well known for his preaching among the Greeks can speak Aramaic causes the crowd to take note.

Brought up in this city (22:3). This expression (*anatethrammenos*) is key for understanding Paul's formative years. Although Paul was born in Tarsus and lived the first few years of his life there, he apparently spent most of his schooldays in Jerusalem. We do not know if his parents moved here when he was young[445] or if they sent Paul here for the purpose of his education. We know from 23:16 that he has a family connection with Jerusalem. Exactly how old he is when he first starts his education in Jerusalem is not known. It would not be suprising if he began schooling there as early as ten or twelve years of age after some elementary-level education in Tarsus in a Jewish context.[446] Paul probably learned Greek as his native tongue and later acquired Aramaic and Hebrew. As a Roman citizen, he may also have learned some Latin.[447] It is improbable that the young Paul has received any formal training in Greek rhetoric and literature in Tarsus. He never hints at receiving a Greek education (*paideia*) that was so widely valued by well-educated Jews (e.g., Philo and Aristeas).[448]

Gamaliel (22:3). Paul studied with this famous teacher of Israel who represented the school of Hillel. Paul's method of interpreting the Old Testament as seen in his letters bears the mark of Hillel influence (see comments on 5:34).

Thoroughly trained in the law of our fathers (22:3). Before his conversion to Christ, Paul knew the Old Testament extraordinarily well. Not only that, he became familiar with the traditions of the Pharisees. This means he would have known all of the purity laws, regulations regarding the Sabbath, procedures regarding the sacrifices and the festivals, and many other rules regulating every part of daily life. Above all, he would have gained a commitment to the Torah (the first five books of the Old Testament) and the temple as central to Jewish life. He would also have acquired an attitude toward the Gentiles as impure, idolatrous people.

There is no doubt that Paul's training in the Law was thorough, but the wording of the text indicates that he received a *strict* training. His instruction was rigorous, meticulous, and accurately reflected the venerable traditions of the Pharisees.

Zealous for God (22:3). Paul clearly displayed a passion for God, but "zeal" implies more than this in a Jewish context. "Zeal" is identified with a willingness to use violence to defend the Torah. In recent Jewish history, the most revered examples of this were the high priest

Mattathias and his sons who rebelled against the blasphemous and impure Gentile rulers and eventually led Israel to a successful war of independence known as the Maccabean revolt (in the second century B.C.). The members of the Jewish movement of Paul's day that were seeking independence from Rome referred to themselves as "Zealots." When he wrote his letter to the Romans (prior to this occasion), Paul expressed his heart's desire to see the salvation of the Jews: "For I can testify about them that they are zealous for God, but their zeal is not based on knowledge" (Rom. 10:2). They are missing Christ.

I persecuted the followers of this Way to their death (22:4). Paul acknowledges he was responsible for the murder of Christians. It is little wonder that he could say, "For I am the least of the apostles and do not even deserve to be called an apostle, because I persecuted the church of God" (1 Cor. 15:9). Paul never forgot his misdirected zeal and his murderous past. It did not paralyze him, however, but gave him a profound appreciation of the mercy and grace of God and moved him to fulfill his commission from Christ with all of his strength until the end of his days.

All the Council can testify (22:5). The entire Sanhedrin is aware of the persecuting activity of Paul. Indeed, together with the high priest, they authorized the persecution.

Suddenly a bright light (22:6). The account of Paul's encounter with Christ is basically the same as Luke previously records (see comments on 9:3–9).

Jesus of Nazareth (22:8). Literally, "Jesus the Nazarene." This is the only one of the three accounts where Jesus refers to himself as "the Nazarene."

Saw the light, but they did not understand the voice of him who was speaking (22:9). In the earlier account, the men traveling with Paul "heard the sound but did not see anyone" (9:7). Some take this as an apparent discrepancy between the two versions of the conversion, mainly because the Greek text literally reads, "but they did not *hear* the voice." The answer lies in the fact that they did not hear the voice with comprehension—as an audible revelation of the resurrected Messiah. They probably heard the voice, but could not make out the words, only sensing it as noise.[449]

A devout observer of the law and highly respected by all the Jews living there (22:12). It is significant that Paul describes Ananias to this crowd of Jews assembled in Jerusalem in this way. It may impress the Jews, but the real difference is that Ananias has already embraced Jesus as the Messiah. This is a significantly abbreviated account of the role of Ananias when compared to the earlier version (see comments on 9:10–19).

The God of our fathers (22:14). Paul's reference to God in this way serves to underline the fact that he has not turned to a false god, but understands himself as maintaining his fidelity to the one true God, but now with a new knowledge.

The Righteous One (22:14). For Paul, Jesus is not only the Messiah, but "the Righteous One" (see comments on 3:14).

Be baptized (22:16). The rite served as a sign of Paul's cleansing from sin. This was all accomplished in the name of the Lord Jesus Christ. Jesus is the agent of God for procuring Paul's salvation and for all people who will call on his name. He has become the present and dominant influence in Paul's life from this point forward.

When I returned to Jerusalem (22:17). Paul's return to Jerusalem does not occur until three years later when he goes for a two-week period to become acquainted with Peter. This follows a period of ministry in Damascus and in Arabia (Nabatea).

Praying at the temple, I fell into a trance (22:17). This is now the third recorded vision that Paul has had since his trip to Damascus. The first is the actual appearance of Christ to him on the Damascus road and the second is the vision that he receives of Ananias's coming to him (9:12). Visions as a means of divine guidance play a crucial role in Paul's Christian experience (see also 16:9; 2 Cor. 12:1–6). Note how the vision comes to him while he is earnestly seeking God in prayer.

Saw the Lord speaking . . . he said to me (22:18). The Lord himself commands Paul to leave Jerusalem because the Jews will not accept his testimony. Paul objects by suggesting that his testimony will be all the more powerful and compelling because he had formerly been one with them in opposition to the Jesus movement, even in the killing of Stephen. How could they not be convinced? The Lord does not argue with Paul, but merely tells him that he will send him far away to proclaim the gospel to the Gentiles. Paul yields to his wise and all-knowing Lord.

The Crowd Reacts Violently (22:22–29)

Once Paul mentions the word "Gentile" and his alleged instructions from God to take salvation to the Gentiles, the crowd becomes enraged. This only confirms in their minds the allegation that he has taken a Gentile into the inner courts of the temple. Paul's address thus comes to an abrupt end whereupon he is taken in for an inquisition by flogging. At this point, he reveals his Roman citizenship to the centurion and averts the terrible ordeal he is about to face.

Throwing off their cloaks and flinging dust into the air (22:23). The crowd becomes so angry and frantic that they begin throwing whatever is available. Just as Paul shakes off the dust of his feet as a symbol of protest against those who oppose the gospel at Pisidian Antioch and shakes out his clothes against the opposition at Corinth (13:51; 18:6), so these Jews symbolically portray their opposition to all that Paul is saying and stands for.

He directed that he be flogged (22:24). The Roman flog (Greek = *mastix*; Latin = *flagrum*) is an instrument designed to inflict a great deal of pain and physical damage to the back. One scholar describes the instruments well and their potential for affliction: "While it sometimes consisted of a handle on which were fixed leather straps, it was often an instrument of brutal innovation. The lashes could be knotted cords or wire having bristled ends or be strung with knucklebones and lead pellets. This method of interrogation, though never overtly construed as punitive, could nevertheless result in crippling or even death before the truth had been arrived at."[450]

Is it legal for you to flog a Roman citizen? (22:25) The Porcian and Julian laws prohibited such a flogging (see comments on 16:37).

Tell me, are you a Roman citizen? (22:27). Roman citizens were given a document *diploma civitas Romanae* recording their citizenship for purposes of identification. It was a hinged wooden tablet with two leaves (a *diptych*). It is not known whether Paul carried this document with him verifying his claim of Roman citizenship; yet, if he was found making a false claim, he could be punished by death.[451]

I had to pay a big price for my citizenship (22:28). Roman citizenships were not sold on the open market. Claudius Lysias is here admitting that he paid a great deal of money to bribe a Roman official to put his name on a list of candidates.[452] The Roman historian Dio Cassius gives evidence that this was a widespread problem during the reign of the emperor Claudius:

> For inasmuch as Romans had the advantage over foreigners in practically all respects, many sought the franchise by personal application to the emperor, and many bought it from Massalina and the imperial freedmen. For this reason, though the privilege was at first sold only for large sums, it became so cheapened by the facility with which it could be obtained that it came to be a common saying, that a man could become a citizen by giving the right person some bits of broken glass.[453]

It appears that Lysias bought his citizenship early in the reign of Claudius. He then took on the Roman *nomen* Claudius, as was the custom of those receiving citizenship during his reign.[454]

I was born a citizen (22:28). There are two plausible theories on how Paul's family came to acquire Roman citizenship, although both are admittedly speculative. The first view suggests that Paul's ancestors settled in Tarsus at some time during the Seleucid era (2d cent. B.C.) as colonists from Israel. Roman citizenship may be bestowed on Paul's father or grandfather by one of the Roman generals—Pompey, Julius Caesar, or Mark Antony—who, successively, were in control of the province of Cilicia in the first century B.C. and engaged in wars. If Paul's father or grandfather rendered an outstanding service to the Roman cause (such as providing tents to the Roman forces in Tarsus or by serving in the mercenary forces), then, as an expression of gratitude, either of the Roman generals may have bestowed citizenship on the family.[455]

The second view is that Paul's grandparents received citizenship after being emancipated from slavery. Under this reconstruction, Paul's ancestors became prisoners and were subsequently enslaved by the Roman general Pompey when he invaded Israel, took control of the country for Rome, and sacked the temple. After a generation or so, the family was emancipated by their Roman owners and extended citizenship, a practice well attested in the Roman era. Sometimes this freedom was purchased by relatives and friends—a lucrative practice for the Roman master.[456]

Ordered the chief priests and all the Sanhedrin to assemble (22:30). Claudius Lysias is not handing the case over to the Sanhedrin. Because of his Roman citizenship, Paul will need to stand trial before the Roman procurator Felix. Lysias orders the Sanhedrin (see comments on 4:13) to meet because he does not understand the nature of the charges against Paul and wants the Jewish leaders to gather the relevant facts for this case.

▶ Paul's Roman Citizenship

Paul possessed the high-status privilege of being a Roman citizen.[A-134] His name was written on a register in Rome and recorded on the citizen registry in Tarsus.[A-135] As a citizen, he was accorded the right of a Roman trial, exemption from certain forms of degrading punishments (such as being beat with a *flagrum*), protection from summary execution, and the right of appeal. Among the responsibilities coming with citizenship were voting rights (*suffragium*), eligibility for Roman offices (depending on wealth status), potential liability for military service, and financial obligation to one's municipality.

It was not always necessary for Roman citizens to show their devotion to the emperor by engaging in emperor worship, worship of the goddess Roma, or by participating in the worship of any of the official Roman cults. Philo reports that the majority of Jews living in Rome were Roman citizens and yet were not compelled to compromise their ancestral laws.[A-136] Even Philo himself, as a wealthy Roman citizen living in Egypt, was never forced to worship the emperor or other gods.

Paul Appears Before the Sanhedrin (23:1–11)

In Paul's hearing before the Sanhedrin, disorder reigns and the facts of the case are never discussed. Part of the blame lies at the feet of Paul, who adeptly changes the focus from himself to the issue of bodily resurrection. Paul's driving concern is not to find some means of being released from custody, but in bearing witness to all of the principal leaders of the Jews.

In all good conscience to this day (23:1). Paul is probably not reflecting back as far as his pre-Christian days—when he rejected Jesus and persecuted the church (although in his conscience at that time, he was convinced he was serving God with zeal). He is here probably thinking of his preaching in the synagogues of Asia Minor, Macedonia, and Achaia that elicited violent opposition, his presentation of the gospel to Gentiles, and the way he explained to them their obligations before God in terms of the law.

God will strike you (23:3). This is not a curse, but rather a simple statement of assurance that God will deal with this injustice (e.g., Ps. 94:23). In some instances, this judgment came rapidly

(Acts 5:9–10; 13:11). Ananias was struck dead by assailants some nine years later.

You whitewashed wall (23:3). Paul is here using a prophetic image from the book of Ezekiel. The intent of the figure is to portray something fundamentally weak, poorly constructed, and unstable yet appearing as new, appealing, and strong. Ezekiel says: "When a flimsy wall is built, they cover it with whitewash, therefore tell those who cover it with whitewash that it is going to fall. . . . I will tear down the wall you have covered with whitewash and will level it to the ground so that its foundation will be laid bare. When it falls, you will be destroyed in it; and you will know that I am the LORD" (Ezek. 36:10–16; see also CD

◀

WHITEWASHED WALLS

Buildings on the island of Mykonos.

▶ The High Priest Ananias

This high priest is not to be confused with the earlier high priest Annas, father-in-law of Caiaphas (see Acts 4:6). This is Ananias, son of Nebedeus, who served as high priest from A.D. 47–59.[A-137]

Josephus portrays Ananias as popular with the people, but corrupt, engorging himself with wealth. At one point he sent his servants to the threshing floors demanding the workers to pay the tithes that belonged to the priests. Any who refused to surrender their money, the servants

beat. Some of the older priests who depended on these tithes for support actually starved to death.[A-138]

Ananias was also well known as a collaborator with Rome much to the vexation of the Pharisees and Jewish revolutionaries. At the outbreak of the Jewish war, Ananias went into hiding in Jerusalem near an aqueduct. The Jewish revolutionaries found him and his brother, Hezekiah, and killed them both.[A-139]

Select List of Jewish High Priests		
Name	**Date**	**New Testament Event**
Annas	A.D. 6–15	• High Priest during Jesus' early life
Joseph Caiaphas	A.D. 18–37	• High Priest during Jesus' earthly ministry, his trial, death, resurrection, and ascension • He was also in office during the early years of the church: Pentecost, the arrest of Peter and John, and the conversion of Paul • High Priest when Saul was persecuting the church
Ananias, Son of Nebedeus	A.D. 47–59	• In office during the Jerusalem Council • Paul's arrest at Jerusalem and hearing before the Sanhedrin
Ishmael ben Phiabi	A.D. 59–61	• High Priest when Festus assumed the procuratorship of Judea
Mattathias, son of Theophilus	A.D. 65–67	• High Priest at the outbreak of the Jewish war
Pinḥas of Ḥabtam	A.D. 67–70	• High Priest during the destruction of Jerusalem and the temple • The last High Priest

8:12). Perhaps Paul's statement is more than an emotional response to being struck; it may be a prophetic announcement of the weakness and instability of Israel's leadership and God's impending judgment.

Violate the law by commanding that I be struck (23:3). Paul may have in mind here Leviticus 19:15, which reads, "Do not pervert justice; do not show partiality to the poor or favoritism to the great, but judge your neighbor fairly."

I did not realize that he was the high priest (23:5). For nearly the past twenty-five years, Paul has been away from Jerusalem. He is not nearly as concerned as he once was about who the influential people were in the city. He has probably never seen Ananias before.

Do not speak evil about the ruler of your people (23:5). This is a direct quotation

of Exodus 22:27. Paul genuinely feels regret about having violated this instruction from the law in spite of how he was wrongly treated. Yet Paul's statement is correct and still may serve as an unwitting prophetic warning by Paul to the assembled Sanhedrin.

I am a Pharisee (23:6). Most noteworthy about this declaration is that Paul does not say, "I *once was* a Pharisee." Paul continues to regard himself as a Pharisee, but one who has rightly recognized Jesus as the Messiah sent from God. By implication, this means that Paul continues to value much of the Pharisaic doctrine he received, their respect for the Scripture, and their zeal for God, as well as many other key features of Pharisaism.

The son of a Pharisee (23:6). Literally, "the son of Pharisees." Apparently, Paul's father and grandfather were also Pharisees. This helps explain his family's commitment to get him to Jerusalem at an early age for training in the law and subsequently to become a disciple of Gamaliel.

I stand on trial because of my hope in the resurrection of the dead (23:6). Although it is to some degree true that Paul is employing a "divide and conquer" approach in his provocative remarks to the Sanhedrin, it is of paramount importance to recognize that this is the central issue for which he is being persecuted and tried.

The Sadducees say that there is no resurrection (23:8). The Sadducees viewed only the Torah as Scripture; none of the other writings, including the Prophets, were binding. Since there is no explicit reference to a bodily resurrection in the Torah, the Sadducees denied this teaching and presumably viewed it as a later, unbiblical, development. Their disbelief in the resurrection is attested by Josephus although he described it for his Greek readers as denying a belief in the immortal soul.[457] Jesus also debated with them over this point (Luke 20:27–40).

There are allusions to the resurrection in a variety of Old Testament passages, but Daniel 12:2–3 is the most explicit: "Multitudes who sleep in the dust of the earth will awake: some to everlasting life, others to shame and everlasting contempt. Those who are wise will shine like the brightness of the heavens, and those who lead many to righteousness, like the stars for ever and ever."[458] Much of Judaism in the time leading up to Christ anticipated a bodily resurrection. This is illustrated well in the story about the Jewish mother and her seven sons who were martyred by the executioners of Antiochus IV Epiphanes.[459] Their belief in the resurrection of the dead enabled

them to face martyrdom with noble spirits. When the second brother was ready to die, he exclaimed to Antiochus: "You accursed wretch, you dismiss us from this present life, but the King of the universe will raise us up to an everlasting renewal of life, because we have died for his laws" (2 Macc. 7:9). The rabbis who put together the Mishnah, the heirs of the Pharisaic school, left no doubt about an importance of a belief in the resurrection: "And these are they that have no share in the world to come: he that says that there is no resurrection of the dead."[460]

There are neither angels nor spirits (23:8). The Sadducees' disbelief in the realm of angels and spirits is surprising given their commitment to the Torah where references to angels abound, such as the angel who appeared to Hagar (Gen. 16:7–11), the two angels at Sodom (Gen. 19:1, 15), the angel of the Lord who kept Abraham from slaying Isaac (Gen. 22:11–15), Jacob's vision of a ladder to heaven with angels ascending and descending on it (Gen. 28:12), the angel who led the Israelites through the desert (Ex. 23:20), as well as references to demons (Deut. 32:17). Luke is the only ancient writer who records this feature of their belief. This may not have been an absolute denial of the existence of angels and spirits, which is more a product of our time than theirs, but a reticence to accept a belief in the multitudinous hierarchies of spirits that some Jewish teachers of their day postulated (such as evidenced in *1 Enoch, Jubilees,* and some of the Dead Sea Scrolls).[461]

We find nothing wrong with this man (23:9). The focus of the debate has remain centered on the issue of the reality of a future bodily resurrection, not on whether Jesus of Nazareth has risen from the tomb.

What if a spirit or an angel has spoken to him (23:9). The Pharisees agreed with Paul to a large extent—belief in a bodily resurrection and the possibility that a divine being could impart information to someone. Yet, as one writer puts it, their agreement "falls far short of recognizing the key point, which is the reality of the resurrection in Paul's experience of Jesus as Lord."[462] It was not an angelic mediator who spoke to Paul on the Damascus road; it was the resurrected and exalted Jesus of Nazareth.

The Lord stood near Paul (23:11). Luke does not say whether Jesus appears to Paul in bodily form or in a dream-vision, but this is certainly a timely appearing. Paul is probably on the throes of discouragement wondering if he will survive, and, if he does, will he be released and be able to fulfill his ambition of going to Rome and on to Spain? Jesus not only previously appears to Paul on the Damascus road, but also at a discouraging point in his ministry in Corinth (see 18:9).

So you must also testify in Rome (23:11). The Lord's comments reassure Paul that he will survive and proclaim the

REFLECTIONS

AFTER JESUS ASCENDED TO HEAVEN and took his place at the right hand of God, he did not cease to be actively involved with his people. He continues to be intimately concerned with the extension and well-being of his church. As "head" of the church, he continues to provide encouragement, direction, guidance, and counsel. Are we hearing him today?

gospel in Rome. What the Lord does not reveal at this time is that it will be two years before he arrives there, that he will be shipwrecked at sea, and that he will testify in Rome bound in chains.

A Plot to Kill Paul Is Discovered (23:12–22)

The Jews formed a conspiracy (23:12). Luke clarifies in the next verse that it is not the Jewish people as a whole who now represent the enemies of the faith, but a zealous group of forty men with a design on Paul's life.

An oath not to eat or drink until they had killed Paul (23:12). This kind of zeal for the law is well illustrated in the Mishnah: "He who stole a sacred vessel of the cult (Num. 4:7), and he who curses using the name of an idol, and he who has sexual relations with an Aramaean woman—zealots beat him up on the spot (Num. 25:8, 11). A priest who performed the rite in a state of uncleanness—his brothers, the priests, do not bring him to court. But the young priests take him outside the courtyard and break his head with clubs" (*m. Sanh.* 9:6).

The expression translated by "oath" here (*anathema*) is used in the Greek Old

Testament to translate the Hebrew term *ḥērem*. It designates something hostile to God and therefore under a ban and to be destroyed. Thus, the idolatrous cities of the Canaanites became *ḥērem* (or *anathema*) and were to be utterly destroyed (see Deut. 13:16; 20:17).

We are ready to kill him before he gets here (23:15). The meeting place of the Sanhedrin was in the center of the city at the *lišhat haggazît* (the "Chamber of Hewn Stone"), just west of the southwestern portion of the temple wall. Josephus calls this place the *Xystos*.[463] It was approximately a quarter-mile from the Antonia Fortress. The group of forty have planned to ambush Paul at some strategic point between the two locations. This was a bold plan since Paul would be escorted by Roman soldiers. The conspirators are obviously prepared to kill one or more of the soldiers to get to Paul.

The son of Paul's sister (23:16). This is a rare and fascinating insight into Paul's family. We do not know whether Paul's sister and her family have taken up residence in Jerusalem or whether the nephew has come to Jerusalem, as Paul had, for his education. Neither do we know if Paul's nephew is a believer. It is clear, however, that he possesses a family affection for Paul and wants to save his life.

He went into the barracks and told Paul (23:16). In his Jerusalem custody, Paul is not kept in a dark inner cell and chained to the floor by leg irons as he had been in Philippi. This is a more honorable custody since the *chiliarch* knows that Paul is a Roman citizen. Apparently, Paul is able to receive visitors.

Take this young man to the commander (23:17). Paul asks the centurion to take

his nephew to the *chiliarch* so he can reveal the conspiracy. The *chiliarch* listens sympathetically to the boy and enjoins him to silence about the plot.

Paul Is Sent to Caesarea (23:23–35)

The plot is not only a serious threat to Paul—a Roman citizen whom Claudius Lysias now has responsibility to protect—but also to Roman soldiers protecting him. Lysias probably also recognizes that there is a risk that this situation might escalate into a much greater problem. The *chiliarch* thus makes the decision to send Paul to Caesarea immediately under a heavy guard and the cover of night.

Get ready a detachment of two hundred soldiers (23:23). The total number of Roman soldiers escorting Paul to Caesarea is 470. Although this seems like an enormous number for protecting one man on his journey, Claudius Lysias rightly recognizes the volatile nature of this situation at a time when Jewish antipathy against Rome has nearly reached a boiling point. The size of this detachment functions as an adequate deterrent to forestall any attack by the forty men and any others they may have pulled into their planned ambush.

Go to Caesarea (23:23). Caesarea, not Jerusalem, was the seat of the Roman proconsul as well as the administrative and judicial center for Judea (see 10:1).

He wrote a letter as follows (23:25). In Greek, this is a technical expression (*typos*) indicating that Luke has available to him the exact text of the letter.[464]

Claudius Lysias (23:26). This is the first reference to the *chiliarch's* name. His *nomen* "Claudius" likely reflects that fact that he received his citizenship under the principate of the emperor Claudius.

To His Excellency (23:26). This is the NIV's translation of the Greek word *kratistos*, the same expression that is used of Theophilus, the recipient of Luke's two-volume work (Luke 1:3). *Kratistos* is a title of respect for Roman citizens of the aristocratic equestrian order and for those who hold high office (usually held by men of the equestrian order).[465]

For I had learned that he is a Roman citizen (23:27). Lysias is guilty of twisting

the facts to some degree perhaps in an effort to portray his actions in the best possible light. In reality, he learned that Paul is a Roman citizen *after* he rescued him from the murderous mob. He also failed to mention that he had Paul stretched out and ready to be flogged.

No charge against him that deserved death or imprisonment (23:29). In spite of the earlier false testimony that Paul had taken Trophimus into the inner courts of the temple, a capital crime, this was never mentioned in the Sanhedrin hearing.

As far as Antipatris (23:31). Antipatris was a city about thirty-five miles northwest of Jerusalem on the main road leading to the port city of Caesarea via Lydda.[466] It was less than ten miles from the coast and situated in the plain of Sharon near the Judean hills at the headwaters of the Yarkon river. The city had

▶
COIN MINTED UNDER ANTONIUS FELIX

▶ Felix

Felix was the Roman procurator of Judea for roughly eight years (A.D. 52–59) and had ruled for five years when Paul was taken into custody.[A-140] He did not come from a background of wealth and status, but was actually a freed slave. Both he and his brother Pallas had been the slaves of Antonia, the mother of Claudius. This was the first time that a Roman procuratorship had ever been held by a freedman.

His reign over Judea, Samaria, Galilee, and Perea did much to stimulate further unrest among the Jews, which eventually led to the war against Rome. The Roman historian Tacitus sums up his leadership with this remark: "Practicing every kind of cruelty and lust, he wielded royal power with the instincts of a slave."[A-141] Elsewhere, Tacitus says that Felix "stimulated outbreaks [of Jewish unrest] by injudicious disciplinary measures."[A-142] According to

Josephus, Felix had his soldiers track down and catch Jewish zealots virtually every day and immediately executed them, many of them by crucifixion. One of his most heinous crimes was conspiring to put to death the Jewish high priest Jonathan.[A-143]

He was ousted from his office by the emperor Nero in A.D. 59 after his inept handling of an uprising in the city of Caesarea. A dispute had arisen between the Jewish population of the city and the Syrian inhabitants' citizenship status in the city. The conflict led to rioting and street fighting. "One day the Jews were victorious, and Felix came into the market-place and ordered them with threats to retire. When they refused, he sent his soldiers against them and killed a large number, whose property was promptly plundered."[A-144] This happened while Paul was in Roman custody in Caesarea.

Selected List of the Roman Procurators of Judea		
Name	Date	NT Event
Coponius	A.D. 6–10	• The first Roman procurator of Judea after the deposition of Herod Archelaus
Valerius Gratus	A.D. 15–26	• Procurator during much of Jesus' life prior to the beginning of his ministry
Pontius Pilate	A.D. 26–36	• Procurator during Jesus' ministry • Jesus is crucified during his administration • Peter and John arrested during his rule
NO PROCURATOR		
Herod Agrippa I	A.D. 41–44	• Herod Agrippa I is made king over Judea, Samaria, and Galilee
Ventidius Cumanus	A.D. 48–52	• Procurator during the time of the Jerusalem Council
Felix	A.D. 52–59	• Paul is tried before him (Acts 24)
Festus	A.D. 60–62	• Paul is tried before him (Acts 25)
Albinus	A.D. 62–64	
Gessius Florus	A.D. 64–66	• Last procurator before the destruction of Jerusalem
Sextus Vettulenus Cerialis	A.D. 70–72	• First procurator after the destruction of Jerusalem

a long history as the ancient Aphek (see Josh. 12:18). Herod the Great renamed the city after his father Antipater: "In memory of his father he founded a city, choosing a site in the loveliest plain in his kingdom with an abundance of rivers and trees, and naming it Antipatris."[467] The distance for the next day's journey to Caesarea was about twenty-seven miles.

They let the cavalry go on with him, while they returned to the barracks (23:32). Now that they are in lands populated predominately by Gentiles and presumably safer from the threat of an ambush by Jewish zealots, the four hundred soldiers are ordered to return to Jerusalem.

Asked what province he was from (23:34). Felix asks this question not out of personal interest, but in an attempt to establish if the case is within his jurisdiction. Since the Roman province of Cilicia falls under the authority of the Roman legate of Syria—to whom Felix

ANTIPATRIS

The site of Antipatris (Aphek) with a seventeenth-century Turkish fortress in the background.
▼

reports—he is therefore responsible for handling the case.[468]

Kept under guard in Herod's palace (23:35). The literal reference is to Herod's *praitōrion*, which is best understood as his palace. Not only has Herod built a remarkable port at Caesarea, but he "adorned it with the most splendid palace."[469] After Herod passed off the scene, the Roman procurators made their residence at the palace. The fact that Paul is held in the palace does not mean that he spends two years living in opulence.

Similar to the Antonia Fortress in Jerusalem, this facility would have had rooms for those kept under light custody.

Paul's Trial Before the Roman Procurator Felix (24:1–21)

Five days after Paul's arrival in Caesarea, a trial is convened. The Roman procurator Felix properly serves as judge of the trial and hears the cases of both the plaintiffs and the defendant. Luke gives a précis of both presentations. The trial is adjourned without a decision so Felix can

HEROD'S PALACE IN CAESAREA

The foreground represents the foundations of Herod's palace by the sea.

▶ Herod's Palace By the Sea

In 1976, Ehed Netzer of Hebrew University of Jerusalem began excavating a site on a rocky promontory of Caesarea. Renewed excavations of this site in 1992 by Netzer and members of an American team led by Kathryn Gleason and Barbara Burell of the University of Pennsylvania have led to a provisional identification of this site as Herod's *praitōrion*—his seaside palace. A-145

A striking feature of the "promontory palace" is a pool measuring 115 feet long and 59 feet wide in the center of the complex. Water channels leading to it suggest that it would have been filled with fresh water. Surrounding the pool on all four sides are the foundations of a large structure with rooms for a range of purposes. The discovery of a variety of Herodian era artifacts—including pottery and lamps—suggest that the palace was built sometime between 22–10 B.C.

await the testimony of the Roman commander of forces in Jerusalem.

The high priest Ananias went down (24:1). The presence of the high priest—the highest authority of the Jewish nation—and some of the Jerusalem elders at this trial underline its importance and significance to the Jewish leaders.

A lawyer named Tertullus (24:1). Nothing is known of this man outside of this passage. He is a *rhētor*, that is, he is a professional attorney. As such, he has knowledge of Roman law and proper court procedure as well as training in the art of rhetoric. Since it is not required for the plaintiff to have a legal advocate, their hiring of Tertullus reveals their determination to win a conviction.

Tertullus presented his case (24:2). Before Tertullus gets to the heart of his case, he gives a laudatory introduction in which he heaps lavish (and, in this case, undeserved) praise on Felix. This type of beginning to a case, known as a *captatio benevolentiae*, was common in the courtroom and often effective in winning the respect and favor of the judge.[470]

A long period of peace under you (24:2). Tertullus begins his case with an empty line of flattery. The only way Felix endeavored to bring peace was by having his soldiers hunt down and kill extremist Jewish freedom fighters (*sicarii*) (see "Felix" at 23:23). In reality, Felix did more than any other governor to disrupt any semblance of peace there might have been in the Holy Land.

Your foresight (24:2). The Greek word *pronoia* ("foresight") was often used of

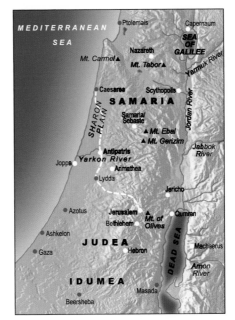

JERUSALEM TO
CAESAREA

the providence of God in Hellenistic Judaism (e.g., *3 Macc.* 4:21; 5:30). It could also be used of Hellenistic rulers who exercised excellent insight in the management of public affairs, as it was used of the Syrian ruler Seleucus IV: "For he [the high priest] saw that without the king's attention [*pronoia*] public affairs could not again reach a peaceful settlement, and that Simon would not stop his folly" (2 Macc. 4:6).

A troublemaker (24:5). "Troublemaker" (*loimos*) is a word that in its literal sense means a "plague" or a "pestilence." It came to be used as a metaphor for a dangerous person—like someone who carries a deadly disease and infects other people. Using a different term but the same image, the emperor Claudius in a letter refers to certain activities of the Jews as "stirring up a universal plague [*nosos*] throughout the world."[471] The "plague" image is used frequently in the Greek Old Testament. *Loimos* refers to the "wicked man" of Psalm 1:1 and the "mocker" in many of the Proverbs.[472] Eli's sons were "troublemakers" because "they had no regard for the Lord" (1 Sam. 2:12).

Stirring up riots among the Jews all over the world (24:5). The Greek word *stasis* is the counterpart to the Latin *seditio* and similar in meaning to our word "sedition." The charge of *stasis* was serious among the Roman authorities who were seeking to maintain peace in the empire—especially in a province where outbreaks of hostility were increasingly commonplace. There is clearly some truth to Tertullus's charge when one considers the reaction to Paul's preaching in synagogues in Pisidian Antioch, Iconium, Lystra, Thessalonica, Berea, and Corinth.

A ringleader of the Nazarene sect (24:5). This is the earliest use of "Nazarenes" as a description of the Christian movement. The origin of this name is rooted in the description of Jesus as from Nazareth (Jesus the *Nazōraios*, see 2:22; 3:6).

Tertullus characterizes this movement as a *hairesis*, the term from which is derived the English word "heresy." The term itself does not necessarily have the kind of negative connotations implied by "heresy." Josephus used the term to distinguish the various schools of thought within Judaism—the Pharisees, Sadducees, and the Essenes.[473] But the term took on pejorative overtones (see 24:14; 28:22); that is how Tertullus seems to use it.[474] Christianity is thus presented by him as an illegitimate or deviant form of Judaism.

Tried to desecrate the temple (24:6). The implication is that Paul brought Trophimus into the inner courts with the intent of desecrating the temple. This was a serious charge for which, if proven, Paul could receive the death penalty. Without the alleged witnesses—Jewish pilgrims from Asia Minor—the charge was without substance.

So we seized him (24:6). Tertullus gives the impression that the temple police apprehended Paul in an orderly fashion. He says nothing about the mob scene. It is possible that he is implying that Lysias exceeded his jurisdiction by taking Paul out of their hands. This is the interpretation of the Western tradition of the text (verse 7 in certain versions), which adds, "but the commander, Lysias, came and with the use of much force snatched him from our hands." Thus, Felix should hand Paul over to the Sanhedrin, who would try him and, if guilty, hand him back over to the Romans for execution.[475]

Paul replied (24:10). After Tertullus finishes, Paul is given the chance to respond to the accusations. This account is given in verses 10–21. As with the case presented by Tertullus, Luke only gives us a summary of the salient points, but possibly bases it on actual court documents.[476] Like Tertullus, Paul properly and politely begins with a *captatio benevolentiae*, but not by bending the truth to endear himself to Felix.

Twelve days ago (24:11). This expression in the original is best interpreted to mean that Paul was only in Jerusalem a total of twelve days.[477] Now having been in Caesarea for five days (24:1), it has only been seventeen days since his arrival in Jerusalem. An extraordinary amount has happened in that brief span of time:

- Day 1: Paul arrives in Jerusalem (21:18).
- Day 2: Paul meets with the leaders of the Jerusalem church (21:18).
- Days 3–9: Paul observes a seven-day ritual of purification (21:27).
- Day 9: Paul is arrested (21:33).
- Day 10: Paul appears before the Sanhedrin (22:30).
- Day 11: The plot against Paul's life is uncovered (23:12).
- Day 12: Paul is taken to Caesarea.
- Days 13–17: Paul awaits trial in Caesarea.

The Way (24:14). See comments on 9:2.

I believe everything that agrees with the Law and that is written in the Prophets (24:14). Paul represents himself as a faithful and observant Jew. He continues to regard himself as a Pharisee (23:6). The difference, of course, is that he sees the hope of Judaism fulfilled in Jesus of Nazareth. In upholding the law, Paul does not necessarily agree with all of the Pharisaic traditions that surround the law and he also reinterprets the meaning and significance of certain key parts of the law (e.g., the law governing circumcision; see Rom. 2:29).

I have the same hope in God (24:15). As an outcome of embracing all that is written in the prophets, Paul claims to share the same future hope as nearly all Jews (with the exception of the Sadducees). At the heart of this is a belief in the coming descendant of David who will be the end-time deliverer for Israel. It also encompasses a belief in the resurrection of the dead (Dan. 12:2).

A resurrection of ... the wicked (24:15). Many texts in the Judaism of the time of Christ affirm a belief in a general resurrection, developing the teaching of Daniel 12:2. For example, the *Testament of Benjamin* 10:6–10 teaches that all will be resurrected and God will judge the nations for all of the wrongs they have committed. Similarly, *4 Ezra* (2 Esdras) 7:32–35 speaks of a day when "the earth shall give up those who are asleep in it" and the Most High will judge all people according to their deeds.[478] According to the Gospel of John, Jesus also affirms this belief in a general resurrection (John 5:28–29). In his letters, Paul never explicitly develops this teaching (though cf. 1 Cor. 15:12–13), but he emphasizes that all people must appear before the judgment seat of Christ (see 2 Cor. 5:10).

After an absence of several years (24:17). Paul's most recent visit was about five years earlier when he briefly visited the Jerusalem church following his Corinthian ministry and prior to his trip to Ephesus (18:22). Prior to that was his trip to Jerusalem for the so-called Apostolic Council in A.D. 49 (Acts 15).

I came to Jerusalem to bring my people gifts for the poor (24:17). This is Luke's only explicit reference to the collection of money Paul has gathered for the impoverished Jewish Christians in Jerusalem (see comments on 21:18). This was the second time that Paul brought relief to the city. The first time was roughly twelve years earlier when he came to Jerusalem as a delegate from the church at Antioch (11:27–30; 12:25). At that time, James, Peter, and John asked Paul to continue to "remember the poor" (Gal. 2:10). Paul was faithful to this request and gathered a substantial relief offering from the churches of Asia Minor, Macedonia, and Achaia "for the poor among the saints in Jerusalem" (Rom. 15:26). The gift was not only motivated by the desire to help those in need, but also expressed thanks from the Gentiles because they now share in the spiritual blessings of the Jews (Rom. 15:27). One can have a glimpse into how Paul gathered this collection from the Macedonian and Achaian churches in 2 Corinthians 8:1–9:15.

And to present offerings (24:17). These offerings must be seen as distinct from the gifts for the poor. This term (*prosphoras*) refers to sacrificial offerings. Paul paid the expenses for four men to purchase animals, bread, grain, and liquid as sacrificial offerings in fulfillment of their Nazirite vows (see comments on 21:22–23). Beyond this, there is no evidence that Paul presented any other offerings as part of the temple worship.

I was ceremonially clean (24:18). Paul had undertaken the seven-day Jewish ritual of purification (see comments on 21:24).

Who ought to be here before you (24:19). A group of Jewish pilgrims from Asia Minor (presumably Ephesus) instigated the disturbance in the temple courts by falsely accusing Paul. Yet they are not present at the proceedings before Felix. Why none of them is present is somewhat perplexing, especially in light of how important this case is to the high priest and members of the Sanhedrin who have accompanied him. Do the Asian Jews know that their testimony will not stand up under close scrutiny? Or are they simply pressed by time to return home to their jobs and their families? Whatever the reason, their absence greatly damages the case of the Jewish leaders. As one expert on Roman law notes, "The Roman law was very strong against accusers who abandoned their charges."[479]

Paul's Caesarean Imprisonment (24:22–27)

Paul remains in Roman custody in Caesarea for two full years (A.D. 57–59) awaiting the resumption of his trial. He is afforded an occasional opportunity to talk with the Roman procurator and his wife, which he takes advantage of for the presentation of the gospel.

Felix, who was well acquainted with the Way (24:22). With the thousands who have become Christians in Jerusalem and the many Christian communities that have developed in Caesarea and throughout Palestine, it is not surprising that this Roman governor is acquainted with the movement. The precise wording here suggests that he is either "well acquainted" with the Jesus movement or "better acquainted" with it than the Jerusalem leaders (it is a comparative adjective). What kind of information he has received about Christianity is unknown. As the Roman procurator of this volatile region, surely his chief concern is to know what kind of security risk this movement posed. He is sufficiently familiar with them to know that they are not insurrectionists or rioters.

When Lysias the commander comes (24:22). Felix formally adjourns the trial until he can obtain further information from the *chiliarch*. Presumably Lysias does come at some point and the trial is resumed, although Luke says nothing about this. If he does, Felix does not find enough information to release Paul or proceed with a conviction.

Give him some freedom and permit his friends to take care of his needs (24:23). Felix orders Paul to be kept in a lightened form of military custody. This does not mean that Paul is unchained; he is probably manacled or chained to his centurion or other military personnel. He is most likely kept in a secure room of Herod's palace (see "Herod's Palace By the Sea" at 23:35). Since the Romans do not take responsibility for providing food and clothing to someone in custody, Paul's friends are given access to him for taking care of his needs. [480] These friends are probably members of the Christian community at Caesarea as well as Luke and any of the other delegates from the churches who may have remained with him for a time. One wonders if Cornelius and members of his household (see Acts 10) might have been among the people who care for Paul during this time.

His wife Drusilla, who was a Jewess (24:24). Drusilla was one of three daughters of Herod Agrippa I, the king of Palestine who died suddenly in Caesarea after appearing to people as a god (see 12:19–23). Drusilla was six years old when her father died in A.D. 44, which means that she was only fourteen years old when she married Felix and nineteen years old at this juncture. [481]

Drusilla was Felix's third wife. One of his previous wives was the granddaughter of Anthony and Cleopatra—a marriage that made Felix a relative of the emperor Claudius. The circumstances of Drusilla's marriage to Felix reveal something of his sordid character. Drusilla had recently been married to Azizus, king of Emesa (a small territory in Syria). When Felix subsequently met Drusilla, he was overcome with desire for her. Josephus says that "she did indeed exceed all other women in beauty." [482] Longing to make this woman his own wife, Felix secured the services of a magician from Cyprus and made every effort to take her away from Azizus. Enticed by the many promises of Felix to make her a happy woman, she was persuaded to leave her husband and become Felix's wife. [483]

He spoke about faith in Christ Jesus (24:24). When Paul is given the opportunity to speak to Felix and Drusilla, he clearly presents his conviction that Jesus is the fulfillment of the messianic hope of Israel. This would have involved an explanation of why he had to suffer and die as

REFLECTIONS

TO SPEAK OF THE COMING JUDGMENT HAS BECOME unfashionable in the evangelistic sharing or preaching of many Christians. We are afraid of turning people off by appearing extremist. The apostle Paul regularly speaks about a time of impending accountability before God in his preaching. Less concerned about how people feel, he is overcome by his feeling of responsibility for clearly informing people that God indeed will call people to account one day.

well as rise from the dead. Paul exhorts them to put their faith in this Jesus.

Paul discoursed on righteousness . . . and the judgment to come (24:25). Jesus taught that when the Spirit came, he would "convict the world of guilt in regard to sin and righteousness and judgment" (John 16:8). Paul continues his presentation of the gospel to Felix and Drusilla by focusing on these themes in concert with the work of the Spirit.

Self-control (24:25). Sandwiched between Paul's themes of righteousness and the coming judgment is the topic of self-control. The term *enkrateia* never appears in the Greek Old Testament (except *4 Macc.* 5:34), but Paul presents it as a virtue that the Spirit produces in the life of a believer (Gal. 5:23). The roots of the use of this term in ethical contexts probably go back to Plato, who emphasizes the cultivation of *enkrateia*, that is, mastery over oneself, especially over sensual desires and pleasures.[484] Socrates, Aristotle, and the Stoics regard self-control as a cardinal virtue. Similarly, the Hellenistic Jew Philo repeatedly stresses the importance of developing self-control.[485] Paul's discourse on self-control, together with his teaching on righteousness and the judgment, is probably intended to help Felix and Drusilla recognize their guilt before God as a means of pointing them to their need for the forgiveness that comes from putting their faith in Christ Jesus.

Hoping that Paul would offer him a bribe (24:26). Felix does not recognize his own lack of self-control with regard to his lust for money. He invites Paul to meet with him periodically not to discuss the problem in his own soul, but to provide Paul with ample opportunity to offer him a bribe. Apparently Felix has the impression that Paul has access to considerable wealth. This probably stems from Felix's awareness that Paul has come to Jerusalem with a sizeable amount of money. Although it was illegal for Felix to accept a bribe, this law was frequently overlooked in the governance of the provinces.

When two years had passed (24:27). Paul remains in Roman custody in Caesarea for two full years. Some think that Paul may have written his letter to the church at Philippi during this imprisonment (see the introduction to Philippians). Luke apparently stays in Caesarea while Paul is in custody; he is with Paul when Festus determines that Paul should be sent to Rome (Acts 27:1). This extended stay in Caesarea would have been invaluable to Luke as he continued to gather information for his Gospel and the book of Acts.

Felix was succeeded (24:27). Felix is recalled because of his inept handling of a flareup of violence between Jews and Greeks in the city of Caesarea (see "Felix" at 23:23). Josephus says that under normal circumstances, Felix would have faced a much greater punishment for this misdeed:

When Porcius Festus was sent by Nero as successor to Felix, the leaders of the Jewish community of Caesarea went up to Rome to accuse Felix. He undoubtedly would have paid the penalty for his misdeeds against the Jews had not Nero yielded to the urgent entreaty of Felix's brother Pallas, whom at that time he held in the highest honour.[486]

Because Felix wanted to grant a favor to the Jews, he left Paul in prison (24:27). Felix is in a precarious position with the

Jews. His killing of many of the insurrectionists (*sicarii*) and his insensitive treatment of many other affairs has embroiled Jewish opinion against him. To release Paul would have inflamed the Jewish leaders even more. Yet to extradite Paul to the Sanhedrin for trial would surely have resulted in the apostle's death. He does not want to face the political implications from Rome for the death of a Roman citizen. The most expedient course for Felix is the continuous postponement of the trial.[487]

Paul Stands Trial Before Festus (25:1–12)

With the change of procurators comes a resumption of Paul's trial. Any hope of a dismissal under Felix evaporates with his recall by the emperor. As soon as Festus arrives on the scene (A.D. 59), the Jerusalem leaders exploit the situation to seek an extradition of Paul to Jerusalem. This does not work and a hearing is convened in Caesarea.

Festus went up from Caesarea to Jerusalem (25:1). Shortly after assuming his new position, Festus travels to the principal city of his domain to become acquainted with the religious and political leaders. As an outsider, he has much to learn about this volatile region.

The chief priests and Jewish leaders appeared before him (25:2). "Chief priests" refers to the current high priest, former high priests, and the priestly group from whom the high priests are chosen. The high priest is now Ishmael ben Phiabi. After he takes office, a terrible schism arises between the ruling elite and the chief priests, resulting in violence.[488] The two groups are united, however, in their opposition to Paul and the Jesus movement. The fact that Paul's case is one of the first items they discuss with the new Roman procurator demonstrates the importance of the case to them.

◀
PORCIUS FESTUS
COIN

▶ Porcius Festus

Nero appointed Festus as the replacement for Felix in A.D. 59 and he governed until his premature death in A.D. 62. In the only portrayal of Festus outside of the New Testament, Josephus represents him as an honorable and capable leader, but facing a set of insurmountable crises.[A-146]

Nothing is known about his background. Upon coming to Judea he was immediately faced with the ongoing strife between the Jews and Greeks in Caesarea, the *sicarii* setting villages on fire and plundering them, a messianic pretender leading people into the desert, and a dispute over a high wall that the temple officials erected that obstructed Agrippa and Festus from observing the inner courts of the temple from the palace. All of these events further contributed to the massive unrest in the country that led to the Jewish war four years after the death of Festus.

Festus was succeeded by Albinus (A.D. 62–64). Josephus says that, "Albinus, who followed him, acted very differently, being guilty of every possible misdemeanor."[A-147]

As a favor to them (25:3). The Jewish leaders quickly attempt to take advantage of the new procurator's natural tendency to ingratiate himself to them. For maintaining security in this region, Festus would certainly want to achieve their goodwill. This is especially important in the aftermath of the Jew-Gentile rioting in Caesarea that led to the demise of his predecessor Felix.[489] The case of Paul—a person with whom he has no prior familiarity—would be a matter of indifference to him. Although it is his duty to uphold Roman law, the rulers of the eastern provinces frequently bent the law to obtain their desired political aims.

They were preparing an ambush (25:3). Luke does not state specifically who is preparing the ambush. Presumably, the forty men who previously took the vow would still want to carry it out (23:13–14). Others also may have joined them in their strategy to rid the Holy Land of the outspoken man they consider to be perverting the law. The plan now is to ambush Paul somewhere on the road from Caesarea to Jerusalem. As with the previous strategy, they would not be able to accomplish their aim without some Roman casualties.

He convened the court (25:6). Festus reopens Paul's case by inviting leaders from Jerusalem to travel to Caesarea and present their charges against him. This time there is no mention of a hired rhetorician/lawyer to represent the Jerusalem side. They apparently raise the same charges, accusing Paul of abandoning the Jewish law and defiling the temple.

I have done nothing wrong ... against Caesar (25:8). In his defense, Paul implies that the Jewish leaders are accusing him of sedition. In a Roman context, this was a serious charge, which could lead to death. It may be an expansion of Tertullus's charge that Paul was a "trouble-maker" (see 24:15). The charge may be based on reports that the priests have heard from Diaspora Jews in places such as Thessalonica (17:6–7), where Paul had run-ins with the Roman authorities.

Festus, wishing to do the Jews a favor (25:9). Luke recognizes that politics has now entered into the trial and that any notion of fair and just proceedings is hopeless.

Are you willing to go to Jerusalem and stand trial (25:9). Festus now changes his mind and reveals an openness to change the venue of the trial to Jerusalem. It may seem odd to us that a Roman ruler would ask his prisoner about his willingness to stand trial in a different city, but as a Roman citizen, Paul has the right to insist on a Roman trial.[490] It is unclear what Festus has in mind: Is he proposing that Paul stand trial in the Sanhedrin and he would be present and merely approve the outcome of their deliberations? Or is he planning to hold the trial in the Antonia Fortress in the presence of the Jerusalem leaders?

I appeal to Caesar (25:11). As a Roman citizen, Paul has the right to make an appeal to have his case heard in Rome by the emperor. There were varied forms of this provision giving citizens the right to appeal at any point during the course of legal action or after a verdict had been rendered.[491] Paul's case has been in limbo for two years and now seems to be moving in a disadvantageous direction. To prevent his case from being moved to Jerusalem, Paul asserts his right of appeal (*provocatio*) at this time. Why he had not done so previously can only be explained on the basis that he assumed the charges against him would eventually be dismissed, whereupon he could travel to Rome (according to his plans) as a free man.

Paul has seen enough to convince him that he will not receive a fair trial in Jerusalem. Because of his nephew's previous warning and the antipathy of the Jewish leaders against him, perhaps he is also suspicious of the very thing that they are plotting against him. The apostle is clearly not fearful of suffering for the sake of Christ—even to the point of death. Yet the overriding concerns of the gospel drive him to use the means available to him to forestall an extradition to Jerusalem so he can travel to Rome and present his case to the emperor himself. The appeal will give him an unprecedented opportunity for presenting the gospel at the highest seat of Roman power. Perhaps Paul now sees his right of appeal as the way the Lord has given him for getting to Rome to testify before the authorities (see 23:11).

Paul will be making his appeal to appear before Nero, who has been emperor for five years by A.D. 59. At this point in Nero's principate, he showed a fair amount of stability as he was still under the influence of his tutor, Seneca (the Stoic philosopher) and Sextus Afrianus Burrus. The horrible atrocities

AERIAL VIEW OF CAESAREA

The theater is visible in the top right. The remains of the hippodrome are in the foreground.

against Christians will take place five years hence after the burning of Rome (A.D. 64).

After Festus had conferred with his council (25:12). Festus has the power to deny Paul's request if it is not reasonable or falls within a list of exceptions.[492] Of course, he has the option of dismissing the charges altogether, though the latter course of action is not in the interest of maintaining order among the Jews. To help him make a decision, Festus meets with his own council—a panel of eight to twenty local Roman citizens, military men, and civil servants who function as an advisory group on judicial matters.[493]

Paul Appears Before Agrippa (25:13–27)

After Paul makes his appeal to the emperor, he must wait for the procurator to write an accompanying report about the case. During this time, the client-king from the northern territories (which includes a portion of the area of modern Lebanon) comes to welcome the new procurator. This king is the grandson of Herod the Great, a valued friend of Rome, knowledgeable about the affairs of the Jews, curator of the temple, and someone in charge of appointing high priests in Jerusalem. If anyone could legally lay claim to the title "king of the Jews," it is Agrippa. For Festus, his arrival presents a fortuitous opportunity to gain additional perspective on the case. Since Agrippa possesses no legal jurisdiction in Judea, the hearing should be regarded as merely an informal inquiry into Paul's case.

Bernice (25:13). Bernice was the younger sister—not the wife—of Agrippa.[494] Yet suspicions abounded that there was an inappropriate relationship between the two.[495] At the time of this hearing with Paul, she and her brother would have been thirty-one and thirty-two years of age.

Bernice was previously married to Marcus Julius Alexander (in A.D. 41), who died shortly afterward, and to her uncle, Herod of Chalcis (whose kingdom Agrippa inherited), who died in A.D. 48. She and her two children from Herod lived with Agrippa for the next fifteen years. It was during this time that rumors circulated that she was having an incestuous relationship with her brother. To thwart the evil gossip, she married King Polemon of Cilicia in A.D. 64 (about five years after the hearing with Paul), but this marriage did not last and she returned to her brother. She later fell in love with Titus, the Roman general who destroyed Jerusalem, and became his mistress. She went to Rome in A.D. 75 and lived with him on the Palatine, but popular sentiment forced Titus to terminate this liason.

She was in Jerusalem at the outbreak of the Jewish war and interceded on behalf of the Jews to the Roman procurator, Gessius Florus (A.D. 64–66), with substantial risk to her own life. She and her brother also made repeated efforts to

---

The Lineage of Herod the Great

Herod the Great
→ Aristobulus
→ Herod (King of Chalcis) and Agrippa I
→ Agrippa II, Bernice, Drusilla (Wife of Felix)

dissuade the Jewish revolutionaries, but were not successful.

To pay their respects to Festus (25:13). The couple comes to Caesarea to meet the new procurator of Judea. They have a vested interest in Judea and certainly want to secure the new procurator's goodwill.

Festus discussed Paul's case with the king (25:14). This is the perfect opportunity for Festus to discuss Paul's case with someone far more knowledgeable about Jewish affairs than he is. In the next eight verses, Luke summarizes Festus's presentation of the case to Agrippa. How Luke knows what is said in this private discussion is difficult to discern unless he has access to informants who

were present and heard what was said.[496] It is also possible that Luke is merely inferring what is said based on what is widely known about the case.[497]

Before he has faced his accusers (25:16). It was an established Roman custom acknowledged as law that the plaintiffs had to make their accusations before a judge in the presence of the defendant: "This is the law by which we abide: No

◄

COIN WITH THE IMAGE OF HEROD AGRIPPA II

▶ Marcus Julius Agrippa (Herod Agrippa II)

Marcus Julius Agrippa was the eldest of four children and only son born to Agrippa I, who died in A.D. 44 in Caesarea when an angel of the Lord struck him down (see Acts 12:23).[A-148] The younger Agrippa was in Rome at the time of his father's death. Emperor Claudius wanted to immediately make Agrippa II the successor to his father's throne, but the emperor's counselors convincingly dissuaded him because the boy was only seventeen years of age. The rule of Judea was once again returned to a procuratorship, and Cuspius Fadus (A.D. 44–46) was appointed.

Six years later (A.D. 50), Claudius bestowed on Agrippa the kingdom of Chalcis (part of present-day Lebanon). Over the next few years, Claudius extended Agrippa's domain to include other territories in the north in addition to important portions of Galilee and Perea while Judea remained under Roman governorship. Claudius also gave him the influential and powerful right to appoint the high priests.[A-149]

Coins and inscriptions demonstrate that Agrippa preferred the title "king" and was often referred to as "the great king" (*megas basileus*).[A-150] Agrippa's loyalties were more stongly aligned with Rome than with the Jewish cause. Nevertheless, he attempted to create goodwill with the Jews. He went so far as to have the city of Jerusalem paved with white marble, in part so that the building workers would not be unemployed.[A-151] When the Jewish war broke out, however, Agrippa did all he could to dissuade the Jewish aggressors while he remained solidly on the side of the Romans.

Because of his loyalty to Rome, Vespasian confirmed him in the rulership of his kingdom after the war and even increased the extent of his reign. The historian Josephus corresponded with Agrippa about the history of the Jewish war he was engaged in writing.[A-152] The precise date of his death is unknown, but he probably lived until the 90s. He apparently never married or fathered any children.

one may be condemned in his [the plaintiff's] absence, nor can equity tolerate that anyone be condemned without his case being heard."[498] Similarly, Appian states, "The law requires, members of the council, that a man who is on trial should hear the accusation and speak in his own defense before judgment is passed on him."[499]

About their own religion (25:19). This is not the common Greek word for "religion," but a term (*deisidaimonia*) often translated "superstition" and can mean "a terrible fear of the gods" or "dread of demons." Although it could be used in a positive sense ("reverence for the gods," as in 17:22), Festus is here being derogatory in his comments about Christianity.

A dead man named Jesus who Paul claimed was alive (25:19). Previously, in his hearing before Felix, Luke records Paul as stating that he is on trial because of his belief in the resurrection of the dead (24:21). Now we know that Paul specifically relates his belief in the resurrection to one particular person whom he believes God has already raised—Jesus of Nazareth.

For the Emperor's decision (25:21). The term here used for emperor is *Sebastos*, the Greek equivalent of the Latin *Augustus*. The word itself means "revered" or "worthy of reverence." It is a title that the Roman Senate first conferred on Gaius Octavius (Caesar Augustus) and was subsequently used for his successors.

Agrippa and Bernice came with great pomp (25:23). "Pomp" is the NIV's translation of the Greek word *phantasia*, a word used in Aristotle for the faculty of the imagination.[500] Here it refers to an ostentatious display that sometimes accompanies the arrival and procession of a king.

With the high ranking officers and leading men of the city (25:23). The high ranking officers are literally, *chiliarchos*, the commanders of the cohorts in the city (the same rank as Claudius Lysias in Jerusalem). According to Josephus, five cohorts were stationed at Caesarea.[501] In addition to the military officers, all the leading civic officials were also present. The apostle Paul would have the chance to address an elite gathering. This continues to fulfill the words of Jesus, who predicted regarding his witnesses: "They will lay hands on you and persecute you. They will deliver you to synagogues and prisons, and you will be brought before kings and governors, and all on account of my name" (Luke 22:12).

The whole Jewish community has petitioned me (25:24). This does not refer to every Jew living in Judea, but rather the

---

REFLECTIONS

THE RESURRECTION OF JESUS IS central and decisive for Paul's preaching and the witness of the early Christians. Paul tells the Corinthians, "If Christ has not been raised, our preaching is useless and so is your faith" (1 Cor. 15:14). When we share the gospel today, it is essential that we not only explain that Jesus died for our sins, but that he also rose from the dead. If Jesus remained in the grave, then we would still be dead in our sins and without hope. But the truth is this: "He is alive!"

legal representatives of the nation, namely, the Sanhedrin and the chief priests.

His Majesty (25:26). Literally, "my Lord [*kyrios*]." The Roman emperors were also referred to by the title "Lord." This was especially true in the eastern Mediterranean region. Egyptian papyri have been discovered where the title *kyrios* is applied to Augustus (P.Oxy. 1143.4), Claudius (P.Oxy. 37.6), and Nero (P.Oxy. 246.30, 34, 37). As one scholar puts it: "The title denoted the status and power that the *Princeps* enjoyed in the Roman world."[502]

As a result of this investigation I may have something to write (25:26). Festus is still at a loss on how to present Paul's case to the emperor. Convinced that Paul is not guilty of sedition against the emperor, he is hopeful that this informal hearing will clarify the issues so that he can write a competent report. Roman law required such a report from Festus: "After an appeal has been made, records must be provided by the one with whom the appeal has been filed to the person who will adjudicate the appeal."[503]

Paul's Explains His Conversion to Agrippa (26:1–23)

This is now the third occasion where Luke chooses to include a recounting of Paul's conversion experience (see 9:1–30; 22:3–21). In this instance, he summarizes the essence of what Paul says as he stands before King Agrippa. This is not a formal court defense, but is rather more of an opportunity for the curious Agrippa to find out firsthand what Paul is proclaiming that is stirring up so much trouble. As in Paul's previous presentation, it is important to consider the distinctive audience and setting, since Paul adapts them to the unique demands of each occasion. Here Paul appeals particularly to Agrippa, who knows better than Festus the traditions and culture of the Jews.

I consider myself fortunate (26:2). Paul begins his address to Agrippa by respectfully expressing his appreciation for the opportunity and by commending Agrippa's grasp of Jewish customs and manners. Paul politely urges him to carefully listen to his entire case.

The Jews all know the way I have lived (26:4). Paul's first line of argument is to demonstrate that he was and remains utterly Jewish in all that he proclaims. He has not broken away from the ancestral faith and embraced something entirely new.

My hope in what God has promised our fathers (26:6). Paul still bases his faith entirely on the Torah, the Writings, and the Prophets (what we now call the Old Testament). The difference is that he has come to believe that the promises throughout the Scriptures have been fulfilled in Jesus the Messiah. On this basis, he then attempts to establish for Agrippa that the central issue is one of interpretation of the Old Testament hope. Has it or has it not been fulfilled in the person of Jesus?

Why should any of you consider it incredible that God raises the dead? (26:8) Paul immediately goes to the key stumbling block for many Jews in accepting what he has to say about Jesus—the issue of his resurrection. There is no Christian faith without the resurrection. Paul previously told the Corinthians, "if Christ has not been raised, our preaching is useless and so is your faith" (1 Cor. 15:14). Paul asks rhetorically why it is so incredible to believe in the resurrection. This is particularly true for Pharisees who, in principle, affirmed a belief in end-time resurrection.

All that was possible to oppose the name of Jesus (26:9). Paul now admits to his own previous unwillingness to recognize Jesus as Messiah and how that resulted in his fervor to persecute Christians. Here he indicates that he had a part in putting many saints to death. We know of Stephen, but history is silent about the names and stories of the others. Paul saw the Jesus movement as "a cancer attacking the vitals of Israel's life; it must be uprooted."504 This is understandable from the vantage point of the Jew since Christianity called into question the traditional role of the temple, the law, the sacrifices, and the purity regulations.

I cast my vote against them (26:10). When Paul says that he cast his vote against those he was persecuting (26:10), this simply means that he approved of their death,505 not that he was a member of the Jewish ruling council (the Sanhedrin). He was too young at this point in his life to be a member of the Sanhedrin.

I went from one synagogue to another to have them punished (26:11). Paul gave vent to his zeal by traveling to a number of synagogues throughout Judea and then on the frontiers of Israel to oppose the spread of Christianity. The synagogues each had their own ruling body that could administer punishments to its members (such as the thirty-nine lashes), but in certain cases Paul sought extradition to Jerusalem. Once in Jerusalem, the

accused were imprisoned and some were found guilty of a capital offence and put to death.

Tried to force them to blaspheme (26:11). One of the methods Paul used when he interrogated the believers was to compel them to repudiate Christ. This apparently met with little success since these believers preferred synagogal punishments, imprisonment in Jerusalem, and even death over denying their precious Lord.

On one of these journeys I was going to Damascus (26:12). Paul goes on to tell of his dramatic encounter with the risen Christ on the road to Damascus. It is told in almost precisely the same terms as it was narrated twice previously in the book of Acts.

In Aramaic (26:14). Paul now makes it explicit that the Lord Jesus speaks to him in Aramaic. But this is previously intimated by the Aramaic form of Paul's name (*Saoul*).

It is hard for you to kick against the goads (26:14). A goad is a long stick with a sharpened, pointed end. It was used by the keepers of livestock, particularly oxen, to prod the animal when it was yoked up to a wagon or farm implement. The animal, of course, did not like being jabbed with the stick and would kick at the object. The kicking was obviously useless and the animal soon learned it was better to submit to the farmer's direction rather than to kick against the goad. This expression came to be used figuratively in a variety of literary contexts. It became proverbial in classical Greek writers to express the futility of struggling against one's destiny. Euripides, for instance, has Dionysus say to Pentheus: "I would control my rage and sacrifice to him if I were you, rather than kick against the goad."[506] The writer of Ecclesiastes says that "the words of the wise are like goads" (Eccl. 12:14). Here the message the Lord was conveying to Paul was that it would be useless for him to persist on the wrong path of resisting what God had accomplished in Christ and what he was now accomplishing through the church.

Appoint you as a servant (26:16). Paul now gives us more details of what the Lord said to him on this occasion than either of the other two accounts. Jesus announced that he was appointing Paul as a "servant." This is a rich expression pointing back to Isaiah's prophecy of the coming "Servant of the Lord," who would be a light to the Gentiles (Isa. 42:1–7). Jesus came in direct fulfillment of this prophecy, constantly referring to himself and his ministry in terms of the language and imagery of "the servant" in Isaiah. The Lord was now commissioning Paul *to continue* the ministry of the Lord Jesus in the world as his agent.

I will rescue you (26:17). The Lord promised Paul protection as he fulfilled his ministry. This does not mean that Paul would be free from suffering; on the contrary, the Lord told him he would face suffering. It did mean that the Lord would protect him sufficiently to carry out his divinely intended mission.

Turn them from darkness to light, and from the power of Satan to God (26:18). Jesus promised to work through Paul to reach many Gentiles with the message of the cross. This redemptive message would save them, fulfilling the terms of Isaiah 42:6–7: "[You will be] a light for the Gentiles, to open eyes that are blind, to free captives from prison and to release from the dungeon those who sit in darkness." This would not be just a simple task, but a real spiritual battle. People had been deceived and were held in bondage by the power of sin and the power of a living, intelligent being opposed to God and his kingdom program.

Forgiveness of sins and a place among those who are sanctified by faith in me (26:18). Two great benefits result from this message of redemption. Both forgiveness and sanctification become key themes in Paul's preaching to the Gentiles. Paul later reflected the language of this passage well when he wrote to the Colossians: "For he has rescued us from the dominion of darkness and brought us into the kingdom of the Son he loves, in whom we have redemption, the forgiveness of sins" (Col. 1:13–14).

I was not disobedient (26:19). Having told Agrippa of his encounter with the risen Christ, Paul now defends his course of actions by insisting that he could not possibly disobey instructions given to him directly by God.

I preached that they should repent (26:20). The essence of what he has been proclaiming to the Gentiles is a message

DARKNESS AND LIGHT

of repentance. This includes a sorrow for sin, but also a reorientation of the whole of one's life around the kingdom of God and the work of the Messiah. True repentance can be seen in a changed lifestyle.

I have had God's help to this very day (26:22). In spite of the many dangers he faced and the threats to his life, not least of which was the Jewish mob that apprehended him in the temple and tried to kill him, Paul has continued fulfilling his commission because of the daily help God provides. Throughout his ministry, he draws on the enabling power of God. A few years later he remarked, "I labor, struggling with all his energy, which so powerfully works in me" (Col. 1:29).

I am saying nothing beyond what the prophets and Moses said would happen (26:22). Summing up his defence to Agrippa, Paul insists that the heart of his message is nothing other than what was announced in the Old Testament: The Messiah would suffer, die, and rise from the dead and this message would bring saving light to both Jews and Gentiles.

The Response of Agrippa and Festus (26:24–32)

Paul is not able to finish his presentation before he is interrupted by Festus, who has now concluded that Paul is no threat; he is simply an educated nut. This opens up a period of dialogue between Festus, Agrippa, and Paul. The apostle does his best to seize this opportunity to clearly communicate the gospel to these men, particularly Agrippa, whom he sees as more open. Spiritually, there is no positive response to Paul's message. Legally, the procurator and the king both recognize Paul's innocence of all charges. It is

significant that both of these officials find nothing illegal about Christianity.

Your great learning is driving you insane (26:24). Festus interrupts Paul's monologue at the point where he is proclaiming the death and resurrection of Christ. Both aspects of this teaching about the Messiah would have been incomprehensible to Festus. First, before coming to Palestine, Festus would no doubt have been briefed about the Jewish expectation of a messiah figure who would come and lead his people in revolt. Surely he has also heard of the many false messiahs who have already surfaced and led uprisings. These are a significant security risk to Roman rule. But now Festus hears an eloquent discourse on how the Messiah must suffer and die—a notion he has never heard from a Jew. Second, for a Roman, the idea of the resurrection of the body after death was ludicrous. The afterlife was a time when the person would finally be free from the bondage of material existence. It is little wonder that Festus concludes that Paul is raving mad.

True and reasonable (26:25). Paul immediately and courteously denies the accusation and asserts the essential truthfulness of what he is saying. For Paul, it is not merely a matter of perspective or personal belief; rather, the gospel is objectively true. But the gospel is also reasonable (*sōphrosynē*)—the precise opposite of madness (*mania*). This characterization of the gospel message was particularly apt for a Gentile since *sōphrosynē* expressed an ideal of philosophy. It had to do with a knowledge of deity and the relationship of oneself to deity.[507]

The king is familiar with these things (26:26). Agrippa possesses a knowledge of the Law and the Prophets as well as the prevailing Jewish understanding of these texts. He is also aware of the Jesus movement and the kinds of things that have been asserted about Jesus.

Not done in a corner (26:26). This is a proverbial expression in Greek philosophy.[508] Paul is stressing that the central events of what he proclaims—namely, the public ministry, death, and resurrection of Jesus of Nazareth—did not take place in some faraway land or even in a set of private visionary experiences. They happened in Jerusalem itself and involved the principal Jewish and Roman leaders of the nation. As such, these events are open for analysis and verification.

Do you believe the prophets? (26:27). For someone who already believes the message of the prophets, Paul can quickly and convincingly demonstrate the fact that the Messiah must suffer and die, that this death would be an atonement for sin, that there is hope of a bodily resurrection, and that the Messiah would rise from the dead. Paul prepares to explain this to Agrippa, but he is abruptly interrupted by the king.

Do you think that in such a short time you can persuade me to be a Christian? (26:28) Without hearing the tone of Agrippa's remark, it is difficult to know if he poses this question sarcastically or with some degree of sincerity. The king knows the direction Paul is headed and clearly does not want to hear him continue on at this point.

I pray God that not only you but all who are listening to me today may become what I am (26:29). In a straightforward

REFLECTIONS

IN SPITE OF PAUL'S ELOQUENT proclamation of the gospel in this august gathering, there was no response. It does not appear that even one of the persons present turned his or her heart to Christ on that day. Like Paul, we will face times when our sharing falls on deaf ears. It is our job to be faithful and to take advantage of the opportunities that God gives us for communicating the gospel.

manner, Paul affirms that it truly is his desire that everyone in this hearing—the procurator, the king, the queen, the military commanders, and the civic leaders of Caesarea—will all become Christians.

Except for these chains (26:29). At this point, Paul may have held up his chains as a dramatic gesture to the audience.

This man is not doing anything that deserves death or imprisonment (26:31). After an informal time of discussion, Festus and Agrippa jointly conclude that Paul has committed no capital offense or even anything worthy of imprisonment.

This man could have been set free (26:32). After declaring Paul's innocence of the charges, Agrippa observes that it is too late to dismiss the charges because of Paul's appeal to the emperor. Strictly speaking, it would not have been illegal to free Paul, but Festus would have risked offending the emperor. An expert on Roman law notes, "No sensible man with hopes of promotion would dream of short-circuiting the appeal to Caesar unless he had specific authority to do so."[509]

The Voyage to Rome and Shipwreck (27:1–44)

Throughout this chapter and part of the next, Luke tells the story of Paul's harrowing voyage to Rome. While Paul's boat skirted the south shore of Crete, it is caught suddenly by a violent northeast wind and driven out to sea. After two weeks of an unrelenting storm and when all on board have lost hope, the boat is shipwrecked on the island of Malta.

Luke relates the account in significant detail and in an engaging way that keeps the reader in constant suspense. Because of the divine promise that Paul will appear before Caesar, the question in the minds of the readers is not *if* Paul will make it to Rome, but *how* he will do so given the overwhelming odds against him. How will the divine plan be fulfilled when it seems that everything is working against it?[510]

Paul and some other prisoners (27:1). No indication is given as to how many prisoners there are or the nature of the crimes for which they are incarcerated. Paul is included with them as just another prisoner.

The Imperial Regiment (27:1). The literal reading here is "the *Sebastos* [or *Augustus*] cohort." Archaeologists have

discovered two inscriptions, one in Latin and one in Greek, that refer to a cohort of this title in the Roman army stationed at Syria (including Judea) in the first century.[511] Nothing more is known about Julius than what is in this text.

We boarded a ship from Adramyttium (27:2). There were no cruise ships or passenger vessels in the first century. It was common for people to travel on cargo vessels. This particular ship comes from a city on the west coast of Asia Minor, about thirty-five miles north of Pergamum and thirty-seven miles due east of Assos (see the map on Acts 20). This is a small privately owned cargo vessel presumably on its way back to its home port. The centurion's intent is to book passage on a vessel that will take them to one of the major ports of south Asia Minor, where they can board a larger grain vessel heading to Rome.

Aristarchus, a Macedonian from Thessalonica (27:2). On Aristarchus, see comments on 20:4. He was among the delegates accompanying Paul with the collection for the Jerusalem believers. Apparently he is the only one of the group who remains with Paul in Caesarea for the two years of his imprisonment and will continue to minister to Paul through his own Roman imprisonment. The text does not say that Aristarchus is also a prisoner at this time, but for some unknown reason (but probably related to his commitment to the gospel) he will be imprisoned in Rome (Col. 4:10).

We landed at Sidon (27:3). Sidon was one of the principal cities of Phoenicia, but now part of the province of Syria under Roman rule. It was located about seventy miles north of Caesarea.

In kindness to Paul (27:3). Literally, Julius shows *philanthrōpia* to Paul. This is the word from which is derived the English "philanthropy," but here simply means "benevolence" or "kindness." This was an esteemed virtue in the Hellenistic world; the word refers frequently in moral exhortation to "civilized" behavior.[512]

Allowed him to go to his friends (27:3). These "friends" are Christians in the city. Some from the first wave of Jewish-Christian missionaries scattered by the persecution in Jerusalem came to Phoenicia and planted churches (11:19). Paul may have already met many of these believers as he passed through the city on one of his trips to Jerusalem (11:30; 12:25; 15:3).[513]

Passed to the lee of Cyprus (27:4). This refers to the side of Cyprus where ships were most protected from the autumnal prevailing winds. Because Luke mentions passing by the coast of Cilicia and Pamphylia, the boat probably traveled north of Cyprus. This was the opposite side of Cyprus Paul passed when he traveled from Miletus to Jerusalem (21:3).

We landed at Myra in Lycia (27:5). Myra was one of the key cities of the territory of Lycia in southern Asia Minor. It was about forty miles east of the other Lycian city, Patara, where Paul had docked in his voyage from Miletus to Jerusalem with the collection (21:1). The city of Myra was actually three and a half miles inland on a plateau.[514] It was served by a port called Andriace, where the boat would have docked. Myra has yet to be excavated, but many Roman ruins are still visible, including the eleven thousand-seat theater and an immense granary built during the reign of Hadrian (A.D. 117–38). Myra was due north of Alexandria, Egypt, and a key stopping point for the grain vessels that traveled on to Rome.

Depending on the precise route the Adramyttium vessel took, the boat covered a distance of 450 to 500 miles from Sidon to Myra. According to a tradition preserved in the western form of the text, the voyage took a total of fifteen days.

bottom left

MYRA IN LYCIA
The theater.

PORT CITY OF ANDRIACE
▼

▶ "Santa Claus": Saint Nicholas of Myra

Myra is perhaps best known for a Christian leader who lived there in the late third and early fourth century: St. Nicholas. In the Netherlands, this saint was venerated as "Sante Klaas" and in America became known as "Santa Claus."[A-153] He was probably martyred during the Diocletian persecutions.

Little accurate historical information is known about his life and ministry in Myra, but numerous legends surfaced and he became popular throught the Middle Ages. The principal legend known in America is based on a story involving his concern over the fate of three daughters of a poor man in his city. Lacking enough money for dowries, the father allegedly planned to sell the girls into slavery to a brothel. Learning of the father's decision, Nicholas secretly tried to enter their house late one night to leave three bags of gold. Finding the doors and windows locked, he dropped the three bags down the chimney. They miraculously fell into the stockings that the girls had hung up to dry.

An Alexandrian ship sailing for Italy (27:6). The centurion is able to locate an Alexandrian grain vessel heading for Rome without any difficulty. With a population of over a million people, Rome was greatly dependent on the regular shipment of grain from Egypt.

Arriving off Cnidus (27:7). The port of Cnidus lay at the tip of a long peninsula at the southwestern portion of Asia Minor (in the territory of Caria) that extended between the islands of Cos and Rhodes. This was about a 150-mile trip from Myra. In his voyage to Jerusalem from Miletus, Paul's boat would have passed within visual distance of this city (see 21:1). The ancient geographer Strabo provides a helpful description of this port city:

> Then to Cnidus, with two harbours, one of which can be closed, can receive triremes, and is a naval station for twenty ships. Off it lies an island which is appoximately seven stadia in circuit, rises high, is theatre-like, is connected by moles with the mainland, and in a way makes Cnidus a double city, for a large part of its people live on the island, which shelters both harbors.[515]

When the wind did not allow us to hold our course (27:7). A westward voyage on a sailboat in the Mediterranean took considerably longer than the same trip eastward because of adverse winds through the entire trip. An eastward voyage that might take ten days could take between fifty and seventy days when traveling

MODEL OF AN EGYPTIAN MERCHANT VESSEL ▼

westward. The difficulty and length was compounded all the more when traveling in the winter.[516]

We sailed to the lee of Crete, opposite Salmone (27:7). The boat journeys southwest toward the island of Crete, where the crew attempts to round the eastern cape. Salmone is a promontory on the easternmost side of the island (today it is called Cape Sideros). Because of the strong northwest winds, the crew of the boat seeks protection by sailing along the southern side of the island. Interestingly, the name "Salmone" is of Phoenician origin and describes a refuge from exposure to the wind.[517]

Fair Havens, near the town of Lasea (27:8). This small port was roughly halfway around the island east of Cape Littinos. The ancient village of Lasea has also been identified. It lay about five miles east of Fair Havens.

Sailing had already become dangerous (27:9). According to ancient sources, sea travel was particularly risky in the fall from September 14 to November 11 and considered extremely dangerous from November 11 to March 10.[518] Visibility (mists and fogs) as well as the constant threat of severe winter storms rendered this period an inadvisable time to travel by sea.

It is not suprising, however, to find a grain vessel traveling during this dangerous period. Suetonius notes that because of regular shortages of grain in Rome, the emperor Claudius "took all possible steps to import grain, even during the winter months—insuring merchants against the loss of their ships in stormy weather (which guaranteed them a good return on their ventures)."[519]

PAUL'S VOYAGE FROM CAESAREA TO CRETE

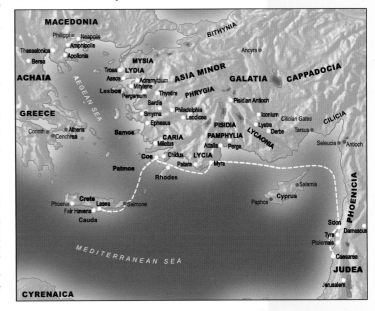

▶ Crete

This island is the fifth largest in the Mediterranean (after Cyprus, Sicily, Sardinia, and Corsica).[A-154] It measures 162 miles from east to west and ranges between nine and thirty-seven miles north to south. At the center of the island, Mount Ida reaches an elevation of 8,058 feet. The principal cities of the island were Cnossus, Gortyn, and Lyttus. During the first century, Crete was part of a Roman province with Cyrene (north Africa). There is literary and archaeological evidence of a Jewish presence on the island. The island was evangelized at some point early in the first century. After his Roman imprisonment, Paul returned to the island and left Titus there to give leadership and assistance to the churches.

By now it was after the Fast (27:9). This is another way of referring to the Jewish Day of Atonement (*Yom Kippur*). A number of passages in Jewish literature connect the day with fasting. The Mishnah, for example, stipulates, "On the Day of Atonement, eating, drinking . . . are forbidden."[520] The date of this festival was on Tishri 10 on the Jewish lunar calendar. In A.D. 59, the observance would have fallen on October 5.[521] The Jewish Feast of Tabernacles (Booths or *Succoth*) fell shortly after this on Tishri 15. Since Luke does not mention the Festival of Tabernacles, it is likely then that the boat arrives in Fair Havens sometime in the five-day period of October 10–15, A.D. 59.[522]

Men, I can see that our voyage is going to be disastrous (27:10). Paul asserts this warning not as a prophetic insight from the Spirit, but as a common-sense observation based on his personal experience at sea (2 Cor. 11:25–26) and his knowledge that sea travel is typically avoided from this time on because of the inherent dangers. Because of the Lord's providential care, there will be no loss of life, as Paul assumes.

right ▶

FAIR HAVENS, CRETE

The pilot and . . . the owner of the ship (27:11). The *kybernētēs* is the "steersman"—essentially, the captain of the ship. The *naukleros* may be the owner of the ship but may also be a representative of the owner and thus concerned about the financial interest of the voyage.[523] The grain vessels are privately owned and the shipowners are free agents. They take advantage of "a healthy private enterprise system conferring great rewards on speculators and adventurous transporters."[524] Both of these men disagree with Paul and decide to press further on.

Hoping to reach Phoenix and winter there (27:12). The owner and the captain of the ship apparently consult others about whether to seek a better port in Cyprus to spend the winter. The group decision is not to take the risk to travel on to Rome, but simply to coast westward along the southern shore of Crete another fifty miles or so to a better harbor. The precise location of this harbor in Crete remains uncertain. Most scholars think it was near the modern coastal village of Loutro.

A wind of hurricane force, called the "northeaster" (27:14). The conditions are fine for reaching Phoenix as long as the

PAUL'S VOYAGE FROM CRETE TO MALTA

▼

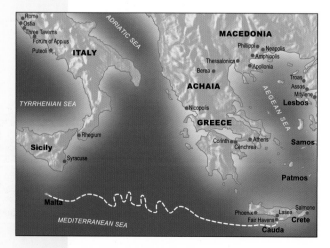

northeast), *euroaquilo* (northeast wind), *vulturnus*, *eurus* (east wind), etc.[526]

Today this wind is called a "Gregale" and can approach hurricane force and endanger shipping. In 1555 it is reported to have caused waves that drowned six hundred persons in the city of Valletta, the principal port city of the island of Malta.[527]

A small island called Cauda (27:16). Caught by the violent wind, the ship is driven south. This island of Cauda is located about twenty-three miles south of Phoenix. Today it is called Gaudos and is the most southerly Greek island. The ancient island did possess a city and a harbor, but there is little chance of this vessel making it.

Make the lifeboat secure (27:16). The lifeboat was normally towed behind the ship. Since towing a boat is dangerous in a storm, the sailors pull the rope and bring the little boat on board. The difficulty in doing so is probably caused by the dinghy taking on water.[528]

They passed ropes under the ship itself to hold it together (27:17). There are a

gentle wind blows from the south, but this abruptly changes. A violent wind from the northeast blows across the island, down from Mount Ida, and howls from the shore south out to the sea. Luke describes this wind as *typhōnikos*, a Greek word from which is derived our English "typhoon." Ancient sailors named this dangerous wind *Euraquilo*, a name with which Luke shows his familiarity. *Euraquilo* is actually a bilingual compound formed from a shortened form of the Greek *euronotos* (east wind) and the Latin *Aquila* (north wind).

Although at one time critical scholars claimed that this hybrid word is found nowhere else and took it as a sign of Luke's literary creativity, the term has been discovered on a Latin inscription found in the city of Thugga in proconsular Africa.[525] It appears on a wind-rose inscribed on a pavement that bears the names of the wind in each direction. Beginning with the north and moving clockwise it reads: *septentrio* (north wind), *aquilo* (north wind; apparently slightly

◀ *left*

STONE ANCHOR

◀

ISLAND OF CAUDA

Modern Gavdos.

variety of views as to what this bracing procedure involves, but the most likely explanation is a practice called "frapping." Heavy ropes or cables were passed under the bow of the ship and secured transversely on either side. The object of this procedure was to keep the planks of the ship tight against the "ribs" (the inner wooden beams that formed the skeleton of the boat). This gave the ship extra protection in the fury of the storm.[529]

The sandbars of Syrtis (27:17). These are "the notoriously dangerous shoals and shallows of the Libyan continental shelf of North Africa from Cyrenaica through Tripolitania to Tunisia: the Greater Syrtis to the southeast and the Lesser off Gabés to the southwest."[530] The Syrtes are 375 miles away from the island of Cauda. Sailors' fears of Syrtis are well summed up by Dio Chrysostom: "Those who have once sailed into it find egress impossible; for shoals, cross-currents, and long sandbars extending a great distance out make the sea utterly impassable or troublesome."[531] Luke's mention of their fear of these treacherous shoals at this point demonstrates that the crew knows it is in for a long, harrowing voyage.

Lowered the sea anchor (27:17). Luke literally says that they lower the "vessel" (*skeuos*). The NIV interprets this to be an anchor, but it probably refers to the sails (the same word was used for the sheet lowered from heaven in 10:11).[532] All the sails are taken down and only a storm-sail is kept up, which is necessary to keep the boat steady.[533]

Finally gave up all hope of being saved (27:20). With the storm showing no sign of diminishing, the sailors and passengers begin fearing the worst possible outcome. They think they may have missed Sicily and will never make it to the North African (Tunisian) coast alive.

The men had gone a long time without food (27:21). In such a storm, anxiety and seasickness would surely eliminate any appetite.

An angel of the God whose I am and whom I serve stood beside me (27:23). After days of being tossed around at sea and at the point when all on board are at the point of despair, God intervenes not to stop the storm, but to communicate a message of encouragement and hope to

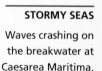

STORMY SEAS

Waves crashing on the breakwater at Caesarea Maritima.

Paul through a divine emissary. The angel specifically tells Paul that the ship will be destroyed, but not one person will die. In communicating the content of this appearance to the passengers, Paul tailors his remarks to be understood by a group of people not familiar with Christianity or Judaism. Greeks and Romans believed in divine intermediaries, however, and would probably not have been skeptical about what Paul was saying. Paul makes it clear that it is not a messenger of Zeus (or any other deity from the pantheon of Gentile gods), but the God he serves.

You must stand trial before Caesar (27:24). This is a new revelation to Paul. When Jesus spoke to him previously in Jerusalem, he simply assured him that he would survive to testify about him in Rome (23:11).

On the fourteenth night (27:27). In a detailed and careful study done over a hundred years ago about this voyage on the basis of interviews with experienced Mediterranean sailors, J. Smith calculated that in a gale such as this, the boat would have averaged about one-and-a-half miles per hour. Given the distance of 476 miles from Cauda to Malta on the course the storm-driven boat would likely have taken, Paul's boat would have been within a few miles of the island on the fourteenth night.[534]

The Adriatic Sea (27:27). Literally, "the sea of Adria." Today the Adriatic Sea refers specifically to the long narrow body of water that extends between Italy and the Balkan Peninsula. In the Roman period that was distinguished as the Gulf of Adria whereas the Sea of Adria extended much further south and from Crete to Sicily.[535]

They took soundings (27:28). It must be remembered that there were no sonar or acoustical instruments available to ancient sailors. The "sounding" referred to here was a depth measurement taken by a hand line. A series of lead weights were attached to the end of the line separated by measured intervals. Archaeologists have discovered some of these weights. The bottom of the weight was hollowed out so that it could be filled with tallow or grease. When lowered and drug on the floor of the sea, the grease would pick up rocks and debris.[536] The use of this kind of line is well illustrated by a passage from Herodotus:

> The nature of the land of Egypt is such that when a ship is approaching it and is yet one day's sail from the shore, if a man try the sounding, he will bring up mud even at a depth of eleven fathoms. This shows that the outpouring of land goes that far.[537]

REFLECTIONS

THERE WAS ANOTHER OCCASION when followers of Jesus were on a boat that was threatened by a tempestuous storm. Just as the boat was ready to be swamped by the waves, Jesus "rebuked the wind and the raging waters; the storm subsided, and all was calm" (Luke 8:24). Jesus could easily have calmed this storm, yet he allowed the storm to rage. In the midst of the storm, however, God gave a sign of his awareness of their plight and a special promise of his protection. In a similar way, God allows us to weather many storms throughout our lifetimes, but he is present with us and extends his protection to us until it is our appointed time to die.

They dropped four anchors from the stern (27:29). The four anchors would have slowed the speed of the ship enough to keep it from careening perilously onto the rocks of the shore. Normally a ship was anchored from the bow. Anchoring it from the stern (the rear) would enable it to continue its forward progress until it reached shore.[538]

An attempt to escape from the ship (27:30). Knowing the extreme danger of being on board a vessel speeding toward the rock shore in ferocious winds and high, choppy surf, the crew decides to abandon ship and take their chances on board the dinghy. The apostle Paul, however, foils their plans by informing the Roman military personnel. The action of the soldiers in cutting the lines holding the dinghy would certainly have occasioned a great deal of tension and bitter emotions of the crew toward the soldiers and Paul.

Just before dawn Paul urged them all to eat (27:33). Paul's appeal would surely help to restore some measure of calm to the passengers, who are waiting impatiently for dawn and the impending prospect of making it to shore.

Not one of you will lose a single hair from his head (27:34). Paul reiterates here the assurance given to him by the angel of God (27:22) by means of a Jewish/Old Testament idiom. The expression is illustrated in the remarks made by Saul to his men regarding Jonathan: "As surely as the LORD lives, not a hair of his head will fall to the ground."[539] This is a way of stressing the certainty that no person would die.

Gave thanks to God in front of them all (27:35). Paul boldly prays and gives thanks to the one true God in the presence of worshipers of numerous other deities. It was typical Jewish custom to give thanks to God before a meal. In spite of some of the language of this passage ("took some bread . . . broke it"), this is not a celebration of the Eucharist or the

---

▶ **The *Isis*: An Immense Alexandrian Grain Vessel**

Underwater archaeologists have not yet recovered an Alexandrian grain vessel, but there is an important literary account by Lucian that describes one of these ships, the *Isis*:

> What a huge ship! 180 feet long, the ship-wright said, and well over a quarter as wide [over 45 feet wide], and from deck to bottom, where it is deepest, in the bilge, 44 feet. Then, what a tall mast, what a yard to carry! What a forestay to hold it up! How gently the poop curves up, with a little golden goose below! And correspondingly at the opposite end, the prow juts right out in front, with figures of the goddess, Isis, after whom the ship is named, on either side. And the other decorations, the paintings and the topsail blazing like

fire, anchors in front of them, and capstans, and windlasses, and the cabins on the poop—all very wonderful to me. You could put the number of sailors at an army of soldiers. She was said to carry corn enough to feed Attica for a year.[A-155]

Other ancient writers attest to ships of immense size. A grain ship called the *Syracusia* (3d c. B.C.) may have had a capacity of nearly two thousand tons according to Athenaeus. The first-writer Pliny speaks about a boat constructed during the reign of Caligula that carried a monument weighing approximately thirteen hundred tons.[A-156] A Roman vessel was recently discovered at Caesarea Maritima that has been tentatively dated to the first century A.D. and measures 147 feet in length.[A-157]

Lord's Supper. Paul is encouraging everyone on board (273 non-Christians) to eat for nourishment and strength; this is not a time of Christian community reflecting on the death of Christ.

276 of us on board (27:37). This is by no means an unrealistic number of people to be aboard an Alexandrian grain vessel. Josephus claims that there were six hundred people aboard a ship he was on that was shipwrecked in the Sea of Adria.[540]

Throwing the grain into the sea (27:38). The explicit mention of grain as the cargo here confirms the impression that this was indeed an Alexandrian grain vessel. Their intent would have been that by lightening the ship, the vessel would travel farther up the beach before it grounded. This would enhance their chances of making it safely to shore. The grain would have been stored in the hull in sacks, not poured in loosely.[541]

They saw a bay with a sandy beach (27:39). A sandy beach, as opposed to a rocky set of cliffs, is the perfect place to land the boat. The crew now does everything they can to reach the beach.

Untied the ropes that held the rudders (27:40). Two large paddles were attached on each side of the stern in ancient ships. When it was necessary to anchor the boat from the stern, these paddles were lifted out of the water and secured by ropes.[542]

Struck a sandbar (27:41). "Sandbar" is an interpretation of the Greek word *dithalassos*, which literally means, "between two seas" or "where two seas meet." That this is a sandy shoal is probably the correct interpretation. Some have suggested that this wording points to a precise identification of the location on Malta where the ship went aground, namely, in a place that is today known as "St. Paul's Bay." This bay is located on the northwestern portion of the island. A small island called Salmonetta is only a hundred yards off the mainland. The channel separating the mainland from the island may have been the place "between two seas."[543] Because of the proximity of Salmonetta to the mainland, it is conceivable that the sailors think the island is simply a promontory from the mainland. By the time they realize there is a narrow and shallow waterway separating the two, it is too late to change directions.

Archaeologists undertaking surveys of the waters around Malta have discovered eight shipwrecks of Roman era boats.[544] In recent years, a British expedition has been searching for Paul's ship.[545]

The soldiers planned to kill the prisoners (27:42). According to the Code of Justinian, a Roman guard who allowed a prisoner to escape could face the same penalty awaiting the accused prisoner.[546] Most of the soldiers do not want to take any risk with the prisoners they are responsible for. Some of these prisoners may have been accused of capital offenses. In the panic of the moment, little thought apparently seems to be given to the potential punishment a soldier might face for killing a Roman citizen.

Paul Spends the Winter in Malta (28:1–10)

The suspense continues in this next section. No sooner has Paul made it safely to shore than he is bitten by a poisonous snake and expected to die. God continues to protect Paul, however, and not only does he survive a venomous snakebite, but he is able to engage in a significant and dramatic ministry on this island during the winter months.

Malta (28:1). Malta, or *Melitē* as it is called in Greek, is a Mediterranean island lying fifty-eight miles south of the island of Sicily and 180 miles north of Libya. It measures about seventeen miles at its longest distance from southeast to northwest and about nine miles at its widest distance from east to west. The island became part of the Roman empire in 218 B.C. and was part of the Roman province of Sicily.

The islanders (28:2). The word translated "islanders" is the Greek word *barbaros*, which is often translated "barbarian." This was the word Greek-speakers used to refer to people who did not know Greek as their native tongue. The term implies that the foreign language sounded like a meaningless set of syllables—such as "bar- bar- bar-"; thus the word was onomatopoetic. The ancestors of the islanders were Phoenician, and they continued to speak a Phoenician dialect. A

number of Punic inscriptions have been found on Malta (Punic was a Phoenician dialect spoken in Carthage, North Africa).[547] Luke's characterization of the islanders as *barbaroi* may reflect some of the voyagers' initial frustration in not being able to communicate with the people. Because of the island's contact with Rome, some would have known Greek or Latin and were able to converse with those coming off the boat.

They built a fire (28:2). It is difficult to imagine what could feel better to 276 cold and wet people on this late October day than a blazing hot fire.

A viper (28:3). The Greek word *echidna* points to a poisonous snake and typically refers to a viper.[548] Jesus uses the word metaphorically to speak of the danger posed by the Pharisees: "You snakes! You brood of vipers! How will you escape being condemned to hell?" (Matt. 23:33). Although there are no poisonous snakes on the island of Malta today, the population may have progressively rid the small island of this danger over the next two thousand years.

Justice has not allowed him to live (28:4). The islanders are referring to the goddess *Dikē* ("Justice"). *Dikē*, the daughter of Zeus, was believed to watch over human affairs and report all wrongdoings to Zeus so the guilty persons could pay for their crimes. In the first century, she was viewed as a goddess of punishment and revenge who would execute judgment from her place in the underworld. In this instance, the islanders interpret the snakebite to reflect the judgment of *Dikē* on Paul for a crime that has gone undetected or unpunished by human authorities.[549]

They changed their minds and said he was a god (28:6). The islanders have seen this type of snake bite people before and know what to expect. When Paul is unaffected by the bite, they assume he must be a god. Luke's abbreviated account changes topics here, but we can assume that Paul once again takes advantage of the situation to deny that he is a god and to proclaim to them the living and true God (cf. what he did in Lystra, recorded in 14:8–20).

Publius, the chief official of the island (28:7). Although nothing else is known of Publius, archaeologists have discovered a Greek inscription on Miletus dating to the first century that refers to the chief official of the island with precisely the same expression that Luke uses here: "*prōtos* of the island."[550]

He welcomed us to his home (28:7). It is difficult to imagine that his home is large enough to accommodate 276 people. Perhaps Luke means that he, Aristarchus, Paul, and Julius are invited to stay at this exquisite estate. This kind of preferential treatment is not surprising since the people of the island have just acclaimed Paul as a god.

After prayer, placed his hands on him and healed him (28:8). Jesus often laid his hands on people when he healed them, and the people sometimes expected him to put his hands on them as part of the process.[551] This is the way Paul's eyes were healed when Ananias ministered to him after he lost his sight on the Damascus road (9:12, 17).

The rest of the sick on the island came and were cured (28:9). God uses Paul in a mighty way on this island to bring healing to numerous people. Assuredly, Paul also shares the gospel with them and at least some people are saved, although Luke does not tell us this part of the story in his highly condensed account.

They honored us in many ways (28:10). The "honor" that Luke speaks of here is probably best understood in the sense of financial support and many gifts, which Luke elaborates in the remainder of the verse. "The grateful inhabitants of the island saw to it that the Christian travelers should not be in need during the rest of their journey."[552]

Paul Arrives in Rome (28:11–31)

Paul arrives safely in Rome after a tranquil voyage from Malta. After fellowshiping with believers in the port city of Puteoli, Paul is met by Christians from Rome on his way to the capital city. Luke does not focus on Paul's ministry to the believers in Rome for the concluding chapter of Acts, but rather describes the apostle's efforts to evangelize the unbelieving Jewish community in Rome.

The book of Acts ends somewhat anticlimactically with no verdict from the Roman court and emperor. Yet, for Luke, the important part of his story has been told. Paul has reached Rome and is there proclaiming the kingdom of God. The full story still remains untold. The church continues to proclaim the gospel as it awaits the return of Christ.

After three months (28:11). All 276 remain on the island for the winter months, probably November and December of A.D. 59 and January of A.D. 60.

An Alexandrian ship (28:11). They are able to book passage on another Alexandrian grain vessel that made it safely into port before the severe *Euraquilo* storm hit. This vessel, its crew, and passengers have also spent the winter on the island with the boat safely docked at the principal port of the island, known as Valletta today. Although it is still early and risky to sail, the captain of the Alexandrian vessel thinks the conditions are favorable for making it the relatively short distance to Sicily and then to Italy.

With the figurehead of the twin gods Castor and Pollux (28:11). This Alexandrian freighter sails under the ensign of the *Dioskouroi*, the twin sons of Zeus and brothers of Helen.[553] They are known by name as Castor and Polydeuces (Latinized

as Pollux). The vessel has been dedicated to the appropriate deities, given the fact that the twins were revered as gods who rescue sailors in their distress. They were also worshiped as the third sign of the Zodiac—Gemini.[554]

Syracuse (28:12). The first port the boat reaches is on the southeast coast of the island of Sicily, about ninety miles north of Malta.[555] Syracuse was the center of government for the Roman province (that included the island of Malta). The city was served by two ports, a large one on the mainland and another smaller one on a diminutive island (Ortygia) closely adjacent to the mainland. Still visible today are the remains of a sixth-century B.C. temple of Apollo (also dedicated to Artemis), a fifth-century Greek theater with a semicircular auditorium hewn from the rock, and a large Roman amphitheater.

Arrived at Rhegium (28:13). After the three-day stop in Syracuse, the boat sails another seventy miles to the southwest coast (at the "toe") of Italy and the port at the city of Rhegium. Rhegium was a strategic Roman city that governed the Strait of Messina, a seven-mile-wide waterway separating Sicily and Italy.

▶ Puteoli

Throughout the first half of the first century A.D., Puteoli was Rome's principal shipping port. The bulk of the enormous shipments of grain from Alexandria and north Africa were unloaded at Puteoli.[A-158] This was a likely destination, then, for the Alexandrian grain vessel, although the emperor Claudius had improved the port of Ostia at the mouth of the Tiber for handling more cargo vessels and had created an additional port (Portus) two miles north of Ostia.

Puteoli, known also by its Greek name *Dikearchia,* was located in the Roman district of Campania on the north shore of what is today called the Gulf of Naples. The same gulf was also served by another port city, Neapolis (modern Naples), about seven and a half miles south of Puteoli. Campania had yet another port, Cumae, which was located about ten miles northwest of Neapolis. Of the three ports, Puteoli was by far the largest and of greatest significance for trade in the first century.

Puteoli's harbor was greatly enhanced in the first century with the construction of a breakwater.[A-159] This mole was nearly a quarter mile in length. It carried fifteen masonry piers with arches (with at least one triumphal arch), columns with statues, and a lighthouse. The total amount of shoreline for docking and warehouses (the *emporium*) extended about one and a quarter miles.

The city itself was large. Some have estimated a population of as much as a hundred thousand people in the first century. The beautiful location made it a popular place with the Roman élite who owned villas there. It was also home to many immigrants from the Eastern provinces of the empire, including Asia Minor, Syria, and Egypt. There is evidence of a sizeable Jewish population in the city.[A-160]

There were two navigational hazards fifteen miles to the north of Rhegium and identified with two sisters in Greek mythology—Scylla and Charybdis. Scylla was a large rocky cliff on the Italian side of the strait and Charybdis was a treacherous whirlpool in a narrow channel of the sea on the Sicilian side.[556]

We reached Puteoli (28:13). With the aid of a southerly wind, the large grain vessel makes the 180-mile trip to Puteoli in just two days.

There we found some brothers (28:14). Paul, Luke, and Aristarchus discover a community of believers in this city. This is not surprising given the volume of travel from the East into Puteoli. The church most likely started from within the Jewish community. These Jews may have been reached by Christian Jews from Rome or just as easily by believers arriving from Ephesus, Alexandria, or elsewhere.

Invited us to spend a week with them (28:14). Since they are making the rest of the journey to Rome on foot, they do not need to stay in the city to wait for the unloading of the boat or to book passage on a different vessel. The Christians in the city graciously open up their homes and extend warm hospitality to the trio as well as to Paul's guard, Julius. The offer of free lodging and meals by these kind people probably incline Julius to accept their hospitality. One certainly wonders what is in Julius' mind after being with the apostle for nearly four months—seeing the miracles, hearing him in prayer and worship, listening to the apostle's discussions with Luke and Aristarchus, and now experiencing Christian hospitality.

And so we came to Rome (28:14). Against all odds—a harrowing voyage lost at sea, shipwreck, and snakebite—Paul arrives at Rome. At this point, he is still on the outskirts, but now it is simply a five- or six-day 130-mile trip up the Via Appia to Rome.

The brothers there (28:15). Believers in the city of Rome—both Jews and Gentiles—have heard about Paul's arrival at the port of Puteoli. Perhaps someone from the church at Puteoli has made a quick journey to Rome to inform the fellow Christians there. Paul had written to the believers in Rome several years earlier with his long letter, informing them of his desire to come to the city. The extensive greetings in Romans 16 demonstrate that Paul already knows many Christians in the city.

▶ **The City of Rome**
IMPORTANT FACTS:

- Population: about 1,000,000
- Multi-Ethnic Cosmopolitan City: Italians from various districts as well as peoples from Greece, Asia Minor, Syria, Judea, Persia, Egypt, North Africa, Spain, Gaul, Germany, Brittania, and elsewhere
- Religion: the entire pantheon of Roman gods, numerous Greek deities, some Asian, Persian and Egyptian deities, the goddess *Roma,* and the ruler cult
- Ports: Ostia, Portus, Puteoli
- Position: Seat of the Roman Government for the empire and Residence of the Emperor

---

▶ **Rome**

Rome was the political, economic, and military center of the enormous Roman empire.[A-161] It was the wealthiest and most powerful city in the world in the first century.

The city was fifteen miles inland from the Tyrrhenian Sea and situated along the banks of the Tiber river. It was divided into fourteen different regions, the most well known being the Circus Maximus and the Forum Romanum. The perimeter of the city measured just over thirteen miles.

The forum was the hub of the political, religious, and economic life of Rome. Here the Senate building was located as well as the Mamertime prison, where prisoners were kept prior to their executions. The Colosseum had not yet been built (it was completed in A.D. 80). Throughout the city were numerous temples dedicated to many deities and to the deified Caesars. The palaces of the Caesars were located in the Circus Maximus and crowned the Palatine Hill.

Only a small percentage of people in Rome enjoyed its great wealth. Many slaves and poor people lived in Rome, dwelling in large blocks of apartment buildings (*insulae*) that ranged from three to five stories in size. Some scholars have estimated that as many as two hundred thousand people relied on a government welfare system that provided free grain to the unemployed masses of the city.

Four years after Paul's arrival in the city, ten of the fourteen districts of Rome burned to the ground (A.D. 64). Nero found the Christians in the city an easy target for blame and began a horrible persecution of these believers, which Tacitus recounts.[A-162]

clockwise from top

ROME

Interior view of the Colosseum.

The Arch of Constantine, which he built to commemorate his military victory in A.D. 312.

The Church of St. Peter in Montorio, west of the Tiber, commemorating the area where he was said to have been crucified upside-down.

Outside view of the Colosseum.

It is reasonable to assume that the nucleus of this church had its start shortly after Pentecost when some Jewish pilgrims filled with the Spirit and embracing Jesus as Messiah returned from Jerusalem and shared their new beliefs and experience in the synagogues (cf. 2:10). If not at this earliest stage, then either Jewish Christians from Palestine or the Diaspora went to Rome and shared the gospel or Jewish pilgrims from Rome encountered the gospel on subsequent visits to Jerusalem.[557] Since the early 30s, the church had presumably grown in numbers, especially with more and more Gentiles coming to faith in Christ. The church faced a major upheaval in A.D. 49 when Claudius ordered all Jews to leave the city (a proscription that would have included all Christian Jews as well; cf. comments on 18:2). According to Suetonius, there had been much consternation and debate in the synagogues about Christ leading up to this edict from the emperor.[558] When

Nero became emperor five years later (A.D. 54), it is safe to assume that many Jews (again, including Christian Jews) began trickling back into the city.

The Forum of Appius (28:15). The delegation of Christians from Rome come to meet Paul and his companions at a small market town in Latium about forty miles south of the city on the Appian Way. The forum was located at the juncture of where a canal came close to the main highway. Taking a boat pulled by a mule while the passengers slept made a nighttime journey possible (Strabo, *Geography* 5.3.6). The famous Roman writer Horace complains about the boatmen and "stingy tavern-keepers" at the Forum of Appius, as well as the poor drinking water (which made him ill), the gnats, and the frogs.[559]

The Three Taverns (28:15). Another group of Christians came as far as *Tres Tabernai* to meet Paul—a distance of

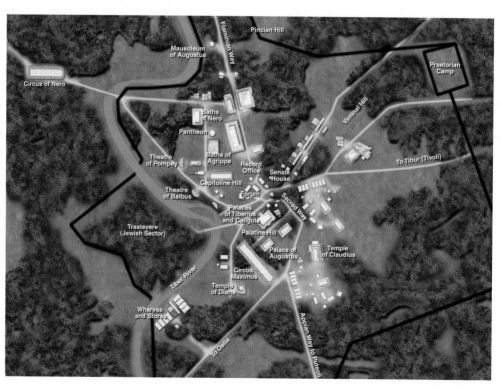

thirty miles south of Rome on the Appian Way. "Tavern" (*tabernus* in Latin) does not have the same connotation in English as it did in Latin. The *tabernai* were probably "a group of inns where travelers could rest, eat, and spend the night."[560]

Paul thanked God and was encouraged (28:15). Three years earlier Paul wrote, "I have been longing for many years to see you. . . . Pray that I may be rescued from the unbelievers in Judea and that my service in Jerusalem may be acceptable to the saints there, so that by God's will I may come to you with joy and together with you be refreshed" (Rom. 15:23, 31–32). Although his circumstances in coming to Rome are significantly different than what he had anticipated, he has finally arrived and is grateful to God for the opportunity to be with these dear believers. Their prayers have been answered.

Paul was allowed to live by himself (28:16). When Paul enters Rome, the centurion Julius would have taken him to a prisoner reception facility most likely

---

▶ Jews in Rome in the First Century

Life was not easy for Jews in Rome in the first century. There was a great deal of anti-Jewish sentiment, which reached boiling points when the emperor Tiberius expelled the Jews from the city in A.D. 19, and then Claudius carried out the same measure in A.D. 49. It is difficult to know if Claudius's eviction extended to literally all Jews in the city, the majority, or a large number of perceived troublemakers. Claudius's edict was issued just eight years before Paul wrote his letter to the Romans and eleven years before he arrived in the city. By the time Paul came to Rome in A.D. 60, there was clearly a substantial number of Jews living in the city again. Because of these vicissitudes, it is impossible to know precisely what the Jewish population in the city would have been at this time. A rough estimate would be twenty to thirty thousand (although some scholars have suggested more).[A-163]

Although there is evidence of a Jewish presence in Rome as early as the second century B.C., the Jewish population swelled significantly after Pompey conquered Judea and Jerusalem in 63 B.C. The general brought back with him thousands of Jewish prisoners, who were sold as slaves. Many of these people were manumitted during their lifetimes and granted Roman citizenship.[A-164] Most of the Jews lived in a Jewish ghetto in the fourteenth district of Rome across the Tiber River—a section called the *Trastevere*.

Philo provides us with the most detailed information about this community:

> He [the emperor Augustus] was aware that the great section of Rome on the other side of the Tiber is occupied and inhabited by Jews, most of whom were Roman citizens emancipated. For having been brought as captives to Italy they were liberated by their owners and were not forced to violate any of their native institutions. He knew therefore that they have houses of prayer (*proseuchai* = synagogues) and meet together in them, particularly on the sacred Sabbaths when they receive as a body a training in their ancestral philosophy. He knew too that they collect money for sacred purposes from their first-fruits and send them to Jerusalem by persons who would offer the sacrifices.[A-165]

Numerous Jewish inscriptions (mainly epitaphs) discovered in the city give evidence of at least ten different synagogues by name, although it is difficult to know how many of these date back to the first century.[A-166] These inscriptions also point to the fact that some Jews had moved from the Trastevere district to other parts of the city, such as Subura, Porta Capena, and the Campus Martius.

located at the military camp in the northeast part of the city (the *Campus Cohortium Praetoriarum*). There it is decided to grant Paul a lightened form of military custody. Rather than confining him to custody in a Roman prison, Paul is given the freedom to rent an apartment and live by himself.

[The centurion delivered the prisoners to the *stratopedarch*, and Paul was allowed to live by himself outside the barracks] (28:16). The manuscripts of the Western form of the text (which, in turn, influenced the Byzantine family of manuscripts and is thus present in the KJV) inserts this historical information. Most scholars, while denying that this insertion was written by Luke, nevertheless believe it contains some valuable historical traditions and regard it as an accurate commentary on the text. The *stratopedarch* is most likely to be identified as the chief administrator of the Praetorian Guard (the *princeps castrorum* or the *princeps praetorii*).[561] The passage also suggests that Paul's apartment would have been located near the Praetorian barracks near the Porta Viminalis in the northeast part

of the city. Paul may have been required to reside close to the military camp, which may explain why he did not move into the home of a Roman Christian somewhere else in the city.

With a soldier to guard him (28:16). Paul is no longer assigned a centurion to guard him—only an ordinary soldier. In spite of his lightened form of military custody, he is still bound to this soldier by a chain attached to his wrist (see 28:20).[562] Why Paul is granted this form of light custody may have to do with the fact that, upon reviewing the charges and speaking with Julius, the *stratopedarch* determines that Paul is neither a dangerous criminal nor a flight risk. It may also have to do with the weakness of the case against him—both Festus and Agrippa think that the charges against Paul should be dismissed.

He called together the leaders of the Jews (28:17). Apparently Paul is unable to travel to the synagogues to present his case for Jesus of Nazareth as the Messiah and hope of Israel. Thus he takes the bold step of inviting the Jewish leaders—pre-

ARCH OF TITUS

(bottom left)
Built by Domitian to celebrate his brother's military victory over Jerusalem and Judea.

(bottom right)
The Via Sacra from near the Colosseum with Titus's Arch in the background.

▼

sumably the rulers of the synagogues and the elders—to come and dialogue with him. There is no evidence of a centralized organizational structure to the Jewish community in Rome such as the Sanhedrin that functioned in Jerusalem or the *gerousia* in Alexandria. Rather, the Jewish community is structured as a loosely networked set of religious associations.[563]

When they had assembled, Paul said to them (28:17). Luke provides us with a concise summary of Paul's address to them, which summarizes the events surrounding his arrest, trial, and appeal. Paul emphatically denies that he has done anything contrary to the core convictions of Judaism.

It is because of the hope of Israel that I am bound with this chain (28:20). Once again, Paul emphasizes that the central issue in his dispute with the Jerusalem authorities is over "the hope of Israel," which, for Paul, is a belief that Jesus of Nazareth is the fulfillment of Israel's messianic hope. Bound up closely with this is the belief that Jesus rose from the dead and that there will be a future resurrection (see 23:6; 24:15; 26:6).

We have not received any letters from Judea concerning you (28:21). It would be surprising if the Jerusalem authorities never made contact with the leaders of the Jewish community in Rome about Paul, especially given the effort they expended to do away with Paul while he was in Palestine. It was probably only a matter of time until they received a letter from Jerusalem. It is yet another question as to whether the Jewish leaders would want to go to the expense and trouble of prosecuting their case against Paul before the emperor in Rome, espe-

cially knowing the weakness of the case with respect to Roman law.

People everywhere are talking against this sect (28:22). The Roman Jewish community has already debated intensely over whether Jesus was "the Christ," which led to violent confrontations and rioting—apparently the final straw leading to Claudius's expulsion of the Jews from the city.[564] Evidently, the Jewish community in Rome continued to hear reports from Jews scattered throughout the empire about how disruptive this messianic sect had been in their own communities.

They arranged to meet Paul on a certain day (28:23). In spite of their initial prejudice against Christianity (based on their own experience with Jewish Christians in Rome and the reports they have heard elsewhere), the Jewish leaders show an interest in hearing Paul and debating with him. They probably also have an innate curiosity about why this formerly prominent Pharisee would join such a sect and become an important leader of the movement.

Came in even larger numbers to the place where he was staying (28:23). The meeting attracts far more people than Paul anticipates. If Paul's rented lodging is near the Praetorium barracks, most of the Jews must travel from across the river on the opposite side of the city to get there. Assuming that Paul rents a room on the third- (fourth- or fifth-) story of a tenement house, the available space for such a meeting would have been rather limited.

From morning till evening he explained and declared to them the kingdom of God (28:23). The theme of the kingdom of God is larger and more expansive than a simple proclamation of the gospel (the *kerygma*). Paul explains the gospel in light of the whole of God's unfolding plan. Not only would Paul have spent considerable time expounding the plan of God from the Hebrew Scriptures (perhaps by using the LXX), but he would have recited the teaching of Jesus about the kingdom.

Tried to convince them about Jesus from the Law of Moses and from the Prophets (28:23). Specifically, Paul wants to convince these Jewish leaders that Jesus of Nazareth fulfills the meaning and the promises of the Law and the Prophets. Reciting the relevant passages from Genesis to Malachi, which Paul would have known by heart, he explains how they are uniquely fulfilled in Jesus. As one scholar speculates: "Paul on this occasion must have exerted all his powerful qualities of mind and heart as he endeavored to persuade the leading Jews of Rome of the truth of the gospel. . . . The debate must have been keen and impassioned."[565]

Some were convinced . . . others would not believe (28:24). This response is typical of Paul's proclamation of Christ in the Diaspora synagogues.[566] The difference this time is that these Jewish leaders have already become exposed to the gospel and are already unfavorably inclined toward the message when they begin listening to Paul. The positive response of some is greatly encouraging to Paul and to the Christian community in Rome.

The Holy Spirit spoke (28:25). This introduction to the passage from Isaiah reveals Paul's belief in the divine inspiration of the Scriptures.

You will be ever hearing but never understanding. . . . For this people's heart has become calloused (28:26–27). When they begin to leave, Paul makes one final statement to the Jewish leaders who remain unconvinced that Jesus is the Messiah of Israel. He recites a passage from Isaiah 6:9–10, which speaks of the unresponsiveness of God's people to divine revelation because of the callousness of their hearts. One can only wonder about the emotion in Paul's voice as he utters this. In applying this passage to the unresponsive hearers, Paul follows the example of Jesus, who also pronounced these words to Palestinian Jews hostile to his message.[567] When Paul wrote to the Roman Christians a few years earlier, he attributed the unresponsiveness of many Jews to their hardened hearts (Rom. 11:7–8).

God's salvation has been sent to the Gentiles (28:28). This does not imply a final rejection of the Jews in favor of the Gentiles. Paul anticipates a time when there will be a massive turning of Jews to Jesus the Messiah (see Rom. 11:25–32). This may represent a departure from his principle of "to the Jews first" and a statement that his priority from henceforth will be to reach Gentiles with the gospel. "Luke may well be presenting him as an

ROMAN APARTMENT BUILDING

The remains of a multi-storied *insula* in Ostia, the port city of Rome.

example for the church generally to follow."[568]

For two whole years (28:30). Arriving in Rome in early A.D. 60 (perhaps March), this means that Paul is in custody at least until early in A.D. 62. Probably during this time Luke writes his second volume. At the conclusion of his writing, Paul still has not faced his trial. Had Paul already been released, it is difficult to explain why Luke would not have recorded the outcome of the trial (unless he was planning to do so in a third volume—a work never completed). Paul has been in custody four years, and his readers await the anticipated acquittal by the emperor. It would have made a better ending to the Gospel and Acts to portray Paul as free from chains and proclaiming the gospel to Gentiles in regions beyond Rome.

One of the activities Paul engages in during this time is letter writing. From his Roman apartment chained to a soldier, he writes Philippians (if it was not written while he was in prison in Caesarea, or even earlier during his Ephesian ministry), Colossians, Philemon, and Ephesians. Philippians may plausibly be explained as having been written just before Paul's trial at the end of the two years since it reflects an approaching crisis that could end in life or death for the apostle (Phil. 1:19–26).[569]

In his own rented house (28:30). It is inappropriate for us to think a single story two-bedroom home on a nice suburban street. Paul rents space on an upper floor of a Roman *insula*—a block apartment in a densely populated urban area. Housing prices were extraordinarily expensive in ancient Rome. Paul's apartment is probably modest—what we may even call a "slum dwelling."

How he is able to afford this is a matter of speculation. It is doubtful that he is able to work at his tentmaking business since he is chained by the wrist to a soldier.[570] It is possible that Paul may be drawing on an inheritance (this is highly speculative), but far more likely his source of income comes from contributions from fellow believers.

Boldly and without hindrance he preached (28:31). When Paul writes to the Ephesians (probably during this imprisonment), he asks these believers to pray that he will be enabled to proclaim the gospel boldly while he is "in chains" (Eph. 6:19–20). Perhaps he faces the threat of discouragement or intimidation from a variety of quarters. Luke, however, represents Paul as proclaiming the kingdom with great boldness.

The Roman authorities and the soldier chained to Paul could have used a variety of means to silence his proclamation of the gospel. Luke claims that the Roman authorities are tolerant of Paul's ministry and message during this period of time.

REFLECTIONS

PAUL WAS NOT IN IDEAL CIRCUM-stances for sharing the gospel. He was confined to his apartment, chained to a Roman soldier, and suffered from some physical limitation (his "thorn in the flesh"). Nevertheless, God strengthened and enabled him to shine brightly in Rome. Do you suffer a physical handicap? Do you feel limited by your circumstances? God delights in empowering the weak to be his witnesses!

ANNOTATED BIBLIOGRAPHY

Commentaries

Bruce, F. F. *The Book of the Acts* (*revised*). NICNT. Grand Rapids: Eerdmans, 1988.

This has been a longstanding classic on the book of Acts. F. F. Bruce had an eye for bringing out helpful historical background information to illuminate the text.

Larkin, William J. *Acts.* IVPNTC. Downers Grove, Ill.: InterVarsity, 1995.

This is an exceptional commentary that properly highlights the strong emphasis on mission throughout Acts. The reader will find valuable insights (especially on cultural issues) and helpful explanations of the text, combined with discussion of practical and contemporary significance.

Marshall, I. Howard. *The Acts of the Apostles.* TNTC. Grand Rapids: Eerdmans, 1980.

This is an outstanding paperback commentary that provides background information, but gives a greater amount of attention to the theological issues and themes. Marshall has long been appreciated for his lucid writing style.

Williams, David J. *Acts.* NIBC. Peabody, Mass.: Hendrickson, 1985.

This is well written and contains many excellent historical and theological insights.

Witherington, Ben, III. *The Acts of the Apostles: A Socio-Rhetorical Commentary.* Grand Rapids: Eerdmans, 1998.

This 874-page volume is perhaps now the best all-around commentary on the book of Acts. It is well written and gives extensive insight into the social and cultural background of each of the passages. Witherington is conversant with the recent scholarship on Acts and makes good use of it for illuminating the meaning of the text.

Special Studies

The Book of Acts in Its First Century Setting. Grand Rapids: Eerdmans, 1993–1996.

The Tyndale Fellowship in Cambridge, England, has sponsored the publication of a massive historical study of the book of Acts that has appeared in five volumes. These are indispensible for anyone wanting to gain a firm and up-to-date treatment of the historical background of Acts. The series consists of the following titles:

1. Bruce D. Winter and Andrew D. Clark, eds. *The Book of Acts in its Ancient Literary Setting* (1993).
2. David W. J. Gill and Conrad Gempf, eds. *The Book of Acts in its Graeco-Roman Setting* (1994).
3. Brian Rapske. *The Book of Acts and Paul in Roman Custody* (1994).
4. Richard Bauckham, ed. *The Book of Acts in its Palestinian Setting* (1995).
5. Irina Levinskaya. *The Book of Acts in its Diaspora Setting* (1996).

Hengel, Martin, and Anna Maria Schwemer. *Paul: Between Damascus and Antioch.* Louisville, Ky.: Westminster John Knox, 1997.

This is a landmark historical study of Acts 6–15, covering the years A.D. 33–49.

Riesner, Rainer. *Paul's Early Period: Chronology, Mission Strategy, Theology.* Grand Rapids: Eerdmans, 1998.

This is an invaluable historical study of the historical events and chronology of the events surrounding Paul's life from his conversion to the writing of 1 Thessalonians.

Main Text Notes

1. Irenaeus, *Against Heresies* 3.1.1.
2. Ibid., 3.14.1.
3. This is also known as an "Anti-Marcionite prologue." Cited from J. A. Fitzmyer, *The Gospel According to Luke* (New York: Doubleday, 1981), 1:38.
4. Eusebius, *Eccl. Hist.* 3.4; Jerome, *De Viris Illustribus* 7.
5. Col. 4:14; 2 Tim. 4:11; Philem. 24.
6. F. G. B. Millar and G. P. Burton, "*Equites,*" *OCD*³, 551.
7. R. F. O'Toole, "Theophilus," *ABD*, 6.511.
8. C. J. Hemer, *The Book of Acts in the Setting of Hellenistic History* (WUNT 49; Tübingen: Mohr-Siebeck, 1989; rpt. Winona Lake, Ind.: Eisenbrauns, 1990), 362.
9. I. H. Marshall, *The Acts of the Apostles* (TNTC; Grand Rapids: Eerdmans, 1980), 21. This conclusion is reaffirmed by D. Peterson, "Luke's Theological Enterprise," in *Witness to the Gospel: The Theology of Acts*, eds. I. H. Marshall and D. Peterson (Grand Rapids: Eerdmans, 1998), 534.
10. J. T. Squires, "The Plan of God," in *Witness to the Gospel*, 19–39, esp. 37–39.
11. D. Peterson, "The Motif of Fulfillment," in *Witness to the Gospel*, 100–101.
12. J. T. Squires, *The Plan of God in Luke-Acts* (SNTSMS 76; Cambridge: Cambridge University Press, 1993), 192–94; Peterson, "Luke's Theological Enterprise," 540.
13. Peterson, "Luke's Theological Enterprise," 540–44.
14. So also Hemer, *Book of Acts*, 365–410, 414.
15. For further discussion and references, see H. J. Cadbury, "Appendix C: Commentary on the Preface of Luke," in *The Beginnings of Christianity. Part I: The Acts of the Apostles*, eds. F. J. Foakes-Jackson and K. Lake (Grand Rapids: Baker, 1979; orig. 1932), 4:491.
16. Josephus, *Ag. Ap.* 2.1 §1
17. See, for example, *Pss. Sol.* 8:15.
18. See N. Avigad, *The Herodian Quarter in Jerusalem* (Jerusalem: Keter Publishing House, n.d.); B. Blue, "Acts and the House Church," in *The Book of Acts in Its Graeco-Roman Setting*, eds. D. W. J. Gill and C. Gempf (BAFCS 2; Grand Rapids: Eerdmans, 1994), 130–38, 140–44.
19. *m. Sanh.* 1:6.
20. See Marshall, *Acts*, 64–65; D. J. Williams, "Judas Iscariot," *DJG*, 408.
21. L. & K. Ritmeyer, "Akeldama: Potter's Field or High Priest's Tomb?" *BAR* 20.6 (Nov./Dec. 1994): 22–35, 76. Their conclu-

sions are also supported by G. Avni and Z. Greenhut, "Akeldama: Resting Place of the Rich and Famous," *BAR* 20.6 (November/December 1994): 36–46.
22. See Luke 10:1; Eusebius, *Eccl. Hist.* 1.12.
23. Lake and Cadbury, *Beginnings of Christianity*, 4:15.
24. W. Reinhardt, "The Population Size of Jerusalem and the Numerical Growth of the City," in *Acts in its Palestinian Setting*, 262–63.
25. J. Jeremias, *Jerusalem in the Time of Jesus* (Philadelphia: Fortress, 1969), 61.
26. Josephus, *Ant.* 7.15.3 §393.
27. Ibid., 16.7.1 §§179–82.
28. See D. Tarler and J. M. Cahill, "David, City Of," *ABD*, 2.64.
29. See H. Shanks, "Is This King David's Tomb?" *BAR* 21.1 (Jan./Feb. 1995): 62–67.
30. See BAGD, s.v.
31. M. Broshi, "The Archaeology of Palestine 63 B.C.E—CE 70," in *CHJ*³, 10.
32. 1QS 6:13–25.
33. See Blue, "Acts and the House Church," *Graeco-Roman Setting*, 140–44.
34. Josephus, *Ant.* 14.4.3 §65.
35. *m. Tamid* 7:3.
36. Jeremias, *Jerusalem*, 116–17.
37. Josephus, *J.W.* Trans. G. A. Williamson (New York: Viking Penguin, 1970), 5.5.3 §201.
38. Ibid., 5.5.2 §§190–92.
39. See, for example, Pss. 22; 69; Jer. 11:19; Dan. 9:26; Zech. 13:7.
40. *m. Sotah* 7:7–8; *m. Tamid* 7:3.
41. Josephus, *J.W.* 2.20.4 §566.
42. Ibid., 2.8.14 §165.
43. Josephus, *Ant.* 18.1.4 §16. On the Sadducees, see Schürer, *HJP*², 2:391.
44. G. Bornkamm, "πρέσβυς," *TDNT*, 6:659.
45. Ibid., 18.4.3 §95.
46. As cited in P. W. van der Horst, *Ancient Jewish Epitaphs: An Introductory Survey of a Millennium of Jewish Funerary Epigraphy (300 B.C.E–700 C.E.)* (Kampen: Kok Pharos Publishing House, 1991), 141.
47. Str-B, 1:876.
48. J. Fitzmyer, *The Acts of the Apostles* (AB 31; New York: Doubleday, 1998), 301.
49. *T. Sol.* 22:7.
50. Plato, *Apology of Socrates* 29D.
51. E.g. Josh. 10:24; 1 Kings 5:3; Ps. 8:6; 110:1.
52. Matt. 22:44; 1 Cor. 15:25–26; Eph. 1:22; Heb. 2:8.
53. Clement of Alexandria, *Stromata* 2.20.112.
54. C. K. Barrett, *The Acts of the Apostles*, 2 vols., (ICC; Edinburgh: T. & T. Clark, 1993–98), 1:259; B. Witherington III, *The Acts of the*

Apostles: A Socio-Rhetorical Commentary (Grand Rapids: Eerdmans, 1998), 209.

55. This is the view of J. Duncan M. Derrett, "Ananias, Sapphira, and the Right of Property," in *Studies in the New Testament*, vol. 1 (Leiden: Brill, 1977), 197–98.

56. Derrett, "Ananias, Sapphira," 198.

57. See Johannes P. Louw and Eugene A. Nida, *Greek-English Lexicon of the New Testament Based on Semantic Domains*, 2d ed. (New York: United Bible Societies, 1989) §11.32, 78.

58. See also Deut. 4:10; 23:2, 3, 4, 9; Judg. 20:2; 1 Kings 8:14; Ps. 22:22; et al.

59. Marshall, *Acts*, 115.

60. Cicero, *Tusc.* 3:12, 26. See P. W. van der Horst, "Shadow," *ABD*, 5.1148–50.

61. Ps.-Aristotle, *De mirabilibus auscultationibus* 145 (157) as reported in P. W. van der Horst, "Peter's Shadow: The Religio-Historical Background of Acts v.15," *NTS* 23 (1976–77): 208.

62. *m. ʿAbod. Zar.* 3:8.

63. *m. ʾOhal.* 2:1–2.

64. Tobit 6:7.

65. *T. Benj.* 5:2.

66. See Luke 4:33, 36; 6:18; 8:29; 9:42; 11:24.

67. K. Lake, "Localities In and Near Jerusalem Mentioned in Acts," in *Beginnings*, 5:478.

68. Gen. 22:11; Judg. 6:11, 12, 21; 1 Kings 19:7; 2 Kings 19:35; Isa. 37:6.

69. See, for instance, Duane Garrett, *Angels and the New Spirituality* (Nashville: Broadman & Holman, 1995), 19–23.

70. Barrett, *Acts*, 1:284.

71. Ibid., 1:289.

72. Deut. 26:7; 1 Chron. 29:18; 2 Chron. 20:6; Ezra 7:27.

73. Josephus, *Ant.* 13.10.6 §297.

74. Hemer, *Book of Acts*, 162, suggests that Josephus rather than Luke may be wrong on the dating of Theudas.

75. Josephus, *J.W.* 2.8.1 §118.

76. Josephus, *Ant.* 18.1.1, 6 §§1–10, 23–25.

77. *m. ʾAbot* 4:11.

78. Josephus, *Ant.* 4.8.21 §238.

79. See M. Wilkins, "Disciples," *DJG*, 176–82.

80. See, for example, Plato, *Meno* 82b; Aeschines, *Or.* 3.172. For additional texts, see Barrett, *Acts*, 1:308.

81. Chrysostom, *Hom. Act.* 21.1; Migne, *PG*, 60:164 (as reported in Hengel, "Between Jesus and Paul," 6).

82. See M. O. Wise, "Languages of Palestine," *DJG*, 434–44.

83. See Witherington, "A Closer Look—The Hellenists," *Acts*, 240–47.

84. J. J. Scott, "The Church's Progress to the Council of Jerusalem According to the Book of Acts," *BBR* 7 (1997): 209–11.

85. See the evidence in M. Hengel, "Between Jesus and Paul," in *Between Jesus and Paul: Studies in the Earliest History of Christianity* (Philadelphia: Fortress, 1983), 16 and n. 109 on p. 147.

86. Jeremias, *Jerusalem*, 131. He cites *m. Peʾah* 8:7 and a variety of texts from the Talmuds.

87. Such a suggestion occurs as early as Irenaeus (*Haer.* 1.26.3; 3.12.10; 4.15.1).

88. Barrett, *Acts*, 1:304.

89. Josephus, *J.W.* 2.20.5 §571.

90. Josephus, *Ant.* 4.8.14 §214.

91. For references, see Barrett, *Acts*, 1:312 and Str-B, 2:641.

92. Irenaeus, *Adv. Haer.* 1.26.3 and Eusebius, *Eccl. Hist.* 3.29.1–3.

93. Ex. 29:10, 15, 19; Lev. 1:4; 3:2, 8, 13; 4:15.

94. For the texts, see Str-B, 2:647–61.

95. Jeremias, *Jerusalem*, 204.

96. See R. Riesner, "Excursus I: An Essene Quarter in Jerusalem?," in *Acts in its Palestinian Setting*, 190–92.

97. Philo, *Embassy* 155.

98. Tacitus, *Ann.* 2.85.

99. M. Hengel, *The "Hellenization" of Judea in the First Century after Christ* (Philadelphia: Trinity Press, 1989), 13.

100. W. Schrage, "συναγωγή," *TDNT*, 7:837

101. *t. Meg.* 3.6; cf. also *y. Meg.* 73d.

102. See Str-B, 2.661–65; Schürer, *HJP²*, 2:76, 445; *b. Meg.* 26b.

103. N. Avigad, "A Depository of Inscribed Ossuaries in the Kidron Valley," *IEJ* 12 (1962): 1–12 (cited in Fitzmyer, *Acts*, 358).

104. *Gos. Thom.* 71.

105. Witherington, *Acts*, 260.

106. See W. A. van Gemeren, "Shekinah," *ISBE*, 4.466–68.

107. Josephus, *Ant.* 12.3.3 §136.

108. On "glory," see C. C. Newman, "Glory," *DLNT*, 394–400.

109. Josephus, *Ant.* 2.8.2 §199.

110. Ibid., 2.9.7 §236.

111. J. Jeremias, "Μωυσῆς," *TDNT*, 4:851.

112. Marshall, *Acts*, 141.

113. *m. ʾAbot* 2:7.

114. See M. Stohl, "Sakkuth," *DDD²*, 722–23; idem, "Kaiwan," *DDD²*, 478.

115. G. C. Heider, "Molech," *DDD²*, 585.

116. 2 Kings 21:62; 2 Chron. 28:3.

117. See R. K. Harrison, "Molech," *ISBE*, 3:401–2; 2 Kings 17:17; 21:6; Ps. 106:38; Ezek. 16:21.

118. Fitzmyer, *Acts*, 383; Bruce, *Acts*, 147 (note 78).

119. Fitzmyer, *Acts*, 384.

120. Witherington, *Acts*, 273.

121. 2 Chron. 24:20–21; Neh. 9:26; Jer. 2:30; 26:20–24.

122. Justin Martyr, *Dialogue With Trypho* 120.5; Tertullian, *De patientia* 14; *Scorpiace* 8.

123. See also Ps. 68:17; Josephus, *Ant.* 15.5.3 §136.

124. For the texts, see Str-B, 3:554–56.

125. See R. Riesner, *Paul's Early Period: Chronology, Mission Strategy, Theology* (Grand Rapids: Eerdmans, 1998), 59–63.

126. Ps. 37:12; see also Lam. 2:16; Ps. 112:10.

127. See also Eph. 1:20; 1 Peter 3:22.

128. See Dan. 7:13; *1 En.* 46–53.

129. Acts 13:21; Rom. 11:1; Phil. 3:5.

130. Based on the use of the word in Philo, *Cherubim* 32 (§114) and Diogenes Laertius 8.10.

131. See Fitzmyer, *Acts*, 394.

132. *m. Sanh.* 6.6.

133. For the references, see Lake and Cadbury, *Beginnings*, 4.88.

134. See F. S. Spencer, "Philip the Evangelist," *DLNT*, 929–31.

135. Eusebius, *Eccl. Hist.* 3.39.9–10.

136. Hengel, "Luke the Historian," 115.

137. Josephus, *Ant.* 13.10.2–3 §§275–83; *J.W.* 1.2.7 §§64–65.

138. Josephus, *Ant.* 14.5.3 §88; *J.W.* 1.8.4 §166. On Herod renaming the restored city, see *Ant.* 15.8.5 §392; *J.W.* 1.21.2 §403.

139. See Irenaeus, *Against Heresies* 1.23.1–4; Origen, *Cont. Cel.* 6.11; Tertullian, *de Anima* 34; *Against All Heresies* 1; Eusebius, *Eccl. Hist.* 2.13–14.

140. See E. M. Yamauchi, "Gnosis, Gnosticism," *DPL* 350–54.

141. See C. E. Arnold, "Magical Papyri," *DNTB*, 666–70.

142. E. Lane, *Corpus Monumentorum Religionis Dei Menis*, part 1 (EPRO 19; Leiden: Brill, 1971), 45–46 (no. 69).

143. So also Witherington, *Acts*, 289; Bruce, *Acts*, 170.

144. Barrett, *Acts*, 1:413.

145. Ibid., 1:416–17.

146. Homer, *Odyssey* 1.22–23.

147. See also Strabo, *Geog* 1.1.6; Philostratus, *Vit. Apoll.* 6.1; Herodotus, *Hist.* 3.114.

148. Josephus, *Ant.* 14.5.3 §§86–88.

149. F. L. Horton and J. A. Blakely, "'Behold, Water!' Tell el-Hesi and the Baptism of the Ethiopian Eunuch (Acts 8:26–40)," *RB* 107 (2000): 56–71.

150. On Ethiopia, see R. G. Morkot, "Ethiopia," *OCD³*, 558; "Nubia," *OCD³*, 1052; R. H. Smith, "Ethiopia," *ABD*, 2:665.

151. BAGD, s.v.

152. Schürer, *HJP²*, 3.1.57–59.

153. *CPJ*, II.432.57–61 (AD 113).

154. A. Segal, *Rebecca's Children: Judaism and Christianity in the Roman World* (Cambridge, Mass.: Harvard University Press, 1986), 93.

155. Spencer, *Portrait of Philip*, 178–80; Barrett, *Acts*, 1:431.

156. See also Barrett, *Acts*, 1:434.

157. Irenaeus, *Haer.* 3.12.8; see also Eusebius, *Eccl. Hist.* 2.1.13.

158. On Azotus, see M. Dothan, "Ashdod," *ABD*, 1:477–82; idem, "Ashdod," *NEAE*, 1:93–102.

159. Hengel & Schwemer, *Paul*, 131; Riesner, *Paul's Early Period*, 87.

160. See McRay, *Archaeology*, 233–34; idem, "Damascus (The Greco-Roman Period)," *ABD*, 2:8.

161. 2 Sam. 7:14; see also Ps. 89:26–27; Ps. 2:7.

162. See Hengel & Schwemer, *Paul*, 106–26.

163. Ibid., *Paul*, 132.

164. See Acts 9:11; 21:39; 22:3.

165. Hengel & Schwemer, *Paul*, 174.

166. See Ezra 2:33; Neh. 7:37; 11:35.

167. Josephus, *J.W.* 32.3.5 §§54–58.

168. Ibid., 2.19.1 §513.

169. See J. Kaplan, "Lod," *NEAE*, 3:917; W. Ewing & R. K. Harrison, "Lod," *ISBE*, 3:150–51.

170. On Joppa, see J. Kaplan & H. Ritter-Kaplan, "Jaffa," *NEAE*, 2:655–59; idem, "Joppa," *ABD*, 3:946–49.

171. Josephus, *J.W.* 3.9.3 §§419–27.

172. Schürer, *HJP²*, 2:110–14.

173. *m. Šabb.* 23.5.

174. *b. Pesaḥ* 65a.

175. See Jeremias, *Jerusalem*, 309–10.

176. On Caesarea, see R. L. Hohlfelder, "Caesarea," *ABD*, 1:798–803; K. G. Holum, A. Raban, A. Negev, A. Frova, M. Avi-Yonah, L. I. Levine, and E. Netzer, "Caesarea," *NEAE*, 1:271–91; K. G. Holum, R. L. Hohlfelder, R.J. Bull, and A. Raban, *King Herod's Dream: Caesarea on the Sea* (New York: Norton, 1988).

177. Josephus, *J.W.* 1.21.7 §414, ed. Williamson.

178. Ibid., 2.18.1 §457.

179. Appian, *Civil War* 1.100.

180. H. M. D. Parker and G. R. Watson, "Centurio," *OCD³*, 310.

181. D. Kennedy, "Roman Army," *ABD*, 5:791.

182. Polybius, *Histories* 6.24.9 (as cited in W. J. Larkin, *Acts* [IVPNTC; Downer's Grove, Ill.: InterVarsity Press, 1995], 153).

183. M. J. Olson, "Italian Cohort," *ABD*, 3:578–79; T. R. S. Broughton, "The Roman Army," in *Beginnings*, 5:441–43.

184. Broughton, "Roman Army," 442.

185. See Acts 5:19; 8:26; 12:7; 27:23.

186. BAGD, s.v.

187. W. Hauck, "κοινός," *TDNT*, 3:790.

188. Midrash on Psalm 146 as cited in Barrett, *Acts*, 1:509.

189. Fitzmyer, *Acts*, 457.

190. *m. ʾOhal.* 18:7.

191. BAGD, s.v.

192. See the discussion in Schürer, *HJP*², 2:81–83.

193. J. J. Scott, "The Cornelius Incident in the Light of its Jewish Setting," *JETS* 34 (1991): 482.

194. Witherington, *Acts*, 356.

195. C. W. Stenschke, *Luke's Portrait of Gentiles Prior to Their Coming to Faith* (WUNT 2/108; Tübingen: Mohr Siebeck, 1999), 153.

196. See R. F. Youngblood, "Peace," *ISBE*, 3:731–33.

197. Barrett, *Acts*, 1:527.

198. On the Roman *familia*, see F. Dupont, *Daily Life in Ancient Rome* (Oxford: Blackwell, 1992), 103–6.

199. Schürer, *HJP*², 3:1:15.

200. Philo, *Embassy* 36 (281–82).

201. BAGD, s.v.

202. Hengel & Schwemer, *Paul*, 205–24.

203. *Didache* 11:7–12; Hermas, *Mandate* 11:1–21.

204. Hermas, *Mandate* 11:3, 17.

205. The best discussion of these famines and the impact they had on Judea is in Riesner, *Paul's Early Period*, 125–36.

206. Winter, "Acts and Food Shortages," in *Graeco-Roman Setting*, 61–62.

207. Dio Cassius, *Hist.* 59.17.2, 60.11.1–4; Suetonius, *Gaius* 39.1; P. Michigan 123, 127; see Riesner, *Paul's Early Period*, 129.

208. Orosius, *Adv. Pag.* 7.6.12.

209. Josephus, *Ant.* 12.8.3, 4, 6 §§272, 274, 284.

210. Suetonius, *Claud.* 2.

211. 1 Cor. 6:1–4; 2 Cor. 8–9.

212. For further support of the view that the visit of Acts 11:30 and 12:25 = the visit of Gal. 2:1–10, see: Witherington, *Acts*, 375 and Appendix 1, 817–20; Bruce, *Acts*, 231; Hemer, *Book of Acts*, chaps. 6–7.

213. On Herod Agrippa I, see Josephus, *Ant.* 18–19. See also D. R. Schwartz, *Agrippa I: The Last King of Judaea* (TSAJ 23; Tübingen: Mohr Siebeck, 1990); Schürer, *HJP*², 1:442–54; D. C. Braund, "Agrippa," *ABD*, 1:98–100; H. W. Hoehner, "Herod," *ISBE*, 2:696–97.

214. Josephus, *Ant.* 19.7.3 §331.

215. See Eusebius, *Eccl. Hist.* 3.1, 20, 23–24.

216. Ibid., 2.1, 9; 3.5.

217. See *m. Sanhedrin* 7:3, 9:3.

218. Riesner, *Paul's Early Period*, 119.

219. On the feast of Unleavened Bread, see: B. M. Bokser, "Unleavened Bread and Passover, Feasts Of," *ABD*, 6:755–65; M. O. Wise, "Feasts," *DJG*, 234–41.

220. As cited in H. Conzelmann, *Acts of the Apostles* (Hermeneia; Philadelphia: Fortress, 1987), 93; Vegetius, *On Military Affairs* 3.8.

221. See B. Rapske, *Paul in Roman Custody* (BAFCS 3; Grand Rapids: Eerdmans, 1994), 206–207; Lucian, *Tox.* 29.

222. Barrett, *Acts*, 1:583.

223. See Blue, "Acts and the House Church," 135–36.

224. Hemer, *Book of Acts*, 227.

225. See also Barrett, *Acts*, 1:584.

226. See M. Noll, *Angels of Light, Powers of Darkness* (Downer's Grove, Ill.: InterVarsity Press, 1998), 170–72.

227. Acts 15:13; Gal. 1:19; 2:9, 12.

228. Josephus, *Ant.* 20.9.1 §200.

229. R. Bauckham, "James and the Jerusalem Church," in *Palestinian Setting*, 434–35.

230. *Code of Justinian* 9.4.4.

231. Ibid., 19.8.2 §351.

232. J. D. G. Dunn, *The Acts of the Apostles* (NC; Philadelphia: Trinity Press, 1996), 173.

233. On Seleucia, see A. H. M. Jones, H. Seyrig, & S. Sherwin-White, "Seleucia in Pieria," *OCD*³, 1380; L. J. Hoppe, "Seleucia," *ABD*, 5:1075–76; W. S. LaSor, "Seleucia," *ISBE*, 4:384–85.

234. H. W. Catling, "Salamis," *OCD*³, 1347; E. Meyer, "Salamis," *Der Kleine Pauly*, 4:1505–1506; C. Gempf, "Salamis," *ABD*, 5:904–905.

235. Barrett, *Acts*, 1:612.

236. See Gill, "Cyprus," 220–23, for a discussion of Paul's likely route.

237. H. W. Catling, "Paphos," *OCD*³, 1108; E. Meyer, "Paphos," *Der Kleine Pauly*, 4:484–87.

238. H. J. Klauck, *Magie und Heidentum in der Apostelgeschichte des Lukas* (SBS 167; Stuttgart: Verlag Katholisches Bibelwerk, 1996), 61.

239. See C. E. Arnold, *Powers of Darkness: Principalities and Powers in Paul's Letters* (Downer's Grove, Ill.: InterVarsity Press, 1992), 71–74; Klauck, *Magie und Heidentum*, 62.

240. Josephus, *Ant.* 20.7.2 §142.

241. Suetonius, *Aug.* 94–98.

242. See G. J. Toomer, "Claudius Thrasyllus," *OCD*³, 343. See also A. D. Nock, "Paul and the Magus," in *Beginnings*, 5:183–84; Suetonius, *Tiberius* 14, 62; *Gaius* 19.

243. Suetonius, *Nero* 36, 40.

244. Pliny, *Nat. Hist.* 30.17; Suetonius, *Nero* 56.

245. *CIL*, 6.31543.

246. On this inscription, now see Nobbs, "Cyprus," in *Graeco-Roman Setting*, 279–89 and Mitchell, *Anatolia*, 2:6–7.

247. W. Ramsay, *The Bearing of Recent Discovery on the Trustworthiness of the New Testament* (Grand Rapids: Baker, 1953 [rep. of 1915 ed.]), 151.

248. Mitchell, *Anatolia*, 2:6.

249. Ibid., 2:6; Nobbs, "Cyprus," 287; S. Mitchell and M. Waelkens, *Pisidian Antioch: The Site and its Monuments* (London: Duckworth, 1998), 12.

250. See Hemer, *Book of Acts*, 227–28.

251. LSJ, s.v.

252. F. F. Bruce, *Paul: Apostle of the Heart Set Free* (Grand Rapids: Eerdmans, 1977), 37–40; idem, *New Testament History* (New York: Doubleday, 1972), 234–35.

253. Riesner, *Paul's Early Period*, 151–54.

254. On Perga, see E. A. Judge, "Perga," *ISBE*, 3:767–68; W. W. Gasque, "Perga," *ABD*, 5:228; G. E. Bean & S. Mitchell, "Perge," *OCD³*, 1139.

255. On Pisidia, see W. H. C. Frend, "Pisidia," *ISBE* 3.873–74; S. Mitchell, "Pisidia," *OCD³*, 1186; W. W. Gasque, "Pisidia," *ABD*, 5:374–75.

256. Mitchell, *Anatolia*, 2.4.

257. Schürer, *HJP²*, 2:441–43.

258. Ibid., 2:447–48.

259. See Schürer, *HJP²*, 2:456–59; Num. 15:37–41; Deut. 6:4–9; 11:13–21; *m. Meg.* 4:3.

260. Philo, *Spec. Laws* 2.62 (Yonge trans.).

261. Witherington, *Acts*, 406–407.

262. *b. Ketub.* 96a.

263. Barrett, *Acts*, 1:658.

264. See also Ps. 69:28; Rev. 13:8; 17:8; 20:12–15; 21:27.

265. Mitchell, "Antioch of Pisidia," 265; Mitchell and Waelkens, *Pisidian Antioch*, 12.

266. Str-B, 1:571.

267. See C. Kruse, "Apostle, Apostleship," *DLNTD*, 76–82.

268. A. H. M. Jones and S. Mitchell, "Lycaonia," *OCD³*, 894; F. F. Bruce, "Lycaonia," *ABD*, 4:420–22.

269. C. Breytenbach, "Zeus und der lebendige Gott: Anmerkungen zu Apostelgeschichte 14.11–17," *NTS* 39 (1993): 399; Mitchell, *Anatolia*, 1:173.

270. Mitchell, *Anatolia*, 1:173.

271. Ovid, *Metamorphoses* 8.618–724.

272. See Mitchell, *Anatolia*, 1:24.

273. Iamblichus, *De misteriis* 1.1.

274. See Hemer, *Book of Acts*, 195–96.

275. See L. H. Martin, "Hermes," *DDD²*, 409; F. Graf, "Zeus," *DDD²*, 939.

276. See Herodotus, *Hist.* 7.197.2.

277. See "Grief," *DBI*, 351–52.

278. Num. 14:6; 2 Kings 18:37; 19:1; 22:11; Ezra 4:1.

279. *m. Sanhedrin* 7:5.

280. Bar. 6:17 (LXX = v. 15), see the extended polemic in vv. 3–72; see also Deut. 4:28; Ps. 115:4–8; Isa. 44:9–20; Wis. 15:15–19.

281. *Letter of Aristeas* 135.

282. See also 1 Sam. 17:36; 2 Kings 19:4, 16; Ps. 42:2; 84:2.

283. Bel and the Dragon 4–5.

284. See Ps. 146:6; 4Q521 5.ii.2.

285. *m. Ber.* 9:2.

286. Breytenbach, "Zeus und der lebendige Gott," 399–400.

287. Foakes-Jackson and Lake, *Beginnings*, 4:162.

288. Barrett, *Acts*, 1:688.

289. Ex. 29:36; 30:10; Lev. 16:30; Isa. 53:10.

290. See Ex. 15:22–27; Num. 14:22.

291. *m. ʾAbot* 3.5.

292. Barrett, *Acts*, 2:721.

293. CD 7:16; 4QFlor 1:12–13.

294. See, for example, Isa. 45:20–23; Jer. 12:15–16; Zech. 8:22.

295. *Vita Greg. Thaumaturg.* 46:944, as cited in Witherington, *Acts*, 462.

296. See, for example, Sir. 23:23; *T. Reu.* 3:3; 4:6; 5:3.

297. See 1 Cor. 6:18; 7:2; Gal. 5:19; Eph. 5:3; Heb. 13:4.

298. Wis. 14:23–27; see also 1 Cor. 10:7–8; Rev. 2:14, 20.

299. See A. J. M. Wedderburn, "The 'Apostolic Decree': Tradition and Redaction," *NovT* 35 (1993): 384–89.

300. Origen, *Against Celsus* 8.30.

301. *Comm. on Isaiah* 236 on 10:11 as cited in Wedderburn, "Apostolic Decree," 385.

302. For a full presentation of this view, see Wedderburn, "Apostolic Decree," 362–89.

303. Philo, *Spec. Laws* 2.15 (§ 62).

304. 2 Cor. 1:19; 1 Thess. 1:1; 2 Thess. 1:1.

305. For example, Witherington, *Acts*, 468; Barrett, *Acts*, 2.741.

306. Deut. 29:28; Jer. 32:37.

307. Str-B, 2:741.

308. See *m. Qidd.* 3:12.

309. C. J. Hemer, "The Adjective Phrygia," *JTS* 27 (1976): 122–26; idem, "Phrygia: A Further Note," *JTS* 28 (1977): 99–101.

310. Mitchell, *Anatolia*, 2:3.

311. See, for example, Fitzmyer, *Acts*, 578.

312. Mitchell, *Anatolia*, 2:3.

313. On Bithynia, see T. R. S. Broughton & S. Mitchell, "Bithynia," *OCD³*, 244–45; and A. Sheppard, "Bithynia," *ABD*, 1:750–53.

314. Eusebius, *Eccl. Hist.* 3.4.

315. Witherington, *Acts*, 485.

316. C. Gempf, "Neapolis," *ABD*, 4:1052.

317. On Roman colonization, see A. N. Sherwin-White and B. M. Levick, "Colonization, Roman," *OCD³*, 364.

318. C. Koukouli-Chrysantaki, "Colonia Iulia Augusta Philippensis," in Bakirtzis and Koester, *Philippi*, 21.

319. See Schürer, *HJP²*, 2:439–41; 3:1:65; Str-B, 2:742; W. Schrage, "συναγωγή," *TDNT*, 7:814; H. Greeven, "προσευχή," *TDNT*, 2:808. For further arguments for this conclusion, see D. L. Matson, *Household Conversion Narratives in Acts* (JSNTSup 123; Sheffield: University Press, 1996), 145–46.

320. Koukouli-Chrysantaki, "Philippensis," 28–35.

321. *m. Meg.* 1:4; 4:3.

322. Hemer, *Book of Acts*, 114.

323. Homer, *Iliad* 4.141–42.

324. Pliny, *Nat. Hist.* 7.56.195.

325. For references, see C. J. Hemer, "Lydia and the Purple Trade," in *New Documents*, 3:54.

326. *IG* 10:2:1:291.

327. Koukouli-Chrysantaki, "Philippensis," 26.

328. Van der Horst, *Ancient Jewish Epitaphs*, 136.

329. See L. Maurizio, "Anthropology and Spirit Possession: A Consideration of the Pythia's Role at Delphi," *JHS* 115 (1995): 69–86, esp. 83–86.

330. On the Python, see J. W. van Henten, "Python," *DDD²*, 669–71. See also C. Arnold, *Powers of Darkness*, 32–33; Plutarch, *De Defectu Oraculorum* 9 (414e).

331. See 2 Kings 22:14; Ps. 54(57):3; 77(78):35, 56.

332. See C. Breytenbach, "Hypsistos," *DDD²*, 439–43; Trebilco, "Paul and Silas—'Servants of the Most High God' (Acts 16:16–18)," *JSNT* 36 (1989): 51–73.

333. *m. Sanh.* 7:7.

334. Origen, *De Principiis* 3.4.5.

335. *Clementine Homilies* 9.16.

336. H. Koester, "Paul and Philippi: The Evidence from Early Christian Literature," in *Philippi*, 52.

337. For the many references, see Schürer, *HJP²*, 3.1.150–56.

338. Tacitus, *Histories* 5.5.

339. As cited in Fitzmyer, *Acts*, 587; Cicero, *De legibus* 2.8.19.

340. Rapske, *Roman Custody*, 126.

341. Ibid., 127.

342. Acts 13:52; Gal. 5:22.

343. Barrett, *Acts*, 2:800.

344. As cited in Rapske, *Roman Custody*, 49; Livy 10.9.4; see also, Cicero, *De Republica* 2.31.

345. Ulpian in *Digesta* 48.6.7.

346. Strabo, *Geog.* 7.7.4; 7. Frag. 24.

347. For more information about Thessalonica, see Gill, "Macedonia," 414–15; H. L. Hendrix, "Thessalonica," *ABD*, 6:523–27.

348. I. Levinskaya, *The Book of Acts in Its Diaspora Setting* (BAFCS 5; Grand Rapids: Eerdmans, 1996), 155.

349. See F. M. Gillman, "Jason," *ABD*, 3:649.

350. Dio Cassius, *Roman History* 56.25.5–6.

351. E. A. Judge, "The Decrees of Caesar at Thessalonica," *RTR* 30 (1971): 3–4; Dio Cassius, *Roman History* 57.15.8.

352. Judge, "Decrees of Caesar," 6.

353. See McRay, *Archaeology*, 295–97.

354. See Gill, "Macedonia," 415–17.

355. See Levinskaya, *Diaspora Setting*, 158–62.

356. See McRay, *Archaeology*, 302–8.

357. For a good description of the characteristics and beliefs of these two philosophical schools, see E. Ferguson, *Backgrounds of Early Christianity*, 2d ed. (Grand Rapids: Eerdmans, 1993), 333–56; T. Schmeller, "Stoics, Stoicism," *ABD*, 6:210–14; E. Asmis, "Epicureanism," *ABD*, 2:559–61.

358. Cited in W. Meeks, *The Moral World of the First Christians* (LEC; Philadelphia: Westminster, 1986), 59; *Epistle to Menoeceus* = Diogenes Laertius 10.13f.

359. See Hemer, *Book of Acts*, 117.

360. On the Areopagus, see H. M. Martin, "Areopagus," *ABD*, 1.370–72; T. J. Cadoux, "Areopagus," *OCD²*, 102–103.

361. C. Hemer, "Paul at Athens: A Topographical Note," *NTS* 20 (1974): 341–50, contends that Paul appeared before a formal session of the court in the agora in the immediate neighborhood of the Stoa Basileios.

362. Thucydides, *History of the Peloponnesian War* 2.38.5 (as cited by Bruce, *Acts*, 332).

363. For an outstanding concise treatment of this speech, see C. Gempf, "Athens, Paul at," *DPL*, 51–54.

364. Williams, *Acts*, 297.

365. *Description of Greece* 1:1:14.

366. *Life of Apollonius of Tyana* 6:3:5.

367. *Lives of Philosophers* 1:110.

368. Quoted in Bruce, *Acts*, 339.

369. Ibid.

370. Eusebius, *Eccl. Hist.* 4.23.3.

371. On the city of Corinth, see J. Murphy-O'Connor, "Corinth," *ABD*, 1:1134–39; idem, *St. Paul's Corinth: Texts and Archaeology* (GNS 6; Wilmington, Del.: Liturgical Press, 1983); idem, "The Corinth That Paul Saw," *BA* 47 (1984): 147–59; J. Wiseman, "Corinth and Rome I: 228 B.C.–A.D. 267," *ANRW*, II.7.1 (1979), 438–548; V. P. Furnish, "Corinth in Paul's Time: What Can Archaeology Tell Us?" *BAR* 14 (1988): 14–27.

372. Strabo, *Geog.* 8.6.20.

373. McRay, *Archaeology*, 315–17, has made a good case supporting the credibility of Strabo's account and the extensive sexual immorality in the city.

374. Bruce, *Acts*, 346 n. 4.

375. See P. Lampe, "Prisca," *ABD*, 5:467–68; idem, "Aquila," *ABD*, 1:319–20.

376. Philo, *Embassy* 159–61; Suetonius, *Tib.* 36.

377. Dio Cassius, *Roman History* 60:6 (as cited in Bruce, *History*, 295).

378. Suetonius, *Claud.* 25.4.

379. See P. W. Barnett, "Tentmaking," *DPL*, 925–27.

380. P. Lampe, "Paulus—Zeltmacher," *BZ* 31 (1987): 256–61.

381. Murphy-O'Connor, "Corinth," 149.

382. *Pirqe ʾAbot* 2.12 (as cited in Barnett, "Tentmaking," *DPL*, 927).

383. See Levinskaya, *Diaspora Setting*, 162–66.

384. On Gallio, see K. Haacker, "Gallio," *ABD*, 2:901–903; see also B. W. Winter, "Gallio's Ruling on the Legal Status of Early Christianity (Acts 18:14–15)," *TynBul* 50 (1999): 213–24.

385. The entire Greek text is given in Foakes-Jackson and Lake, *Beginnings*, 5:460–64. An English translation of the text can be found in C. K. Barrett, *The New Testament Background: Selected Documents*, rev. and exp. ed. (San Francisco: Harper, 1989), 51–52.

386. The translation is from Barrett, *Background*, 51–52. The brackets indicate places where the text has been restored. In the original, the text is broken away at these points.

387. Winter, "Gallio's Ruling," 222.

388. Ibid., 221.

389. Jewish traditions about the Nazirite vow are contained in the tractate "Nazir" in the Mishnah (see the English translation by H. Danby, *The Mishnah* [Oxford: Oxford University Press, 1933], 280–93).

390. On Apollos, see B. B. Blue, "Apollos," *DPL*, 37–39 and L. D. Hurst, "Apollos," *ABD*, 1:301.

391. For more information about Ephesus, see Trebilco, "Asia," 302–57; R. Oster, "Ephesus," *ABD*, 2:542–49; and C. E. Arnold, "Ephesus," *DPL*, 249–53. Serious students will also want to consult, Helmut Koester, ed., *Ephesus: Metropolis of Asia* (HTS 41; Valley Forge, Penn.: Trinity Press, 1995).

392. Strabo, *Geog.* 14.1.24.

393. Aelius Aristides, *Orat.* 23.24.

394. Marshall, *Acts*, 306; Witherington, *Acts*, 570.

395. S. M. Baugh, "Paul and Ephesus: The Apostle Among His Contemporaries," Unpublished Ph.D. Dissertation (Irvine, Calif.: University of California Press, 1990): 81–82.

396. Levinskaya, *Diaspora Setting*, 146; *Inschriften von Ephesos* 1251.

397. This was granted by Antiochus II Theos (287–246 B.C.); Josephus, *Ant.* 12.4.10 §225.

398. For a discussion of Jews in Ephesus, see Levinskaya, *Diaspora Setting*, 143–48.

399. *Inschriften von Ephesos* 1676, 1677; D. Knibbe and B. Iplikcioglu, "Neue Inschriften aus Ephesos IX," *JOAIW* 55, Hauptblatt 107 no. 4101 (1984). See the discussion in Baugh, "Paul and Ephesus," 82–86.

400. Baugh, "Paul in Ephesus," 99.

401. Trebilco, "Asia," 312–14.

402. This translation is from: H. D. Betz, ed., *The Greek Magical Papyri in Translation* (Chicago: University of Chicago Press, 1986), 96; *Papyrus Graecae Magicae* 4:3007–3025.

403. See Acts 24:17; Rom. 15:25–31; 1 Cor. 16:1–4; 2 Cor. 8–9.

404. The key study on this theme has been written by R. Oster, "The Ephesian Artemis as an Opponent of Early Christianity," *JAC* 19 (1976): 24–44.

405. See R. A. Kearsley, "Asiarch," in *ABD*, 1:495–97; Baugh, "Paul in Ephesus," 132–64.

406. Cited in Trebilco, "Asia," 347; Dio Chrysostom, *Orationes* 34.33.

407. Bruce, *Acts*, 381.

408. See Riesner, *Paul's Early Period*, 316.

409. See N. Purcell, "Houses, Italian," OCD³, 731–32.

410. Bruce, *Acts*, 387.

411. See the chart in Witherington, *Acts*, 610.

412. See Witherington, *Acts*, 616; Mark 10:41–45; Rom. 12:16; 2 Cor. 10:1; Phil. 2:3.

413. Ezek. 33:2–5; see also Ezek. 3:18–21.

414. Homer, *Odyssey* 8163.

415. H. Beyer, "ἐπίσκοπος," *TDNT*, 2:610; Plato, *Leges* 8.849a.

416. G. A. Deissmann, *Bible Studies* (Edinburgh: T. & T. Clark, 1923), 230–31; MM, 244–45.

417. Philo, *Heir* 30.

418. 1 Tim. 1:19–20; 4:1–3; 2 Tim. 2:17–18; 3:1–9.

419. 1 Cor. 9:12–15; 2 Cor. 11:7–11; 1 Thess. 2:9.

420. For references, see Barrett, *Acts*, 2:983.

421. Witheringon, *Acts*, 626.

422. On Cos, see W. A. Laidlay and S. Sherwin-White, "Cos," OCD³, 403–4.

423. Hemer, *Book of Acts*, 125.

424. Barrett, *Acts*, 2:990–91, reaches a similar conclusion.

425. On Ptolemais, see M. Dothan & Z. Goldmann, "Acco," *NEAE*, 1:16–17; M. Dothan, "Acco," *ABD*, 1:50–53; Schürer, *HJP²*, 2:121–25.

426. Josephus, *J.W.* 3.3.1 §35.

427. Ibid., 2.18.5 §477.

428. Eusebius, *Eccl. Hist.* 3.31; 5.24; see also 3.39.

429. Isa. 20:2–4; see also 1 Kings 11:29–39; Jer. 27:1–22; Ezek. 4–5.

430. Lake and Cadbury, *Beginnings*, 4:269.

431. Xenophon, *Hellenica* 5.3.1.

432. On Mnason, see J. Paulien, "Mnason," *ABD*, 4:881–82.

433. Barrett, *Acts*, 2:1003.

434. For example, Bruce, *Acts*, 404–405.

435. See Acts 24:17; Rom. 15:25–27, 31; Gal. 2:10; 1 Cor. 16:1–4; 2 Cor. 8:1–7; 9:1–5.

436. Josephus, *Ant.* 19.6.1 §§293–294.

437. Fitzmyer, *Acts*, 694; *m. ʾOhal.* 2.3.

438. Jeremias, *Jerusalem*, 210.

439. Josephus, *J.W.* 5.5.8 §244.

440. Ibid., 5.5.8 §243.

441. Rapske, *Roman Custody*, 140.

442. See Rapske, *Roman Custody*, 141–42.

443. Philostratus, *Life of Apollonius* 6.34.

444. G. H. R. Horsley, "The Fiction of 'Jewish Greek,'" in *New Documents*, 5:23.

445. This is the conclusion of W. C. van Unnik, *Tarsus or Jerusalem: The City of Paul's Youth* (London: Epworth Press, 1962), 52.

446. See Hengel, *Pre-Christian Paul*, 18–39.

447. H. W. Tajra, *The Trial of St. Paul* (WUNT 2/35; Tübingen: Mohr Siebeck, 1989), 86.

448. Barclay, *Diaspora*, 383.

449. Marshall, *Acts*, 355.

450. Rapske, *Roman Custody*, 139.

451. Suetonius, *Claudius* 25; Epictetus, *Disc.* 3.24.41.

452. Sherwin-White, *Roman Law*, 154–55.

453. Dio Cassius 60.17.5–7.

454. Tajra, *Trial*, 75.

455. W. M. Ramsay, *St. Paul the Traveler and Roman Citizen* (New York: G. P. Putnam's Sons, 1896), 30–32; Bruce, *Paul*, 37–40; idem, *New Testament History*, 234–35; C. J. Hemer, "The Name of Paul," *TynBul* 36 (1986): 183; Tajra, *Trial*, 83.

456. Hengel, *Pre-Christian Paul*, 11–14.

457. Ibid., 2.8.14 §165.

458. E.g. Ps. 49:15; Isa. 26:19; Hos. 6:1–3; 13:14.

459. See 2 Macc. 7:9, 11, 14, 22–23, 29; see also 2 Macc. 12:43–44; 14:46.

460. *m. Sanh.* 10.1.

461. Dunn, *Acts*, 304, takes a similar position.

462. Johnson, *Acts*, 399.

463. See Schürer, *HJP*², 2:223–25; A. J. Saldarini, "Sanhedrin," *ABD*, 5:977–78.

464. E. A. Judge in *New Documents*, 1:78.

465. LSJ, s.v.

466. On Antipatris, see Murphy-O'Connor, *Holy Land*, 161–63; Schürer, *HJP*², 2:167–68; M. Kochavi, "Antipatris," *ABD*, 1:273–74.

467. Josephus, *Ant.* 1.21.9 §417.

468. Rapske, *Roman Custody*, 155.

469. Josephus, *J.W.* 1.21.5 §408.

470. See Tajra, *Trial*, 120. See also B. Winter, "The Importance of the *captatio benevolentiae* in the Speeches of Tertullus and Paul in Acts 24:1–21," *JTS* 42 (1991): 505–31.

471. Cited in Sherwin-White, *Roman Law*, 51.

472. E.g. Prov. 19:25; 21:24; 22:10.

473. Josephus, *J.W.* 13.5.9 §171.

474. Tajra, *Trial*, 122; Fitzmyer, *Acts*, 734.

475. Tajra, *Trial*, 124.

476. B. Winter, "Official Proceedings and the Forensic Speeches in Acts 24–26," in *The Book of Acts in Its Ancient Literary Setting* (BAFCS 1; Grand Rapids: Eerdmans, 1993), 334.

477. E. Haenchen, *The Acts of the Apostles* (Oxford: Basil Blackwell, 1971), 654, n. 2 (based on an explanation by Adolf Schlatter). See now also Witherington, *Acts*, 654; Hemer, *Book of Acts*, 192.

478. For a discussion of the many Jewish texts that teach a general resurrection, see Str-B, 4:2:1166–98.

479. Sherwin-White, *Roman Law*, 52.

480. Rapske, *Roman Custody*, 172.

481. Josephus, *Ant.* 19.9.1 §354; Schürer, *HJP*², 1:461.

482. Ibid., 20.7.2 §142.

483. Ibid., 20.7.1 §§139–43.

484. Plato, *Republic* 390b; 430c.

485. For the many references, see W. Grundmann, "ἐγκράτεια," *TDNT*, 2:340–41.

486. Josephus, *Ant.* 20.8.9 §182 [Loeb edition].

487. See Tajra, *Trial*, 134.

488. Josephus, *Ant.* 20.8.8 §179.

489. Tajra, *Trial*, 135.

490. Ibid.,140.

491. Rapske, *Roman Custody*, 186–89; Tajra, *Trial*, 145–46.

492. Rapske, *Roman Custody*, 188.

493. Tajra, *Trial*, 148.

494. On Bernice, see D. C. Braund, "Bernice," *ABD*, 1:677–78; Schürer, *HJP*², 1:474–79.

495. Josephus, *Ant.* 20.7.3 §145.

496. This is the view of Larkin, *Acts*, 349.

497. Hemer, *Book of Acts*, 348–49.

498. As cited in Fitzmyer, *Acts*, 750; Ulpian, *Digest* 48.17.1.

499. As cited in Bruce, *Acts*, 457, n. 28; Appian, *Civil War* 3.54.

500. LSJ, 1915–16.

501. Josephus, *Ant.* 19.9.2 §365.

502. Fitzmyer, *Acts*, 752.

503. Ulpian, *Digest* 49.6.1.

504. Bruce, *Acts*, 464.

505. Williams, *Acts*, 417.

506. Euripides, *Bacchae* 795.

507. For a discussion and numerous references in Greek literature, see U. Luck, "σώφρων κτλ.," *TDNT*, 7:1098–1100.

508. Epictetus, *Discourses* 2.12.17; Plato, *Gorgias* 485D; Plutarch, *Moralia* 777B.

509. Sherwin-White, *Roman Law*, 65.

510. C. J. Thornton, *Der Zeuge des Zeugens: Lukas als Historiker der Paulusreisen* (WUNT 56; Tübingen: Mohr Siebeck, 1991), 366.

511. *ILS* 2683 (= *CIL* 3.6687) and *IGRR* 3.1136 (=*OGIS* 421). For a discussion of these texts, see Broughton, "Roman Army," 443–44; Hemer, *Book of Acts*, 132–33, n. 96.

512. See the references in Barrett, *Acts*, 2:1183; Johnson, *Acts*, 445.

513. Witherington, *Acts*, 761.

514. On Myra, see S. Mitchell, "Myra," *OCD*³, 1016; E. M. Yamauchi, "Myra," *ABD*, 4:939–40.

515. Strabo, *Geog.* 14.2.15.

516. Hemer, *Book of Acts*, 135, note 102 (summarizing the study of L. Casson).

517. Ibid., 135–36.

518. Rapske, "Acts, Travel and Shipwreck," 22; Vegetius, *De re militari* 4:39; Pliny, *Nat. Hist.* 2.47.122.

519. Suetonius, *Claudius* 18.

520. See also Josephus, *Ant.* 17.6.4 §165; Philo, *Moses* 2.23; *Spec. Laws* 1:186; 2:193; *m. Yoma* 8:1.

521. Rapske, "Acts, Travel and Shipwreck," 23–24; Hemer, *Book of Acts*, 137–38.

522. Riesner, *Paul's Early Period*, 224–24; Hemer, *Book of Acts*, 137–38.

523. Barrett, *Acts*, 2:1190.

524. Rapske, "Acts, Travel, and Shipwreck," 28.

525. *CIL* 8.26652.

526. See Hemer, *Book of Acts*, 141–42; idem, "Euraquilo and Melita," *JTS* 26 (1975): 100–11.

527. "Gregale," *Encyclopædia Britannica Online*. http://www.eb.com:180/bol/topic?idxref=386818 [Accessed 1 January 2001].

528. Lake and Cadbury, *Beginnings*, 4:332.

529. For a description of the various views, see H. J. Cadbury, "Note XXVIII. Ὑποζώματα," in *Beginnings*, 5:345–54. Taking the view presented here is Hemer, *Book of Acts*, 143, n. 120.

530. N. Purcell, "Syrtes," *OCD³*, 1466.

531. Dio Chrysostom, *Orationes* 5.8–9.

532. This is the view of Barrett, *Acts*, 2:1197.

533. Hemer, *Book of Acts*, 143.

534. J. Smith, *The Voyage and Shipwreck of St. Paul*, 4th ed. (Grand Rapids: Baker, 1978), 126–28. His calculations are accepted by most commentators.

535. M. Cary and W. M. Murray, "Adriatic Sea," *OCD³*, 14; Hemer, *Book of Acts*, 145–46.

536. Hemer, *Book of Acts*, 147 (in reliance on a study by L. Casson).

537. Herodotus, *History* 2.5.

538. On the various anchors used on Greek and Roman vessels, see D. Haldane, "Anchors of Antiquity," *BA* 53.1 (1990): 19–24.

539. 1 Sam. 14:45; see also 2 Sam. 14:11; 1 Kings 1:52.

540. Josephus, *Vita* 3 §15.

541. Hirschfeld, "Ship," 28.

542. Smith, *Voyage*, 141, n. 2.

543. Bruce, *Acts*, 494; Hemer, *Book of Acts*, 150; Smith, *Voyage*, 143.

544. E. A. Yamauchi, "On the Road With Paul: The Ease—and Dangers—of Travel in the Ancient World," *CH* 14.3 (1995): 19.

545. J. M. Gilchrist, "The Historicity of Paul's Shipwreck," *JSNT* 61 (1996): 29.

546. *Code of Justinian* 9.4.4.

547. Hemer, *Book of Acts*, 152; Bruce, *Acts*, 497.

548. BAGD, s.v.

549. P. W. van der Horst, "Dike," *DDD²*, 251–52.

550. *IGRR* 1.512 = *IG* 14.601; see C. J. Hemer, "First Person Narrative in Acts 27–28," *TynBul* 36 (1985): 100.

551. Mark 6:5; 8:23, 25; Luke 4:40; 13:13; Mark 5:23.

552. Barrett, *Acts*, 2:1226.

553. On these gods, see K. Dowden, "Dioskouroi," *DDD²*, 258–59; R. C. T. Parker, "Dioscuri," *OCD³*, 484.

554. See G. J. Toomer, "Constellations and Named Stars," *OCD³*, 382.

555. On Syracuse, see A. Betz, "Syracuse," *ABD*, 6:270–71.

556. Homer, *Odyssey* 12.101–102; Horace, *Carmina* 1.27.19.

557. R. Brändle and E. W. Stegemann, "Die Entstehung der Ersten 'Christliche Gemeinde' Roms im Kontext der Jüdischen Gemeinden," *NTS* 42 (1996): 10–11.

558. Suetonius, *Claud.* 25.

559. Horace, *Satirae* 1.5.3–6.

560. J. D. Wineland, "Three Taverns," *ABD*, 6:544.

561. Sherwin-White, *Roman Society*, 110; Rapske, *Roman Custody*, 176–77; Tajra, *Trial*, 179.

562. Rapske, *Roman Custody*, 181.

563. Schürer, *HJP²*, 3:1:95–96.

564. Suetonius, *Claud.* 25; see comments on Acts 18:2.

565. Bruce, *Acts*, 507.

566. See Acts 13:43; 14:1–2; 17:4–5, 12.

567. See Matt. 13:13; Mark 4:12; Luke 8:10; John 12:39–40.

568. Marshall, *Acts*, 425.

569. So also Hemer, *Book of Acts*, 190.

570. Rapske, *Roman Custody*, 325–26.

Sidebar and Chart Notes

A-1. See J. Murphy-O'Connor, "The Cenacle—Topographical Setting for Acts 2:44–45," in *The Book of Acts in Its Palestinian Setting*, ed. R. Bauckham (BAFCS 4; Grand Rapids: Eerdmans, 1995), 303–21.

A-2. Epiphanius, *De mensuris et ponderibus* 14 (as cited in J. Murphy-O'Connor, "The Cenacle," 307).

A-3. See M. Broshi, "Excavations in the House of Caiaphas, Mount Zion," in *Jerusalem Revealed: Archaeology in the Holy City 1968–1974* (New Haven, Conn.: Yale University Press, 1976), 57–60.

A-4. For additional information about the "Cenacle," see "Cenaculum," *ODCC³*, 313, and J. Finegan, *The Archaeology of the New Testament: The Life of Jesus and the Beginning of the Early Church* (Princeton, N.J.: Princeton University Press, 1969), 147–52; J. Murphy-O'Connor, *The Holy Land*, 4th ed. Rev. and expanded, *OAG* (Oxford: University Press, 1998), 105–6.

A-5. See J. Huehnergard, "Languages (Introductory)," *ABD*, 4.155-70.

A-6. See the discussion of evidence for Jewish presence in most of these countries in Schürer, *HJP²*, 3.1-86; Jeremias, *Jerusalem*, 58-73.

A-7. On the languages of Asia Minor, see S. Mitchell, *Anatolia. Land, Men, and Gods in Asia Minor*, 2 vols. (Oxford: Clarendon Press, 1993), 1.173-76.

A-8. Philo, *Embassy* 282.

A-9. F. Millar, *The Roman Near East: 31* B.C.–A.D. (Cambridge, Mass.: Harvard University Press, 1993), 401-2.

A-10. Schürer, *HJP²*, 3:16-17; Millar, *Roman Near East*, 404-5; M. Hengel & A. M. Schwemer, *Paul: Between Damascus and Antioch. The Unknown Years* (Louisville, Ky.: Westminster John Knox Press, 1997), 110-26.

A-11. Josephus, *Ant.* 18.2.33–35 §37.

A-12. Josephus, *J.W.* 5.4.2 §144.

A-13. *b. Yoma* 25a (as cited in Schürer, *HJP³*, 2:224).

A-14. Finegan, *Archaeology*, 132.

A-15. Str-B, 2:637.

A-16. *m. Soṭah* 9:15.

A-17. Josephus, *Ant.* 20.5.1 §97–99.

A-18. *m. Mak.* 3:12–14.

A-19. For discussion, see R. Riesner, "Synagogues in Jerusalem," *The Book of Acts in Its Palestinian Setting* (BAFCS 4; Grand Rapids: Eerdmans, 1996), 192–200; P. W. van der Horst, "Was the Synagogue a Place of Sabbath Worship Before 70 CE?" in *Jews, Christians, and Polytheists in the Ancient Synagogue: Cultural Interaction During the Graeco-Roman Period*, ed. S. Fine (BSHJ; New York: Routledge, 1999), 18–43; Hengel, "Between Jesus and Paul," 17–18.

A-20. *Corpus Inscription Judaicarum*, 2:333 (no. 1404). Translation from Riesner, "Synagogues," 193.

A-21. Riesner, "Synagogues," 197–98.

A-22. M. Hengel, *The Pre-Christian Paul* (Philadelphia: Trinity Press, 1991), 68–69; Riesner, "Synagogues," 205; Hemer, *Book of Acts*, 176.

A-23. F. F. Bruce, *The Book of Acts*, rev. ed. (NICNT; Grand Rapids: Eerdmans, 1988), 134.

A-24. Philo, *Moses* 1.5 (§20–24) (de Jonge edition).

A-25. On the Samaritans, see Schürer, *HJP²*, 2.15–20; Jeremias, *Jerusalem*, 352–58; R. T. Anderson, "Samaritans," *ABD*, 5.940–47; H. G. M. Williamson, "Samaritans," *DJG*, 724–28; K. Haacker, "Samaritan," *NIDNTT*, 3.449–67.

A-26. See also Josephus, *Ant.* 9.14.3 §288.

A-27. Josephus, *Ant.* 12.5.5 §§258–61.

A-28. Sir. 50:25–26.

A-29. Jeremias, *Jerusalem*, 354; *Pirqe R. Eliezer* 38.

A-30. Justin, *First Apology* 26.

A-31. See J. Scheid, "Semo Sancus Dius Fidius," *OCD³*, 1383.

A-32. P. Lond 121.560–71 (= *PGM*, VII.560–71).

A-33. On eunuchs, see the excellent discussion in F. S. Spencer, *The Portrait of Philip in Acts: A Study of Roles and Relations* (JSNTSup 67; Sheffield: JSOT Press, 1992), 166–72.

A-34. Herodotus, *Hist.* 8.104–106; Lucian, *The Eunuch* 6.

A-35. Josephus, *Ant.* 4.8.40 §§290–91.

A-36. This is adapted from Ajith Fernando, *Acts* (NIVAC; Grand Rapids: Zondervan, 1998), 287–91.

A-37. On Damascus, see Hengel, *Paul*, 55–61; J. McRay, *Archaeology & the New Testament* (Grand Rapids: Baker, 1991), 232–34.

A-38. Schürer, *HJP²*, 2.36.

A-39. Josephus, *J.W.* 2.20.2 §561; 7.6.7 §368.

A-40. On Tarsus, see W. W. Gasque, "Tarsus," *ABD*, 6.333–34; Hengel & Schwemer, *Paul*, 151–77; Hengel, *Pre-Christian Paul*, 1–6; Hemer, "Tarsus," *ISBE*, 4:734–36.

A-41. Strabo, *Geog.* 14.5.13.

A-42. McRay, *Archaeology*, 235.

A-43. S. Mitchell, "Archaeology in Asia Minor 1990–1998," *AR* 45 (1999): 190.

A-44. See Holum, et al., "Caesarea," *NEAE*, 1:271–91.

A-45. R. L. Hohlfelder, "Herod the Great's City on the Sea," *National Geographic* 171/72 (1987): 260–79. The video was featured on National Geographic's "Explorer," but, unfortunately, is not available for purchase from the society.

A-46. See http://digcaesarea.org/ [Accessed 1 January 2001].

A-47. Josephus, *J.W.* 1.21.5–8 §§408–15.

A-48. On Antioch of Syria, see: F. W. Norris, "Antioch," *ABD*, 1:269; J. M. McRay, "Antioch on the Orontes," *DPL*, 23–25; R. E. Brown and J. P. Meier, *Antioch and Rome* (New York: Paulist Press, 1983); G. Downey, *A History of Antioch in Syria from Seleucus to the Arab Conquest* (Princeton, N. J.: Princeton University Press, 1961); W. A. Meeks and R. L. Wilken, *Jews and Christians in Antioch in the First Four Centuries of the Common Era* (SBS 13; Missoula, Mont.: Scholar's Press, 1978).

A-49. Strabo, *Geog.* 16,2:5; cf. Diodorus Siculus 17:52 and Pliny *Nat. Hist.* 6:122. See Hengel & Schwemer, *Paul*, 186.

A-50. Hengel & Schwemer, *Paul*, 196.

A-51. Ibid.,184; Riesner, *Paul's Early Period*, 113–14 (the ancient account is in the *Chronicle of Malalas*).

A-52. Hengel & Schwemer, *Paul*, 205, argue for a much longer period of ministry in Antioch and Syria. Witherington, *Acts*, 83 and F. F. Bruce, "Paul the Apostle," *ISBE*, 3:709, suggest a much longer time in Tarsus and a shorter time in Antioch and Syria.

A-53. For the entire account, see Philo, *Flaccus*; see also Schürer, *HJP²*, 1:389–98.

A-54. See Josephus, *Ant.* 18.8.1–9 §§257–309.

A-55. This account of hostilities in Antioch is only recorded in the *Chronicle* of Malalas (10:315). See the discussion in Hengel & Schwemer, *Paul*, 184–86.

A-56. Suetonius, *Claud.* 18.

A-57. Josephus, *Ant.* 20.2.5 §§51–53.

A-58. Eusebius, *Eccl. Hist.* 6.14.

A-59. Ibid., 3.39.

A-60. Ibid., 2.16.

A-61. On Mark and Egyptian Christianity, see B. Pearson, "Christianity in Egypt," *ABD*, 1:954–60.

A-62. See also Hemer, *Book of Acts*, 359–62.

A-63. Eusebius, *Eccl. Hist.* 2.25.

A-64. Josephus, *Ant.* 19.8.2 §§343–50.

A-65. On Cyprus, see J. McRay, "Cyprus," *ABD*, 1:1228–30; H. W. Catling, "Cyprus," *OCD³*, 419–20; A. Nobbs, "Cyprus," in *Graeco-Roman Setting*, 279–89; D. W. J. Gill, "Paul's Travels Through Cyprus (Acts 13:4–12)," *TB* 46 (1995): 219–28.

A-66. See 1 Macc. 15:23; 2 Macc. 12:2; Philo, *Embassy* 282.

A-67. Schürer, *HJP²*, 2:68–69; Dio Cassius 68.32.1–3 .

A-68. *PGM*, IV:930–55.

A-69. On Roman names, see H. Solin, "Names, Personal, Roman," *OCD³*, 1024-26.

A-70. On Antioch near Pisidia, see Mitchell and Waelkens, *Pisidian Antioch*; S. Mitchell, "Antioch of Pisidia," *ABD*, 1:264–65; idem, "Antioch," *OCD³*, 107; idem, *Anatolia*, 2:7–8; B. van Elderen, "Antioch (Pisidian)," *ISBE*, 1:142.

A-71. A. N. Sherwin-White and B. M. Levick, "Colonization, Roman," *OCD³*, 364.

A-72. Mitchell, "Antioch of Pisidia," 264.

A-73. Josephus, *Ant.* 12.3.4 §§145–53.

A-74. Mitchell, *Anatolia*, 2:10.

A-75. Mitchell & Waelkens, *Pisidian Antioch*, 32–33.

A-76. Schürer, *HJP²*, 2:433–37; 3:92–103; *New Documents*, 4:213–20 (§113).

A-77. On Iconium, see W. W. Gasque, "Iconium," *ABD*, 3:357–58; D. A. Hagner, "Iconium," *ISBE*, 2:792–93.

A-78. Bruce, *Acts*, 272.

A-79. D. H. French, "Acts and the Roman Roads of Asia Minor," *Graeco-Roman Setting*, 52, 55.

A-80. C. Breytenbach, *Paulus und Barnabas in der Provinz Galatien. Studien zu Apostelgeschichte 13f.; 16,6; 18,23 und den Adressaten des Galaterbriefes* (AGJU 38; Leiden: Brill, 1996), 162–63.

A-81. Breytenbach, *Provinz Galatien*, 163–64.

A-82. On Lystra, see D. S. Potter, "Lystra," *ABD*, 4:426–27; D. A. Hagner, "Lystra," *ISBE*, 3:192–93.

A-83. Breytenbach, *Provinz Galatien*, 165.

A-84. See B. van Elderen, "Some Archaeological Observations on Paul's First Missionary Journey," in *Apostolic History and the Gospel: Biblical and Historical Essays Presented to F. F. Bruce on his 60th Birthday*, eds. W. W. Gasque and R. P. Martin (Grand Rapids: Eerdmans, 1970), 156–61.

A-85. *Jubilees* 15:26.

A-86. Josephus, *Ant.* 13.9.1 §254.

A-87. Judith 14:10; see also Est. 8:17 in the LXX version.

A-88. R. G. Hall, "Circumcision," *ABD*, 1:1027; Martial, *Epigrams* 7.35, 82.

A-89. 1 Macc. 1:48, 60–61; 2 Macc. 6:10; *4 Macc.* 4:25.

A-90. See the discussion in J. M. G. Barclay, *Jews in the Mediterranean Diaspora: From Alexander to Trajan, 323 BCE–117 CE* (Edinburgh: T. & T. Clark, 1996), 438–39; Philo, *Spec. Laws* 1.2.

A-91. Barclay, *Jews*, 1027.

A-92. For more extensive discussion, see the following sources: Advocates of the view that Acts 15 = Gal. 2:1–10 (the "North Galatia" view): Barrett, *Acts*, 2:xxxvi-xli; Fitzmyer, *Acts*, 538–39; Dunn, *Acts*, 195–97; D. J. Williams, *Acts* (GNC; San Francisco: Harper, 1985), 246–50. Advocates of the view that Acts 11:27–30 and 12:25 = Gal. 2:1–10 (the "South Galatia" view): Mitchell, *Anatolia*, 2:5; Witherington, *Acts*, 440–45; Bruce, *Acts*, 283–85; Hemer, *Book of Acts*, 277–307; Riesner, *Paul's Early Period*, 286–91; Marshall, *Acts*, 244–47.

A-93. On Troas, see C. J. Hemer, "Alexandria Troas," *TynBul* 26 (1975): 79–112; E. M. Yamauchi, "Troas," *ABD*, 6:666–667; Trebilco, "Asia," in *Graeco-Roman Setting*, 357–59.

A-94. Strabo, *Geog.* 13.1.26.

A-95. Mitchell, "Archaeology in Asia Minor," 138–39.

A-96. On Macedonia, see D. W. J. Gill, "Macedonia," in *Graeco-Roman Setting*, 397–417; F. Papazoglou, "Macedonia Under the Romans," in *Macedonia: 4000 Years of Greek History and Civilization*, ed. M. M. Sakellariou (Athens: Ekdotike Athenon S. A., 1983), 192–221.

A-97. Papazoglou, "Macedonia Under the Romans," 204–7.

A-98. On Philippi, see H. L. Hendrix, "Philippi," *ABD*, 5:313–17; McRay, *Archaeology*, 283–88; and, especially, C. Bakirtzis and H. Koester, eds., *Philippi at the Time of Paul and After His Death* (Harrisburg, Penn.: Trinity Press International, 1998).

A-99. As cited in Rapske, *Roman Custody*, 125 n. 55; Cicero, *In Verrem* 2.5.142.

A-100. An outstanding article has been written on this topic: see K. P. Donfried, "The Cults of Thessalonica and the Thessalonian Correspondence," *NTS* 31 (1985): 336–56.

A-101. On this term, see G. H. R. Horsley, "The Politarchs," in *Graeco-Roman Setting*, 419–31; idem, "Politarchs," *ABD*, 5:384–89.

A-102. O. Broneer, "Athens: 'City of Idol Worship'," *BA* 21 (1958): 1–28.

A-103. Seneca, *Ad Marciam* 26.6 (as cited in N. C. Croy, "Hellenistic Philosophies and the Preaching of the Resurrection [Acts 17:18, 32]," *NovT* 39 [1997]: 34).

A-104. Lucretius, *De rerum Natura* 3.624–33 (as cited in Croy, "Hellenistic Philosophies," 30).

A-105. Epicurus in the Sovereign Maxims (in Diogenes Laertius, 10.139) as cited in Croy, "Hellenistic Philosophies," 30.

A-106. D. W. J. Gill, "In Search of the Social Élite in the Corinthian Church," *TynBul* 44 (1993): 333–34.

A-107. Wiseman, "Corinth and Rome," 516.

A-108. Described in a presentation made by Dr. James Wiseman on Nov. 21, 1999 in Boston, Mass. at the annual meeting of the Society of Biblical Literature.

A-109. On Alexandria, see A. K. Bowman, "Egypt," in *The Cambridge Ancient History*, vol. 10: *The Augustan Empire, 43 B.C.–A.D. 69*, 2d ed. (Cambridge: Cambridge University Press, 1996), 699–701; B. A. Pearson, "Alexandria," *ABD* 1.152–57 and D. W. Rathbone, "Alexandria," *OCD³*, 61–62.

A-110. The entire account is written up by Philo in his *Flaccus*.

A-111. The journal is *Jahreshefte des Österreichischen Archäologischen Instituts in Wien*.

A-112. H. Engelmann, D. Knibbe, and R. Merkelbach, eds., *Die Inschriften von Ephesos*, Inschriften Griechischer Städte aus Kleinasien (Bonn: Rudolf Habelt, 1980–84).

A-113. There is an extensive bibliography on Jewish magic in antiquity. See especially, P. S. Alexander, "Incantations and Books of Magic," in Schürer, *HJP²*, 3:1:342–79; idem, "Jewish Elements in Gnosticism and Magic c. CE 70–CE 270," *CHJ³*, 1052–78;

M. Simon, *Verus Israel* (Oxford: Oxford University Press, 1986).

A-114. Josephus, *Ant.* 8.2.5 §§41–49.

A-115. For an English translation of the *Testament of Solomon*, see D. C. Duling, "Testament of Solomon," in *The Old Testament Pseudepigrapha*, vol. 1 (Garden City, N.Y.: Doubleday, 1983), 935–87.

A-116. For additional discussion, see C. E. Arnold, *Power and Magic* (Grand Rapids: Baker, 1997), 14–20.

A-117. Plutarch, *Quaestiones Convivales* 7.5.

A-118. M. Meyer and R. Smith, *Ancient Christian Magic* (San Francisco: Harper, 1994).

A-119. Pausanias, *Description of Greece* 4.31.8.

A-120. Numerous pictures of the extant cultic images of the Ephesian Artemis have been collected and published by R. Fleischer in two publications: *Artemis von Ephesus und verwandte Kultstatuen aus Anatolien und Syrien* (Leiden: Brill, 1973) and in "Artemis Ephesia," in *Lexicon Iconographicum Mythologiae Classicae*, vol. 2, Parts 1 & 2 (Zürich & München: Artemis, 1984).

A-121. For an extended discussion of this inscription, see *New Documents* 4:7–11; *Inschriften von Ephesos*, 6:2212.

A-122. *Inschriften von Ephesos*, 2:547.

A-123. As cited in Baugh, "Paul in Ephesus," 114; *Inschriften von Ephesos*, 2:585.

A-124. On Miletus, see E. Yamauchi, *The Archaeology of New Testament Cities in Western Asia Minor* (Grand Rapids: Baker, 1980), 115–27; Trebilco, "Asia," 360–62.

A-125. Josephus, *Ant.* 14.10.21 §§ 244–46.

A-126. Trebilco, *Jewish Communities*, 159–62.

A-127. Josephus, *J.W.* 2.12.2 §§229–30.

A-128. Josephus, *J.W.* 5.5.2 §§193–94.

A-129. An English translation is given and discussed in Barrett, *Background*, 53 (no. 50). See also the discussions in D. R. Edwards, "Gentiles, Court of the," *ABD*, 2:963; Schürer, *HJP²*, 2:222.

A-130. Josephus, *J.W.* 2.13.5 §§261–63; see also *Ant.* 20.8.6 §171.

A-131. Fitzmyer, *Acts*, 700.

A-132. On the Sicarii, see Schürer, *HJP²*, 1:463–64.

A-133. Josephus, *J.W.* 2.13.3 §§254–57.

A-134. On Roman citizenship, see A. N. Sherwin-White, *The Roman Citizenship*, 2d ed. (Oxford: Oxford University Press, 1974); idem, *Roman Law and Roman Society* (Grand Rapids: Baker, 1992), 144–62; Hengel, *Pre-Christian Paul*, 6–15; Rapske, *Roman Custody*, 83–90.

A-135. Sherwin-White, *Roman Law*, 147; Tajra, *Trial*, 83.

A-136. Philo, *Embassy* 155–57.

A-137. Josephus, *Ant.* 20.5.2 §103.

A-138. Ibid., 20.9.2 §§206–207.

A-139. Josephus, *J.W.* 2.17.9 §441.

A-140. On Felix, see Schürer, *HJP²*, 1:460–66.

A-141. As cited in Schürer, *HJP²*, 1:461; Tacitus, *Historiae* 5.9.

A-142. Tacitus, *Ann.* 12.54.

A-143. Josephus, *Ant.* 20.8.5 §160–65.

A-144. Josephus, *J.W.* 2.13.7 §270.

A-145. See B. Burrell, K. Gleason, and E. Netzer, "Uncovering Herod's Seaside Palace," *BAR* 19.3 (May/June 1993): 50–57, 96; L. I. Levine and E. Netzer, "Caesarea (Excavations West of the Theater: The Promontory Palace)," *NEAE*, 1:280–82.

A-146. Josephus, *Ant.* 20.8.9–11 §§182–96; *J.W.* 2.14.1 §271; on Festus, see Schürer, *HJP²*, 1:467–68; J. B. Green, "Festus, Porcius," *ABD*, 2:794–95.

A-147. Josephus, *J.W.* 2.14.1 §272.

A-148. On Agrippa II, see Schürer, *HJP²*, 1:471–83; D. C. Braund, "Agrippa," *ABD*, 1:99–100.

A-149. Josephus, *Ant.* 20.5.2 §104.

A-150. See Schürer, *HJP²*, 1:475, for references.

A-151. Josephus, *Ant.* 20.9.7 §§219–22.

A-152. Josephus, *Life* 65 §§362–67.

A-153. See "Nicholas, St.," *ODCC³*, 1148.

A-154. On Crete, see W. A. Laidlaw, L. F. Nixon, & S. R. F. Price, "Crete, Greek and Roman," *OCD³*, 408–9 and F. W. Bush, "Crete," *ISBE*, 1:813–15.

A-155. Lucian, *Navigium (The Ship or the Wishes)* 5; I have altered the translation of K. Kilburn (*Lucian* [LCL 6; Cambridge, Mass.: Harvard University Press, 1968], 435–36) slightly by changing cubits (which I reckoned as 18 inches) to feet.

A-156. See N. Hirschfeld, "The Ship of Saint Paul: Historical Background (Part I)," *BA* 53.1 (March, 1990): 27–28. See also M. Fitzgerald, "The Ship of Saint Paul: Comparative Archaeology," *BA* 53.1 (March, 1990): 31–39.

A-157. Fitzgerald, "Ship," 36; idem, "The Ship," in *The Harbours of Caesarea Maritima: Results of the Caesarea Ancient Excavation Project, 1980–1985*, ed J. P. Oleson (BAR International Series 491, 594; Center for Maritime Studies, University of Haifa, 3, 5; Oxford: Tempus Reparatum, 1989).

A-158. On Puteoli, see H. K. Lomas, "Puteoli," *OCD³*, 1280–81; S. T. Carroll, "Puteoli," *ABD*, 5:560–61; G. H. Allen and A. F. Harris, "Puteoli," *ISBE*, 3:1059–60; see Seneca, *Epistulae* 77.1–2.

A-159. Strabo, *Geog.* 5.4.6.

A-160. Josephus, *Ant.* 17.12.1 §§23–25; *J.W.* 2.7.1 §§101–105.

A-161. On Rome, see J. F. Hall, "Rome," *ABD*, 5:830–34; M. Reasoner, "Rome and Roman Christianity," *DPL*, 850–55; H. F. Vos, "Rome," *ISBE*, 4:228–36.

A-162. Tacitus, *Ann.* 15.44.

A-163. Brändle and Stegemann, "Die Christliche Gemeinde in Rom," 4.

A-164. Schürer, *HJP²*, 3:1:73–75.

A-165. Philo, *Embassy* 23 §155–56.

A-166. Ibid., 3:1:95–98.

CREDITS FOR PHOTOS AND MAPS

Arnold, Clinton E. . . . . pp. 157, 168, 174, 186, 191, 199(3), 200, 201(2), 202, 241

Bredow, Dennis . . . . pp. 75, 102, 155, 163, 171, 181, 189, 236, 268

Claycombe, Hugh . . . . p. 24

Dunn, Cheryl (for Talbot Bible Lands) . . . . pp. 105, 127, 134, 149(2), 153, 204, 206(2)

Franz, Gordon . . . . pp. 72, 119(2), 132, 157, 172, 258, 262, 272

Haradine, Jane (public domain photos) . . . . pp. 10, 92(3), 210, 249

King, Jay . . . . pp. 71, 161, 221

Kohlenberger, John R. III . . . . pp. 10, 16, 35, 51, 62, 68, 73, 74, 80, 82, 84, 86, 100, 101, 114, 118, 124, 131, 137, 138, 148, 150, 151, 163, 166, 178, 185, 187(2), 188, 197, 203, 205, 212, 235, 255, 256

Konstas, Ioannis . . . . pp. 156, 167, 176, 183, 207, 257

McRay, John. . . . . pp. 81, 153, 165, 166, 179, 211, 264

Radovan, Zev . . . . pp. 14, 23(2), 31, 34, 38, 41, 45, 48, 54, 58, 67, 71, 87, 90, 91, 106, 109, 111, 133, 140, 141, 155, 156, 168, 173, 182(2), 214, 219, 232, 234, 235, 252, 254, 257

Rigsby, Richard . . . . pp. 212, 256

Ritmeyer, Leen. . . . . pp. 7, 25, 27, 110, 220

Tabernacle. . . . . p. 56

University of Michigan . . . . pp. 4, 146, 195

Wilson, Mark . . . . pp. 51, 282, 122, 126, 128, 129, 253

Zondervan Image Archive (Neal Bierling) . . . . pp. 2–3, 8, 11, 12, 13, 26, 37, 44(2), 53, 55, 63(2), 67, 69, 76, 77, 80, 82, 85, 88(3), 91, 93, 94(2), 97(2), 99, 105, 115, 120(2), 124(2), 133, 137, 140, 145, 154, 158(2), 160(2), 164, 168(2), 169, 170, 174, 180(3), 186, 209, 213, 215, 222, 227, 230, 233, 242, 243, 253, 264, 267(4), 270(2)